D1478992

EKPHRASIS

The *ouroboros*, emblem of the alchemical *prima materia*, holder of the secret of the universe

"The visual emblem and the verbal emblem are complementary languages for seeking the representation of the unrepresentable. Ekphrasis is the poet's marriage of the two within the verbal art." P. 22

EKPHRASIS

The Illusion
of the
Natural Sign

Murray Krieger
Emblems by Joan Krieger

THE JOHNS HOPKINS UNIVERSITY PRESS
Baltimore and London

© 1992 The Johns Hopkins University Press
All rights reserved
Printed in the United States of America

The Johns Hopkins University Press
701 West 40th Street
Baltimore, Maryland 21211-2190
The Johns Hopkins Press Ltd., London

The paper used in this book meets the minimum requirements of American
National Standard for Information Sciences—Permanence of Paper for
Printed Library Materials, ANSI Z39.48-1984.

Library of Congress Cataloging-in-Publication Data

Krieger, Murray, 1923–
    Ekphrasis : the illusion of the natural sign / Murray Krieger ; emblems by
Joan Krieger.
        p.   cm.
    Includes bibliographical references and index.
        ISBN 0-8018-4266-2
    1. Poetry—History and criticism.   2. Ut pictura poesis (Aesthetics)   I. Krieger,
Joan.   II. Title.
PN126.K75   1991
809.1—dc20   91-21526

To Diane and Eliot

Contents

Acknowledgments

Early and less developed versions of some of these chapters have appeared in *Philosophy and Literature,* ed. Doug Bolling (New York: Haven Publishing, 1987); *The States of "Theory": History, Art, and Critical Discourse,* ed. David Carroll (New York: Columbia University Press, 1990); and *Aesthetic Illusion: Theoretical and Historical Approaches,* ed. Frederick Burwick and Walter Pape (Berlin and New York: Walter de Gruyter, 1990). I am grateful for permission to use these materials in this substantially revised form.

This book has been so many years in preparation and writing that my debts are too numerous and longstanding for all of them to be singled out. I think of many stimulating students in seminars at Irvine and at the School of Criticism and Theory, who forced me to press my ideas beyond where I thought they might be allowed to rest. And I think of many colleagues over the years as well. But there are a few individuals—and I am thinking of those closest to the completed book—to whom special thanks are due: to Lisa Ness for devoted service to the project, to Anne Rosse Gokhale for valuable technical assistance, to Joanne Allen for very useful editorial help with the final version of the manuscript, to Paul Davis for suggestions concerning classical sources of *ekphrasis,* and to Theodore Brunner, of the *Thesaurus Linguae Graecae,* for furnishing source materials. Among my many helpful colleagues I should especially cite William Lillyman, who for many years as executive vice-chancellor and for many more as friend gave constant support to my work; Wolfgang Iser, who has always responded to my writings generously and with patience, and with whom I have continually discovered many common theoretical objectives; and Stephen Nichols, Michael Riffaterre, Frederick Burwick, and Marshall Brown, who encouraged this study at crucial moments in its later development.

About my collaborator in this work I need add nothing here except my deepest thanks, since the evidence of her remarkable contributions runs throughout this volume.

No single contribution to the completion of this work was greater than that made by the Bellagio Study and Conference Center at the Villa Serbelloni, where, during five marvelous weeks in the spring of 1990, the bulk of this work was brought close to its final form and most of the emblems were conceived and executed. I am very grateful to the Rockefeller Foundation for providing that most productive residency.

FOREWORD
Of Shields

It [the "Ode on a Grecian Urn"] is first of all a description of an urn—that is, it belongs to the genre, known to Occidental literature from Homer and Theocritus to the Parnassians and Rilke, of the *ekphrasis*, the poetic description of a pictorial or sculptural work of art, which description implies, in the words of Théophile Gautier, "une transposition d'art," the reproduction, through the medium of words, of sensuously perceptible *objets d'art* ("ut pictura poesis").

Leo Spitzer, "The 'Ode on a Grecian Urn,' or Content vs. Metagrammar"

M y fore-word, the word before the words of the text, is *shields*, and that too is its theme. My book opens, on the page opposite, with two widely separated, wonderfully ingenious, though equally vain, attempts to represent visually Homer's description of the shield of Achilles in book 18 of the *Iliad*. Both seek to create what is, in effect, a reverse *ekphrasis* in that they seek in the visual arts to produce an equivalent of the verbal text instead of the other way around. One is an engraving by Nicolas Vleughels that appears in Alexander Pope's rhymed English version of Homer's *Iliad* (1715–20) and furnishes the visual text for Pope's lengthy commentary on Homer's description of the shield; the other rendering is a gilt silver cast in bas-relief by Abraham Flaxman (1821).[1]

Further, each of the eight chapters of my book is introduced by the representation of an emblem shaped as a circular shield, created by Joan Krieger and constructed around each, in turn, of the Greek

1. The print at the top of the page was reproduced for Pope's *Iliad* after Vleughels's engraving, which appeared in Jean Boivin's *Apologie d'Homère et Bouclier d'Achille* (Paris, 1715). This depiction accompanies Pope's lengthy justification and description of Homer's passage on the shield in his "Observations on the Shield of *Achilles*," which is appended to his rendition of book 18. See vol. 8 (*The Iliad of Homer*, bks. 10–24) of *The Poems of Alexander Pope*, ed. Maynard Mack et al. (New Haven: Yale University Press, 1967), pp. 358–70. For information about the engraving I am indebted to Professor Mack's notes on the plate on p. xiii of the volume. The second representation of the shield is taken from a photograph of Flaxman's effort to reproduce the shield as a gilt silver cast in bas-relief (originally modeled in plaster, 1821). There is of course some distortion produced by translating this imagined equivalent of Homer's words, in its three-dimensionality, onto the two-dimensional page. Nevertheless, the extraordinary attempt to convey the elaborate detail and motion should come through. The photograph was made available through the courtesy of the Huntington Library and its past director, James Thorpe.

letters of *ekphrasis* (ΕΚΦΡΑΣΙΣ).[2] Those letter-emblems, those shields, are meant to call attention to what I hope may become evident by the end of Chapter 7, below: that I have tried to shape my book as an imitation of that word *ekphrasis* (an ekphrasis of *ekphrasis*) and thus of the circle designating the Homeric shield that is its most celebrated representation. (My final chapter, reacting against this formalist pressure for enclosure, is something of a retreat, drifting off with the postmodern into its own uncertainties.)

It is also fitting, in view of the history of this manuscript, that I begin the book with the shield of Achilles, since I began my explorations of this subject with the shield of Achilles by way of Jean Hagstrum's dealing with it in his pioneering work, *The Sister Arts*.[3] Perhaps, as my epigraph seeks to recognize, it was a stimulus shared by Keats's Grecian Urn, with which Leo Spitzer first introduced me to *ekphrasis* by using that object and that poem as an extraordinary example of it.[4] What these poetic descriptions, Homer's and Keats's, shared was a word-ridden and time-ridden attempt not only to portray visual representations but to create verbal "pictures" whose complexity utterly resists their being translated into visual form.[5] Indeed, the divine source of the shield of Achilles wrought for him by Hephaestus is emphasized ("My mother, the god has given me these weapons; they are such as are the work of immortals. No mortal man could have made them"–bk. 19). This superhuman genesis justifies our conviction that such a thing could never be rendered adequately, so that any attempt at a reverse *ekphrasis* by a graphic artist or sculptor–like that which we see in the

---

2. I call them "emblems," but they are intended as free adaptations, in modern computer graphics (composed on Macintosh SE and PC 386), of the practice of designing illuminated letters to ornament medieval manuscripts. At the beginning of each chapter below, they are balanced by my epigraphs as twin attempts (one visual, one verbal) to emblematize the discussion that follows.

3. Jean H. Hagstrum, *The Sister Arts: The Tradition of Literary Pictorialism and English Poetry from Dryden to Gray* (Chicago: University of Chicago Press, 1958), pp. 19–22.

4. In Leo Spitzer, "The 'Ode on a Grecian Urn,' or Content vs. Metagrammar," in *Essays on English and American Literature*, ed. Anna Hatcher (Princeton: Princeton University Press, 1962), pp. 67–97. The quotation that makes up my epigraph to this Foreword is taken from p. 72.

5. Pope would disagree. In his defense of Homer's use of the shield (in his "Observations"–see n. 1, above) he claims that Homer's verbal artifact does indeed succeed as a painting, indeed "as a complete *Idea* of *Painting*, and a Sketch for what one may call an *universal Picture*" (his italics). But Pope's attachment to the idea of *ut pictura poesis* allowed him to make an easy equation that most commentators have resisted.

Vleughels engraving or in the Flaxman bas-relief—must be vain, and may very well have been undertaken partly in order to reveal the impossibility of an adequate rendering because of the unmatchable superiority of the verbal text. The time-ridden and paradox-ridden character of such texts precludes our being able to "see" them in any but textual form.

I want to make something of the fact that discussions of *ekphrasis* often begin, as mine has, with Homer's version of—or rather invention of—the shield of Achilles, and sometimes accompany it with its strangely altered echo in the shield, forged by Vulcan for Aeneas, that Virgil verbally invents in book 8 of the *Aeneid*. In each case the shield has two characteristics, and these make it doubly protective: it functions, through its body, as a heavy and invulnerable physical protection, and, through the sacred image represented on its face, it functions as a symbolic protection. But of course, as the shields are introduced in these poems, we are led yet one further step away from them into the realm of representation, since we have only the verbal descriptions of these imagined objects with the wrought images they bear upon themselves. Not only do these objects not exist independently of their verbal depictions, but the narrative—the before-after—character of their described images defies any attempt by the plastic artist to produce an object that is totally answerable to the words as their visual equivalent. From the first, then, to look into *ekphrasis* is to look into the illusionary representation of the unrepresentable, even while that representation is allowed to masquerade as a natural sign, as if it could be an adequate substitute for its object. And this leads me from my title to my subtitle.

Let me return, however, to speculations about the dual protective function of the represented shield, Achilles' or Aeneas', both as material barrier and as sanctified icon. And let me concentrate on the second, the shield as sanctified icon. Since we are dealing in either poem with a verbal representation of a fictional visual representation, and thus representation at a second remove, we must concentrate on the symbolic, for the material dissipates into the airiness of words. What the shield bears on its face—the full breadth of Greek culture on Achilles' and the past and future of Roman imperial history on Aeneas'—is to ward off all enemies. As emblem of the bearer of the shield, it defines who he is as representative and defender of his culture against all outsiders, and representative too of the gods who protect that culture through him. Its protection is thus wrought by means of the emblematic decoration as well as the invulnerable material, both of which have been wrought by the divine artificer. The shield is of the same order as the Palladium, the statuary representation of Pallas Athena that serves as her surrogate and—sacred icon that it is—as the divine protector of Troy.

Indeed, we can generalize the notion of palladium as the protection afforded by the force of art serving as an empowered surrogate of divine presence. Thus, for example, Dr. Johnson's satiric reference in "The Vanity of Human Wishes" to the protection of fawning followers by the picture of the godlike statesman in his momentary prime, given godlike attributes, at least until his fall:

> From every room descends the painted face,
> That hung the bright Palladium of the place,
> And, smoked in kitchens or in auctions sold,
> To better features yields the frame of gold.

The painting—his or, after him, his successor's—turns the room into a sanctuary, a sacred place.

In the spirit of Jacopo Mazzoni we can speak quite literally of this sort of mimesis as the representation of an "idol" and treat it as a would-be palladium, a shield against an invasion from outside, a sealing off from weapons that would enter the unprotected body. It thus would shut out the consequences of the world's actions, the world and its actions conceived as unremitting warfare. The shield, like art conceived as shield and as palladium, secures the soldier (reader) in his separateness. As he holds it in front of him, it bears with artful decoration on its face a likeness that, as magic protection, keeps off the world and its threatening dangers.

Dare we generalize upon the shield as palladium, or palladium as shield, and see the palladium as a figure for art itself, idol of the gods and the constructed sign that summons their protection? And what shall we say about the verbal creation of such a shield—an *ekphrasis*—though only with words that defy visual transfer in their appeal to the temporal as well as the spatial imagination of their readers? No wonder the object of such an *ekphrasis* (the shield, the urn) cannot be found: it could not exist, if it was to satisfy all the actions that we are told are being pictured on it.

What is being described in *ekphrasis* is both a miracle and a mirage: a miracle because a sequence of actions filled with befores and afters such as language alone can trace seems frozen into an instant's vision, but a mirage because only the illusion of such an impossible picture can be suggested by the poem's words. The poet, with divine verbal forging, may induce us to imagine—in the pages we painstakingly pass through—that on one shield we can perceive the moving breadth of Greek culture or on the other, from past to future, the glorified history of the Roman empire, all spread out before us to be taken in, as on an emblem, all at once. But we must stay with the poem and with the imagined object it inspires in us, since its supposed object of imitation is only that imagined object. It is our unattainable dream of a total verbal form, a tangible verbal space. We may see it as the poem's miracle, and that seeing is our mirage. This peculiar—and paradoxical—jointly produced experience of *ekphrasis* allows it to function as the consummate example of the verbal art, the ultimate shield beyond shields.

EKPHRASIS

1

PICTURE AND WORD, SPACE AND TIME

The Exhilaration
—and Exasperation
—of *Ekphrasis*
as a Subject

The poet's eye, in a fine frenzy rolling,
Doth glance from heaven to earth, from earth to heaven;
And as imagination bodies forth
The forms of things unknown, the poet's pen
Turns them to shapes and gives to airy nothing
A local habitation and a name.

Theseus, in *A Midsummer Night's Dream* 5.1

Ever since it beckoned to me some two dozen years ago, I
have found ekphrasis both a maddeningly elusive and an
endlessly tempting subject. At that moment it led me,
almost overnight, into the most easily written—and I think the most
lyrical—critical essay I remember having written, but one whose
very lyricism surrounded itself with a theoretical evasiveness that
seemed to demand expansion into a book-length project—the most
exciting I have ever seen on my horizon. That original essay, reprinted below as an appendix to this volume, bore the title *"Ekphrasis* and the Still Movement of Poetry; or *Laokoön* Revisited."[1] From
the moment of my finishing it in a frenzy, one night in 1966 only a
night or two after I had begun it, I began to plan the book toward
which that taunting subject drew me.

It was to be a book about the picture-making capacity of words in
poems, except that from the first that capacity was to be challenged

1. See the Appendix. The essay was originally published in *The Poet as Critic*, ed.
Frederick P. W. McDowell (Evanston: Northwestern University Press, 1967), pp.
3–26. When I reprinted it in my book *The Play and Place of Criticism* (Baltimore: Johns
Hopkins Press, 1967), in its title I substituted for *"Ekphrasis"* the phrase "The Ekphrastic Principle" in order to indicate the broader application I was seeking. I am still
unsure about which of the two titles I prefer—just one more unresolved issue in my
dealings with the subject, or rather in its dealings with me. For a perceptive study of
that original essay and the extension of its themes in my later work see Gwen Raa-
berg, *"Ekphrasis* and the Temporal/Spatial Metaphor in Murray Krieger's Critical Theory," *New Orleans Review* 12 (1985): 34–43.

I am including my essay as an appendix to this volume not only to document the
early version of my interest in the subject and to exhibit my own development in treating it but also to suggest some applications of the ekphrastic principle to what we
used to call primary literary works. Finally, I should point out that because of an
increasing number of discussions surrounding the word since my 1967 essay, ekphrasis has come into sufficiently common use to shed the italics that I gave it in that
essay. So, from this point on, I will not italicize it in this volume.

by the obvious fact that words are many other things but are not— and happily are not—pictures and do not, even illusionarily, have "capacity." How can words try to do the job of the "natural sign" (i.e., a sign that is to be taken as a visual substitute for its referent), when they are, obviously, only arbitrary—though conventionally arbitrary—signs? All the complexities of my subject, its unanswered questions, follow from the need to sustain the two opposed halves of this puzzle. What, in apparently pictorial poetry, do words, *can* words, represent? Conversely, how can words in a poem be picturable? Or do they somehow manage, instead, to represent the unrepresentable, or at least the "un-picturable"?[2] I can put the issue another way by asking how we can reconcile the several blurred meanings attributed to that tricky word "image" as it recurs persistently throughout the history of criticism from Plato to Mazzoni to the moderns (Pound and the "imagists"). It is a term that, in its several simultaneous applications—ambiguously literal and metaphorical—to mental pictures and to words, both carries and hides the theoretical confusions it masks. Finally, because this is a study in criticism rather than in poetry itself, the most important question for me behind all these asks, how can the theorist—how *have* the theorists—made sense out of this set of paradoxes?

I could not then have imagined that the book deriving from an essay that seemed with such ease to write itself could be so difficult and resistant and prolonged an activity. For all these years I have felt ekphrasis drawing me, taunting me, putting me off—the one unyielding subject I have found among the books I have planned and written, both before and after my initial encounter with ekphrasis. Finally arrived at the moment that I have marked as a provisional end of my struggles with it (I will not speak of arriving at the light at the end of the tunnel, here where darkness empties into darkness), I think it would be useful to my reader as well as myself to provide a prospectus of what I have distilled into this troubled text: let it be at once summary and promissory note.

What follows, then, is a run-through of the problems with which I believe a systematic treatment of ekphrasis would have to deal, a rough synopsis of the story it would have to tell. In effect, it is the argument of my book. I acknowledge that I have now finished with these endless problems without solving them, that I have come to the end of my reach while leaving them still just beyond my grasp,

---

2. I borrow this term from Lessing (see Chapter 2, below).

though I am content with their ultimate elusiveness as a guarantee of the powers of literature to defy all attempts by the discursive categories of the critic to tame them.

Hard as it has been to satisfy the demands of the enquiry I undertook so long ago, I felt that I had to continue to struggle with ekphrasis and its network of complications because I was convinced that such an enquiry goes to the very heart of the language—which is to say, the habit of metaphor—that, throughout its history, has shaped and directed our literary criticism. We at once recognize the spatial origin of most of our terms of formal criticism, even in that very word "form"; but there is also an opposing tradition of criticism that fights against such spatial impositions on poetry as a temporal art. So we will find, in the history of our criticism, that there are those moments in which it is molded by the pictorial in language and those moments in which it is molded by the purely verbal as non-pictorial; moments in which it is dedicated to words as capturing a stillness and moments in which it is dedicated to words in movement; or even moments dedicated to the more difficult assignment of words as capturing a *still movement*. Thus I see my enquiry here as going to the heart of the varied practice of criticism itself.

A study that parades under the name ekphrasis can be many things. So perhaps at the start I should make clear what this study is *not*. Several likely subjects offer themselves, each of them satisfying interests that might seem consistent with ekphrasis and, consequently, with ideas traditionally associated with the phrase *ut pictura poesis*. For one, we could investigate literary paintings or pictorial poems—say, narrative pictures and detailed verbal descriptions—and conduct our study either historically or generically, depending on the sort of conclusion we hoped to reach. A specialized version of this interest would have us compare pictures and related words as they come together in illustrated texts, whether in poems or in prose fiction. Or we could compare theories of painting with theories of the verbal arts, again either by relating them historically or by seeking to apply general aesthetic principles. As yet another alternative, we could relate the actual painting being produced in a given period with the poetry being written and trace the relationships, if any, between these products. As a slight variation of such a study, we could look at the attitudes of individual poets or schools of poets toward paintings or contemporary painters, or the reverse, the attitudes of painters toward poems or contemporary poets, tracing friendships and enmities, influences and aversions.

All of these are potentially exciting subjects; many important studies have explored them and others will explore them further. (In recent years I think especially of the remarkable work of W. J. T. Mitchell and Wendy Steiner.)[3] But my own interests here carry me in a different direction, perhaps more general in some ways, though always, I hope, with a systematic focus that would reveal important consequences for the history of theory. I am primarily interested here in the notions put forth by literary theorists about the capacity of language to do the work of the visual sign: whether it can, whether it should. So, instead of these other subjects, what follows is intended as a study of the language of literary criticism and theory throughout its varied history in the West, but only as that language is shaped by its relation—positive or negative—to the injunction *ut pictura poesis*, broadly interpreted. I will be tracing the fortunes of the favored metaphors of critical and theoretical discourse about literature, metaphors shaped for many centuries mainly by a conception of the verbal arts that has them sharing characteristics of the plastic arts as arts of space and of visual appeal, but in the past two centuries more frequently shaped by a conception of the verbal arts that distinguishes them by their special relation to time and to the non-visual word.

Indeed, the matter may even be totally reversed, so that the other arts come to be spoken of in terms we normally would reserve for the verbal arts. In other words, instead of asking all the arts—even the verbal—to seek to become natural signs, we are told to move beyond the naiveté of such a semiotic, to accept the arbitrary and conventional character of *all* aesthetic signs—even the visual—and make the most of it, recognizing that pictures, no less than verbal structures, are human inventions and, as such, are products of an artificial making process. There thus would be no representational transparency, so that all the arts would come to be seen as emerging from a mediated activity.

I will be asking, then, about what others have termed the pictorialist or the anti-pictorialist character of critical and theoretical discourse, as well as about the attraction to that discourse of the language of space or the language of time, in the long history of crit-

---

3. Among their other works see esp. Mitchell, *Iconology: Image, Text, Ideology* (Chicago: University of Chicago Press, 1986), and Steiner, *The Colors of Rhetoric: Problems in the Relation between Modern Literature and Painting* (Chicago: University of Chicago Press, 1982) and *Pictures of Romance: Form against Context in Painting and Literature* (Chicago: University of Chicago Press, 1988).

icism in the arts, which has seen one or another art take the lead, at different moments, in creating a model language for the criticism of more arts than itself. One might even conduct a historical tour of our criticism by tracing—in the dominance now of the spatial and the visual, and now of the temporal and the verbal—the ascendancy and the fall of one art after another as the model art for its rivals to ape.

It should be conceded that these two oppositions, space versus time and picture versus word, do not necessarily collapse into a single theoretical issue, though they have many times been made to do so. As the history of criticism has treated them, the spatial and the pictorial are often, even usually, seen as coupled in opposition to the temporal and the verbal, but the two can be treated as distinct oppositions as well, with the debates about one pair not always involving the other. Indeed, they are not necessarily dependent on one another. For example, we shall see that Gotthold Ephraim Lessing concentrates exclusively upon the opposition between the spatial and the temporal, since his only concern with the word is with its capacity to yield moving rather than still pictures: he does not explore its peculiarly verbal—as *non-pictorial*—character. He concedes the opposition between natural and arbitrary signs only to dismiss its importance to his argument against a poetry of space and in favor of a poetry of time. On the other hand, at much the same time, Edmund Burke (as we shall see in Chapter 4) is far more concerned with the word's suggestive—*because non-pictorial*—powers and does not directly engage the issue of temporal versus spatial representation.[4] (It may well be that within the dynamics of Burke's "sublime" there is a flight from stasis and thus the implication of a temporal—to the exclusion of a spatial—dimension, at least in the percipient's response. Still, his argument is explicitly addressed to one of the two debates without addressing the other.)

But to pursue such matters here is to leap far ahead of these introductory suggestions about what this study intends. In dealing with such niceties I meant primarily to make it clear at the outset that I will be concentrating on critical and theoretical discourse, as it reflects my special concern, rather than on the practice of the arts themselves, since, as I acknowledge from the first, the latter would lead me to tell quite a different story. Further, my treatment makes no pretense of being historically exhaustive; I will be selecting only

---

4. See Chapter 2 for the major discussion of Lessing and Chapter 4 for the major discussion of Burke.

a small number of representative landmark texts across the centuries, and returning to them again and again to search further within
them and among them, as I create my own narrative to account for
a series of striking developments in the language of theory and criticism. Whatever its shortcomings, I hope that this narrative, however partial and selective, will mark off the dimensions of the specific problems that define my subject and point the direction in
which solutions to them might be found, or at least eliminate directions that are less likely to lead to solutions.

I enter upon this enquiry by way of ekphrasis because I see ekphrasis as the most extreme and telling instance of the visual and spatial potential of the literary medium. Let me at the outset define my
sense of ekphrasis or rather, more broadly, set the limits on the ways
I will suggest in which the term might be profitably used, although
these limits will prove rather elastic since I intend to suggest an
increasingly expansive reach for the verbal manifestations of the ekphrastic principle. I initiated this enquiry by accepting the narrow
meaning given ekphrasis by Leo Spitzer (see the epigraph to my Foreword, above) as the name of a literary genre, or at least a *topos*, that
attempts to imitate in words an object of the plastic arts.[5] As the most
commonly accepted use of the word, this remains the heart of the
word's meaning for me. Ekphrasis, under this definition, clearly presupposes that one art, poetry, is defining its mission through its
dependence on the mission of another art—painting, sculpture, or
others. From the first, the study of ekphrasis, resting on that dependence, seemed to me the most extreme—and most useful—way to put
into question the pictorial limits of the function of words in poetry.[6]

5. Let me advise at the outset that I will use the phrase "the plastic arts" as aestheticians have traditionally used it: to refer to those arts in which the artist shapes or
fashions or molds a material into a perceptible physical object, principally sculpture
or painting. The more recent connotations associated with "plastic" in our culture,
mainly derogatory, may well preclude the neutral designation "plastic arts" from continuing long in use, but its conventional generic use in aesthetics makes it a helpful
shorthand that I am not quite ready to give up.

6. An even more restrictive meaning, one that I will *not* use, is given the term by
Jean Hagstrum. In *The Sister Arts: The Tradition of Literary Pictorialism and English
Poetry from Dryden to Gray* (Chicago: University of Chicago Press, 1958), Hagstrum
reserves ekphrasis for only those poems in which the represented art object, like
Keats's Grecian urn, "speaks out" to the reader. When objects are only described and
have no verbal message, as in the case of Homer's shield of Achilles, Hagstrum calls
the poem "iconic" as his more generic category. See *The Sister Arts*, pp. 18–29, esp.
18n.

However, I came to feel free to play with the expansiveness of the meaning and application of ekphrasis in view of a fuller history of the term's usage. The early meaning given "ekphrasis" in Hellenistic rhetoric (mainly in the "second sophistic" of the third and fourth centuries A.D.) was totally unrestricted: it referred, most broadly, to a verbal description of something, almost anything, in life or art.[7] Whatever the object it was to describe, and whether in rhetoric or poetry, it consistently carried with it the sense of a set verbal device that encouraged an extravagance in detail and vividness in representation, so that—as it was sometimes put—our ears could serve as our eyes since "[ekphrasis] must through hearing operate to bring about seeing."[8] More flagrantly than other rhetorical devices of the second sophistic, the ekphrasis, as an extended description, was called upon to intrude upon the flow of discourse and, for its duration, to suspend the argument of the rhetor or the action of the poet; to rivet our attention upon a visual object to be described, which it was to elaborate in rich and vivid detail. It was, then, a device intended to interrupt the temporality of discourse, to freeze it during its indulgence in spatial exploration.[9]

Although works of the plastic arts—including illustrated cups and vases and urns and embroideries as well as paintings and sculptures or reliefs—were often cited among the many sorts of objects of ekphrastic description, there was no suggestion that ekphrasis was confined to them; indeed, they were not usually privileged among the unlimited sorts of objects on the visual horizon that were candidates for being converted into words. It is true that the *Imagines* of Philostratus the Elder in the third century was a series of descriptions of pictorial works of art and that, in his own derivative series of

7. I am grateful to Paul Davis both for helpful research into the classical sources of "ekphrasis" and for his useful conversation with me about them.

8. The quotation is from Hermogenes, "Ecphrasis," *The Elementary Exercises (Progymnasmata),* in Charles S. Baldwin, *Medieval Rhetoric and Poetic* (Gloucester, Mass.: Peter Smith, 1959), pp. 35-36. In this broad assignment of its function, ekphrasis would seem to overlap, almost totally, the rhetorically encouraged virtue of *enargeia,* which is also defined as vivid description addressed to the inner eye. I introduce the notion of *enargeia* later in this chapter; and in Chapter 3, from its title on, I use *enargeia* as my starting point for tracing the critical tradition that defined itself by its encouragement of verbal painting (*ut pictura poesis*).

9. As we shall see in Chapter 5, this rhetorical tradition of the second sophistic contributes importantly to the extensive list of precedents that Jacopo Mazzoni cites to back up his own definition of poetry as an "image" or "idol," the transformation of words into the spatial.

similar descriptions, also entitled *Imagines,* Philostratus the Younger refers to such description as ekphrasis. But the term is hardly being used as a technical reference to a genre, nor is there any attempt to argue more generally for such a restriction of objects. And when, during the same general period, Hermogenes, in the work already cited,[10] lists examples of objects for ekphrasis, he does not talk separately about works of art at all.

Yet the narrowing of the objects of ekphrasis to works in the plastic arts does eventually occur, probably influenced by the fact that some of the most striking examples of ekphrasis were devoted to objects, real or imagined, from the plastic arts—perhaps beginning with Homer's shield of Achilles, but also including many other frequently cited examples from Homer and succeeding classical poets and orators. The range of reference of the word "ekphrasis," as it becomes a technical generic term, seems to become restricted in order to conform to those examples, those diverting descriptive interludes, that commentary habitually selected as the great ekphrases.[11] And the connection of ekphrasis to works of pictorial art gradually becomes a firm one and continues into the modern era.

The advantages of having a work of art as an object of ekphrasis are, I think, obvious. If an author is seeking to suspend the discourse for an extended, visually appealing descriptive interlude, is he not better off—instead of describing the moving, changing, object in nature—to describe an object that has already interrupted the flow of existence with its spatial completeness, that has already been created as a fixed representation? Surely so: if he would impose a brief sense of *being,* borrowed from the plastic arts, in the midst of his shifting world of verbal *becoming,* the already frozen pictorial representation would seem to be a preferred object. His ekphrastic purpose would seem to be better served by its having as its object an artifact that itself not only is in keeping with, but is a direct reflection of, that purpose. Further, if one justification for the verbal description is to have it—for all the uncertainties of its words and our reading of them—compete with the visual object it would describe, the comparison would seem to be stabilized on one side by fixing that object so that, as an actual artifact, it can be appealed to as a constant, unlike our varying perceptual experiences of objects in the world.

10. See n. 8, above.

11. Since, by removing the italics, I have brought "ekphrasis" into the language, I will not use the original Greek plural form, *ekphraseis.*

I have acknowledged the special theoretical value of using works of art as ekphrastic objects in order to examine, in its most extreme form, the capacity of words to transmit pictures. But the interest in the pictorial capacities of the verbal art would then once again open onto the broader consideration of ekphrasis as the sought-for equivalent in words of any visual image, in or out of art. Backed by historical precedent, then, I want also to summon this original, more universal sense of ekphrasis. Even while deferring to the special connection between ekphrasis and works in the plastic arts, I will broaden the range of possible ekphrastic objects by re-connecting ekphrasis to all "word-painting." I want to trace the ekphrastic as it is seen occurring all along the spectrum of spatial and visual emulation in words.

But I must also move even beyond such emulation—and beyond historical precedent—as I press all the dimensions I can find in ekphrasis. Because my interests lead me to extend the literal interest in ekphrasis to the widest possible probing of the ekphrastic principle, they lead me to search for a theory that would account for all the spatio-temporal possibilities within the poetic medium. Thus, even more than the verbal representation of the pictorial, I must include those other manifestations of the spatial impulse within poem-making that seek to fulfill the original ekphrastic impulse in the history of the verbal arts in the West, if the ekphrastic is to include every attempt, within an art of words, to work toward the illusion that it is performing a task we usually associate with an art of natural signs. At the far side of this extension of the ekphrastic principle, I see it at work also in the attempted construction of a literary work, whose words shape it into the verbal equivalent of an art object sensed in space. That is, the ekphrastic principle may operate not only on those occasions on which the verbal seeks in its own more limited way to represent the visual but also when the verbal object would emulate the spatial character of the painting or sculpture by trying to force its words, despite their normal way of functioning as empty signs, to take on a substantive configuration— in effect to become an emblem. What is at stake in all these diverse attempts at ekphrasis is the semiotic status of both space and the visual in the representational attempt by the verbal art—an ultimately vain attempt—to capture these within its temporal sequence, which would form itself into its own poetic object.

Ekphrastic ambition gives to the language art the extraordinary assignment of seeking to represent the literally unrepresentable. Yet

every tendency in the verbal sequence to freeze itself into a shape—
or we can use "form" or "pattern" or some other metaphor borrowed from the spatial arts—is inevitably accompanied by a counter-
tendency for that sequence to free itself from the limited enclosure
of the frozen, sensible image into an unbounded temporal flow. Is
it any wonder that I insist on words like "elusive" and "taunting"
to characterize ekphrasis as a subject for theoretical placement?
Whence this sense of inadequacy, of irresolution, of incompleteness, this challenge that seems to resist my attempts to find a critical
language that can wrestle ekphrasis to the ground? I believe the
difficulties arise out of the unresolvable tension, the mutual blockage, at the very base of the ekphrastic aspiration.

The ekphrastic aspiration in the poet and the reader must come
to terms with two opposed impulses, two opposed feelings, about
language: one is exhilarated by the notion of ekphrasis and one is
exasperated by it. Ekphrasis arises out of the first, which craves the
spatial fix, while the second yearns for the freedom of the temporal
flow. The first asks for language—in spite of its arbitrary character
and its temporality—to freeze itself into a spatial form. Yet it retains
an awareness of the incapacity of words to come together at an
instant (*tout à coup*), at a single stroke of sensuous immediacy, as if
in an unmediated impact. Their *incapacity* is precisely what is to be
emphasized: words cannot have capacity, cannot be capacious,
because they have, literally, no space. The exhilaration, then, derives from the dream—and the pursuit—of a language that can, in
spite of its limits, recover the immediacy of a sightless vision built
into our habit of perceptual desire since Plato. It is the romantic
quest to realize the nostalgic dream of an original, pre-fallen language of corporeal presence, though our only means to reach it is
the fallen language around us. And it would be the function of the
ekphrastic poet to work the magical transformation.

The second of these impulses, on the contrary, accepts a modest,
unpretentious, demystified language that claims no magic, whose
arbitrariness and temporal succession can escape the frozen momentary vision that, in seeking the momentous, would belie the
fleetingness of the moment in an anti-pictorial blur. To this impulse
the notion of ekphrasis, as a threat to language's temporal promise
and the critic's conforming aspirations, can only be exasperating. In
the conflict between these two impulses, between the attraction to
ekphrasis and the aversion to it, what we are feeling is, on the one

side, what I call the semiotic desire for the natural sign and, on the other, the rejection of any such claim to the "natural," for fear of the deprivation it would impose on our freedom of internal movement, the freedom of our imagination and its flow in its arbitrary signs.

This is one doubleness in language as a medium of the verbal arts. And there is another: language in poems can be viewed as functioning transparently, sacrificing its own being for its referent; and it can be viewed as functioning sensuously, insisting upon its own irreducible there-ness. Yet I believe that as the Western imagination has seized upon and used the ekphrastic principle, it has sought—through the two-sidedness of language as a medium of the verbal arts—to comprehend the simultaneity, in the verbal figure, of fixity and flow, of an image at once grasped and yet slipping away through the crevices of language. This sense of simultaneity is sponsored by our capacity to respond to the verbal image as at once limitedly referential and mysteriously self-substantial. The aesthetic dream of our culture has long been of a miracle that permits these opposed impulses to come together in the paradoxical immediacy of ekphrasis, whether as a verbal replacement for a visual image or as its own verbal emblem that plays the role of a visual image while playing its own role. In either case, the dream of miracle remains even if its illusionary ground suggests it is no more than mirage. Perhaps this claim to miracle is only a way of specifying Coleridge's claim that in poetry the imagination serves as the "balance or reconciliation of opposite or discordant qualities," or Wolfgang Iser's search in the aesthetic for "the simultaneity of the mutually exclusive," not unlike Louis Marin's or my own pursuit of the duplicity of what we both have termed the "metonymic metaphor." Still, this specification by ekphrasis is important despite its inevitably paradoxical character: indeed, in the deference it pays to the anti-spatial impulse while holding out for the spatial object, it can help cover the break between what we call the modern and the postmodern.

I can now suggest in a preliminary way the directions that following chapters will take and the shape they are intended to give my subject. In speaking of ekphrasis, or at least of the ekphrastic impulse, I have pointed to its source in the semiotic desire for the natural sign, the desire, that is, to have the world captured in the word, the word that belongs to it, or, better yet, the word to which *it* belongs. This desire to see the world in the word is what, after Derrida, we have come to term the logocentric desire. It is this naive desire that leads us to prefer the immediacy of the picture to the mediation of the code in our search for a tangible, "real" referent that would render the sign transparent.[12]

Thus ekphrasis, as the ultimate translation of such a desire into the language arts, rests, in its most obvious form, on a verbal pictorialism—the belief in the natural-sign basis for all the arts—and was most attractive as a device when, in literary theory, pictorialism was in flower. Yet it is not altogether resisted when anti-pictorialism becomes dominant, although its character as ekphrasis is radically modified and sophisticated. Throughout the history of the ekphrastic temptation, we sense the desire to overcome the disadvantage of words and of the verbal art as mere arbitrary signs by forcing them to ape the natural signs and the natural-sign art that they cannot turn themselves into. As readers, we are to use the free play in our minds of the words' *intelligible* character to allow us to indulge the illusion that they create a *sensible* object, though an intelligibly—and hence only figuratively—sensible object, of course.

Throughout its history, at the heart of a poetics of ekphrasis has been the opposition between natural and arbitrary signs. (I will be tracing the steps by which this opposition came to be perceived as no longer tenable, a perception generally agreed upon for some time.) For many centuries this opposition overlapped crucially the related opposition derived from Plato between so-called sensible and intelligible signs (and it is with this opposition that I begin in Chapter 2). In the poetics of ekphrasis we find an ambivalence between, on the one hand, the defensive concession that language, as arbitrary and with a sensuous lack, is a disadvantaged medium in need of emulating the natural and sensible medium of the plastic arts and, on the other hand, the prideful confidence in language as a medium privileged by its very intelligibility, which opens the sensible world to the free-ranging imagination without being bound by the limitations of the sensible as revealed in the visual field. The superior access of natural signs to the sensible world received by our eyes can be countered by the superior access of language, com-

12. I should note parenthetically here that the conception of the picture as natural sign rests on a naively "realistic" assumption of an unproblematic relation between the painting and its object of imitation. Since this conception does not take into account the making of the mimetic painting as a thing of pigment and canvas, it bypasses the use of these materials to create the optical illusion of objects and persons. The narrow, literal doctrine of ekphrasis would seem to require this primitive notion of the pictorial as the naively representational.

posed of arbitrary signs, to the intelligible world received by our inner vision, conceived figuratively as "the eyes of the mind." Such is the cluster of oppositions, and the attempts by language to over-run them, that for me help define the domain of ekphrasis, or at least the ekphrastic, as it has functioned in the Western aesthetic since Plato.

Behind these matters lurks the central question, What theory of representation, what semiotic, is required in order to argue that imi-tation is the same operation in the visual and verbal arts? Ever since, in his *Cratylus*, Plato, however playfully, made what is in effect our first distinction between natural and arbitrary signs, but made it utterly within the precincts of an aesthetic—indeed, a metaphysic—that rested on a doctrine of mimesis, the language arts have had a lengthy struggle to free themselves, because of their visually disad-vantaged medium, from the secondariness assigned to them in their non-naturalness of representation. I believe the history of this struggle, which culminated first in rescuing language from beneath the yoke of visual signs that it could try in vain to emulate, and then in privileging language as supreme among representational media, is important to our understanding of how the ekphrastic principle has functioned and can function in the Western poetic.

But before tracing that history, we have to comprehend the bur-den of the natural-sign aesthetic under which the language arts labored for so long. It is an aesthetic in which, within a commitment to a "visual epistemology," representation can be nothing other than literal imitation and thus poses no problems.[13] Under the aegis of this aesthetic, and with the eye as the privileged sense (as it was for Plato), the model art is of course the pictorial art to which the ver-bal art is to adapt its program. And the poetics, accordingly, is built out of the spatial and visual language of the pictorial art, though, as applied to the *verbal* arts, that language can be no more than roughly and uncritically metaphorical in its attempt to force those verbal arts to take on alien (i.e., spatial and visual) characteristics, if only by analogy.

In spite of Plato's anti-aesthetic, puritanical intentions, his basic and unwavering notion of the unproblematically mimetic character

13. My use of the phrase "visual epistemology" derives from Forrest G. Robinson, *The Shape of Things Known: Sidney's Apology in Its Philosophical Tradition* (Cambridge, Mass.: Harvard University Press, 1972), esp. pp. 1–59. I pursue the consequences of this theory of representation in Chapter 3.

of signs bestowed a privilege on the natural-sign arts, as if they could represent their imitated objects (as objects of our limited perceptions) without disparities eventuating from the making process. Within such a theoretical setting, as Plato's followers were to make clear for centuries, words, on the other hand, could do their mimetic best, but they could not avoid their inferiority as an instrument of faithful representation. It is not surprising that this sort of semiotic produces the device termed *enargeia* as a major virtue for the language arts to attain. To create *enargeia* is to use words to yield so vivid a description that they—dare we say literally?—place the represented object before the reader's (hearer's) inner eye. This is as much as a verbal artist could hope for: almost as good as a picture, which in turn is almost as good as the thing itself. We can understand the original use of *enargeia* as a rhetorical device to enable an advocate to reproduce before his hearers in court the scene or incident he needs them to picture in order to persuade them to judge favorably. As my earlier historical examination indicated, *enargeia* develops into becoming one with the ekphrastic principle as poetry's principle. It is thoroughly in accord with the phrase originally attributed by Plutarch to Simonides that described poetry as a "speaking picture" or, much later, with the unfortunate, though generally accepted, misinterpretation of Horace's *ut pictura poesis.* Art in general is seen as a mnemonic device meant to reproduce an absent reality, and deprived of sensuousness, poetry is art at yet a further remove.

As I argue in detail in Chapter 2, where the drama is excepted from the sensory incapacities of language, it is only because dramatic representation, as the interaction of apparently real people, is itself a sort of natural sign in its illusionary immediacy. Lessing reminds us of drama's special role, a natural-sign role, as a visual art (a "moving picture") and, by implication, concedes the greater mimetic distance that occurs in non-dramatic poetry. For the dramatic mode of representation is not altogether dependent on the invisibilities of language, as the lyric and narrative modes are.

In view of non-dramatic poetry's mimetic objective and the handicaps of its medium to attain it as directly as its more obviously mimetic rival arts, it is no wonder that, as a language art, poetry developed and pursued an ekphrastic ambition, seeking to emulate those arts whose naturalness makes them appear to be reality's surrogate. That ambition expresses itself, its commitment to *enargeia*, in a variety of ways as we follow it from ancient Greece through the

Renaissance. Let me follow that development as a narrative that moves from epigram to ekphrasis to emblem. It is in the latter, the emblem, that the ekphrastic principle, even more than in ekphrasis itself, fully realizes itself. In moving from epigram to ekphrasis to emblem, I do not mean to impose a chronological sequence so much as to suggest the alternative emphases that consistently reflect a complicated, if not confused, mixture of motives and epistemologies as the visual and the verbal interact in these strangely hybrid products.

In its early versions in Greece the epigram, in its primary use as a verbal inscription on sculpture or tombstone, implicitly acknowledged and set in place the subsidiary relation of its words to the work of plastic art that it accompanied (*epi-gram*), often as little more than a legend. But, sometimes restive in this subsidiary role, the epigram could use its words to challenge the primacy of the physical object it adorned. That is, not only could it try to function as a verbal representation — indeed as a verbal equivalent — of its spatial object, but it could also perform in several ways unavailable to its object:[14] it could introduce an awareness of passing time — as only words can do — as a contradictory commentary upon the unmoving, unchangeable monument; it could speak for its object, giving it a voice, whether directly or enigmatically; it could point to the illusionary effects of artifice in the plastic construct; and it could, as an act of interpretation, allegorize the impact of the eternalizing shrine. In these ways the epigram could complicate the apparently unambiguous material representation that it was supposed only to complement; it could drive a wedge between the monument and its referent, thus undermining any pretense that the material object was a natural sign.

On the other side, the epigram was, perhaps more often — and more appropriately — confined to the self-effacing function of calling attention to the illusionary effectiveness of its plastic-art companion as a natural sign ("just *like* the live person"), thereby relegating itself to mere verbal explanation and emphasizing its own arbitrary-sign service as no more than a gloss on the tangible and successfully illusionary primary object. In this acknowledged secondary role, it reinforced the disadvantaged place for literature that we have seen to be dictated by mimetic theory.

14. No one dealing with my subject can fail to be in the debt of Jean Hagstrum's *The Sister Arts*. I again register my own indebtedness in the present discussion, though it will be reflected in many other places in this chapter and others.

Still, the impact of the epigram could go either way: especially in its funerary role it could also insist upon the deceptive consequences of the material object, immobile and unchanging, an illusion that, in its stasis and apparent permanence, belied the transience of human life – and death. That insistence suggests, paradoxically, the unreality of the very eternalizing monument and its now-dead referent that the epigram was to celebrate, thus suggesting also the fraudulence of the pretense of the would-be natural sign. Where the consciousness of time is admitted, there the complexities of the verbal universe also enter, undermining the immediate assurances otherwise given by the pretender natural sign. What has actually re-entered the scene is the spirit of Plato that insists on turning the material world into the deceptive realm of appearance, leaving reality to the invisible ideas that transcend the senses. The epigram has turned into a metaphysical allegory on human vainglory. Once reality is freed from the sensible to soar into the realm of the intelligible, the would-be natural sign and its material object must lose all priority, and the possibility of representing the transcendentally "real" must be vested in the invented codes of language alone. The unchallenged belief in the authority of natural-sign representation will have to wait for the late seventeenth and eighteenth centuries, when the doctrine of imitation could rest securely in the spatial solidity of the material world that produced its firmly standing objects for imitation, unthreatened by any consciousness of the loosening flow of temporality.

Despite the complications into which the epigram could lead, in its early moment it was to function primarily as a pointer to the accompanying monument, for the most part accepting a second-place role for the arbitrary signs of language. (Of course, the epigram pursues its own more ambiguous role as it later emerges into its distinguished career as an independent work of verbal art.) When we move from epigram to ekphrasis and lose the presence of the companion object, we find language no longer yielding any primacy to its (apparently) visual object, but seeking an equivalence with it – and more. The ekphrasis is, in effect, an epigram without the accompanying object, indeed without any object except the one it would verbally create. The visual image that the ekphrasis seeks to translate into words is of course lost in the translation, as gradually the verbal representation, no longer leaning on another, extra-textual, tangible representation, takes on the power of a free-standing entity.

Frequently, as we find in obvious examples of ekphrasis such as the shield of Achilles in the *Iliad* (bk. 18) or—to invoke the most familiar, even if belated, example—Keats's Grecian urn, the object of the ekphrasis does not exist except as it is invented in its verbal description, subject to the special character that only its verbal form can exploit.[15] I suggest that in such cases the poet prefers the object to be fictive so that his ostensible verbal description can make free with it. Indeed, in the verbal representations of both the shield and the urn, the ekphrases take their special meaning by exceeding their fictive spatial objects in a number of ways.

The most obvious way in which each verbal description overruns its object is in the opening it provides, within what is presumably a spatial construct, for movement into the realm of human time. There is this difference between Homer's shield and Keats's urn as objects for the poet exercising the magic of his craft: the first is a fictional "impossible" object that only a poet could transcribe,[16] while the second is a fictional *possible* object that the poet, and only a poet, can move beyond. That is, the invented shield supposedly represents temporal sequences that could not appear on it (hence its miraculous making, which could be performed only by a divine maker), so that only an ostensibly mimetic verbal narrative can convey them to *us*; by contrast, the invented urn accepts the spatially frozen limits of its represented scenes (representative also of metaphysical, or at least aesthetic, stasis), so that it is up to the poet, whose language is in tune with the wretchedness of the human temporality ("all breathing human passion") that we all share, to break through and move beyond into the unfolding incompleteness of mortal time. The two ekphrases thus speak differently in their effort to represent what the fictive art object could not, but the effect is

15. I would argue that even if we found an urn that seemed to be the one that is the ostensible occasion for Keats's poem, it would seem, for all its beauty, a poor thing so long as we expected it to account for all that the poem makes us aware of with respect to the urn. The ability of Keats's language to exploit the paradox of the urn's multidimensional "still"-ness at once leads us beyond the circular enclosure of the urn itself.

16. I borrow (and distort) the word "impossible" as it has been applied to M. C. Escher's misleading architectural pictures, which force us into two simultaneous and contradictory ways of perceiving spatial relationships. I have found E. H. Gombrich's discussion of Escher's "visual paradoxes" especially valuable (see "Illusion and Visual Deadlock," in his *Meditations on a Hobby Horse and Other Essays on the Theory of Art* [London: Phaidon Press, 1963], pp. 154–56). See Chapter 7, below, for an extension of this concept to the verbal arts.

similar: as the hundreds of lines in Homer permit us to take in the extended accumulation of anthropological and narrative detail that could not coexist on a single shield, so Keats's poem gives voice to all that the urn cannot say. Using its speech to break through the "stillness" of the urn's circularity, it points us to what must transpire beyond the seized moments represented on its fictive object, the moments that the urn and the poem (like the urn) would contain, but that the poem also (*un*like the urn) must dissolve.

Both the verbally pictured urn and shield, then, by superimposing our awareness of the accidents of human time upon the fixed completeness of formal stasis, demonstrate the inevitable mixing—through the indulgence in paradox—of the existential in the aesthetic. Keats constantly reminds us of the unhappy befores and afters that cannot appear in the frozen pictures on the urn he is presumably describing: the unpictured moments beyond the wooing and, just beyond the frame of the second scene, both the unpictured past—the absent and abandoned town—and the unpictured future, the sacrificial "green altar" to which the heifer is being led. Linear history and circular art can both be sustained in the poem as they cannot be on the urn. Similarly, in describing what appears on the shield, Homer seeks to give us at once both the elaborately ornamented metal artifact and the routine material life of ancient Greece (together with its mythological divine overseers) that he both represents and *mis*represents: "The earth darkened behind them and looked like earth that has been ploughed / though it was gold. Such was the wonder of the shield's forging" (Lattimore). Black earth in gold, and both at once: it is, rather, the alchemical wonder of the *words'* forging, which in this ekphrasis collapses time and space, earthy life as lived and its divine transmutation into a golden art. In these two ekphrases, then, we are given, not a visual image of a golden shield or an urn, but a verbal shield or a verbal urn *and* the textual intimations of an existence beyond: what only words can give us by revealing the two at once. It is an aesthetic alchemy revived for our time in the golden bird of Yeats's Byzantium.

So the claim of naive imitation no longer applies, not even in a genre like ekphrasis, which seems to have been created expressly for mimetic purposes. The genre is thus used to allow the *fiction* of an ekphrasis, a make-believe imitation of what does not exist outside the poem's verbal creation of it. Literal ekphrasis has moved, via the power of words, to an illusion of ekphrasis. The ekphrastic principle has learned to do without the simple ekphrasis in order to explore more freely the illusionary powers of language.

By the time we arrive at the emblem poetry of the Renaissance, we find that the relationship between visual image and word, which was both established and undermined in the epigram, has completed its reversal. As visual companion to the poem, the emblem, which is no longer anything like a mimetic representation, seems cryptic and in need of explication, so that it leans upon a text whose verbal completeness now permits *it* to claim primacy. Though visual, the emblem has taken on a mysterious complexity that makes it function less as an imitation than as itself a text in need of interpretation, so that we welcome and depend upon the words as the literal code, spelling out as its own what is only hinted at in the opaque pictorial signs of another, figured code.

As I hope to show in Chapter 5, the pressures of Renaissance Neo-Platonism made it increasingly objectionable for the artist to indulge the sensible world or imitations of it. Instead, esoteric symbols were to be taken as an allegorical code to allow us access to a reality that was only intelligible, accessible to the mind alone. According to the mystifications summoned by Marsilio Ficino, for example, we need the symbolic immediacy of things, and the representation of things, rather than the mediation of empty words; but those representations – thanks to an ontological hermeneutic that allows us to interpret them as essential symbols – serve as our threshold to an intelligible reality.[17] So it is a picture, but it is also a language rather than a natural-sign representation. Yet, as language, it is not arbitrary since the signs are firmly tied to their referents through the unalterable allegorical system rooted in that ontological hermeneutic.

In this way, according to Ficino, the hieroglyphs of the Egyptians, though a language of pictures, are an emblematic code rather than a direct imitation of objects presumably being represented. So, on one side, pictures as natural signs are rejected as imitations of the lowly sensible, and on the other, language-as-words, though seeking the intelligible, is rejected as symbolically empty. Between them are pictures-as-language – a sacred language of presence – which, essentially locked into the ontological hermeneutic, indirectly reveal

17. Gombrich is uniquely valuable to us in his dealings with these materials. See his "*Icones Symbolicae*: Philosophies of Symbolism and Their Bearing on Art," reprinted in his *Symbolic Images: Studies in the Art of the Renaissance* (London: Phaidon Press, 1972), pp. 123–95. For my discussion here, see esp. pp. 157–72; the translation from Ficino that shortly follows appears on pp. 158–59.

intelligible reality to us by speaking the unmediated language of
God as the only possible sensible representation of Platonic ideas.
Within this perspective, the dependence on words is part of the
curse on us as fallen creatures, who have access only to signs that
are arbitrary and conventional ("multiple and shifting," Ficino
would say), since we are denied the power to speak the immediate
language of God.

> When the Egyptian priests wished to signify divine mysteries, they did
> not use the small characters of script, but the whole images of plants,
> trees or animals; for God has knowledge of things not by way of multiple
> thought but like the pure and firm shape of the thing itself.
>
> Your thoughts about time are multiple and shifting, when you say that
> time is swift or that, by a kind of turning movement, it links the begin-
> ning again to the end, that it teaches prudence and that it brings things
> and carries them away again. But the Egyptian can comprehend the
> whole of this discourse in one firm image when he paints a winged ser-
> pent with its tail in its mouth, and so with the other images which Horus
> described.

The visual emblem, then, is devised, as "one firm image," to transmit an all-at-once, enclosed meaning—as enclosed as the image of
the "winged serpent with its tail in its mouth," a conventional figure of closure, though for the Egyptian (according to Ficino) it is temporality itself, in its winged form that would escape closure, which
is in this emblem being figured, however paradoxically, as the ultimate closure.[18] Here, in the magical *ouroboros* (or "tail-eater") the
image, functioning here as an emblem, as a code, must be treated as
a language to be interpreted rather than as a natural-sign imitation
to be seen through to its object.[19] This is so even if the code is ren-

18. I have anticipated this sustaining of the paradoxical coexistence of the wings of
linear time and its circular enclosure in what I have said earlier in this chapter about
the shield of Achilles and Keats's urn. The conflict between linear and circular concepts of time is a major issue in Chapter 7. There I take up the need in the ekphrastic
tradition to hold onto the circular and yet to break through it to the linear. It is one
advance I have tried to make on what I now see as the overemphasis on circular secur-
ity in my earlier essay (in the Appendix) and in the source of that essay, the Spitzer
review article that provides my epigraph as well as the grounds for the discussion
that closes Chapter 7.

19. There is a different, even more cosmic significance assigned to the tail-eater by
Horapollo (referred to by Ficino as "Horus" in the above quotation), who is the pre-
sumed (but questionable) author of the *Hieroglyphica*, the most influential list of em-

dered hermeneutically (as well as hermetically) inevitable rather than arbitrary by virtue of its being ontologically secured, thanks to a metaphysical equation.

The desire to shift art's responsibility from objects to be re-presented to a code to be interpreted helps turn all art into interpretable texts, even if—for a world confident of its metaphysical grounding—the interpretation was pre-scribed. This desire is related to the Puritan war on idolatry, which results in a rejection of the deceptive seductions of the worldly—and hence of visual representation as transparent idols of art. Once, like the Neo-Platonists, one pursues Plato's quest for ontological objects seen by the mind's eye rather than phenomenal objects seen by the body's eye, then the superiority of interpretable—and hence intelligible—symbols, visual or verbal, over the immediately representational arts, is assured. Instead of being limited to the sensed world about us, as a visual and natural sign through which that world's objects are to be perceived, the arbitrary, though conventional, signs of a visual or verbal language can give us the insensible illusion of an existing object while actually moving freely to the intelligible realm beyond the senses.

Ficino himself, we saw, distrusted the symbolic powers of signs as arbitrary as words and thus called instead for a language of visual symbols. Despite Ficino's doubts, however, his support of an interpretive system of symbols—though symbols mysteriously multiple in their intelligible meanings—helped clear the ground for claims of the superiority of the verbal arts to emerge. The Neo-Platonic argument led to a view of the verbal arts as the purest version of symbolic structure—the freest from any dependence on sense—so that they could claim all the advantages of the visual arts while enjoying

---

blematic identifications used in the Renaissance. He uses it to symbolize the universe itself, the heavens, the four elements, and human life in the circularity of youth and age, generation and diminution (see *The Hieroglyphics of Horapollo*, trans. George Boas [New York: Pantheon, 1950], pp. 57-58). As it is sometimes used in medieval and Renaissance alchemical literature dominated by Christian Neo-Platonism, the tail-eating serpent has yet another, more moralistic kind of allegorical significance. It is still a paradoxical image expressing the mutually exclusive, but it now encloses the simultaneity of good and evil, of poison and cure, thanks to the magical transmuting properties of mercury (related, of course, to Hermes and, beyond, to the divine master, Hermes Trismegistus). A redemptive metamorphosis of the serpent of Eden, the *ouroboros* is seen in the hermetic reading as consuming his own venom and converting it into a miraculously virtuous balm (see Kurt Seligmann, *The History of Magic* [New York: Pantheon, 1948], pp. 134-35).

a freedom from their limitations: they function, in effect, as a higher but unworldly analogue of the contemned arts of the natural sign. Yet it is the dream of a return to the idyll of the natural sign, the lingering semiotic desire for the natural sign, that presses the poet to resort to the verbal analogy to it in the realm of the intelligible by struggling to create an emblem out of words.

The verbal artist, then, is authorized to have it both ways, dealing with the words of the world and taking advantage of their intelligibility to claim a realm beyond. Some of those who earlier maintained the primacy of the natural sign nostalgically saw an Edenic origin in it, so that our need for the mediation of words was a result of the Fall; but those we have now turned to would privilege the intelligible reach of language over natural-sign images, condemning the latter on the grounds of idolatry and their confinement to the sensible world. The final trick is for language to complete its bid for supremacy by taking on the here-ness of the plastic arts, turning itself into a form that creates the illusion of becoming its own emblem, an internal ekphrasis, *almost* sensuous after all, though without touching the earth. But of course it is the *almost* that stimulates its complex, paradoxical attractiveness.

Once the shift from natural-sign picture to picture-as-code has occurred, it is a short step to a configuration of words that would turn themselves into a form that is the self-enclosed equivalent of an emblem, in effect a verbal emblem. The visual emblem and the verbal emblem are complementary languages for seeking the representation of the unrepresentable. Ekphrasis is the poet's marriage of the two within the verbal art. As we shall see, in the more complex manifestations of the ekphrastic impulse, we find the paradoxical search for a language that can force itself into satisfying a demand for "spatial form." Following the lead of a sacred iconographic tradition, with its dependence on a belief in word magic, the poem appears to convert its language—despite the evanescent way in which words normally seek to function—into an emblematic enclosure. It seeks to defy the mediating properties and the temporality of language by finding in language a plasticity that, as in the plastic arts, turns its medium into the unmediated thing itself, as if it were the word (Word?) of God. The poem as emblem, in effect supplanting its visual accompaniment, becomes the ultimate projection of the ekphrastic principle by representing a fixed object which is itself. The extreme example of George Herbert's poems-as-figures is only a baroque exaggeration of this tendency.

The movement from epigram (with the word as subsidiary to the object it accompanies) to the minimal notion of ekphrasis (with the word attempting an equivalence to a described object) achieves its ultimate claim in the poem-as-emblem (with the word as itself the primary object). It is in the latter that the ekphrastic principle would most fully realize itself. Thus I see the ekphrastic principle, which I have traced here from the "visual epistemology" of Plato and the consequent call for *enargeia*, as completing itself in the verbal emblem of the Renaissance. This development from Plato's *enargeia* to the Renaissance emblem is for me the first major extended moment—and the most complex—in the history of my subject.

As I suggested earlier, by the late seventeenth century and through the first half of the eighteenth, the well-ordered semiotics of the untransforming mirror, differently sponsored by rationalism and by empiricism, restores the dominance of the doctrine of a literalistic imitation and with it, thanks to the continued appeal to "visual epistemology," the authority of the *ut pictura poesis*. This second moment in the history of my subject, a more uncomplicated moment that treats poetry as verbal painting, is taken up in detail in Chapter 3. The medium of the verbal arts is to be thinned to utter transparency in their effort, as a disadvantaged relation, to emulate the natural-sign arts, now restored to primacy as the model for all the arts.

When, for example, Joseph Addison, as a faithful follower of John Locke, projects a spectrum—or, should I rather say, a hierarchy?—of the arts, he moves from sculpture, as "the most natural" art in that it is "likest the object that is represented," to painting, with its illusionary use of the two-dimensional picture plane, and only then to verbal "description," with "letters and syllables" that, unlike a picture, bear no "real resemblance to its original."[20] He is on his way to music as the extreme version of the non-natural sign, furthest from any obvious sort of mimetic representation. By contrast, in the literary there is still some chance for the emulation of visual meanings through the attempt to make verbal pictures, especially since Addison restricts the role of the literary to "description" in the attempt to realize the visual task even with its handicapped arbitrary signs.

It is no wonder that having given the verbal arts the impossible task of painting pictures with their non-pictorial signs, Addison must insist that those signs seek transparency, turning aside from

20. *Spectator* 416 (1712). I quote this passage in full and discuss it at much greater length in Chapter 3.

any play with letters or words that permits them to call attention to themselves *as* letters or words, instead of pointing self-effacingly, without interference, to their meanings. The word, then, should behave as a medium that, in its vain search for a natural-sign transparency, seeks to obliterate our awareness of its being there by suppressing all of its mediating properties.[21] Under such stringencies, any ekphrasis would have to be slavishly other-regarding with respect to the natural-sign object it is imitating (via description): it is not only to imitate the natural sign as its object but also to imitate (i.e., to emulate) the semiotic intention of that object as well.

But this neoclassical moment, which celebrates the "sister arts" while designating literature as the deprived sister, can also sponsor a second—and opposed—tendency (treated in Chapter 4) that acknowledges and even encourages the thickening of the verbal medium and appreciates its opacity. It celebrates the *in*capacity of words to yield natural signs and, instead, relates poetry to the temporal condition of our inner life. We find this tendency even in the same *Spectator* paper of Addison's when, having established the hierarchy of the art objects based on naturalness or resemblance to their referents, he moves on to speak, even if contradictorily, on the other side: of those occasions on which language, as if discovering and exploiting its other-than-natural-sign function, permits the poet not only to gain effects beyond the reach of the painter but even to "get the better of nature."

Edmund Burke, we will see, extends this tendency to invert the hierarchy of the arts in order to privilege the literary. He argues that natural-sign representation is the handicapped one because it is limited by the physical confines of its object of imitation, while language, in the vagueness, the unpredictability—but also the suggestiveness—that emanates from its arbitrary signs, can have a virtually unlimited emotional appeal precisely because language can paint no pictures. In valorizing the "sublime" at the expense of the "beautiful," Burke would have us break through the finite dimensions of the merely pictorial to the limitless potentialities of unpicturable emotions. If I may anticipate the language of a more influential, later thinker who in this distinction was indebted to Burke, the

---

21. See *Spectator* 62 (1711) for the conclusion of Addison's extended definitions of, and comparisons among, "true wit," "false wit," and "mixed wit," based mainly on the degree of activity or passivity in the role of the verbal medium and, consequently, our awareness of its visibility. This issue is pursued in Chapter 6.

"Apollonian" should be supplanted by the "Dionysian." This shift from the externally directed natural sign to internal human expression creates a third moment for my narrative, one that springs from an anti-formal impulse.

Once Burke has shifted our interest from the reproductive picture to the affective sequence of words, we are ready for the general shift of literary theory into the realm of temporality at the expense of visual form. Hence, as Burke himself suggests, the model art toward which the hybrid art of literature is now to move is no longer painting or sculpture, but music. The spectrum we saw introduced by Addison from sculpture through painting to literature and finally to music is reversed as the realm of sound enters the debate, and the total dependence of poetry on a visual epistemology comes to an end. At an end too is the indulgence in that sort of ekphrasis which has a visually mimetic basis. If we see poetry as a two-sided art positioned between the representational visual arts on the one side and music on the other, having referential meaning like the former and temporal sonority like the latter, we would recognize the partial and mutually exclusive character of the aesthetics based on metaphors borrowed from only one (either one) of these two model arts. And the two would have opposite attitudes toward the ekphrastic principle. The analogy to the visual arts would encourage ekphrasis as a simple mimetic procedure, totally ignoring the problematic character of verbal representation, while the analogy to music would appear to preclude ekphrasis altogether as an effective instrument of representation.

But I have already observed another aesthetic that would collapse this opposition and enrich the possibilities for ekphrasis beyond its function within a natural-sign aesthetic. The Renaissance, I suggested, provided such a subtler possibility that could comprehend the ambiguities of poetic language and the emblematic ambitions of some poems. And this is a version that, thanks to the shift away from the natural-sign aesthetic in the later eighteenth century, begins to reappear in a more sophisticated, less ontologically dependent form. I seek to trace its development in Chapters 6 and 7 as my fourth moment, which returns to form on a new basis—on a different notion of what it is to emulate nature, now taken to be one with the natural process.

Some romantic theories, in the wake of Burke, pursue into the twentieth century the quest for an anti-formalistic literary sublimity, indulging language in its anti-pictorial—and anti-spatial—character, which tends toward music. Further, the shift in the nine-teenth century from spatial to temporal models, from metaphors of orderly world machines to metaphors of evolution, tends to give the arts of temporality free movement, as if there were no formal inhibitions to be imposed upon the dispersive tendencies of our responses to language. There are moments in Burke that suggest as much. But almost at once, modifications come to be introduced that shape the major formalist tradition from Herder to Coleridge to the New Critics. What emerges seeks to harness the unleashing of the dynamics of language to create a new emblematics. So hardly has the literary art been freed, in the direction of the temporal, from neo-classical spatiality, before these critics begin, on literature's behalf, to work their way back to space, though only on new and shifting grounds that never quite come to rest.

The emphasis on the sound of language, especially as reflected in the major verse traditions, helps such critics argue that the literary medium, long conceded to be intelligible, can, after all, be made sensible too, like the media of the other arts. Here is yet another way to take up the older argument that language can have it both ways: it can claim the advantages of the sensible arts, and yet in its intellig-ibility it need not suffer the limitations imposed by the phenomenal world. If words in poems can use their aural dimension to give shape to the sequence they form, then through the mutual influ-ence of their sounds they can deepen or even transform the mean-ings they bring to the text. Through such manipulation in the poem, the sensible—because it is aural rather than visual and thus leaves the mind free to range—is able to serve and enrich the intelligible instead of displacing it.

Through such enhancement the language arts could hope to rep-resent what from the merely sensible or natural-sign perspective would appear to be unrepresentable. So here again the two-sided-ness of poetry, using a medium that is conceived as at once mean-ing and sound, was to confer a privilege that would make *it* the model art. As we approach our own time, not only is primacy be-stowed upon the arts of the word and of time (instead of upon the arts of the picture and of space) but the spreading semiotic interest in texts absorbs all the arts, subjects them all to temporality and makes them all ripe for reading. This is the ultimate imperialistic move by literature and literary criticism to subject to its terms all the arts and all the arts of discourse alike.

The efforts of formalist criticism to create a dynamic unity in texts that could reconcile the temporal and the arbitrary into the created inevitabilities of spatial form are reflected in the movement that leads to high modernism in literature and ultimate organicism in high New Criticism. Under the aegis of this movement the paradox of an internal ekphrasis can flourish anew as the mark of a spatial form that can coexist with the flowing character of words as an aesthetic medium.[22] Whatever phonemes, syllables, words, passages, tropes, characters, actions, or even themes may be seen as serial repetitions are to be treated by the formalist as if they were spatial juxtapositions, except that their sequential character allows them to be both the one and the other. The poem as emblem, under the ekphrastic principle, seeks to create itself as its own object.

And yet no object: for all of its intelligible richness, there is, in this set of arbitrary signs, nothing there. Here is an invulnerable duplicity that can claim so much only because, in the end, it claims so little. In examples of it, such as the urn of Keats or the Tennessee jar of Stevens, the verbal representations are described as containing formally what is at the same time seen as dribbling away. Like Stevens's jar, they must give the lie to the very claim to spatial enclosure that their being (i.e., their verbal representation) would for the formalist enact. In this they are another version of the winged serpent with its tail in its mouth, each a verbal emblem that has become its own ekphrasis—and its own undoing.

In my final chapter I look at our current moment, which is my fifth and last: the negative postmodern skepticism that is its reaction to such ambitious claims for poetry. The various—and they *are* varied—literary movements that we think of as postmodern, some of them seeing themselves as theoretical successors to the still maligned New Criticism, have, in their anxiety to press their own anti-formalism, clearly declared such claims to be deceptive self-mystifications resulting from the sacralizing or fetishizing impulse of a long reactionary moment. No one more forcefully than Paul de Man argued for a rhetoric of temporality that would dissolve the would-be emblem—that ekphrastic gesture—and let the string of allegories, like life's unrepeatable moments, keep running, at least until they have an arbitrary stop. But he is only one of many. They have

22. The explicit extension of the principles of main-line New Criticism to the doctrine of spatial form is the contribution of Joseph Frank's original series of essays, "Spatial Form in Modern Literature" (1945), reprinted in *The Widening Gyre: Crisis and Mastery in Modern Literature* (Bloomington: Indiana University Press, 1963). I discuss at length these essays and the issues they raise in Chapter 7.

preferred to ignore the complex possibilities opened by their pre-cursor-antagonists: that is, they have preferred to ignore the slippery version of the ekphrastic poetic which presses for a verbal play that acknowledges the incompatibility of time and space, while collapsing them into the illusion of an object marked by its own sensible absence.

Hence these last decades have seen the increasing dominance of a number of diverse and often embattled interpretive emphases, each shaped by different metaphorical borrowings that project their own anti-aesthetic hierarchies. But in common they suggest a different constellation of the arts, having used a semiotic model to reduce them all to a textuality under the dominion of time. Further, a disdain for what is falsely referred to as the "natural" in sign or ideology—together with an insistence on seeing the "natural" as a deceptive projection of the conventions dictated by sociopolitical power— has consigned all verbal attempts to capture space to a suspect rhetoric sponsored by bad faith.

Such an impatience with the spatial is hardly conducive to a poetics of ekphrasis. Thus an exasperation with the ekphrastic has replaced the exhilaration of those earlier critics of mid-century who were stimulated by formal closure and its illusion of at once representing an object and being an object. Even in the face of this recently flourishing antagonism, however, I wonder whether the semiotic desire for the natural sign can, despite the archaism of that notion and the violently deconstructive character of our time, be quite overcome, though it may be only the unrepresentable itself— an abyss, or an abyss beyond an abyss—that the ekphrastic impulse can now address. An abyss, or an abyss beyond an abyss: since those early self-denying attempts by the verbal art to make its sequence stop long enough to manage to represent—and to fail to represent—has it, like that Egyptian serpent, ever had any other object?

2
REPRESENTATION
AS ILLUSION
Dramatic
Representation
and the
Natural-Sign Aesthetic

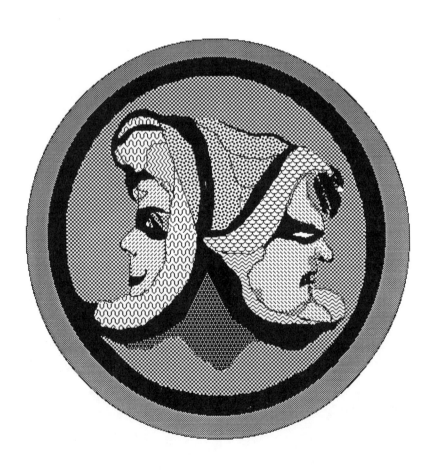

Suit the action to the word, the word to the action; with this special obser-
vance, that you o'erstep not the modesty of nature: for anything so o'erdone is
from the purpose of playing, whose end, both at the first and now, was and
is, to hold, as 'twere, the mirror up to nature; to show virtue her own feature,
scorn her own image, and the very age and body of the time his form and
pressure.

Hamlet to the players, 3.2

Our subject, as established in my introductory chapter, is the use of visual and spatial effects in the arts of the word, or rather the literary critic's attempt to observe such use. The borrowing by literary critics of descriptions of response conventionally assumed to be appropriate to the plastic arts is so common that we often fail to observe it and to be concerned about its *in*appropriateness. For such borrowing is a crossing over of the language appropriate to one art in order to characterize another to which it either is inapplicable or can be applied only figuratively.

It has long seemed inevitable for the language of literary criticism, despite the temporality of both the reading experience and the successiveness of the discourse, to suffer the intrusion of spatial metaphors. Even the critic who knows and cares nothing for the spatial and visual arts has, in the history of our criticism, usually been unable to avoid a language that would freeze the flow of the poem, almost as if it *were* a visual and spatial object. The flat-footed language of the critic reveals its helplessness in capturing the temporal dynamics of verbal play as it resorts to the metaphors of space that it imports to tame its object.

When this difficulty is rationalized into system by critics, it may well account for the widespread dependence upon formalism found in much of our criticism. Indeed, the very word "form," like "shape," "pattern," and—perhaps most striking of these—"structure," reflects the metaphorical borrowing of terms that seem better suited to the spatial arts, to which we should expect to see them applied (although conventions of literary criticism have for some time inured us to their use here as well). The critics' habit of spatializing literary texts accounts also for the primacy often given the visual in their dealings with the effects of the verbal arts, however distant words would seem to be from the literally pictorial. For example, how literally can we take the term "image" as applied to words, or, for that matter, the term "imitation" in relation to the things to which the words in the poem are to refer? Words as combinations of letters can hardly be images and cannot literally be said to imitate anything (except perhaps, as in drama, words being spoken by others). Of course, once we shift our attention from the outer to the inner world, to our minds and their free response to the verbal stimuli, we can make almost any pictorial metaphor for that operation vaguely relevant, although its theoretical power is pretty well depleted.

But as Henri Bergson instructed us, language generally, and not just the critics', is prone to indulge in the spatializing distortion of our temporal experience. As the philosopher who perhaps most strenuously revealed the deceptions and inadequacies of the spatializing habit of language generally, Bergson yet found a special role for poetry precisely in the way *its* language could be so manipulated as to permit it to break through that spatializing habit in order to reveal the temporal dynamics of our inner life. And from Russian Formalism through the New Criticism, modernist poetics may be viewed as a development of Bergson's claim, even though, ironically, many modernist theorists themselves lapsed into the spatializing habit as their language also failed to resist the temptations of "spatial form." (But this is a subject to be pursued in Chapter 7.)

This arresting of the potential plasticity of language is an inherited burden borne by the Western critical tradition since Plato. As we shall see, Plato absorbed literary issues into issues pertaining to the visual arts with an ease only increased by the special place he accorded to the sense of sight and the mental "images" of inner sense. (It is this limited perspective that very likely accounts for Plato's dwelling upon drama as the most blameworthy, because the most literally mimetic, of the verbal arts.) He tried to look past language as a manipulable poetic medium in order to treat it exclusively as an *im*mediate, and an immediately transparent, container of its meaning. Because his metaphysic required a naive theory of representation that rested totally on the doctrine of literal imitation, he had to assume a one-to-one relation between an element in the art work and the object of its imitation in the real world. The word, then, is a belated equivalent for the image that stands for its object as its origin—as if all words were nouns. And the temporality, the coming after, that characterizes the relationship between the word and the object it would represent, like the more obvious temporal relations between word and word in the sequence that constitutes a text, is overlooked, or at least elided, once it has been transformed into an analogue for the spatial.

In dealing with the problems surrounding the intrusion of the spatial upon literature's temporality, we also are confronted with the intrusion of the picture upon the word, despite what appears to be the vast semiotic distance between the ways in which the two function. This distance is as great as what used to be termed the difference between natural signs and arbitrary-conventional signs. However outmoded, this is a difference that will much concern me, since it led to the quest for an aesthetic that privileged the natural sign as its agent, even extending this quest to the poetic word. It is no wonder, in such a quest, that space invaded time and the pictorial invaded the verbal. And it is in Plato that this strange conversion of the literary into natural-sign transparency is first pressed, although— like many theorists after him—he has difficulty converting language to this use. Because of this difficulty, he frequently resorts to drama as his principal instrument for this conversion, because he recognizes in drama a form of verbal art that, as performance, has space for its apparently natural signs built into its very mode of representation.

Thus Plato, like many of those who followed his lead for well over a millennium in constituting the Western aesthetic, has two rather different ways of urging the effort of the verbal arts to move toward the natural sign in emulation of the visual arts. The more general way of emulating the natural-sign arts is to use words to paint a picture for the "eyes of the mind," thus seeking to force the medium of language—in spite of its "nature"—to do what comes naturally for those arts whose more immediate representations serve the body's eye. The second and more specific way of emulating the natural-sign arts, a way available only to drama as a performance art of the word, is to have its signs resemble its referents by standing in for them, the actors in a play like the pictured objects in a painting. In this second way the problem of the arbitrary sign is bypassed, since the use of words is secondary to the mode of representation itself. In the present chapter I pursue in detail the development of theory built around this second sort of emulation of the natural sign, the representation of pictures through live persons, and in Chapter 3 I pursue the first sort, the representation of pictures through words.

From the dawn of systematic thought about the arts in the West, illusion has been treated as the source of the appeal of the arts, even of the verbal arts, whether for good or ill. It was on the grounds of its special illusionary power that, ever since Plato, drama was separated from the other literary genres as a special case that demanded its own theory. And that theory has been granted a history in some crucial ways distinct from the history of literary theory at large. At some moments in that history, where the theory of drama has overlapped the general theory of literature, drama was encouraged, as the model genre, to absorb the other genres within its own norms, to seek to turn literature itself into greater and lesser forms of dramatistics, with drama itself the ideal form to be aped by the others. At other moments drama has been forced, by self-exclusion, to go its own way, separate from—but more than equal to—its rivals, narrative and lyric, among the verbal arts. But always its peculiar character as a performance art—that is, as an *imm*ediately representational art—allowed it to be treated as different from the other verbal arts in that it was uniquely free from the limits that language placed on the representational powers of the others.

In brief, the apparent presence—the tangible presence—in drama of the objects of representation gave it an immediacy denied to words alone. No matter how forceful the conjuring power of verbal images, only drama could claim to produce a *sensible* illusion of reality. For words, strictly speaking, must always, at the source of our experiencing them, be intelligible only—transmitting their images and objects only through the mediation of mind—and not sensible, with their images and objects, as with pictures, grasped immediately as they are sensed. What is being appealed to in this oversimplified opposition between the sensible and the intelligible arts is the dubious distinction to which I earlier alluded, the distinction—as old as the philosophical study of language, or, more broadly, of all symbolic systems—between natural signs and signs that, though conventional, are arbitrary.

In book 3 of the *Republic* Socrates makes a sudden, unanticipated move whose repercussions literary theory may still be feeling. In book 2 he had prepared for the application of his general theory of imitation to the arts, including, of course, all the verbal arts, without regard to differences among the literary kinds: imitation is the same operation, "equally to be observed in every kind of verse, whether epic, lyric, or tragic."[1] Socrates is laying the ground here

---

1. All my quotations in this chapter are from *The Dialogues of Plato,* trans. Benjamin Jowett, 4 vols. (New York: Scribner's, 1901), vol. 2 for the *Republic* and vol. 3 for the *Sophist.* This quotation is from 2:202.

for an attack upon all poetry as a mode of imitation in book 10: "I do not mind saying to you that all poetical imitations are a sort of outrage on the understanding of the hearers, and that the only cure of this is the knowledge of their true nature" (p. 425). He proceeds to the well-known epistemological-ontological arguments about the inability of "poetical imitations," without regard to differences in genre, to gain or transmit such "knowledge." Since Homer is his prime target, there can be little question that his target is far broader than dramatic tragedy. But despite the fact that his working definition of "imitation" allows it to characterize all the arts, including, of course, all the verbal arts, in book 3 he surprisingly restricts it to one verbal art, the dramatic, apparently exempting the lyric and many moments of narrative from the mimetic arts. A theory of poetic genres, distinguished by the manner (what we have come to call the "point of view") of representation, replaces a single universal characterization of the arts as mimetic. Without warning, Plato here is confining "imitation" to the dramatic (whether it occurs constantly in tragedy or occasionally in the epic), which is for him the one mode of representation that seeks to become a total illusion, and for this occasion stops using the term to define all the modes of representation.

Socrates introduces this division within the verbal arts by stating a simple three-way choice for the poet: "All mythology and poetry is a narration of events, either past, present, or to come. . . . And narration may be either simple narration, or imitation, or a union of the two" (p. 215). In the first case

> the poet is speaking in his own person; he never leads us to suppose that he is anyone else. But in what follows [in the opening lines of the *Iliad*] he takes the person of Chryses, and then he does all that he can to make us believe that the speaker is not Homer, but the aged priest himself. . . . But when the poet speaks in the person of another, may we not say that he assimilates his style to that of the person who . . . is going to speak? . . . And this assimilation of himself to another is the imitation, either by voice or gesture, of the person whose character he assumes? . . . Then in this case the narrative of the poet may be said to proceed by way of imitation. . . . Or, if the poet everywhere appears and never conceals himself, then again the imitation is dropped, and his poetry becomes simple narration. (P. 216)

All that follows in both the *Iliad* and the *Odyssey,* Plato concludes, is cast in this mixed form ("simple narration" when in Homer's voice and language, *and* imitation when in the voices and language of others). This mixed form mingles the two purer possibilities: the poet's simple narration (without any dialogue or even monologue in a character's voice) *and* "imitation," in which, as in dramatic tragedy or comedy, there is nothing but the speeches of characters, uninterrupted by a narrative voice.

In this diatribe against imitation as a falling away from the archetypal source of truth and virtue, Socrates must outlaw both the purely imitative art in this narrow sense (drama) and that which from time to time descends to imitate the imperfect characters (the mixed narrative). These three manners of writing, "the two styles, or the mixture of the two, comprehend all poetry and every form of expression in words" (p. 220). Throughout this discussion there seems to be no ambiguity about the definitions being given to "imitation" and pure "narration," which are mutually exclusive, though a writer like Homer mixes them and is condemned for mixing them. Of course, the unworthy attempts at illusion produced by the dramatic parts of the epic are exacerbated by the role of the rhapsode, who, in the oral performance of Homer, must mimic one character after another when he is not speaking in (i.e., imitating) the narrative voice of Homer.[2]

The sins that Homer commits in parts of his works, the tragic poets extend to all of theirs. Because of the shifting meaning of Plato's "imitation" (when we compare book 3 with book 10), it is difficult to be certain of the grounds on which Socrates links Homer to the tragic poets, although the role of "imitation," whichever meaning he ascribes to it, seems central to his condemnation. When Socrates refers in book 10—not without irony—to Homer as "the great captain and teacher of that noble tragic company" (or, elsewhere, to "tragedy and its leader, Homer") and several times lumps him with

2. Because the rhapsode serves not only as the imitator of Homer (in the purely narrative moment of the epic) but also as the imitator of the speaking characters (in the dramatic moments of the epic), Socrates is persuaded at moments to make Homer a member of the mimetic tribe of tragic poets, indeed their leader. At other moments (as in book 3) he clearly separates them when speaking of the narrative moments in Homer. Socrates appears to see the presentational device of the rhapsode as an elocutionary performance of Homer, a mimetic art that has much in common with the drama. Thus he is led to confuse his categories when he at times associates Homer with writers of tragedy and at times distinguishes him from them.

the "imitative tribe" of tragic poets, Plato may be revealing not so much his awareness that Homer has furnished the tragic poets with their master story as his concern—in accordance with his narrow definition of "imitation"—that Homer's free indulgence in those mimetic moments of quoted speech opened the way for the total indulgence in the dialogue form of tragedy. (It must also be conceded that there may be a perhaps more obvious reading: that rather than distinguishing one kind of verbal art, the dramatic, from the others and making Homer responsible for it, Socrates is simply returning to his broader definition of "imitation," which characterizes all the representational arts regardless of genre, so that he is doing no more than echoing his usual charge that Homer, as one of the tragic poets and chief among them, is representing imperfect and unworthy actions of gods and humans.)

These several interpretations can all be justified, although I emphasize the role of dramatic imitation as the controlling one in order to call attention to the special theoretical power of the distinctions made in book 3. In those passages Socrates unambiguously singles out the drama, or the dramatic moments that interrupt the narrative voice, as warranting the term "imitation," with all other forms of verbal artifice—mere words—apparently non-mimetic.[3] This point is worth laboring because dramatic theory can be said to begin when, without warning, in book 3 "imitation" has been narrowed to the one sort of representation that seeks to become a total illusion, instead of being allowed to describe all the modes of verbal representation, including the more mediated forms, as is the case elsewhere when its use is dominated by metaphysical concerns.

But in book 3 poetry itself could be literally and even visually mimetic—as much involved with illusion as painting is—but only so long as that poetry was dramatic. As we will see in Chapter 3, below, Plato invokes painting as the model art only when dramatic poetry can no longer serve as model because the mimetic interest in poetry

3. It should be pointed out that Plato's attack on the mimetic art of dialogue—the employment of speaking characters whose voices are distinct from the author's—should not be taken as inconsistent with his own dialogistic practice, as is sometimes charged. We must remember that his own dialogues are not viewed by him as drama—whatever their apparent form on the page—simply because they are only to be read, and not performed. So dependent does Plato seem to be on the literal manner of representation that he can attack as mimetic a narrative poem elocuted by a rhapsode, while remaining oblivious to a piece of writing (his own) composed only of characters' speeches, so long as they are never to be actually delivered.

wants to cover its non-dramatic forms as well. So the confusion about the relation between painting and poetry, as well as about the relation between the several poetic genres and imitation, reflects Plato's primary confusion about which aspect of poetry he sees as responsible for its mimetic character: is it poetry's capacity in all its forms to give us verbal equivalents of visual images, or is it its capacity, through speaking and acting characters in drama, to duplicate actual persons speaking and acting in the world of actual experience? Only one of these is literally imitative in the way that painting is; hence the narrowing to drama (or to the dramatic aspect of narrative, especially as, in the oral tradition, the narrative is represented in the mimicking elocution of the rhapsode).

The literally mimetic, then, which normally would seem to be the province of sculpture or painting, can also be made to include poetry, so long as we speak only of the dramatic mode of representation (in drama or epic) as circumscribed by the narrow meaning given to "imitation" in book 3. But of course the literally mimetic in art is being carefully delineated only in order to be condemned, condemned because it is false, in every way deceiving its audience. It is its dependence upon illusion that for Plato enables art to practice its deception, and it is only in drama that the verbal arts can find a wholly illusionary form, as illusionary as what we find in sculpture or painting: only in drama are we encouraged to see a representation as if we were witnessing real experience. Thus it is especially culpable among the verbal arts.

This separation of the dramatic from the rest of poetry while allying it to the visual arts—all in the subversive interest of illusion—is echoed in the *Sophist,* one of Plato's late dialogues, which searches for the sophist and finds the poet, who constantly resorts to the deceptions of illusion, as one of the guises that the sophist assumes. After dealing negatively, early in the dialogue (pp. 470–71), with the visual artist as illusionist (to be discussed in Chapter 3, below), Plato's Eleatic Stranger extends the falseness of aesthetic illusion to cover the poet as well. As he recapitulates his argument late in the dialogue (pp. 505–10), he presents a sequence of distinctions and choices that lead him to the poet as sophist: first the distinction between the productive and acquisitive arts, with the former chosen as appropriate for an art of imitation; then, within the productive, between those that are humanly produced and those of nature (divinely produced), again with the former chosen; then, within the humanly produced, between the production of real things and

the production of images (imitations) of things, with the choice between them permitting the Stranger to reach the subclass of image-
making. Within the made images there is a further distinction
between true ("icastic") and "phantastic" images, with the search
for the sophist leading the Stranger to choose the "phantastic," pro-
ducer of false and illusionary images.

Within the "phantastic" the Stranger presents a further subdis-
tinction that will allow him to condemn the ventriloquist-poet or
ventriloquist-rhapsode as sophist: a distinction between the "one
kind of phantastic image which is produced by instruments and
another in which the creator of the apparition is himself the instrument" (p. 508). This would seem to be the distinction between the
plastic artist, who uses external materials and implements, and the
impersonating actor of drama or the rhapsode of the dramatic portions of narrative (using his own person to play, one after the other,
each of the several roles). As it did within the narrow focus of book
3 of the *Republic,* this act of impersonation becomes the sole criterion
of literary "imitation" here: "When anyone makes himself appear
like another in his figure or in his voice, imitation is the name for
this part of the phantastic art. . . . Let this, then, be named the art
of mimicry" (p. 508). Through the illusion produced by the act of
impersonation, a language art seeks to turn itself into a natural sign,
and into a mode of what Mazzoni was to term "sophistic," conceding that he was following Plato in doing so.

When viewed within this mimetic perspective, the drama, together with the dramatic elements in narrative, stands alone among
the verbal arts (though together with the visual arts) as would-be
natural-sign arts, apparently leaving the other verbal arts outside
the definition of imitation and thus exempt from being condemned
as mimetic. Nevertheless, I do not mean to ignore the full reading
of the *Sophist* that argues for two different ways in which artists may
be condemned as mimetic, one less applicable to poets than the
other; but neither is directed against non-dramatic poetry, poetry
that does not indulge in impersonation. In the several parts of the
dialogue there are two grounds for reducing artists into sophists:
visual artists because they produce distorted images of reality (their
works in effect falsely impersonating reality), and poets of several
voices because they indulge in actual impersonation. In its pursuit
of the sophist, the dialogue progresses from the first to the second
of these, from those whose work tries to delude us into believing
that the appearance they present is the reality (that which is not, *is*)

to those ("dissemblers") who use themselves to make us believe
that others are speaking and acting. This is the Stranger's last in this
series of distinctions: between those who have knowledge of what
they imitate, however deceiving that imitation may be, and those
who know nothing of what they are imitating (impersonating), who
know nothing except the art of impersonation itself. And it is in this
latter, in the "ironical imitator" rather than the "simple imitator,"
that "the true and very sophist" is found (p. 510).

But the second of these two ways of relating art to mimesis, which
seems applicable exclusively to the dramatic mode of representation, has a crucial consequence for the history of literary theory, particularly for the place of drama in the history of that theory. Despite
the utterly negative cast of Plato's discussions of mimesis and the
specially mimetic character of drama, more positive theorists pursued the theoretical attractiveness of the semiotic analogy between
dramatic poetry and the visual arts, which has its source in book 3
of the *Republic,* and so gave drama its own theoretical history apart
from the history of literary theory at large. Through the centuries
they also felt the illusionary force of the drama as an immediate visual presence, while reserving for another class of considerations
those problems deriving from poetry (primarily non-dramatic) as a
temporal art. Once thus cut off by Plato, drama continued its lone,
privileged path as a special (and spatial) mode of representation,
one requiring its own poetic, to be distinguished from the poetic for
the other kinds of verbal art. I repeat that this difference between
the developing poetic of the drama and the poetic of the other literary genres reflects the differing demands of the natural-sign arts
and the arbitrary-conventional-sign arts; and this familial separation within literature echoes the more general separation between
the plastic arts and literature as a family. Thus Plato should help remind us, in our observations of later theorists, that for many centuries the distinction between the sensible and the intelligible is what
the distinction between natural and arbitrary-conventional signs
was all about.

We may after all understand Plato's singling out of drama, the special vituperation that he reserves for the "mimetic tribe" (the writers
of dramatic tragedy), once we recognize that his antipathy to "imitation" is metaphysically and thus morally rooted in his concern
about the sensuous (usually for him the visual) consequences of the
world of appearance. Hence his desire to expel it as a threat to the
Republic's health. But it is surprising—and instructive—to find that

even Aristotle, who responds to Plato with a profound defense of *literary* imitation, in an unguarded moment borrows from Plato, his precursor-antagonist, the narrow definition of "imitation" that isolated drama from its sister verbal arts.

It is the more surprising, in view of the care with which Aristotle, from the start of the *Poetics*, defines "imitation" as his central term and concept, giving it a broadly inclusive coverage. It explicitly includes all the "various kinds" of poetry, however they may differ from one another in the "medium" of imitation, the "objects" of imitation, or the "manner of mode" of imitation. In chapter 3 Aristotle clearly distinguishes drama from the other kinds by virtue of the difference in its "manner," even if the "medium" and the "objects" are the same. Drama, as that kind which, whatever its "medium" and "objects," presents all the "characters as living and moving before us," is distinguished from "narration," which is of two types, depending on whether the poet decides to "take another personality as Homer does, or [to] speak in his own person, unchanged."[4] Obviously, these distinctions in Aristotle's third chapter repeat Plato's in *his* third book; but unlike Plato, Aristotle insists that the poet does "imitate by narration" as much as he does by representing the action in drama. These are equally modes of imitation, since the "objects" of their imitation are "men in action," and narrative as well as drama imitates men in action, though in its own "manner." Imitation, then, does not have the restriction to one mode of direct representation that it has for the Plato of book 3 and, I would add, of the *Sophist*. (I have acknowledged that Plato's own definition is similarly broadened elsewhere, but in the place where he makes the distinctions among literary kinds that Aristotle clearly takes up, he restricts "imitation" to dramatic impersonation. Hence Aristotle's departure is significant.)

But after clearly using "imitation" throughout the *Poetics* in a way that includes all the "various kinds" of poetry, in chapter 24 Aristotle suddenly reverts to Plato's narrower meaning, that which would restrict imitation to dramatic representation, whether in plays or in the dialogue portion of narratives. Speaking approvingly of Homer for staying out of the action as much as he does, Aristotle asserts, "The poet should speak as little as possible in his own person, for it is not this that makes him an imitator. Other poets [unlike Homer]

4. I am using the S. H. Butcher translation of Aristotle. Since the chapters of the *Poetics* are so brief, citations that refer only to chapter numbers should suffice.

appear themselves upon the scene throughout, and imitate but little and rarely." The dramatist, needless to say, does nothing but imitate. In this passage all the parts of the poem delivered in the voice of the poet, rather than in the voices of the characters, are not imitations. For it is the poet's speaking in the persons of others "that makes him an imitator."

This passage occurs in the midst of Aristotle's discussion of epic, begun in chapter 23, and his attempt to judge it as a rival to tragedy.[5] Aristotle wants to counter Plato's condemnation of drama by arguing for a preference of the dramatic "manner" over the narrative "manner," so that it should not be surprising that he allows "imitation" to be reduced to its purest form in drama, with tragedy becoming a synecdoche for general poetic mimesis, as his scientific analysis gives way to the privileges of hierarchy. With the unmediated representation of tragedy as the model, that variety of epic which most closely approaches it—in spite of the lingering handicaps of its own "manner"—is best. Since for Plato imitation was bad and drama was the most extreme version of imitation, he charged Homer with speaking too little in his own voice and too much in the voices of his characters; since for Aristotle imitation is salutary and drama is the most extreme version of imitation, he praises Homer for hiding himself behind his characters as much as he does. Both see Homer's narrative moving toward drama; Plato deplores it, while Aristotle applauds. Both are conceding to drama, at least momentarily, an unmediated representation that seems to make only *it* deserving of having the word "imitation" applied to it, converting it into the one literary kind that can overcome the handicap of language as an arbitrary-conventional medium and can truly, "naturally," imitate, even as the plastic arts do.

What makes this momentary lapse in Aristotle's use of "imitation" significant (aside from its indication of the hold Plato has upon him even in his dissent) is the fact that it runs counter to a main objective of the *Poetics*—Aristotle's formalist desire to transcend Plato's limited concern for the separate, imitated objects by concentrating upon the poem itself as one integral, formed object. For Aristotle "imitation" refers to the created structure that over-

---

5. I must in fairness add that by the start of chapter 25, Aristotle again speaks of the poet as "an imitator" in the broad sense that characterizes all forms of poetry, just as it characterizes art produced by "any other artist." The Plato-like aberration caused by the comparison of tragic to epic "manner" is behind him and out of sight.

rides the individual elements in it (hence his preference for the probable impossibility over the possible improbability). So "imitation" for Aristotle derives from the "formal cause."

But the Platonic restriction of imitation to impersonation, borrowed by Aristotle in his chapter 24, limits the power of imitation to taking advantage of the peculiar capacities of the dramatic "manner"—even in epic!—at the cost of the larger, formal notion of imitation as poetic structure. The dependence on characters visibly in action means that Aristotle, at least in this context, is limiting "imitation" to his "efficient cause" so that it may be applicable to drama only, that is, to the one natural-sign manifestation in poetry. It is this Platonic hangover, given Aristotelian sanction, that—we shall see—will be carried over to the "verisimilitude" version of "imitation" that characterizes French dramatic criticism in the seventeenth century, in which the natural-sign character of drama is carried to its farthest consequence.[6]

Except for Aristotle's formalist diversion, what we are confronting—at moments in Aristotle and through most of Plato—is an aesthetic directed toward an ideal of pure natural-sign representation. Its basis in imitation theory led to its assigning aesthetic value to the extent that the imitation approximated its object of imitation. I put it this way despite the fact that Plato, as moralist, rather insisted that the greater the aesthetic value—that is, the more mimetic, the more illusory and deceptive the representation—the more it was to be condemned on both moral and metaphysical grounds. But once—after Plato, but hardly in accord with him—a higher worth was put on our phenomenal experiences, a more positive view of aesthetic value, and of mimetic fidelity, took over our judgments of all the arts, with drama leading the way.

As we shall see in Chapter 3, below, from late classicism through much of the eighteenth century the pictorialist view of non-dramatic

---

6. As I argue in greater detail in Chapter 5, Aristotle here is giving the epic—because it is not limited to what is representable on the stage—the freedom to introduce the element of "wonder." Yet this difference is not intended to raise the epic above the drama. Indeed Aristotle is here comparing the two genres to demonstrate the superiority of the drama—on the grounds of its compactness, its capacity to accomplish its end more efficiently, within a smaller, more contained compass. So the freedom from representational restriction, the freedom to wander into the wonderful, is, within these Aristotelian criteria, no virtue. What is not representable within the constraints of stage "imitation" is a threat to the formalist strictures of the Aristotelian system.

poetry, of poetry as vivid description—as verbal painting—commanded a wide following as *its* way of arguing for poetry's attempt to function as if it were a natural sign. Of course, the "as if" acknowledges the metaphorical character of this attempt: it must be conceded that for non-dramatic poetry to function this way would be for it to emulate the natural-sign function of painting with the handicap of not being able literally to claim a "natural" status for its signs. We have seen that this view could also claim support from Plato, although not from the special and limited concept of imitation as dramatic illusion that we find in book 3 of the *Republic*. Clearly, any claim to the natural sign for non-dramatic poetry seems weak next to the natural-sign claim for a separate notion of dramatic representation, for which Plato—and Aristotle after him—furnished so forceful a precedent.

Of course, it is only by implication that I have been attributing the phrase "natural sign" to Plato's semiotic, since while he clearly sets forth the concept, he does not use these words. But when, in the later eighteenth century, Lessing extends this semiotic—though he would incorporate some Aristotelian modifications—he uses the phrase "natural sign," and its distinction from "arbitrary sign," to help create an ultimate justification of drama. That is, he attempts to convert poetry into an unqualifiedly natural-sign art and can do so only because he is a protagonist for the drama. Strangely, because his argument seems aimed *against* the notion of pictorial poems, it appears—but only appears—to undermine the application of the natural-sign aesthetic to poetry, at least so long as what is at issue is poetry in its other than dramatic forms—the use of words for poetic description. Indeed, in his *Laokoön* (1766) he is expressly committed to oppose the use of poetry to make verbal pictures. In spite of this commitment, however, we will find him to champion that very aesthetic in its application to poetry.

The opening lines of the Preface to the *Laokoön* repeat in explicit terms the usual first principle of the mimetic, illusionary objective of painting and poetry: "Both represent what is absent as if it were present, and appearance as if it were reality; both deceive and the deception of both is pleasing."[7] Here again is the appeal to art's mnemonic character; here again what Plato found vicious in the imita-

---

7. My quotations are taken from the translation of *Laokoön* by E. C. Beasley and Helen Zimmern (London: G. Bell and Sons, 1900).

tive arts has been converted into their virtue, thanks to an aesthetic validated by an empiricist psychology that accepts appearance, for all its deceptiveness, as reality enough. But Lessing goes on to establish a mimetic function for poetry that differs from that of painting as the temporality of verbal sequence differs from the spatiality of the pictorial instant. And he enjoins poetry to shun any attempt at static description, the proper business of painting, in order to indulge the kind of consecutive images appropriate to poetry as a temporal art. Consequently, he has been credited with helping to undermine the neoclassical injunction *ut pictura poesis*, though in doing so he by no means releases poetry from its literally mimetic obligation, no less obligatory than painting's.

Poetry is indeed freed from the obligation to provide "descriptions" (in Addison's sense of the word) that yield pictures for the painter, but it yields its own sort of pictures nonetheless—in effect moving pictures. This critical attitude would support the proscenium-arch theater, in which the action is framed in a way that makes it the moving analogue to the framed painting as a "still life." Drawing a distinction between the "picturesque" *(malerisch)* and the "picturable" *(malbar)*, Lessing argues that poetry can be the former, though without being the latter, since it is full of time.[8] And he proceeds to distinguish between those pictures that emphasize the movement among objects and those that dwell upon statically disposed objects themselves, the first properly the poet's and the second properly the painter's. Each may impose upon the other's proper realm to its own detriment, but the *Laokoön* is dedicated to setting the matter straight. Indeed, it is Lessing's consequent emphasis on action as poetry's realm that makes him a faithful Aristotelian in spite of his lingering pictorialism: "Although both objects, as visible, are alike capable of being subjects of painting in its strict sense; still, there is this essential difference between them, that the action of one [poetry] is visible and progressive, its different parts happening one after another in sequence of time; while on the other

---

8. *Laokoön*, chap. 16. Lessing uses the inevitable example, Homer's description of the shield of Achilles (*Iliad*, bk. 18), to demonstrate his defense of *literary* images as images of objects that are in motion and hence are "picturesque" rather than at rest and hence "picturable" ("Where Homer paints, the artist finds least to employ his pencil"). See my related discussion of Homer's treatment of the shield, as well as of Virgil's similar treatment of the shield of Aeneas as time-ridden, in the Foreword and Chapter 1, above.

hand, the action of the other [painting] is visible and stationary, its different parts developing themselves in juxtaposition in space."⁹

However forcefully Lessing may argue for the distinction between time arts and space arts and thus the need to keep separate their mimetic functions, he insists (in chapter 14) that the poet, with his "power of setting forth picturesquely the most unpicturable," should still produce that which inspires the reader to mental reproduction of the visible world. At the same time, we must remember, "a poetical picture is not necessarily convertible into a material picture." It turns out, then, that for Lessing also, the mimetic function of poetry leads us to reduce the role of the verbal medium to self-effacing transparency: "The poet makes his object so palpable to us, that we become more conscious of this object than of his words." Even though this picturesque object is in motion, "it brings us nearer to that degree of illusion of which the material picture is especially capable, and which is most quickly and easily called forth by the contemplation of the material picture." Still, the poet creates his own illusionary object in his own slightly less effective way to the extent that we "become more conscious of this object than of his words." So it is a verbal illusion that allows our mind the pictorial conversion, however different the kind of picture: how far has theory progressed from Addison's more conventional passages after all?

At the start of chapter 17 Lessing freely grants that words are arbitrary signs only, so that they differ from painterly images in two ways: first, words are progressive, and second, they are arbitrary instead of being static and natural as visual images are. As verbal sequences rather than still pictures, poems can be treated as moving pictures only by a sort of metaphor that characterizes the way in which the reader's receptivity acts upon them.

> The poet does not merely wish to be clear; the prose writer is contented with simply rendering his descriptions lucid and distinct, but not the poet. He must awaken in us conceptions so lively, that, from the rapidity with which they arise, the same impression should be made upon our senses which the sight of the material objects that these conceptions represent would produce. In this moment of illusion we should cease to be conscious of the instruments—his words—by which this effect is obtained.

9. Chap. 15. It is because Lessing is defending an Aristotelian commitment to a progressive sequence of action that he writes the *Laokoön* in order to do battle with the static universality of Johann Joachim Winckelmann's Platonism.

This was the source of the explanation of poetic painting which we have given. But a poet should always produce a picture.

In this key passage of a document presumably dedicated to undermining the *ut pictura poesis* tradition, we find echoes of the age-old pictorial injunctions controlled by the rhetorical device of *enargeia*, which in the Renaissance culminated in the presentational aesthetic of Jacopo Mazzoni: here too the poet, unlike the orator (Lessing's "prose writer"), is required to figure forth "images" or "idols" instead of engaging in discursive description.[10] These may all be seen as extensions of Aristotle's (or even Plato's) separation of those kinds (or portions) of literary works in which words are forced into functioning as something like natural signs.

If the poet leads us to "cease to be conscious of the instruments— his words," then, under the spell of the illusion, we seem to substitute the object itself for its representation, so that the medium itself disappears into its transparency. This suppression of the medium, and with it all consciousness of the artistic process, seeks to turn arbitrary signs—despite themselves—into the illusions of natural signs. It may seem odd that despite Lessing's concern to keep the medium out of it, it is for him the medium of the particular art that, because of its intrinsic limitations, defines what the art can or cannot do. The temporal character of words and the spatial character of pictures determine what kind of object each art is capable of imitating:

I reason thus: if it is true that painting and poetry in their imitations make use of entirely different means or symbols—the first, namely, of form and color in space, the second of articulated sounds in time—if these symbols indisputably require a suitable relation to the thing symbolized, then it is clear that symbols arranged in juxtaposition can only express subjects of which the wholes or parts exist in juxtaposition; while consecutive symbols can only express subjects of which the wholes or parts are themselves consecutive. (Chap. 16)

10. Chapter 3, below, is devoted to the development of static pictorialism out of the notion of *enargeia*. The relation of this development to the different version of it in Mazzoni is pursued in Chapter 5. We will see an earlier version of Lessing's distinction between "prose" writing and poetry, between mere clarity and a special intensity, in Mazzoni's distinction between "rhetoric" and "poetry." The roots of this distinction can be found in Longinus (see Chapter 4), and this privileging of poetry above rhetoric can be traced forward to Russian Formalism in our own century.

Lessing terms the first of these objects of imitation "bodies" and the second "actions." Consequently, just as the medium of painting requires that it avoid the telling of stories that are appropriate to the verbal arts, the medium of poetry requires that it avoid the description of objects that are appropriate to the visual arts. Otherwise "the coexistence of the body comes into collision with the consecutiveness of language," so that the illusion, which depends on this one-to-one relationship between medium and object of imitation, must fail. So, in poetry as in painting, the medium is the determining factor of the art after all, though only because it functions in accord with an objective so purely mimetic (time for time, space for space) that it determines also that any awareness of itself be eliminated.[11]

It is clear that for Lessing art's mimetic purpose requires that all the arts (though in different ways) seek a natural-sign status so complete that—as if the medium were not there—they may become illusionary substitutes for the objects of imitation. In his letter to Friedrich Nicolai of May 26, 1769, Lessing pursues the distinction between natural and arbitrary signs, basing it on the argument developed in the *Laokoön:* "The more painting gets away from natural signs, or mixes natural signs with arbitrary signs, the more it gets away from its highest point of perfection; while poetry approaches perfection the more nearly, the more its arbitrary signs approximate natural signs. Thus the higher painting is that which uses only natural signs in space and the higher poetry that which uses only natural signs in time."[12] When we remember that the *Laokoön,* as we can see from the subject announced in its title, is mainly concerned with the epic (Virgil's and, of course, as the inevitable master, Homer's) as its literary example, we better understand why, in his letter shortly afterwards, Lessing will bring in the drama to

11. As I point out in Chapter 7, Diderot, Herder, and many modernists reject Lessing's claim that poetry, because its medium is sequential, is bound exclusively to the temporal. They argue, rather, for an instantaneity of effect that creates a spatial dimension for the poem.

12. It was René Wellek, in his *A History of Modern Criticism: 1750–1950,* vol. 1, *The Later Eighteenth Century* (New Haven: Yale University Press, 1955), pp. 164–65, who most shrewdly excised this passage and those that follow from the May 26, 1769, letter to Nicolai and called attention to their crucial significance. At several points over the next paragraphs I have altered his translations where a more literal rendering suited my purpose. The letter can be found in Lessing's *Sämtliche Schriften,* ed. K. Lachmann and F. Muncker, 23 vols. (Leipzig: G. J. Göschen'sche Verlagshandlung, 1886–1924), 17:289–92.

complete the move of the verbal arts toward the natural sign.

I originally introduced Lessing by promising that he would extend and complete the framework of the natural-sign aesthetic by using drama to convert poetry into a natural-sign art.[13] Until now we have seen him urge this conversion while being unable to make good on it. Nor can he until he moves beyond the relation of words to picture-making, and thus beyond narrative poetry.[14] Let me recapitulate. In narrative, we have seen, poetry must deal with the visible without describing it in a way that creates possible subjects for the painter or for our inner eye as mental painter. It must yield pictures—moving pictures—though these are not to be confused with what we normally take to be pictures as spatially bound entities, symbols in juxtaposition. Finally, it consists of arbitrary signs and not—like paintings—of natural signs, and yet it must be capable of creating a sensible illusion not unlike that created by natural signs. Though a narration that must avoid static description, it yet creates an illusionary presence for its described action, even if that illusionary presence, however "picturesque" it may be, is not "picturable." The attempt by the language arts to describe a static picture leads only to the work of the prose writer rather than the poet: it is a use of arbitrary signs that does not permit them to rise beyond themselves. How, then, in poetry, can arbitrary signs do more? How can they yield an illusion of moving life comparable to what a painting does for a static object? Enter the drama.

In his letter to Nicolai, Lessing proposes various poetic devices that move toward naturalizing the arbitrary signs: "Poetry must try to raise its arbitrary signs to natural signs: only that way does it differentiate itself from prose and become poetry. The means by which this is accomplished are the tone, the words, the position of words, the measure, figures and tropes, similes, etc. All these bring

13. I must concede that there are many places in Lessing's dramatic criticism (his *Hamburgische Dramaturgie*) and in his debates with his fellow critics, where—in contrast to the naive commitment to the natural sign that I am stressing—Lessing indicates his awareness of the need for the drama to be self-conscious about the illusionary character of its medium. But Lessing's place in my historical narrative leads me to dwell upon his firmly stated claims for drama as the ultimate—and the only—natural-sign verbal art and to make that aspect of his theory the ultimate statement of the natural-sign aesthetic, even if he does display significant qualifications elsewhere.

14. I should note again that the tradition I trace in Chapter 3 does focus on the picture-making power of words, the very power that Lessing, coming at the end of that tradition, reinforces while working to reject it.

arbitrary signs closer to natural signs, but they don't actually make them into natural signs." Lessing here is anticipating the efforts of recent critics—Sigurd Burckhardt comes most immediately to mind,[15] though there are many others, several Russian Formalists among them—who seek to account for ways in which poems become poems by forcing their words to create a presence within themselves, in effect to corporealize themselves. These are strange demands to be made of the medium by a critic like Lessing, who asks the poetic medium to be self-effacingly transparent. Even so, these devices are not in the end sufficient to make the transformation he seeks, since as he acknowledges, the arbitrary signs do not quite change into natural signs—not this way. The quest for a fully mimetic poetry in the *Laokoön,* then, must be incomplete: narrative poetry cannot transcend its arbitrary means totally, nor can the completeness of illusion be attained, however high the hopes Lessing reveals in that treatise.

Having exhausted the naturalizing possibilities of narrated poems, Lessing must, if he is to culminate his quest for poetry as a natural-sign art, abandon our epic masterpieces and follow the lead of Plato and Aristotle in his discovery of the special semiotic role of drama. By now the history of criticism has enabled him to use the terms "natural sign" and "arbitrary sign," toward which Plato and Aristotle, in dealing with drama and narrative, were groping (although, I repeat, I have freely imposed these terms in my treatment of their arguments); and it is their specially narrowed notion of imitation, as applicable only to dramatic representation, that is borrowed by Lessing now to make his own special case for poetry as a natural-sign art.

After speaking, in his letter to Nicolai, of those poetic devices (verbal and figural manipulations) that "bring arbitrary signs closer to natural signs, but . . . don't actually make them into natural signs," Lessing continues: "Consequently all genres that use only these means must be looked upon as lower genres of poetry; and the highest genre of poetry will be that which transforms the arbitrary signs completely into natural signs. That is dramatic poetry; for in it words cease to be arbitrary signs, and become natural signs of arbitrary objects." Because of its peculiar mode of representation— flesh-and-blood creatures (actors) impersonating made-up poetic creatures (characters) who represent real people (objects of imita-

15. See my extended treatment of Burckhardt in Chapter 6.

tion)—drama converts literature's words into the moving pictures of a visual art. The words of a play, though arbitrary, like all words, are an imitation of an actual speech act: the words of a dramatic speech constitute a natural representation—in the mouth of a natural-sign speaker who speaks like his or her real counterpart—of our use of words as arbitrary signs. Thus the arbitrary signs of language, like the arbitrarily named fictional creatures who speak them, function within a mimetic operation in which actions and speeches are viewed by us as natural signs. In this way "words . . . become natural signs of arbitrary objects [*Dinge*]."

Drama has thus defied and triumphed over literature's inherent disadvantage as an arbitrary-sign art; but it also demonstrates its superiority to the spatial visual arts because only it can marry the natural sign to temporality, thereby imitating the sequence of lived moments. In this ultimate extension of the natural-sign aesthetic to literature, dramatic poetry alone becomes the most perfectly realized representation of the consecutiveness of human experience: because the fact that it is only a representation is most completely hidden, the illusion is most effective. In view of the real gesturing bodies on the stage, occupying three-dimensional space and moving in time as experience moves, there would appear to be no medium at all required to make the illusion do its work upon us. In non-dramatic poetry, the poet's attempt to produce something like (but not quite) natural-sign illusion requires a struggle to make words produce extraordinary effects; in drama the poet can relax in the assurance that the very mode of representation carries the illusionary effect within itself. It is as if the ancient verbal attempt to produce ekphrases as gestures to the superiority of the natural sign has been realizing itself all along in drama: in it without verbal effort we come upon the uncomplicated production of walking ekphrases, those living, moving, flesh-and-blood sculptures (pace Addison) who strut before us in their own space, so reminiscent of our own. After all, an art of moving life must be more satisfactorily mimetic of our actual temporal experience of living than an art of still life.

This argument for drama as the hybrid art that has overcome the inherent disadvantages of the verbal arts was anticipated in the previous century in the aggressive theoretical defenses of the most extreme practices of the neoclassical French theater, although it took Lessing to create a systematic rationalization for them. While most French dramatists and even their apologists may have been less rigid

than their mythical, totally restrictive counterparts created for po-
lemical purposes by a Dryden or a Johnson, the most consistent version of French neoclassical theatrical theory, as it affects the history
of criticism, has certain logical consequences for which Lessing's
natural-sign commitments are a systematic justification.

I do not at all mean to suggest that Lessing intended such support, since in his criticism he strongly objected to this French theater and the theory that sought to justify it. It is true that the restrictions of French neoclassicism are usually looked upon—and were
surely looked upon by Lessing—as arising out of a narrow and legalistic formalism rather than out of a natural-sign interest in the drama.
They were sometimes—though not by that faithful Aristotelian,
Lessing—taken to be an inheritance from, and an extreme extension
of, Aristotle's formal analysis converted into prescriptive rules. It
must be conceded that Aristotle's preference of tragedy to epic, toward the end (chap. 26) of the extant version of the *Poetics*, rests upon
the greater compression permitted by the dramatic form: "The art
attains its end within narrower limits; for the concentrated effect is
more pleasurable than one which is spread over a long time and so
diluted. . . . It plainly follows that tragedy is the higher art, as attaining its end more perfectly." Lessing alludes to these grounds for
Aristotle's preference in his letter to Nicolai: "Aristotle said that dramatic poetry is the highest, even the only, poetry, and he assigns
second place to the epic only insofar as it is for the most part dramatic or can be dramatic." In Aristotle this compactness is a virtue
drama can display only by sacrificing the freedom of the epic—because the epic does not actually show us what it narrates—to treat
the marvelous, even the monstrous, to tell grandiose lies with im-
punity.[16] Reversing Plato's hierarchy, Aristotle approves the restrictions of the drama that inhibit the more reckless elements of the
poet's imagination. This recklessness, with its consequent freedom,
leads the epic into a formal diffuseness and looseness that, for Aristotle, make it inferior to tragedy.

But Aristotle sees the compact system of internal relations in tragedy, bound by the laws of probability, as an intrinsic characteristic
of the poem, *not* as an attempt by the play to imitate the time-space

16. "The irrational, on which the wonderful depends for its chief effects, has
wider scope in epic poetry, because there the person acting is not seen. . . . It is
Homer who has chiefly taught other poets the art of telling lies skillfully" (*Poetics*,
chap. 24).

conditions of the members of the audience in order to trick them into viewing it as a real part of their world. A strange transformation of Aristotle's "probability," which the Renaissance had already turned into "credibility," allowed it to slip further into "verisimilitude." Hence the narrowly conceived unities of time and place, instrumental in producing "verisimilitude" for the French neoclassicists, should not be traced back to Aristotle as coordinates of his highly prized unity of action. Aristotle's central concern for the "formal cause" as the primary stimulus of the tragic effect is shifted by the French to an expanded notion of the "efficient cause," "the manner of imitation," which is a less important factor for Aristotle. Indeed, French neoclassicism has the efficient cause take over the role of the formal as it, in effect, creates a semiotics of drama that changes what is being represented: since the stage is taken to be the real world itself, the words in the text can be taken to refer to the limited stage space and stage time (within a picture-frame stage), instead of, as in Aristotle, referring to the world of people, their acts in their time and their space, even if they must be contracted by form for their effective representation before us.

The extreme tightness of French dramatic prescriptions may be traced to an almost perverse naturalism of semiotic desire. (I repeat that I am referring here to the extreme version of French seventeenth-century dramatic theory rather than to the actual productions of a more interestingly varied dramatic practice.)[17] The restrictive enforcement of the doctrine of "verisimilitude" could be and was interpreted as treating drama, from the viewer's perspective, as the ultimate natural sign; treating it, in other words, as a mimesis that literalized the viewer's imagination by reducing the play to the audience's reality as bodies in the theater. The doctrine could be made to rest on the insistence that the play should approach a one-to-one relationship between stage time and space and audience time and space, between, that is, the passage of time represented onstage and the amount of elapsed time in the theater, as well as between the one place to be represented onstage and the singleness of the framed stage itself. Otherwise, the argument runs, the presen-

17. In dealing with such extremes of natural-sign theory, we should remain aware of the countertendencies in the arts of the seventeenth century and beyond. The extravagance of the baroque, for example, helped create opera as a rich and utterly artificial mélange of the arts. In opera, with its mix of song and speech, and the occasional intrusion of masque and orchestral music and dance, we find little attempted illusion of reality in dialogue or action.

tation would not be "verisimilar" and would not be credited by an audience who knew how little their time had advanced and that their space had not changed at all.

The absurdity that this theory cultivated rested on the supposed desire to remove from the drama any obstacle of convention that would prevent us from mistaking the play for the real thing: this mistaking is what Lessing thought of as "illusion," though Johnson would call it "delusion," saving "illusion" for a more self-consciously aesthetic activity.[18] The deliberate confusion that required the time and space of the represented fiction to be one with the "real" time and space in the theater can be seen as arising from a desire to rid the play of all intrusions by a medium that, in calling attention to artifice, threatened the play's credibility: would keep members of the audience from believing it to be a real-life happening they had come upon. Such a suppression of the medium for the immediacy of illusion (in the sense attributed to "illusion" by Lessing and the French, though not by Johnson) is precisely in accord with Lessing's objective in moving poetry toward becoming a natural-sign art.

The paradox is that French neoclassical drama accomplished the very opposite of this intent, since, as Dryden and others—including Corneille himself—freely point out, it is just where such rules of verisimilitude are closely followed that the plays seem reduced to an extreme of unlifelike artifice. That which is intended to make them "natural" has turned them "conventional" as well as "arbitrary," beyond all chance of being "credited." And, ironically, these plays had no critic more disparaging of them on this score than Lessing himself. For how can one hope to produce his desired illusion of reality when the rules imposed by the French version of verisimilitude maximize the artificial and minimize the "natural," instead of the other way around?

For example, the *liaison des scènes*—which dictates that the stage not be left vacant, since a character is to remain onstage to link one scene to the next—is a device intended to prevent any gap in the represented time sequence, so that members of the audience would feel that their own temporal continuity, where they sit, is not being violated onstage. Thus, it could be argued, the natural signs they ob-

18. My use of Johnson's views here and later rests primarily on his introduction of the theater of illusion, as contrasted to delusion, in his defense of Shakespeare's violation of the French unities in the "Preface" to his *Shakespeare*. A more extended discussion of Johnson appears later in this chapter.

serve have their naturalness reinforced, as no intervening dramatic conventions are needed to account for the leap forward from one time period to another or from one place to another. Yet obviously the play that restrains its represented actions in order to observe the *liaison des scènes* must resort to considerable artifice, and—alas—very evident artifice, to do so; what is represented onstage is sometimes so awkwardly restricted that the unnaturalness of the compression of what we are permitted to see demonstrates the strain it imposes on the representation, thereby revealing all too clearly that it is only a conventional representation and not life at all. The paradox, then, is found in the obvious artificiality that accompanies devices intended to produce the illusion of reality, thereby emphasizing the strange failings of the distorted and even impossible search after "nature," or rather the search after the apparently "natural" in order to command our belief that the signs we see do not merely represent nature, but *are* "nature."

I have been observing from Plato onward the conflicting discussion of the two modes of representation, the dramatic and the narrative, and I have observed the tendency to ally one (the dramatic) with the visual arts as potential natural signs and to resign the other (the narrative) to the realm of the verbal arts that cannot rise beyond being arbitrary and conventional signs. Now, we have seen in Lessing the privileging of drama (in the Aristotelian tradition that sought to reverse, though on familiar grounds, Plato's special condemnation of drama) as *the* way to convert arbitrary signs to natural signs. Consequently, Lessing must want to expand that portion of the drama that *shows* the audience and hence functions as natural signs and must want to reduce that portion that *tells* the audience, since this portion is only narrative in disguise, no more than arbitrary signs after all. Indeed the best play, as a perfect structure of natural signs, would only show and never tell.

These observations lead to another and more striking paradox, linked to the first, that lurks within this restrictive dramatic practice. As witnesses to an illusion of "natural" action, we should see it all as if it were a "real" action happening before us; consequently everything should be directly represented. But the dramatist, despite the desire to delude us into this belief that what we are witnessing is "real," is forced severely to restrict the stage space and time if all gaps are to be avoided: consequently he is forced to limit what may be directly represented. He thus must exclude much in the ac-

tion that we ought to *see* happening before us and, as a consequence, must yield to the temptation of having the characters *tell*
one another (and us) *about* what has happened or is happening elsewhere; for he must let us in on the action one way or another. As the
extreme version of French neoclassical theater demonstrates, the
more the collapsing of stage time and stage space reduces what may
be *shown*, the more it expands what must be *reported* by one character or another for the audience's benefit. The more exclusive the
quest for natural signs, the greater the need to resort to arbitrary
signs as supplements. The desperate struggle to compress the stage
action, so that its verisimilitude may deceive the audience into seeing it as real, leads instead to a severity that necessitates the increased employment of reported offstage action. This narrative intrusion on the dramatic, the theatrical, makes the members of the
audience more and more aware of themselves as listeners, auditory
recipients of a story being told, engaging in *verbal* activities that preserve their function within the conventions of a mediated aesthetic
transaction; they cease being fully engaged onlookers (even voy-
eurs) of a real happening they have come upon.

The restrictions that were to have produced an unalloyed structure of natural signs end by producing more and more supplemen-
tation by arbitrary signs to the point that drama becomes converted
into mixed media, a mélange of the shown and the reported, the
would-be natural and the arbitrary-conventional. Such a dramatist
employs supplementary narrative, just as, on the other side of the
generic boundary, a narrative poet like Homer—as we have been
reminded since Plato—produced supplementary dramatic (that is,
quoted) episodes. But both have both, both mixed—neither "natural." The search for the dramatic purity of the natural sign inadver-
tently turns drama into a hybrid that betrays its *un*naturalness.

Of course, all drama—even the least restrictive, the most wandering—inevitably displays some mixing of genres in its need, from time
to time, to resort to narration; but the stringencies of seventeenth-
century French dramatic theory, however contrary to their intention,
are forced to exaggerate the need for narrative intrusion until it sometimes appears to play the primary role in getting the plot represented, though it must do so verbally rather than dramatically. The
very act of pressing the dramatic into its narrowest enclosure leads to
breaking it open in an extreme fashion that demonstrates the mixed
character of *all* drama in its dependence, at whatever cost to its illusionary objective, on the narrative supplement. As a consequence of

such revelations about the quest for the natural sign in the French
dramatic model of the seventeenth century, the way was opened for
the questioning of that quest in less severe examples of drama.[19]

We can well understand Lessing's attacks on the French theater of
the preceding century, since—whatever its mission was or could be
interpreted as being—he had to see it as artificial, obviously so, and
hence unlikely to produce in its audience the natural-sign illusion
he sought as the objective of all drama. Yet we have seen how the
arguments made in defense of the French theater were aimed, however self-deludedly, at that very objective. Perhaps what Lessing
saw as the failure of that theater should have persuaded him of the
futility of pursuing the myth of art—even drama—as a natural sign.
This pursuit is self-defeating because in the very making of art (even
if as a would-be natural sign) the employment of various illusionary
devices, and hence of artifice, must intrude, and with effects that
should be seen as part of a transaction with the viewer-hearer from
which the aesthetic (as non-real, as fictional) cannot be excluded.
We have seen that this turns out to be the case even if the work of
art is a would-be natural sign; indeed, my examination of French
neoclassicism suggests that it is all the more the case as the work
seeks to be a natural sign. If by saying this I am consigning the natural-sign aesthetic to the realm of self-deluding myth, I am only
anticipating what subsequent thinking about art has done—and
shrewdly and effectively done—in our own century.

Johnson's well-known response to the seventeenth-century French
version of the unities dwells precisely on the extent to which the
doctrine of verisimilitude can be exposed as a most naive version of
what I have called the myth of the natural sign. In returning us to
the drama as a created fiction, Johnson is also, in effect, answering
Lessing a year in advance of Lessing's major statement. (Johnson's
"Preface" to his *Shakespeare* appears in 1765, a year earlier than *Laokoön.*) Johnson frees dramatic representation from a mimetic subservience to our empirical reality, since such a subservience would
deny the representation its own constructive power: "It is false that
any representation is mistaken for reality; that any dramatic fable in
its materiality was ever credible, or, for a single moment, was ever
credited." The key phrase, it is clear, is the qualification "in its mate-

19. In Chapter 7 we will see modernist critics argue for self-referential features that
display themselves even in ostensibly "realistic" works of art, whether in painting or
drama, to disrupt any natural-sign appeal.

riality": echoing Aristotle's material cause, it points to the difference between the stuff of the world and the make-believe of stage
illusion. It is not that the credibility of the drama as dramatic representation is being denied; what is being denied is our literal belief
in the stage happening *in its materiality* as a real happening. We believe in it not *as* reality but *as if* it were reality. I quote again the often
quoted lines:

> The truth is that the spectators are always in their senses, and know,
> from the first act to the last, that the stage is only a stage, and that the
> players are only players. . . . It will be asked how the drama moves, if it
> is not credited. It is credited with all the credit due to a drama . . . rep-
> resenting to the auditor what he would himself feel if he were to do or
> suffer what is there feigned to be suffered or to be done. . . . The delight
> of tragedy proceeds from our consciousness of fiction; if we thought
> murders and treasons real, they would please no more.[20]

Here, in the tradition of Aristotle, the arbitrary inventions of the
playwright, subjected to the conventions of the generic literary occasion, presumably are made to achieve a propriety of their own that
allows the auditor to receive the experience they impose as an
acceptable substitute for nature, though hardly as the thing itself. It
is in accordance with this view that Johnson acknowledges the purely nominal and conventional—in contrast to the ontological and
"natural"—status of dramatic genres:

> Out of this chaos of mingled purposes and casualties [the mixed nature
> of human experience that he refers to as "the real state of sublunary
> nature"] the ancient poets, according to the laws which *custom* had pre-
> scribed, selected some the crimes of men, and some their absurdities;
> some the momentous vicissitudes of life, and some the lighter occur-
> rences; some the terrors of distress, and some the gaieties of prosperity.

20. This quotation and those in the rest of the paragraph appear in the "Preface"
to *The Plays of William Shakespeare,* in *Samuel Johnson,* ed. Donald Greene (New York:
Oxford University Press, 1984), pp. 430–32. It must be conceded that this extended
argument in Johnson is not altogether consistent with Johnson's writings elsewhere.
Even in the "Preface" I find three Johnsons: a realistic and particularizing Johnson,
who can confound drama with the world of immediate experience; a moralistic and
universalizing Johnson, who would have drama improve upon the way things go in
the world; and the Johnson I am describing here, who celebrates our consciousness
of the artifice of art as fiction. See my "Fiction, Nature, and Literary Kinds in
Johnson's Criticism of Shakespeare," *Poetic Presence and Illusion* (Baltimore: Johns
Hopkins University Press, 1979), pp. 55–69.

Thus rose the two modes of imitation, known by the *names* of *tragedy* and *comedy* (my italics).[21]

Unlike these ancients who accepted such customary distinctions, "Shakespeare has united the powers of exciting laughter and sorrow not only in one mind, but in one composition." Thus, Johnson's justification of Shakespeare maintains, though contrary to the rules, this procedure is *not* contrary to nature. Indeed there is always an appeal open "from criticism to nature," though obviously this is a more complex nature than that which gives rise to natural signs.

Johnson's poet is giving us, though in another form, that "other" or second nature that Renaissance critics like Sir Philip Sidney recommended ("Only the poet . . . lifted up with the vigor of his own invention, doth grow in effect into another nature, in making things either better than Nature bringeth forth, or, quite anew, forms such as never were in Nature").[22] As a precursor to Johnson, Sidney in his *Apology for Poetry* also finds in drama an exemplary genre as he seeks to distance all poetry, and especially the epic, from the truth of a *literal* mimesis in order to support his concept of poetry as a feigned fiction, a concept springing from the distinction between poetry and history that he borrows from Aristotle:[23]

> The historian, affirming many things, can, in the cloudy knowledge of mankind, hardly escape from many lies. But the poet . . . nothing affirmeth. The poet never maketh any circles about your imagination, to conjure you to believe for true what he writes. He citeth not authorities of other histories, but even for his entry, calleth the sweet Muses to inspire into him a good invention. (P. 124)

Consequently, since

> the poet's persons and doings are but pictures what should be, and not stories what have been, they [readers or auditors] will never give the lie

---

21. "Preface" to *Shakespeare*, p. 423. This passage appears in Johnson's defense of Shakespeare's violation of the neoclassical doctrine that calls for the purity of genres.

22. Sidney, *An Apology for Poetry or The Defence of Poesy*, ed. Geoffrey Shepherd (Manchester: Manchester University Press, 1973), p. 100.

23. I do not at all deny that Sidney's major attachment is to Plato rather than Aristotle, but as is often the case with sixteenth-century critics, his Platonism did not prevent him from borrowing enough from Aristotle to free poetry from historical reality, even if largely on metaphysical, and thus Platonic, rather than formalistic grounds.

to things not affirmatively but allegorically and figuratively written. And therefore, as in History looking for truth, they go away full fraught with falsehood, so in Poesy looking but for fiction, they shall use the narration but as an imaginative ground-plot of a profitable invention. (P. 124)

As Aristotle demonstrated long before, one cannot press the history-poetry distinction without freeing poetry from nature and from the succession of actual events, and subjecting it to the rules of its own operations. Indeed, the power and influence of the *Poetics* over the centuries have been due in large part to its shrewd instructions about how to impose humanly formed fables upon the casual sequences of history and to do so with forms that will move audiences despite their factual untruth. Clearly, the several sequential parts of such dramatic forms are governed by principles of internal relations that are anything but naturally derived.

In the midst of the discussion I have quoted, Sidney explicitly introduces drama as his example to prove poetry's freedom from literal truth. And he does it by summoning stage illusion as his prima facie argument: "What child is there that, coming to a play, and seeing *Thebes* written in great letters upon an old door, doth believe that it is *Thebes*?" (*Apology*, p. 124). This passage surely anticipates Johnson's similar defense (in the midst of the passage I have referred to) of the auditor's power to entertain dramatic *i*llusion, though without *de*lusion. The enemy for Johnson is the French insistence that the stage cannot successively represent different places because the spectator "knows with certainty that he has not changed his place, and he knows that place cannot change itself; that what was a house cannot become a plain; that what was *Thebes* can never be *Persepolis*" ("Preface," p. 430).

Johnson answers with his enthroning of our imaginative power to entertain dramatic illusion and, consequently, to resist being deluded about what is art and what is reality. The crucial sentence is the one I have quoted before: "It is false that any representation is mistaken for reality; that any dramatic fable in its materiality was ever credible, or, for a single moment, was ever credited" (pp. 430–31). Certainly one should be able to entertain the change on the stage from one place to another, once having granted the initial make-believe time and place of the first scene. (As Sidney said, no child believes he is in Thebes—in time and place—when he sees the name written as the denomination of what the stage represents.)

After all, the leaps licensed by the imagination, if we are to grant the play its initial premises of time and place, make subsequent demands for shifts in time and place seem slight indeed. Or, in Johnson's powerful simplicity, "Surely he that imagines this may imagine more. . . . Delusion, if delusion be admitted, has no certain limitation" (p. 431). For we know we are actually in none of those places but only in "a modern theatre," watching "players" pretending to be characters who are themselves artful creations and not real people. In opposition to narrowly restrictive neoclassicism, Johnson justifies the great variety that can be admitted onstage to be represented because place and, even more, time are utterly "obsequious to the imagination." How far, with this splendid phrase, we have come from the literal, surrogate function of the natural sign. In an argument that has been echoed many times, even in recent years, Johnson—after Sidney and with much more detailed argument—speaks for dramatic illusion rather than dramatic delusion. In what sense "illusion" and in what sense "delusion"? He sees illusion as a wilful version of delusion, a deception that is aware of itself even as it indulges itself. The spectator sees the duplicity in the play but is complicitous in allowing it to function both ways. The sign in drama is no longer viewed as natural, but it does not totally lose its relation to the natural-sign myth. The make-believe in the play requires that we respond to the sense in which it apparently claims to be a natural sign even while it ministers to our common-sense knowledge of it as anything but natural—as an artifact constructed out of arbitrary and conventional materials. In effect, the stage illusion is a fake imitation of the natural sign it pretends to represent, and as audience we share both in its pretension and in the acknowledged deception behind that pretension.

The common-sense liberation from the artificial strictures of neoclassical theory, most brilliantly formulated by Johnson, spread beyond England. Indeed, as if to qualify the excesses of his precursors, it was a Frenchman, Denis Diderot, who soon after Johnson's "Preface" echoed the rejection of any association of the stage with empirical reality.[24] Diderot (at least the later Diderot of the *Paradox*

24. Diderot, *Paradoxe sur le comédien* (Paris: Garnier-Flammarion, 1967), pp. 123–91. This witty extended dialogue was probably written—or at least started—in 1769, though it was only published posthumously in 1830. Its authorship, at one time challenged, is no longer in question. The translations of the quoted phrases are my own.

Strangely enough, the position that Diderot persists in taking throughout the dia-

of the Actor) is, in effect, rejecting the French neoclassical idea of a century before, although he is doing it primarily from the standpoint of the actor rather than from that of the audience. Indeed, he finds his argument particularly applicable to the French theater—to the very plays that were presumably sponsored by earlier doctrine but often succeeded in spite of it. Diderot argues that the actor is to be always aware of the difference between the stage situation and the real one: he is not to surrender to the "real" feelings of the character being portrayed, as if the situation were an actual one, but, instead, is at all times to be conscious of his own extra-theatrical person and circumstances, as well as of the conventional demands of the theater and the art of acting. The "paradox of the actor" is precisely that he does not seek to become the person he imitates, but, as a self-conscious and hence conventional performer, remains himself, though only himself *as* an imitator. In a curious way Diderot's "paradox" serves as a forerunner to Bertolt Brecht's notion of the "alienation effect," discussed in Chapter 8, below.

Diderot approaches Johnson even more closely as he suggests that the audience responds accordingly: the fictional scene of domestic pathos will move us more than a real scene it may be said to imitate, because, he argues, neither the actor *nor we* have "perfectly forgotten ourselves" (pp. 180–81). The actor, then, should not actually be moved to tears, "because one does not come [to the theater] to see tears, but to hear discourse that draws forth tears, because this truth of nature does not accord with the truth of convention" (p. 187). With no intention to delude, the play is to remain a play: "The actors impress the audience, not when they are furious, but when they play fury well" (p. 190).

From this perspective—Johnson's and, after him, Diderot's (and later Brecht's)—the myth of the natural sign is a temptation that must be exposed as a theoretical deception. In the arts it perhaps tempts us most in the deliberate falseness of the stage illusion, which from the standpoint of a natural sign betrayed can be read as

---

logue is diametrically opposed to his earlier claims, consistent with the French defense of a theater of delusion, that the dramatic spectacle persuades the spectator to believe that what is before him is the action itself rather than an imitation of the action. His movement from the pursuit of the natural sign to the Johnsonian acceptance of the cool conventionality of dramatic signs is a manifestation of the skeptical character of late neoclassicism in its final resistance to the romanticism for which it is, hardly intentionally, helping to prepare.

dramatic delusion: here stand apparently real people apparently interrelating as in life, except that their actions and speeches are directed by structural and theatrical requirements both arbitrary and conventional, playing within the realm of appearance, with the representations *as* in life always belied by the representations *as if* in life. From Plato through Lessing, the theorist who professes the natural-sign aesthetic seems to have been taken in by what the drama pretends to, and would even try to extend that deception to all the verbal arts; but theorists in the Johnson mold know better on both counts.

So unless we take the Johnsonian path, the semiotic on which we ground our aesthetics will fool us as seventeenth-century French theory—and even, in his own way, Lessing—wanted the drama to fool us.[25] The myth of the natural sign, prompted by the example of drama, may have deceived the innocent mimetic theorist about the semiotic of the literary work of art, while in Johnson's view of drama, which converts both audience response and the semiotic itself, viewers, in complicity with the ambiguous aesthetic occasion, help to deceive themselves, to welcome the illusion in its duplicity, so that their response is anything but innocent. The drama, given its peculiar character and the peculiar history of its theorists, may be viewed as the example par excellence of how the natural-sign aesthetic turned its deceived worshipers into willing victims of the temptation to convert aesthetic illusions into their delusions. And it is Johnson's corrective view, as developed through the nineteenth century and into our own time, that permits us to see that naive conversion and to resist it. It is an unfortunate consequence—but should not be a surprising one—that once the natural-sign aesthetic is displaced, the drama appears to suffer its own decline among competing literary genres as a newer theory authorizes a semiotic that privileges more unbounded kinds of verbal representation, mainly the novel and the lyric.

25. Again I remind the reader that the early Diderot (see n. 24, above) seemed to defend just such a natural-sign doctrine. Thus, from *Les bijoux indiscrets* (1748), "I know still that the perfection of a spectacle consists in so exact an imitation of an action that the spectator, deluded without interruption, imagines that he is observing the action itself." His later position in the *Paradox* thus represents a most significant correction. I have translated this passage from *Oeuvres complètes de Diderot*, ed. J. Assézat, vol. 4 (Paris: Garnier Frères, 1875), pp. 284–85.

A SUPPLEMENTARY NOTE

Well beyond the central city, occupying a large estate on one of the many islands that make up greater Stockholm, is the palace of Drottningholm, home of the Swedish royal family. A neighboring structure on the compound is the wonderfully preserved eighteenth-century court theater and its companion building, the theater museum. One large room in the museum is devoted mainly to pictures of old stage sets, theatrical representations of both interior and exterior "realities," some of which are urban scenes, filled with houses, streets, people. But the one side of the room that backs against the windows provides a significant contrast to the others: mounted against the windows are several old prints, nineteenth-century drawings of actual European urban scenes, even identified by the names of the cities being represented. Of course, since all the drawings around the room are also aesthetic representations, these pictures of actual cities also appear to us, in effect, as a series of sets, not very unlike the invented theater sets pictured on the other walls of the room: all of them are, similarly, artful reductions of "reality."

But there is a strangely paradoxical effect in the scenes of the ostensibly "real" cities (in contrast to the stage cities) being represented. In each of them we seem to be seeing a night scene, though the drawings are not darkened and it is still daylight in the room. Indeed, we seem to be seeing a night scene only *because* it is daylight. In the city scenes all the windows of the pictured houses are cutouts covered by a transparent film, so that the daylight pours through the film to create the illusion of interior nighttime illumination. In this way nature's own daylight, entering through the windows, is transformed into—or at least is made to appear as—artificial night lights, the many bright dots of lighted windows shining into what now appears to be a night scene.

Here is a strange conjunction indeed, one that turns nature's day into art's night, forcing nature to change its "nature" in order to serve its artful opposite. Observing this paradoxical conjunction, I suddenly saw figured in it all the collisions and interchanges that occur between our attraction and our resistance to the illusion of the natural sign: an allegory of what I am struggling to describe and account for in this chapter—and in this entire study.

3

REPRESENTATION AS *ENARGEIA I*

Verbal Representation and the Natural-Sign Aesthetic

To me be Nature's volume broad displayed;
And to peruse its all-instructing page,
Or, haply catching inspiration thence,
Some easy passage, raptured, to translate,
My sole delight. . . .

James Thomson, "Summer," *The Seasons*

W e saw in the preceding chapter that the need for Plato's metaphysic to deprecate all that contributed to the illusionary, as the deceptive, led him to condemn the arts insofar as they were mimetic, since he equated mimesis with illusion. In the *Sophist* he used the illusionistic tendencies of contemporary sculpture and painting to justify this judgment, since they permitted him to see all illusion as delusion and, consequently, to denounce the realm of appearance on metaphysical grounds. But his sense of the illusionary in poetry and hence his desire to outlaw poetry at large as an illusionary art were at some moments insecure enough to force him to reduce the object of his attack to the dramatic art of tragedy, which, despite its material base in words, could be treated as a natural sign by virtue of its mode of representation. Since the non-dramatic verbal arts, in this special sense non-mimetic, could not be so reduced, these moments in Plato's attack opened the way to a separation between the poetics of drama and the poetics of the less literally representational verbal arts, a separation that persisted throughout much of the history of literary criticism. And as we have seen, it helped to produce a poetics of drama heavily dependent on the myth of a natural-sign aesthetics, so that the place of drama in the literary hierarchy declined as the natural-sign aesthetic came to be abandoned.

But we saw in other places that Plato's attack on poetry as a mimetic art could also, despite the arbitrary character of words, spread out beyond dramatic representation to include the descriptive power of language to paint images for the mind, though not, of course, for the eyes. With this power poetry could seek to produce the effect of the natural sign even if—except in the drama—it could not quite *be* a natural sign. For the most part in Plato this picture-inducing power of words enables poetry at large—and not just drama—to be condemned as dangerously mimetic. In this chapter

I will pursue the development of this version of the theory of poetry as would-be natural sign.

The capacity of words to describe with a vividness that, in effect, reproduces an object before our very eyes (i.e., before the eyes of the mind) defines the rhetorical trope of *enargeia;* and once we assume, as Plato does, that the writer or speaker has this trope as his objective and at his best can manage to achieve it, the danger of the verbal art in wedding us to the world of appearances can approach that of the visual arts, despite the difference between words and pictures. In Chapter 1, I suggested that later classicism, looking for a device that would break into and halt the temporal flow of discourse by forcing us to pause over an extended verbal picture, develops the notion of ekphrasis (as an elaborate description of any visible entity) out of this earlier call for *enargeia.* It is to the later pictorialist tradition that emerges from *enargeia* that I will turn in this chapter, though only after once more dwelling on its sources in Plato.

Despite those lapses in which Plato narrows his attack on verbal imitation to dramatic poetry, we have several times noted that since he usually allows "imitation" to refer to all the modes of representation, it must usually refer to all the modes of verbal representation as well. And it is the broader definition of "imitation" toward which Plato consistently works in book 10 of the *Republic,* so that it is clear, as he moves back and forth between poetry and painting, that he means to overlook the generic distinctions within poetry that are so central to book 3, once he turns to examine the nature of artistic representation generally, finding all versions of that representation wanting, both cognitively and morally. By the time he has arrived at his definition in book 10, drama and narrative have come to be companion mimetic sinners confronted by the same charges, rather than opponents, one the many-voiced imitator and the other the unchanging, single-voiced teller. And similarly, poetry of whatever kind is a companion sinner with the visual mimetic arts.

It is significant that though book 10 begins by referring agreeably back to the damning judgment made against "the imitative kind of poetry" in book 3, it rapidly shifts to the world of things and the representation of them by the painter. What is also shifted is the grounds on which Socrates has declared himself to be hunting for "a general definition of imitation": "imitation" now is to rest, not on a natural-sign relation between an illusionary visual equivalent and its original, but on the one-to-one-ness of the referential relation between a thing and its representation. From the general idea to a generic noun that "imitates" it, to a particular example of it in a thing, the passage that leads our mind from one to the other is a direct one.

Plato's argument is based, of course, on an unproblematic view of representation that Derridean theory has in recent years taught us to think of as "logocentric": a word, a generic noun, in effect contains the substantive idea within itself, as the idea contains all its particular representatives within *it*self. Hence Plato opens book 10 by accepting an assumption that, in our ontological insecurity, we would question rather than assume: "Whenever a number of individuals have a common name, we assume that there is one corresponding idea or form." From here he moves to his well-known metaphysical divisions among beds and tables: the universal "ideas or forms" of them, the particular examples of them made for use in our world, and the imitations of them by the painter.

We must note that the ground for establishing this sequence rests primarily on visual resemblances, what Socrates hastens to call "appearances." Indeed, he only half-seriously invokes the metaphor of the mirror to make his point. How may one be a universal maker, a maker of all things, even "the earth and heaven, and the things which are in heaven or under the earth . . . the gods also"? "There are many ways in which the feat might be accomplished, none quicker than that of turning a mirror round and round—you would soon enough make the sun and the heavens, and the earth and yourself, and other animals and plants, and all the other creations of art as well as nature, in the mirror."[1] When it is objected that these so-called creations would only be "appearances," Socrates eagerly agrees, labeling the painter just such "a creator of appearances," appearances of particular beds, each of which is in its turn only an appearance, a "semblance" of "the idea which according to our view is the real object." In this semblance-making at a second remove, there must be as much distortion of the "true object" as there is in any of the tricks our eyes play upon us. He reminds us how we are fooled by the refraction of objects in water and suggests that similar effects are achieved in us by the painter's art of conjuring.[2]

1. "The Republic," bk. 10, *The Dialogues of Plato*, trans. Benjamin Jowett, 4 vols. (New York: Scribner's, 1901), 2:426.
2. "And the same objects appear straight when looked at out of the water, and crooked when in the water; and the convex becomes concave, owing to the illusions about colors to which the sight is liable. There is no end to this sort of confusion in the

Given his objective of discovering the "general definition of imitation"—the realm of apparently hard things and their visible representations—we can understand why Plato has Socrates shift his primary target from the verbal to the visual arts, from poetry to painting. This general definition of "imitation" rests on art's capacity to mirror the thing we perceive (with its distortions) by making an illusionary substitute for it, so that the visual-spatial art is clearly a more appropriate model for his claims than is the verbal and temporal art. But when Socrates returns once more to include the poet as well, he still wants to retain the advantages of the definition that he derived from the painter even though within such a definition the poet could be included only as he is—if no more than metaphorically—a lesser painter.

Once again it is Homer he focuses upon, even though now what gives Homer his status is not his habit of speaking through the mouths of others but the fact that he is "an image-maker, that is, by our definition, an imitator."

> The poet is like a painter who . . . will make a likeness of a cobbler though he understands nothing of cobbling; and his picture is good enough for those who know no more than he does, and judge only by colors and figures. In like manner the poet with his words and phrases may be said to lay on the colors of the several arts, himself understanding their nature only enough to imitate them; and other people, who are as ignorant as he is, and judge only from his words, imagine that if he speaks of cobbling, or of military tactics, or of anything else, in meter and harmony and rhythm, he speaks very well—such is the sweet influence which melody and rhythm by nature have. (P. 431)

There are few better examples of the position that later critics wrongly read into Horace's phrase *ut pictura poesis*.[3] Yet here, clearly, the common ground between painter and poet depends not at all

---

mind; and there is a similar deception about painting in light and shade, and juggling, and other ingenious devices, which have quite a magical power of imposing upon our weakness" (bk. 10, p. 433).

3. A bit later in book 10 Socrates himself questions his relying "on a probability derived from the analogy of painting" but after further argument concludes by affirming the justness of that analogy: "And now we may fairly take him [the poet] and set him up by the side of the painter, for he is like him in two ways: first, inasmuch as his creations have an inferior degree of truth—in this, I say, he is like him; and he is also like him in being concerned with an inferior part of the soul" [because

on the poet's attempt, through dramatic dialogue, to imitate the
voices of his characters. Instead, it depends on the poet's capacity
to create a "likeness," an image, though in his verbal—other than
sensible—way, different as that way must be from the painter's. To
the example of Homer Socrates now can even add Hesiod, whom
he would have had to exclude so long as he relied only upon the
poet's habit of speaking primarily through the voices of others.

So the definition of imitation *is* "general" and consequently is far
removed from the limited definition of book 3. It would include all
the varieties of poetry—dramatic, narrative, lyric—so long as they
were characterized by the poet's misleading power as "image-
maker." Still the poet's mission, however misguided, must require
him to use his more indirect medium to follow as best he can
(though with an inferior instrument) in the footsteps of painting,
the model art that produces duplications directly, as visual substitutes for its objects.

Since Socrates has invoked painting in order to emphasize the visual character of mimetic illusion, he can, for purposes of emulation,
bring together the several varieties of the verbal arts that have in
common the image-making power of their words: poetry thus
creates mimetic images for the mind's eye as painting does for the
body's eye, in accordance with a consistent theory of mental imagery. But he can use this theory only by borrowing a word like
"image," which can be applied to the visual arts in its literal sense,
and applying it to poetry as an unacknowledged metaphor or
empty analogy, in order to elide the differences between the verbal
and the visual. This metaphorical transfer from the visual to the verbal arts, together with the free use of the word "image" in poetic
commentary, will be a common practice in the pictorialist aesthetic.
That aesthetic, which is also dedicated to the primacy of the natural
sign and of the visual arts that are that sign's literal embodiment,
develops—though with welcome interruptions by dissenters—over
the centuries right up to the eighteenth.

If, then, in book 3 dramatic impersonation was seen as the one
literal way for poetry to produce imitations like those of the painter,
Plato's general devotion to what has been called "visual epistemology" usually leads him to attribute image-making to less immediate

---

he imitates the imperfections of character and behavior that are "easily imitated"]
(pp. 434–36).

means.[4] Nevertheless, since poetry at large, and especially the non-dramatic genres, consists of conventional (though no more than arbitrary) signs, it can produce internal pictures only through our interpretation of the words, mediating signifiers that must be converted into meaning—and, presumably, into mental images—in accordance with a controlling code. With signs in the verbal arts there is no *im*mediacy of movement from physical stimulus to mental image such as a natural-sign art like painting permits. I noted at length in Chapter 2 that in a definition of poetry-as-imitation contained within the domain of *dramatic* illusion (as in book 3 and as confirmed in the *Sophist*), poetry can be permitted to join with painting in the mimetic function of aesthetic signs as natural signs, even if only to be charged and exiled by the priggish moralist. The confusion that arises from these readings of Plato's "imitation" in books 3 and 10 leads me to concern myself further with the way (or ways) in which Plato would relate the verbal arts—and especially the non-dramatic verbal arts—to the arts of the natural sign.

It is important to note that Plato deals at length and painstakingly with the relation of language at large to natural signs in the *Cratylus*, that strange and ambiguous dialogue in which he tries in every way to avoid giving up the mimetic function of words. That dialogue, despite its confusing playfulness, still persistently urges the "natural" fitness of words to their meaning, their more than arbitrary, more than conventional character. At moments almost tempted to see them as approaching a natural-sign status just this side of onomatopoeia, Plato has Socrates draw back from the claim to natural signs as from the start he rejects any claim that signs are merely arbitrary signs. Plato rather leaves the claim for language as natural signs to be made by Cratylus—though as an absurdity to be rejected—and only fleetingly and wistfully by Socrates, who, when it counts, must deny that "a name is a vocal imitation of that which the vocal imitator names or imitates. . . . Because then we should be obliged to admit that the people who imitate sheep, or cocks, or other animals, name that which they imitate." Thus a name is "not a musical imitation," and "the art of naming" has nothing to do with "forms of imitation" like music and drawing.[5]

Yet Socrates maintains to the end that "the name is an imitation

4. I refer again to Forrest G. Robinson, *The Shape of Things Known: Sidney's Apology in Its Philosophical Tradition* (Cambridge, Mass.: Harvard University Press, 1972).

5. "Cratylus," *The Dialogues of Plato*, 1:662–63.

of the thing": "the true name indicates the nature of the thing" (p. 667). Or even more strongly elsewhere: "Have we not several times acknowledged that names rightly given are the likenesses and images of the things which they name?" (p. 679). Although the name, then, has the obligation to represent accurately the nature of the thing—and, even more telling, should be a likeness and even an image of the thing—Socrates still concedes "that pictures are also imitations of things, *but in another way*" (p. 669, my italics). Now, "likenesses" and "images" are strong words for our primary philosopher of mimesis to apply to "names"; and yet he must allow that he does *not* here mean them quite to be "pictures." This difference (between verbal likeness and visual pictures) is all-important to the conclusion of this baffling dialogue.

Socrates' developing argument makes clear his commitment to the distinction between sensible signs (as in pictures) and intelligible signs (as in words). And it is this distinction that underlies the further distinction made over the centuries between the natural sign and the arbitrary-conventional sign (arbitrary with respect to its object, though conventional, as a code, with respect to its community of users). This distinction, resting on the resemblance between signifier and signified in the natural sign and the lack of that sensory relation between them in the arbitrary-conventional sign, has assumed that the natural sign functions immediately, while the arbitrary-conventional sign requires a translating mediation in order to function. The distinction is retained, though Plato is clearly reluctant to abandon altogether some fit relationship between name and thing, even if the hope of a literal mimesis in words must be abandoned.

So Plato can claim a natural and imitative fitness between picture and thing, as he makes this claim in the realm of the sensible when speaking of pictures, though—if only by analogy—he wants not altogether to give up the claim to an analogous fitness in the realm of the intelligible when speaking of words. It is in either case a "visual epistemology" yielding internal pictures, though this mental imagery must occur through very different processes in the two cases. He does not permit this distinction to prevent him from speaking of poetry as mimetic in the broad sense of verbal representation in book 10 of the *Republic*. Nevertheless, when, in book 3 or in the *Sophist*, Plato equates "imitation" with literal impersonation, he yields to the temptation that he often feels in dealing with the fallen world of art—the temptation that worries about sensible appearances—as he tries to bring poetry into the sensible world of natural-sign immediacy that characterizes the visual arts.

Where Plato discusses the artist in the earlier portion of the *Sophist*, he emphasizes the deceptive character of those visual distortions, those misrepresentations related to perspective, which cater to our interest in appearances, to our absorption by *apparent* accuracy. In Chapter 2 I pointed out that his transference, later in that dialogue, of these illusionary sins to the poet-as-sophist leads him to impersonation as *the* illusionary verbal art. But once we have watched Plato broaden the visual (by analogy to the intelligible) realm to include verbal images, the *Sophist*'s attack on aesthetic deception can be applied to all poetry as versions of those misleading disciplines that Mazzoni will term "sophistics."

I have before noted the extent to which Plato's entire conception of natural-sign imitation rests upon an unproblematic notion of how pictures represent and how the viewer reacts to the representation: from thing to picture of the thing to our internal image of the picture as if it were the thing. In moving to the intelligible mental imagery produced by words as pictorial translations, the semiotic rests upon an equally simple view of transparency, only slightly less immediate. The process must merely tolerate a middle (mediating) but still *un*transforming element to intrude itself: from thing to its equivalent word to its idea to our internal image of our pictured idea as if it were the thing. So whichever way one conceives poetry as mimetic—as an intelligible surrogate for the sensible or as itself a sensible impersonation—the one-to-one simplism remains as the basis for the conception.

As a consequence, the mimetic object would yield to a similarly simplistic analysis. It would be treated not as *an* object but rather as a collection of separately imitated objects, with the emphasis falling not on their collectivity but on the accuracy of the individual imitations. Clearly, the semiotic basis of such an aesthetic assumes the unproblematic character of individual representations, so that there seems to be no need to ask how these are to be *made*. The *making* of a representational object intended to *match* its existential archetype presents no problem, since we are assuming an unerringly representational visual art that intends to be nothing else and encounters no difficulty in realizing that intention. In other words, we need worry about no medium's interfering with the making process and thereby clouding the transparency of the reproduction. As an analogy to this process in the verbal arts, the uninhibited representation

of an object in words—as the ultimate triumph of *enargeia*—is to proceed without being inhibited by the resistance of the verbal medium. What is being ignored is the very plasticity of the plastic arts,
or—in the verbal arts—the intransigence of words, in our consideration of the artist's or the poet's labors to bend the materials at hand
to a prior intention.

Plato's broad view of literary imitation seemed enough to allow
him to condemn poetry merely because, as an intelligibly based art,
it creates mental images through its verbal representation. So we
may wonder why, as if not content with this broad attack that he can
make despite his acknowledgment that poetry cannot be a natural-
sign art, Plato should feel the need for those moments when he collapses poetry's mimetic guilt into the dramatic, using drama's peculiar representational character as an impersonator of reality to open
it to his attack upon it as if it were a natural-sign art indeed. During
such moments the drama, or even the dramatic elements in narrative, may seem separated from the other verbal arts—though allied
with the visual arts—as all these leave the other verbal arts outside
the definition of imitation and thus exempt from condemnation as
mimetic. But the non-dramatic verbal arts can be condemned in
other places and for other reasons, reasons that recognize that
though they are intelligible rather than sensible, they can be condemned nonetheless. The dramatic art may be most like a visual art
because it too would create a sensible illusion; but though the non-
dramatic verbal arts, with their arbitrary signs, are semiotically unlike a visual art, they *seek* to emulate that art in the way they would
function, thereby using the visual arts as their model in their attempt, despite their disadvantaged (because invisible) medium of
words, to create pictures in their readers' minds. Their objective is
to be like the sensible arts, to emulate their effects, even if they are
only intelligible. Here, then, in their emulation of natural-sign arts,
are the grounds on which poetry, as non-dramatic, can be condemned by Plato even when in its mode of representation it accepts
its status as an art of arbitrary signs. When poetry, as dramatic, mimics or impersonates, then its imitative intention is patently objectionable, but the anti-aesthetic moralist can change definitions to allow
for objections even to image-making poems of a single voice.

The reason behind the lapses in Plato's doctrine of mimesis, I suggest, is that they represent his attempt to find a place for poetry
within the spatial and visual categories of art generally, because of
his special concern for the sense of sight—external and internal—

and thus his desire to include poetry among the arts to be condemned for their exclusive traffic with the realm of appearance, and hence of illusion. Why not, then, seize upon that mode of poetry, the dramatic, which seems calculated to deceive our senses? And so he does. But he clearly leaves the way open, though only within another argumentative context, to charge non-dramatic poetry as well with catering to the realm of appearance by its concentration upon its representational powers, its powers to produce *enargeia*. If, as we saw in Chapter 2, the dramatic, in its illusionary intention, seems to be the only analogue among the verbal arts to the natural-sign status of the visual arts, Plato's introduction of his additional analogy between the eyes and the eyes of the mind allows him to include the narrative and lyric also among the objectionable arts, so long as their appeal to the eyes of the mind has an objective as mimetic as the appeal to the eyes themselves made by the visual arts. With this analogy he has opened the way for the pictorialist tradition that uses the visual arts as the model for the functioning of the poem.

We have already seen, in Chapter 2, the extent to which Aristotle seemed burdened with the spatial and pictorialist consequences of Plato's "imitation" even as he tried to free poetry (or at least tragedy) from the obligations to *enargeia* that the static representations of Platonic theory imposed. It is clear that Aristotle's metaphysical commitment to teleological process led him to see the dramatic poem as a single organic object whose unfolding form was to transcend and redispose every element (each of Plato's imitated "objects") within it. Aristotle counteracts the visual and spatial implications of *enargeia* with his own temporal interest in the very different term *energeia*, which characterizes the force that drives the developing plot, whose system of probabilities strives for the realization of all that is potential within it.

Now, it must be conceded that Aristotle's formalistic concern with sequence yielded only an apparent temporality, since that sequence, as fixed within its form, had its own sort of stasis: the phrase "temporal structure," which one might apply to the Aristotelian plot, proves to be no more than a deceptive oxymoron. For Aristotle the poem, for all its consecutiveness, was, in effect, replaced by the architectural framework that served as its spatial icon. This was projected onto the dramatic action that, with its dialogue, could only fill that framework. That action was an unwinding, but one always trapped in advance by its closed form. Despite this deceptive commitment to spatiality, there was in Aristotle's poetic a crucial advance over the restrictive Platonic concern with individually imitated objects. The sense in which the Aristotelian action still represented human action—still could claim to be an "imitation"—was much less literal-minded, much more subtle and complex, and it led to quite another sort of theoretical tradition.

Yet here and there the deadening hand of Plato's analogy to the spatial and the visual intrudes to flatten Aristotle's supple definitions of a unique art form and return poetry to being a poor relation of the visual arts, struggling to mimic them by analogy. For example, in arguing for the primacy of plot over character in chapter 6 (11–15), Aristotle more than once uses the analogy to painting to make his point: "it is the same in painting," or "a similar fact is seen in painting." The point being argued is that the diction and thought through which a character is expressed in the drama have no more primacy than do the colors used in a painting to fill in the "outline" of the portrait, on which its quality principally depends. The relation of the outline to the total picture is analogous to the relation of the sequence of incidents—the plot—to the total play: each is the primary feature on which all else depends, to which all else is subordinated. We should note here, if only parenthetically, the naive theory of drawing-as-imitation that is being assumed as the aesthetic example for the drama to follow: "The most beautiful colors, laid on confusedly, will not give as much pleasure as the chalk outline of a portrait."

The notion of a portrait as the filling in of an outline, with the outline as the essence of the work and the fill as secondary, will often be borrowed by those who will treat character or figures or diction as external garments, pleasing decorations, for what comes first— the plot—as the "soul" of the literary work. Thanks to the analogy to painting, and perhaps to its source in the Platonic doctrine of "imitation," we have here a far more primitive—and static—theory of the making process or of the finished work than the more dynamic Aristotelian notion of organic development should encourage. His use of this analogy only reinforces my claim that beneath his call to action-as-sequence Aristotle is dependent upon the notion of dramatic form as a spatial icon.

Despite Aristotle's emphasis on *energeia*, there is even an explicit, if momentary, call for *enargeia* in the *Poetics*. In chapter 17.1, Aristotle uses the conventional code words associated with *enargeia* to invoke this mimetic obligation, and with the usual appeal to the visual:

"The poet should place the scene, as far as possible, before his eyes . . . in this way seeing everything with the utmost vividness, as if he were a spectator of the action." Even in this appeal to *enargeia*, it must be conceded, Aristotle shifts in mid-sentence from the object of inner vision (the scene) to a vision of the scene as an action. His primary concern with a sequential plot (as the projection of *energeia*) somehow has the Platonic appeal to *enargeia* imposed upon it as a visual appendage in conflict with a system dependent upon the principle of progression. While he remains faithful to that progressiveness, he cannot altogether resist the continuing influence that the visual character of mimesis, even with his alteration of its meaning, carries with it.

It is true that Aristotle's most obvious borrowing from Plato is that literalistic version of "imitation," as applied to the dramatic mode of representation (in his chapter 24), which we traced in Chapter 2. Still, we see in the passages cited here how much the spatial implications that Plato imposed upon that word "imitation" could inhibit the attempts to break free of them even by later critics struggling to do so. But most later critics were far less uncomfortable with Plato's inclination toward the spatial, since they found in it ample precedent for their own similar inclinations.

I am leading us to the most obvious and faithful adherents of the tradition in which Horace's phrase *ut pictura poesis* serves as an injunction to guide a poetic art that, in spite of its resistant verbal resources, seeks to emulate the spatial and visual arts—the arts of the natural sign—to which the visible world is immediately accessible. As is generally acknowledged, that key Horatian phrase was able to serve this way only because it was utterly misread, or was lifted out of context in order to be misread—and misread in a way that violates the easy, informal, and unsystematic tone of the *Epistle* in which it appears.[6]

One can argue, however, that the static nature of the injunctions that Horace proposes throughout the *Epistle*—whether concerning conventions of character, plot, diction, or didactic function—does in any case suggest a flat conception of the literary work that reveals consistently spatial thinking, so that, it may be claimed, the partic-

6. By referring to the treatise as the *Epistle to the Pisos*, I am bypassing its more pompous but less appropriate alternative title, *Ars Poetica*, in order to emphasize its unsystematic informality. Unhappily, the history of criticism records the extent to which the more theoretical impositions upon the treatise were responsible for its continuing importance.

ular misreading of his *ut pictura poesis* is less of a disservice to him than our literal complaints against such a misreading might charge. Nevertheless, it must be acknowledged that in the passage in question Horace is doing no more than considering similarities in audience (or reader) response to works from different arts: some (as with a picture, so with poetry: *ut pictura poesis*) to be seen close up and some from a distance, with attention paid in the first to petty faults and in the second to a grand scheme, with the faults overlooked. But there is here no suggestion, however remote, that poetry is to be made in order to function like a picture. Horace's words hardly present a position that warrants all that the pictorialist tradition claimed to make it responsible for, whatever we may grant concerning the static tendencies of Horace's continual fidelity to convention and its decorum.

Of course, Horace's phrase, however read or misread when it was picked up in the Renaissance, was hardly needed to establish the pictorialist tradition, though it of course served to reinforce it. Those who invoke the phrase can—and do—freely refer to the much earlier maxim, attributed to Simonides of Ceos by Plutarch, that speaks of poetry as a speaking picture, as well as the reverse, also speaking of the picture as mute poetry. And many in later antiquity—Lucian, Philostratus, and others—often invoke their precursors and add their own claims to make up an impressive anthology of such sayings for those looking for precedents. It is an easy matter for Horace's phrase, though utterly misread, to be forced into service to capture the intent of an already strongly held position to which Horace's essential spirit is made to lend support. But it is hardly a crucial matter, since that tradition must already be securely in place for the misreading to occur.

Further, once the phrase was ready for use (or misuse), the scholar-grammarian created an additional authority to reinforce the phrase by reworking the text in order to justify the misreading. Much has been written on the punctuation of the sentence in which the phrase occurs, with the placement of the comma crucial to the strength of the injunction that later scholars read into it. When, as in the generally accepted text, the comma immediately follows the phrase *ut pictura poesis*, the usual meaning, like the one I offer above, is attributed to it: as with the picture, so with poetry, in the ways in which we observe and judge the art object at a distance or close up. The verb *erit* comes after the comma and begins the next clause to explain how the observing and judging works ("it will be that"). But when the comma is placed after *erit,* the verb controls the preceding phrase, *ut pictura poesis,* and turns it into a firm statement of how it will be: poetry will be like a picture.[7]

With this reading, *ut pictura poesis* was just the phrase that Renaissance and neoclassical pictorialists could seize upon as the motto that summed up their view of poetry.[8] It helped them insist on analogous relations among the arts, but with the visual art as the semiotic model and the verbal art as being adapted to that model, as emulating it despite the handicaps inherent in its own medium; above all, it helped pictorialists insist on the special role of the natural sign as criterion for all the arts. Thus, by the mid-eighteenth century, theorists could move to the notion of a general aesthetic, a theory of the fine arts (*les Beaux Arts*) as analogous to one another. It was, needless to say, primarily a natural-sign aesthetic. By the mid-eighteenth century (1746) the title of an important treatise by Abbé Batteux contains just the wording that characterizes this program: *The Fine Arts Reduced to a Single Principle.* That principle is, of course, the imitation of nature—yet another, belated reminder of Plato's insistence that imitation cannot help but be, at bottom, the same thing in all the arts. (As we shall see in Chapter 6, Diderot shortly afterwards addressed Batteux in a treatise that reacts against this general tendency by urging a loosening of his single principle in a way that would produce significant theoretical consequences for the powers of poetry.) There was ample precedent for Batteux's title, as well as his emphasis, in the work of earlier neoclassicists in the seventeenth and earlier eighteenth centuries: among many I will mention only Abbé Du Bos's *Critical Reflections on Poetry and Painting* (1719) and, earlier, Dryden's "Parallel of Poetry and Painting" (1695).

The latter serves as a preface to Dryden's translation of Du Fres-

7. Once again I record my debt to Hagstrum's *The Sister Arts: The Tradition of Literary Pictorialism and English Poetry from Dryden to Gray* (Chicago: University of Chicago Press, 1958), which first made me aware of this issue. See esp. his discussion on pp. 59–62.

8. At the same time I must observe that some major eighteenth-century commentators, such as Pope and Roscommon, give evidence of having read the Latin carefully, so that they clearly understand the limited application of the original passage that contains the Horatian *ut pictura poesis* and do not misuse this phrase as a precedent for general pictorialist claims, though they sympathize with these claims. See, e.g., Pope's *Essay on Criticism,* lines 169–80, which paraphrase much of the Horatian passage in its original restricted sense, though without even translating the phrase that proclaims the analogy.

noy's *De Arte Graphica* (1637), a poem in Latin reflecting the extremely conservative mimetic doctrine and leaning upon the *ut pictura poesis erit* formulation. In sympathy with the text that furnishes his occasion, Dryden's prefatory essay strongly urges the typical naive analogies between the two arts, accepting with them the need to turn poetry into something like a natural sign: "To imitate nature well in whatsoever subject, is the perfection of both arts; and that picture, and that poem, which comes nearest to the resemblance of nature, is the best."[9] How can the words of a poem manage to create a "resemblance of nature" as pictures do? Dryden does not address the issue but continues to apply such borrowings from the visual arts metaphorically. Indeed, he acknowledges his indebtedness to "all the particular passages in Aristotle and Horace which are used by them to explain the art of poetry by that of painting" (p. 138).

The "Parallel" echoes in its major argument Aristotle's passing analogy, which I have summarized above, between the plot of a poem and the outline of a picture, and consequently between poetic diction and painterly filling in. Dryden uses the term "design" as the creation of the painting's outline, its basic "posture," and then borrows the term for analogical use by the poet. That design is created in a play's scenario ("scenary"): "To make a sketch, or a more perfect model of a picture, is, in the language of poets, to draw up the scenary of a play" (pp. 144–45). Once the design or outline is set, the painter can proceed with the filling in, what is termed the "coloring," another term that Dryden metaphorically adapts for the poet: "Expression, and all that belongs to words, is that in a poem which coloring is in a picture. . . . Thus in poetry, the expression is that which charms the reader, and beautifies the design, which is only the outlines of the fable" (pp. 147–48). He sees the need to compare a painting's "lights and shadows" to a poem's "tropes and figures" and exemplifies such comparisons with the statement that "strong and glowing colors are the just resemblances of bold metaphors" (p. 149). Late in his preface Dryden adds this comparison to a second, the customary metaphor introduced to describe ornament, whether in painting or in poetry, as attractive but superficial garments: "The words, etc., are evidently shown to be the clothing of the thought, in the same sense as colors are the clothing of the design" (p. 152).

9. "A Parallel of Poetry and Painting," in *Essays of John Dryden*, ed. W. P. Ker, 2 vols. (New York: Russell and Russell, 1961), 2:136.

In Chapter 2 we saw how neoclassical dramatic theory adapted the illusionistic version of Platonic mimeticism to the natural-sign aesthetic. In it the drama is championed (no longer singled out for censure as it was by Plato) as the most "natural"—and thus the most obvious—way for poetry to join the natural-sign arts. But deriving from Plato's other reason for condemning poetry—its inevitable habit of imitating unworthy objects—we have found neoclassical theory looking another way: by assuming a semiotic process that moved, almost automatically, from verbal description to mental images conjured up by the "idea" stimulated by the words, it could champion poetry as description, so that poetry was to seek, despite its obvious handicaps as a language art, to become the verbal equivalent of painting. And this mission led poetic theory to emphasize the Horatian strain.

The influence of a restrictive Latin tradition, founded on the notion of the Enlightenment as a second coming of Augustan Rome, is evident enough. But besides this principal source of support, neoclassicism, with its notion of a static mimesis, was sustained by a number of different philosophic perspectives, all of which, however much they might be opposed to one another, contributed to the exclusively spatial imagination that characterized the period aesthetic. From the recent past the rationalistic metaphysic provided a full and fully perceptible mechanism of universals that constituted an all-inclusive cosmic architecture. From the opposite end of the epistemological spectrum, an emerging empiricism, for all of its antithetical impact on rationalism, set forth an image of the mind as a storehouse of pictures that only reinforced the theory of poetry as visual imitation. At much the same time, as a late residue of a pallid Platonism, now resurgent with the revival of interest in Greek culture, the static version of a universal classic idealism associated with Winckelmann worked to lead the verbal arts in much the same direction.

Thus by the eighteenth century, which produced several comfortable epistemologies and a set of spatial metaphors for an uncritically mimetic theory, with the visual arts leading the way, the slogan *ut pictura poesis* was totally to absorb the non-dramatic poetic. As James Thomson, in his epigraph to this chapter, puts it, the Book of Nature ("Nature's volume") is to be converted into the poet's book. But for Thomson nature's is a "book" only in the figurative sense because its signs are immediately visible, while the poet's, with its arbitrary signs, must indeed be a book. Still, Thomson's poet is dedicated to converting the one "book" into the other, his own, as an act of literal translation ("Some easy passage, raptured, to translate, / My sole delight"). This poet must spatialize his temporal object by trying to naturalize his arbitrary instrument, so that he might compete in an aesthetic drawn to the specifications of another art, a natural-sign art. He was to proceed, in short, as if the mediating element of language could obliterate itself, or at least render itself transparent, so that the verbal object also could be naturalized. It is not so much that he is converting nature into a text as that he means to convert his text into nature: he can approach the Book of Nature (which is not a book) only by fighting against the bookishness of his own.

There is perhaps no clearer application of the natural-sign aesthetic to non-dramatic poetry than we find in a few paragraphs of Addison's *Spectator* 416, from his series on "The Pleasures of the Imagination" (1712). The distinctions Addison makes there clearly derive from Locke's definition of words—in contrast to natural signs—as "arbitrary" and "voluntary" signs that, by an indirection modified by convention, work to bring back to our consciousness those "ideas" (i.e., prior sensations) that are stored in the mind: "Words, by their immediate operation on us, cause no other ideas but of their natural sounds; and it is by the custom of using them for signs that they excite and revive in our minds latent ideas, but yet only such ideas as were there before. For words, seen or heard, recall to our thoughts those ideas only which they have been wont to be signs of."[10]

By adapting Locke's epistemology too uncritically, Addison—as is so often the case—allows his popularizing intent to denude the more carefully drawn distinctions he has borrowed and to press them toward an extreme, though commonplace, statement; but the special virtue of such simplification is its capacity to expose the posi-

---

10. John Locke, *An Essay Concerning Human Understanding*, ed. Alexander Campbell Fraser, vol. 2 (Oxford: Clarendon Press, 1894), p. 417. It is earlier in his *Essay*, throughout the lengthy book 3 ("Of Words"), that Locke worries in great detail about problems with language as our arbitrary-sign instrument. In dealing with words, he consistently emphasizes that "their signification [is] perfectly arbitrary" (2:12), since he does not find "any natural connexion . . . between particular articulate sounds [which are, for Locke, all that *is* "natural" about language] and certain ideas" (2:8). Yet, he must concede, "it is true, common use, by a tacit consent, appropriates certain sounds to certain ideas" (2:13). This is his way of rescuing language as an instrument for understanding: by recognizing its conventionality, its responsiveness to what, in the quotation cited in the text, he calls "custom."

tion with the clarity that its very extremity affords. I referred to this passage briefly in the summary that my introductory chapter was intended to provide, but I believe it is worth quoting in full here:

> Among the different kinds of representation, statuary is the most natural, and shows us something *likest* the object that is represented. To make use of a common instance, let one who is born blind take an image in his hands, and trace out with his fingers the different furrows and impressions of the chisel, and he will easily conceive how the shape of a man, or beast, may be represented by it; but should he draw his hand over a picture, where all is smooth and uniform, he would never be able to imagine how the several prominencies and depressions of a human body could be shown on a plain piece of canvas that has in it no unevenness or irregularity. Description runs yet further from the things it represents than painting; for a picture bears a real resemblance to its original, which letters and syllables are wholly void of. . . . It would be yet more strange to represent visible objects by sounds that have no ideas annexed to them, and to make something like description in music.

Addison is setting forth a spectrum running from the art closest to being a natural sign to the art that is farthest from it, and clearly is assuming the advantaged position of the natural-sign art. Not unexpectedly, his first art is sculpture, the art which, in its three-dimensionality, could almost be mistaken for that which it imitates. "Among the different kinds of representation, statuary is the most natural, and shows us something *likest* the object that is represented" (his italics). His second art, painting, comes close to being as natural an art as sculpture, but the difference between them is a significant one: although in painting there still is, from any distance, an appearance of similarity between the imitation and its "real" object, the two-dimensionality of the representation of a three-dimensional object creates in physical, touchable reality a marked difference between them.[11] One might argue that because

11. It is, then, the sense of touch that allows sculpture to be perceived as more "natural" than painting and hence as the closest to a natural-sign art. The sense of touch is commonly associated with sculpture in early distinctions made among the sensuous arts, although the dominance of the visual in the *ut pictura poesis erit* claim usually leads to the distinctions between touch and sight being overlooked in theoretical conclusions drawn about natural signs in art. Thus, for the convenience of my argument, my subsequent discussion will, to some extent inaccurately, also tend to collapse discussions of the two senses and speak, for the most part, of sculpture and painting as twin visual (and spatial) arts.

of this difference, there is a greater need in painting than in sculpture for the medium to create an illusionary naturalness in the art
work as sign—which is all it is. Yet, from a distance beyond our
touching, the *appearance* of naturalness persists. As we move further
along the spectrum to Addison's third art, the verbal art, we seem
to have left art as natural sign well behind, even though Addison—
for good reason—restricts his interest to the art of verbal "description," the use of words to create a mental picture: "Description runs
yet further from the things it represents than painting; for a picture
bears a real resemblance to its original, which letters and syllables
are wholly void of." As Addison completes his spectrum, only music, in which, he concedes, mimetic meanings (if any) are "confused" and "imperfect" at best, remains to move us toward the
extreme of totally arbitrary signs. It is evident that he does not quite
know how to deal with music within this scheme, though even in
this case he does not altogether surrender his mimetic objective.

Addison's spectrum of the arts, carrying an implicit hierarchy
within it, seems to urge that poetry, reduced to verbal "description," should look to the natural-sign "sister arts" to define for it its
representational function. And that function, clearly, is still what
from Plato onward has been termed *enargeia:* to use words to reproduce in the hearer or reader the perception of the natural object
itself in all its vividness. But might I not also claim that a subsidiary
mission is also justified, one that would reinforce the semiotic claim
of the natural-sign aesthetic by reinforcing the mimetic relation of
poetry to the natural-sign arts that were to be its model: that is, to
reproduce in words a natural-sign art object in the absence of that
object—in short, to make a literal ekphrasis? As the third art in line
along Addison's spectrum and emulating the first two, poetry thus
would also seek to imitate—in this case, to represent—the art object,
in effect performing an ekphrasis by way of *enargeia*. This would
thus provide a verbal equivalent, in all its vividness, of the sensuous experiencing of sculpture or painting, using *enargeia* to emulate,
by representing, the most natural of natural signs as an alternative
to nature itself. In a period such as the early eighteenth century, in
which nature and art can be conceived as substitutes—mutually reflecting signs—for one another, such alternatives seem justifiable.

This concept of natural-sign representation as the ideal end of all
the arts rests on Addison's mimetic definition of the "secondary
pleasures of imagination." These secondary pleasures, Addison reminds us at the start of *Spectator* 416, arise from recollections in our

mind of our original sensory experiences, including those recollections that have been strengthened through the stimulation of an art
object ("I at first divided the pleasures of the imagination into such
as arise from objects that are actually before our eyes [primary], or
that once entered in at our eyes, and are afterwards called up into
the mind, either barely by its own operations, or on occasion of
something without us, as statues or descriptions [secondary]").
This is, of course, Addison's extension of Locke's basic distinction
between "sensation" and "idea" ("sensation" as original sense perception of an object, and "idea" as mental image, the recollected
"sensation" in the absence of the object). Thus those secondary
pleasures deriving from art, rather than from unaided memory, proceed "from that action of the mind, which compares the ideas arising from the original objects, with the ideas we receive from the
statue, picture, description, or sound that represents them." This
mimetic view seems to value the art object largely because of its
function as a mnemonic object, an aid to memory, serving to
remind us of the primary object of actual sensation which it seeks
to imitate. (In the case of ekphrasis, mnemonics would function at
two removes: the verbal description of a visual representation of
nature.) The art object is to help us restore the liveliness of the original sensory experience within the idea that preserves the fading
memory of that experience inside us after we have been removed
from it. The pleasures of art are not called "secondary" pleasures
for nothing.

So literal a sense of imitation (as natural-sign imitation) must assume that the original sensory perception is superior to its reproduction in art: the "real" object is superior to the imitation whose
role, primarily, is to point toward that object as its "origin," recalling
for us the stored mental snapshot of our sensory experience. Consequently, this reductive notion of artistic mimesis assumes—as
Plato did—that the work of art can be no more than a collection of
individually represented objects, each related, separately, to its original rather than to the other represented objects that accompany it:
the art work is to consist of discrete objects as imitated rather than
being itself a single, made object. This is why it is more accurate to
speak of the origins of the work of art as those "real" objects of experience out there rather than as the creative mind of its author as
maker, since that mind is given little enough to create, especially
when the artistic process is to seek representational *immediacy*. In
the case of the poet, such immediacy must be emulated even though

it seems folly to maintain that a verbal entity can avoid the intrusions of a medium in its attempt to represent an object.[12]

In this aesthetic such fidelity to external, "real" origins in experience is what makes the natural sign the highest achievement of the work of art. It also dictates that the visual arts, as natural-sign arts, are to be the model arts for the other arts—source of the metaphors that are to govern our criticism of them—so that the disadvantaged art of literature must struggle against its handicap as an arbitrary-conventional-sign art and still try to imitate as best it can, seeking to do in *its* way what comes naturally to sculpture and painting: the providing of "images" to match "reality." Hence *ut pictura poesis erit*. It is no wonder that Addison in this passage speaks only of "description" as the product of the verbal arts and that "landscapes" and "portraits" were treated in the eighteenth century as poetic genres as well as painterly genres.

If we extend this line of argument, nature itself, the prime mover, is itself as much superior to the visual arts as those arts are superior to literature. With us still are the descending values associated with Plato's doctrine of imitation, which projects a downward succession of objects and imitations of those objects, with each object of imitation better (in the sense of being closer to its origin) than its imitation, the latter becoming in its turn an object for yet another, and more distant, imitation. Logic would suggest that given the absence of the original thing itself, as is the case in art, the best art object is the one that tends toward self-effacement as art in the apparent attempt to appear to be the natural object itself. All works of art try to become a reality-substitute without difference; all would, if they could, approach the *trompe l'oeil*. We should therefore accept the special virtue of sculpture and the special disadvantage of the verbal arts, unless, of course, arguing from the Platonic precedent, we claim an exception for the special mimetic immediacy of the drama, as Addison does *not* in this discussion.

So confident a doctrine of pure and unimpeded representation rests not only on a self-assurance about the transparency of representational media (the visual ones easily and automatically, and the verbal ones insofar as possible by emulation) but also on an ontolog-

12. Addison himself, in the same *Spectator* paper and, indeed, almost immediately after the passage I have quoted, will give ground before this difficulty, as we will see in Chapter 4, in which we see him in retreat from the extreme position I am attributing to him here.

ical assurance about "real experience" that even the epistemological doubts suggested by empiricism could not shake. The spatial fix on the object caught in the visual snapshot of our phenomenal experience is secured in the frozen image drawn by the painter or by the poet who seeks to adapt his words to the painter's objective.

My focus upon the total surrender to the visual and the spatial in the late seventeenth and eighteenth centuries, with poetry creeping after painting as its model, may seem to overlook the reverse tendency, which was also common in this period, to make painting like literature. For all my insistence on poetry as a "speaking picture," I should give due emphasis to the attention paid to the other half of the mutual crossovers attributed to Simonides—to painting seen as "mute poetry." We should not ignore the widespread indulgence in narrative and genre painting, and the critics' encouragement of it. If I have been addressing only the encouragement of poetry to emulate the arts of portraiture and static description, I cannot fail to mention—in addition to the painting that represented spatially fixed objects—the painting that was to emulate literary narrative. This latter emphasis would seem to be working the opposite way, with the visual seeking to forgo the spatial in pursuit of temporality, of sequence.

Does my recognition of this reverse tendency undo my argument? On the contrary, once we examine it, I believe it will provide only reinforcement. As Lessing never tired of reminding us, the theoretical support for narrative painting had to come to terms with the need for the artist to select out of a narrative sequence the single moment to be represented. The spatial art had to settle upon the one point of time (referred to again and again in the eighteenth century as the *punctum temporis*) that it was to represent.[13] But it was hardly to be any random point of time. Instead, it was to be carefully and wisely selected as the "pregnant moment," the one moment to which all preceding moments in the narrative sequence led and from which all succeeding moments descended. In effect, it was the narrative's spatial equivalent—*the* moment that held the en-

13. E. H. Gombrich provides a most helpful and perceptive summary of the arguments surrounding the formulation of the *punctum temporis* from Lord Shaftesbury (in his *Characteristics*, 1711) to James Harris (in his *Three Treatises*, 1744) to Lessing and to modern painting and film (see Gombrich, "Moment and Movement in Art," *Journal of the Warburg and Courtauld Institutes* 27 [1964]: 293–306, reprinted in *The Image and the Eye: Further Studies in the Psychology of Pictorial Representation* [Ithaca: Cornell University Press, 1982], pp. 40–62).

tire narrative—full with potential, awaiting the inevitability of realization. Aristotle, the architect of dramatic and narrative form, was
reinvoked to be adapted to an aesthetic of painting that could proclaim that superiority of the picture to the poem in attaining the purity of a story's necessity and probability. So long as the choice is
right—and the judgment of the work will rest in large part on the
shrewdness of that choice—the high moment of that one pregnant
instant, the *punctum temporis,* can in the picture have all the lines of
narrative flowing into and out of it without the trivial and minor
and barely relevant (or, even worse, irrelevant) moments in the sequence detracting from its eminence. It is the representation of the
soul of the narrative because it is *the* representative moment of it.

Here is a forceful reminder of my earlier suggestion that Aristotle's
alternative to Plato's call for stasis was only deceptively temporal,
since the sequence he called for, in its formal perfection, was a
frozen sequence and not freely temporal at all. Those who defended
the capacity of the picture to portray the essence of narrative seized
upon that formalizing, and hence spatializing, of the temporal by
Aristotle to argue for the painter's or the sculptor's power to take
over the poet's province. Thus, far from introducing temporality
into painting, the justification of narrative painting only reinforced
the triumph of aesthetic spatiality by extending it beyond still persons and still lifes and landscapes into the domain of moving life—
but only by stilling that movement. The *ut poesis pictura,* in this version of it, was no less founded on the principle of spatial reduction
than was the *ut pictura poesis.*

Before moving beyond the picture-poetry analogy as I have traced
it across the centuries, I should make explicit the misleading grounds
on which that analogy was formulated and broadly accepted. In
their desire to read one art in terms of the other—poetry in terms of
painting—the critics we have observed have repeatedly been comparing elements in the two arts that do not correspond with one
another. Because it is assumed that the picture can reproduce its
object without any distortions being introduced by the making process, an unmediated, one-to-one relationship between the sign and
its referent is also being assumed. But in poetry as a verbal art what
is at stake is the character of mediation itself, which keeps the interpreting mind at some distance from the would-be referent. So
picture-making and poem-making are being compared on misleading grounds: on the side of the visual arts critics are forced to speak
of the natural objects themselves (even if by means of their painted

surrogates) as if there were no medium, while on the side of poetry critics must speak with an awareness of a medium that, unable to reproduce literally, can only indirectly represent an object. They seem to assume that there is no work in pictorial representation, which is the model that the descriptive poet must work to emulate. Thus pictorialist literary critics are not comparing one art with another so much as they are comparing nature itself, in an unmediated reflection, with the workings of words in a struggle to represent. Nevertheless they treat these incomparable characteristics as if they permitted a proper comparison between the two arts—indeed, permitted a translation of one into the other.

Because the elements of their comparison are not comparable, their supposed comparison turns out to be no more than a loose analogy (*ut pictura poesis*) that unjustly forces one art to deny its own characteristics in order to try to behave in the terms of the other, even if it is incapable of doing so. Further, their ontological commitments contribute to the same consequence by conferring upon nature the sacramental status of an all-controlling origin, thereby reducing what claims to be a comparison to the emulation of a superior by a disadvantaged inferior. They thus are led to collapse one art into the other rather than to sustain any balance between them. Yet it was on such a false claim to comparison that the pictorialist aesthetic was founded.

This aesthetic could no longer be maintained (though the comparison between pictures and poetry could be made the more cogent) once drawing and painting and sculpture also came to be seen as working processes; once, that is, criticism admitted both the conventional character of visual signs and the artists' struggle to manipulate their materials in order to make perceptual structures of them. This recognition that such processes obstructed the easy immediacy of representation led to the rejection of any claim to natural-sign transparency. The grounds were thus cleared for proponents of the arts of the word, now able to champion their conventional medium instead of masking it, to claim a comparison with the other arts that, thanks to arguments similarly slanted by their self-interest, could invert the hierarchy to favor the primacy of their own subject. As if to follow their lead, recent critics of the visual arts, often applying to paintings the techniques we associate with literary interpretation, have come increasingly to treat them as texts to be read, embracing them as conventional-sign systems.

4
REPRESENTATION
AS *ENARGEIA II*
Nature's Transcendence
of the
Natural Sign

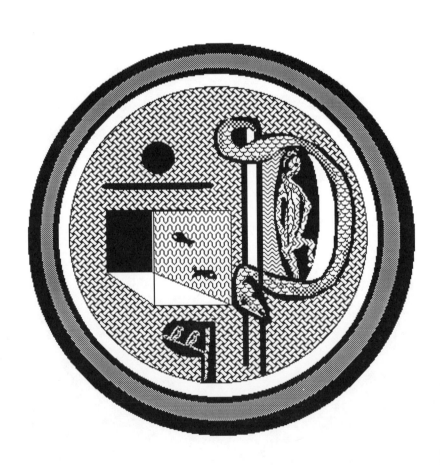

Ah! Then, if mine had been the Painter's hand,
To express what then I saw; and add the gleam,
The light that never was, on sea or land,
The consecration, and the Poet's dream.

William Wordsworth, "Elegiac Stanzas"

One of the most explicit appeals to *enargeia* among the ancients occurs in *On the Sublime,* the treatise attributed to Longinus. Because his use of this term can also lead in another direction, I have postponed dealing with it until this chapter. When we first meet Longinus's version of *enargeia* at the start of chapter 15, it is given its familiar characteristics and is expressed in the language conventionally reserved for it. Since chapter 8 Longinus has been dealing with the principal sources of the sublime, and of these he now is turning to "images," an appropriate term for the visual appeal of the figure the ancient rhetoricians called *enargeia.* Longinus's definition of "image" is to the point: "At the present day the word is predominantly used in cases where, carried away by enthusiasm and passion, you think you see what you describe, and you place it before the eyes of your hearers." After quoting two examples from Euripedes, he comments, "In these scenes the poet himself saw Furies ['Yon maidens gory-eyed and snaky-haired'], and the image in his mind he almost compelled his audience also to behold."[1] From this statement there might appear to be nothing unusual in this description of the successful operation of *enargeia.* But since it is the Furies – mythical rather than real creatures – that are being described, Longinus is carrying us beyond the realm of the sensible description typically expected in *enargeia.* This extension, further modified by the emphasis Longinus places, in his initial definition of "image," on being "carried away by enthusiasm and passion," suggests that he is thinking of a far different sort of *enargeia* indeed. His language ("you think you see what you describe, and you place it before the eyes of your hearers") seems familiar enough, but the fantastic object of description and the dependence on emotional intensity will produce a conflict between the

1. My quotations are from the commonly used translation by W. Rhys Roberts (1899). Since the chapters are brief, quotations should easily be found by reference to chapter numbers only.

mimetic objective of that language and the affective uses to which it is being put.

The conventional sense of *enargeia,* already strained by this introduction of the "image" of the Furies, is utterly transformed in the comments that follow a number of additional examples Longinus later quotes, even though it still seems to be *enargeia* that is being invoked. Hence I have designated the conventional sense of the word, which I discussed at length in Chapter 3, as *enargeia I* and turn now to what I will term *enargeia II.* I have noted the intrusion of Longinus's special interest in the role of "enthusiasm and passion" even into the vividness he attributed to *enargeia* (still being described as if it were *enargeia I*) in his first quotations. In the subsequent quotations the sense of the writer's being thus "carried away" leads Longinus explicitly to shift our attention from the reader's or hearer's vivid mental perception of what is being described to the writer's vicarious participation in it: "Would you not say that the soul of the writer enters the chariot at the same moment as Phaeton and shares in his dangers and in the rapid flight of his steeds? For it could never have conceived such a picture had it not been borne in no less swift career on that journey through the heavens."

The shift here is of significant theoretical consequence: instead of presenting a vivid picture for us to apprehend as spectators in front of, but at a distance from, a tableau, this second *enargeia* collapses distance between subject and object, in effect subjectifying the experience, since we obviously are being called upon to identify ourselves with the poet in participating similarly (or rather identically) in the described experience. What we are seeing in the difference between what I am terming *enargeia I* and *enargeia II* is the difference between the cool aesthetic based on distance between audience and object and the heated aesthetic based on fusion, or empathy, between audience and the object into which they enter (feel themselves into) as imaginary subjects. This becomes the basis of a strikingly different aesthetic, one that is emotionalist rather than mimetic, that dissolves the dimensions of a structured object into the free-ranging consciousness of the reader: an aesthetic that, consequently, would find any suggestion of the natural sign undesirable. We are on our way to Edmund Burke's Longinian distinction between the beautiful and the sublime (and his clear preference for the latter), which in turn foreshadows Nietzsche's distinction between the Apollonian and the Dionysian.

There may well seem to be something perverse in my insistence on broadening the range of the term *enargeia* so that it may also cover the tradition emerging from this second use of the term by Longinus. After all, *enargeia* is supposed to refer to the intensity of visual representation rather than to the intensity of emotional response; indeed, the latter—as we shall see—can lead to rejecting the value of accurate representation altogether. My claim is that by focusing only on the qualities (in *enargeia*) of vividness and intensity as psychological stimulants, psychologically measured, Longinus makes the shift to an audience- or reader-response theory inevitable. He expands the literal notion of *enargeia*, born in mimetic theory and referred to in his own initial definition of "images," to cover its internal effectiveness as it arouses an empathic response— the impulse to identification—in the audience or reader. What more intense awareness of the object could there be? Hence, by reducing the impact of precise visual outlines if the effect can be better produced by other means, *enargeia* loses its original connection with visual representation and eventually becomes an instrument to attack mimetic theory. Therefore, while I may be charged with misusing the term—or, at least, of shepherding its misuse—I would argue that in Longinus it does start out as an alternative *enargeia* by concentrating on our intense awareness of the verbally described object and that, though he does sharply change its direction, there is value in using the same word to demonstrate this inverse tradition, so long as the distinction between *enargeia I* and *enargeia II* is clearly maintained.

The appeal to *enargeia II*, as I will now freely call it, carries special privileges for the poetic power to go beyond the merely mimetic in its need to assert its power over the audience to make their subjectivity one with its own. Even in the midst of his initial reference to *enargeia* in what seemed its conventional sense (in my first quotations, above), Longinus makes a distinction between the use of images in poetry and their use in rhetoric. It is a distinction that seems to free the poet from the obligation to reproduce what he sees. In the sentence following his instruction, quoted above, for the writer to "see" what is being described and to place it "before the eyes" of the audience, he distinguishes between the ways in which the poet and the rhetorician would carry out that instruction: "Further, you will be aware of the fact that an image has one purpose with the orators and another with the poets, and that the design of the poetical image is enthralment, of the rhetorical— vivid description." Strict adherence to *enargeia I*, then, is below the loftier capacities of poetry. This distinction is the more striking in that it introduces generic differences between objectively determined literary kinds (poetry and rhetoric), almost in Aristotelian fashion, despite the fact that Longinus's entire undertaking seems to be addressed to a desirable characteristic (the sublime) of passages that may occur anywhere in speech or writing of whatever kind. Such an ad hoc distinction argues that the need to free some writers (the poets) from the mere reproduction of images must have been as important to Longinus as it later was for those following in the Longinian tradition. Later in this chapter he reinforces this distinction as he summarizes the effectiveness of the image: "It is no doubt true that those [images] which are found in the poets contain, as I said, a tendency to exaggeration in the way of the fabulous and that they transcend in every way the credible, but in oratorical imagery the best feature is always its reality and truth." Further, Longinus forbids the orator to borrow this specially transcendent poetic power: "Whenever the form of a speech is poetical and fabulous and breaks into every kind of impossibility, such digressions have a strange and alien air." Consequently, he complains of contemporary orators who use images "like the tragedians."

In the "fabulous" poetic power that Longinus encourages "the tragedians" to display but denies to the orators, we may be reminded of the special freedom Aristotle gave to epic poets to wander into the domain of the "wonderful." We will be reminded too of Longinus's elevation of the "marvelous" over the merely "credible," which is central to his distinction between poetry and rhetoric, when we come to the more systematic version of that distinction that we will find in Mazzoni in Chapter 5, below.[2] We must remember that Plato assigned the mimetic function to all the arts as part of his program to condemn them as illusionary and deceptive. It is understandable that once succeeding critics, free of Plato's puritanical strictures, sought instead to justify the mimetic character of the arts, many of them, even if still aware of the poet's pictorial obligation, are yet devoted to the poet's special power to give us verbal objects that are something more than nature's substitutes.

The mimetic theorist has as an inevitable dilemma the desire to

2. In the chapters that follow I will track this claim of a special role for poetry, in contrast to non-poetry (whether "rhetoric" or "prose" or whatever term is used), as it is developed in Mazzoni, Diderot, Lessing, Coleridge, Bergson, the Russian Formalists, and the New Critics. It is this common theme that helps mark the postmoderns by their fervent opposition to it.

account for poetry's power to be loftier than nature while wanting it to emulate painting's power to reproduce nature. Many a mimetic theorist reacts to this dilemma with apparently contradictory claims: sometimes lauding poetry as a mimetic art with reproductive powers that rival painting's, sometimes lauding poetry as the art that leads us beyond mere copying, improving upon nature and leading us beyond, into the realm of wonder, of human alchemy. Where possible, the attempt may be made to make the two claims compatible by finding a way to claim the two, nature and the beyond-nature, as reconcilable by the poet.

Even as conventionally conservative a critic as was the Dryden who translated Du Fresnoy and wrote the preface I have discussed in Chapter 3, above, finds himself drawn beyond the mere imitation of nature to the imitation "of the best Nature, of that which is wrought up to a nobler pitch."[3] This latter phrase should sound familiar to us, as an echo of its often-noted use in Dryden's earlier and more liberal "Essay of Dramatic Poesy" (1668). Late in that essay he qualifies his continuing insistence on poetry's mimetic obligation as "a just and lively image of human nature": "a serious play . . . is indeed the representation of Nature, but 'tis Nature wrought up to a higher pitch."[4] Given the desire to justify poetry—often on behalf of a Platonic moralism that contemns the state of nature, as well as on behalf of the desire to find functions for the verbal art that allow it to exploit all that language can open for us—it is not surprising that we can find within the mimetic tradition many such examples of divided attitudes toward the objects being represented in the words of a poem.[5] In what may appear to be a philosophically innocent precursor of the Kantian dualism between nature and freedom, this tradition spawns critics who, without seeing any conflict between the two objectives, seem to want poems to paint nature and yet to improve upon it with a freer human vision, which can be projected only from beyond it.

But the introduction of this second power eventually has to come at the expense of the first. This special licensing of the poetic art, for

3. "A Parallel of Poetry and Painting," in *Essays of John Dryden*, ed. W. P. Ker, 2 vols. (New York: Russell and Russell, 1961), 2:137.

4. John Dryden, "Of Dramatic Poesy: An Essay," in *Of Dramatic Poesy and Other Critical Essays*, ed. George Watson, vol. 1 (London: J. M. Dent, 1962), p. 87.

5. Chapter 5 deals with the extraordinary modifications produced by Renaissance thought in its exploitation of the special privileges of language as an alternative to picture-making.

those critics anxious to follow it to its consequences, might well mean forsaking the *ut pictura poesis* command. To the extent that pictures were seen as unproblematic representations of existing things, the verbal art might well claim to do more, and in that *more* might lie its superiority. Under this dispensation, it is not merely that poems, because of their arbitrary and conventional medium, cannot be pictures but that they are better off—indeed enjoy a special liberty—by virtue of this incapacity. This is the shift I have begun to mark in Longinus.

Strangely perhaps, it is in Addison, who seems to be influenced as much by the Longinian tradition as by the Horatian—and by both as much as by Locke—that we find a striking example of this division of attitude between the power of the picture and the power of the word, between the need of the word to emulate the natural sign and the need of the word to do its own special thing.[6] I cited the passage that I discussed in Chapter 3, above, as the ultimate example of the aesthetic of the natural sign, with the arts, from sculpture to music, arranged as a spectrum from the most natural-sign art to the most arbitrary-sign art. And we saw literature there viewed only insofar as it could use its words to emulate sculpture, or at least painting. We saw Addison expand on those secondary pleasures of the imagination associated with the comparison of "the ideas arising from the original objects, with the ideas we receive from the statue, picture, [verbal] description, or [musical] sound that represents them." He thus was recapitulating his spectrum of the arts and reaffirming the natural-sign model that controls it. Thus he could echo in *Spectator* 416 his attack on "false wit" (*Spectator* 58–62), which he defined as the poet's self-indulgence that permits words to call attention to themselves and thus to obscure the clarity of the ideas they are to represent.

Yet Addison cannot adhere consistently to this rigid, and rigidly self-denying, view of the effects of language, not even for the balance of *Spectator* 416. Only a few lines later—perhaps because he recalls himself to his fidelity to literature as a verbal art, or perhaps he recalls himself to the influence of Longinus—he appears to reverse himself and to dwell upon the power of words to have more of

6. The strangely joint allegiance to the contradictory traditions seen as sponsored by Horace and by Longinus is scattered through Addison's work, as it is through that of many of his contemporaries. Indeed, we see it earlier—and perhaps most influentially—in Boileau, who in the same year (1674) published his imitation of Horace (*L'Art poétique*) and his translation of Longinus.

an effect upon us than faithful pictures of nature can, perhaps even more than nature itself can:

> Words, when well chosen, have so great a force in them, that a description often gives us more lively ideas than the sight of things themselves. The reader finds a scene drawn in stronger colors, and painted more to the life in his imagination, by the help of words, than by an actual survey of the scene which they describe. In this case the poet seems to get the better of Nature; he takes, indeed, the landskip after her, but gives it more vigorous touches, heightens its beauty, and so enlivens the whole piece, that the images which flow from the objects themselves appear weak and faint, in comparison of those that come from the expressions.

He thus can examine the other side of the pictorial disadvantage of words in order to give the verbal art an unanticipated ascendancy, despite all he has done earlier to subject it to both the visual arts and nature. Indeed, the verbal art suddenly emerges as potentially their superior, and precisely *because* of its arbitrary (non-natural) signs. The very fact that verbal description is not limited to what we are able to view at a given point in space and time allows it to range freely beyond what a picture, as a natural sign, permits: "In the survey of any object, we have only so much of it painted on the imagination, as comes in at the eye; but in its description, the poet gives us as free a view of it as he pleases."

Further, the property of words is such that they can stimulate "stronger colors" in the imagination than a faithful reproduction can. The fact that language, as made up of arbitrary signs, *is* a mediating instrument means that it permits—indeed requires—interpretation, thus leading to a response not altogether under the control of the text, so that readers "have a different relish of the same descriptions" because of "the different ideas that several readers affix to the same words." This capacity of words as medium to stimulate the interpreting reader to a breadth of response not available to the observer of the faithful picture—or even to the observer of nature itself as the source of the picture—allows Addison to reverse the privileged place among the arts: in allowing "the poet to get the better of nature," Addison is, *a fortiori*, claiming poetry's superiority to natural-sign representation in sculpture or painting.

These notions are expanded and systematized by that prime Longinian, Edmund Burke, in his *Philosophical Enquiry into the Origins of Our Ideas of the Sublime and the Beautiful* (1757). Since Burke is far less divided than Addison in his consistent championing of the special effectiveness of words as a medium of art, he argues less ambiguously for the verbal arts in his extravagant rejection of pictorialism. Burke denies that the effect of words arises out of their giving our imaginations pictures of the objects they would represent. Consequently, unlike visual media, words are free from the limited function of the pictorial arts to mirror finite objects. He even suggests that words, as arbitrary sounds, are divorced from the need to be faithful to an external reality. But what they fail to give us descriptively they are freer to give us emotionally.

For this reason Burke attacks as false the claim of Abbé Du Bos, made as a natural-sign theorist on behalf of the visual arts, that the pictorial clarity of painting gives it a greater emotional impact than poetry does.[7] Burke bases his refutation on the proposition that "a great clearness helps but little towards affecting the passions, as it is in some sort an enemy to all enthusiasms whatsoever."[8] "The images raised by poetry are always of this obscure kind; though in general the effects of poetry are by no means to be attributed to the images it raises. . . . But painting, when we have allowed for the pleasure of imitation, can only affect simply by the images it presents" (pp. 106–7). "But let it be considered that hardly anything can strike the mind with its greatness, which does not make some sort of approach toward infinity; which nothing can do whilst we are able to perceive its bounds; but to see an object distinctly, and to perceive its bounds, is one and the same thing. A clear idea is therefore another name for a little idea" (pp. 107–8). While Burke agrees with Du Bos about the greater clarity of painting and the greater obscurity of words, he reverses what, according to Du Bos, the effects of the two are likely to be on the passions of the observer or reader.

Burke tends to isolate and exaggerate Longinus's occasional association of the sublime with the arousal of terror in the reader or hearer, since terror is seen as the strongest of our passions, and pas-

7. In *Réflexions critiques sur la poésie et sur la peinture* (1719). An influential English translation by Thomas Nugent appeared in 1748. I refer to this treatise by its English title in Chapter 3.

8. Burke, *A Philosophical Enquiry into the Origin of Our Ideas of the Sublime and the Beautiful* (New York: Garland Publishing, 1971 [facsimile]), pp. 102–3. It is worth noting how different this call for verbal obscurity is from Lessing's call for verbal clarity (see Chapter 2), though both are major influences in the anti-pictorial tradition. This difference is a measure of the distance between the visual and the verbal grounds for giving literature a special place.

sion is the proper objective of the sublime for Burke. As "an enemy
to all enthusiasms" (a word—borrowed from contemporary Protestant teachings—that for Burke includes the passions), clarity, like
the pictorial art that produces it, is left for the more trivial category
of the "beautiful," while the necessarily "obscure" character of
words, with their less predictable and less controlling—and hence
less limiting—effects, can stimulate the wild grandeur of the "sublime" in the Protestant world of private enthusiasm.

> It is one thing to make an idea clear, and another to make it *affecting* to the
> imagination. If I make a drawing of a palace, or a temple, or a landscape,
> I present a very clear idea of those objects; but then (allowing for the
> effect of imitation which is something) my picture can at most affect only
> as the palace, temple, or landscape would have affected in the reality. On
> the other hand, the most lively and spirited verbal description I can give,
> raises a very obscure and imperfect *idea* of such objects; but then it is in
> my power to raise a stronger *emotion* by the description than I could do
> by the best painting. This experience constantly evinces. The proper man-
> ner of conveying the *affections* of the mind from one to another, is by
> words; there is a great insufficiency in all other methods of communica-
> tion; and so far is a clearness of imagery from being absolutely necessary
> to an influence upon the passions, that they may be considerably oper-
> ated upon without presenting any image at all. (Pp. 101–2)

Burke's extreme conclusion is that poetry—in flight from imagistic
precision or even from images themselves—"with all its obscurity,
has a more general as well as a more powerful dominion over the
passions than any other art" (p. 104).

A similar argument appears, ironically enough, in the later work
of Du Bos's countryman Diderot, which is very likely indebted to
Burke. We find in it the same association of the sublime with terror,
and of both with the obscurity that is the proper atmosphere for
both poet and reader.

> Everything that astonishes the soul, everything that impresses a feeling
> of terror leads to the sublime. A vast plain does not astonish as the ocean
> does, nor the quiet ocean as the wild ocean does. Obscurity adds to the
> terror. . . . Clarity is good if one wants to be convincing; it is worthless
> if one wants to move. Clarity of any kind hurts enthusiasm. Poets—speak
> continually of eternity, of infinity, of immensity, of time, of space, of
> divinity, of tombs, of manes, of hell, of an obscure heaven, of the deep

seas, obscure forests, thunder, flashes of lightning that tear the clouds.
Be dark. . . . There are, in all these things [the list has continued at some
length], inexplicable terror, grandeur and obscurity.[9]

This passage makes it clear that Burke had a profound influence in
France, home of the excessive commitment to a natural-sign aesthetic, besides his more obvious and more widely studied influence
in Germany. But it is in Burke himself that we can trace the most
forceful theoretical consequences of this counter-aesthetic — or is it,
in its condescension toward the "beautiful" and the usual formal
virtues associated with the "beautiful," an anti-aesthetic?

Burke insists that the language arts can have a special hold on our
emotions, our inner reality, in contrast to the visual arts, whose
power is limited to presenting exact, if unmoving, reflections of
outer reality. Free of the pictorial artist's need to represent finite
objects with visual precision, and equally free of any obligation to
emulate that way of representing, the poet can use the connotative
vagueness of his instrument — the fact that different readers will interpret words differently, will *see* different things, have different
"ideas," on hearing the identical words — to work upon the reader's
emotions. And the more suggestive, the less precisely definitive the
words, the better.

It is on these grounds that Burke's preference for the sublime over
the beautiful must follow. He must prefer the sublime poem, whose
very lack of precision permits it to spread its suggestive aura, to the
beautiful poem, which can do little more than emulate the precision
of the visual arts, with their natural-sign pictorialism, thus failing to
exploit its own potential freedom from the mimetic. The vagaries of
the idiosyncratic associations triggered by the words stimulate the
production of a suggestive aura that looses the reader's imagination.
We can see that such stimulation can account for those characteristics
in the gothic novel, as well as in much of the poetry of the age of sen-
timent and of the romantics, that aroused the contempt shown such
work by formalist critics closer to the spirit of Aristotle, anxious to preserve a classic distance between the controlling poem and its objective observer and to condemn those works whose verbal looseness
encouraged the vague unpredictabilities of subjective exuberance.

9. *Salon de 1767*, in *Oeuvres complètes de Diderot*, ed. J. Assézat, vol. 11 (Paris: Garnier
Frères, 1876), pp. 146–47. These pieces were not published until 1798. The translations
are mine.

In Burke, as less single-mindedly in Addison, once the critic moves from the pictorial imperative—moves, that is, from the obligations of the *ut pictura poesis* tradition that accompanies the mimetic theory of representation—language takes on major affective advantages unavailable to the visual, natural-sign arts. The very weakness—nay, the incapacity—of language as a surrogate natural sign is the source of its strength as a stimulus of emotion. Because language only suggests, but does not direct, how it is to be interpreted, the poet should play up that suggestiveness and exploit its inevitable vagueness instead of trying to force it to paint pictures that each reader would in any case construct differently from the hints cast by the poem's words.

In Plato it was assumed that the reader or hearer was controlled by the verbal object, being led by it to the idea it represented as a transparency. In Aristotle it was assumed that the audience was controlled by the verbal object, being coerced into the appropriate response through the precise stimulation by its strategically manipulated formal components. But in Burke, after Longinus, control passes from the object to the subject, from poem to reader. Burke himself, obviously embracing the emphasis on *enargeia II* by Longinus, proposes, as the appropriate response to the literary sublime, the term "sympathy" (the term "empathy" is not invented until more than a century later as an English translation of the German *Einfühlung*).[10] Through sympathy, Burke tells us, "we enter into the concerns of others; . . . are moved as they are moved, and are never suffered to be indifferent spectators. . . . [It is] a sort of substitution by which we are put into the place of another man, and affected . . . as he is affected" (p. 70). This "feeling-into" is just what the term "empathy" later is invented to signify: it is the word that expresses what in subjective theory has replaced the classic notion of aesthetic distance. For Burke it is this "sympathy" that in our response to the sublime replaces what in the beautiful is given to "description" ("We yield to sympathy, what we refuse to description").

I mean here, as I did in my discussion of Longinus, to indicate how profoundly the development of theory was to be affected by this shift from the aesthetics of distance, in which the observer coolly measures the object, to the aesthetics of empathy, in which

10. The British psychologist Edward Titchener invented the English translation of this term in his *Experimental Psychology of the Thought Processes* (New York: Macmillan, 1909), pp. 21–22, 205.

the observer merges his subjectivity into—and becomes one with—
the object, transforming it into himself as subject.[11] As Burke addresses Du Bos, he puts the opposition, and his preference, bluntly:
"I know several who admire and love painting, and yet who regard
the objects of their admiration in that art with coolness enough, in
comparison of that warmth with which they are animated by affecting pieces of poetry or rhetoric" (p. 104). The tendency to treat the
object as spatially fixed—as inevitably there within the mimetic
impulse that produced the natural-sign aesthetic and saw the picture as the model aesthetic object—must give way under the impact
of an aesthetic that begins with the primacy of the word.

This vision of language breaking free of the trap of spatiality
arises as part of the desire to break eighteenth-century ideas free of
the spatial enclosure of the neoclassical world view, both literary
and philosophical. Time-consciousness, and the theories of evolution that accompany it, can claim a mimetic fidelity to the moments
of our living that is urged at the expense of spatiality, which is subsequently taken to be only a false human superimposition upon
human experience, and a fundamental misrepresentation of it.
With the increasing dependence for our metaphors on time rather
than space, there is a movement away from natural signs and
toward arbitrary signs. Indeed, painting, so long guaranteed its
place as the model art by the *ut pictura poesis* assumptions of the pictorialist tradition, yields up this place as the spectrum gradually
reverses itself, so that what was the least likely art at the far end of
Addison's spectrum now finds itself in the position of the model art.
From Burke to Nietzsche to Pater we can trace the movement toward
the radical universal claim that "all art constantly aspires towards
the condition of music."[12]

Because of its temporality, language flows as the frozen tableau

11. This sense of identification may be seen as working against drama criticism
that would be conscious of the stage as moving picture, the framed proscenium that
preserves fictionality. For to be such an audience presupposes a crucial sense of
difference between the observer and the observed. Enemy of all forms of representation that would make us into observers of supposed imitations of nature, the
empathic tradition, inevitably, becomes a major sponsor of the lyric.

12. Walter Pater, "The School of Giorgione" (1877), in *The Renaissance: Studies in Art
and Poetry* (London: Macmillan, 1935), p. 124. The entire essay (pp. 120–43) seeks to
expand on this claim. Earlier, Burke had used the effect of music as "proof" of the
way to move the passions without any image at all (*Sublime*, p. 102); Shelley, like
other romantics, invoked the wind-harp to help suggest the immediacy of expression; and Nietzsche's *Birth of Tragedy* (1871) rests largely on the claim that "music is

cannot and thus has deeper affinities with the dark rhythms of primal existence out of which the emotions grow. In Nietzsche's extension of the sublime into the Dionysian, and in Bergson's adaptation
of the latter for his less dark notion of the *élan vital*, one finds – still
in keeping with the attitude we found in Burke – this special authen-
ticity given to the moving dynamic of the temporal and denied to
the flat, visual finitude of the spatial. The special affinity found
among language, the disorderly, and the flux of inner experience
and the attention paid – more and more paid, even, or especially, to
our day – to the category of the "sublime" testify to the power of
Burke's distinction and, after him, to Nietzsche's: a power that elevates a sense of something vague but profoundly primal with which
we can be put in touch, provided the clean power of the "beautiful," the Apollonian, will be surrendered. The "music of our inner
being," to which Bergson so often appeals, can be released through
an engagement of our consciousness, next to which the distancing
act of "objective" aesthetic judgment pales as a less than human response. In the telling opposition put forth much later by Müller-
Freienfels, as an echo from Nietzsche, the virtues of being a *Mit-
spieler* (participant) more than balance those of being a *Zuschauer*
(observer).[13] One must join in the dance; must, as dancer, become
one with the dance, as a great post-Nietzschean poet tells us.

Behind this shift that I have been observing – from Longinus to
Addison to Burke and beyond – in the respective positions of the
verbal and visual arts, we have seen the development of a major
challenger to the natural-sign aesthetic. But because it insists on the
arts as an unrestrained expression of human internality, it too must
insist upon a claim to being the natural art, the expression of nature,
the nature of *human* nature. This claim to an alternative aesthetics of
nature can, I believe, be traced back to Longinus. In an important
passage in *On the Sublime*, Longinus may be seen as reversing the
respective positions of the plastic arts and poetry as they relate to
nature, for he rejects the exclusion of language from the domain of
the natural (despite the fact that since it consists of arbitrary signs,
language was always assumed by the natural-sign tradition to be an
other-than-natural medium). Indeed Longinus suggests the con-

the essential idea of the world" (C. P. Fadiman translation, in *The Philosophy of Nietzsche*, intro. W. H. Wright [New York: Modern Library, n.d.], p. 1069).

13. Richard Müller-Freienfels, *Psychologie der Kunst*, vol. 1 (Leipzig and Berlin:
Tuebner, 1922), pp. 66–67; idem, *Poetik* (Leipzig and Berlin: Tuebner, 1914), pp. 44–46.

trary: that it is language alone that can properly be considered as a natural and immediate material for art.

Late in his argument on behalf of flawed greatness in preference to moderate perfection (chaps. 33–36), Longinus introduces a comparison between sculpture and the verbal arts as these relate to "mere" perfection on the one hand and greatness, with whatever flaws, on the other. In chapter 36 he distinguishes between art and nature, characterizing the plastic arts as "art" and human discourse as "nature." Although he concedes that "the faulty Colossus is not superior to the Spearman of Polycleitus," the judgment does not bother him, because "in art the utmost exactitude is admired" and these are works of art (i.e., plastic art). But different criteria are required for the arts of discourse because "grandeur [rather than utmost exactitude is admired] in the works of nature; and . . . it is by nature that man is a being gifted with speech. In statues likeness to man is the quality required; in discourse we demand, as I said, that which transcends the human." Thus Longinus associates perfection ("freedom from failings") with "art" and elevation (even if "unevenly sustained") with "nature." And the verbal arts, as a natural emanation—like speech itself—from the human being as author, must reach toward grandeur, whatever it may sacrifice in the exactitude of representation.[14] Presumably those arts, like the plastic arts, which require the employment of implements external to the artist— and the training, the know-how, and the decision to use them—are conceived as crafts and are derived from artifice rather than nature, since the latter is reserved as the source for language, as a spontaneous human gift, and hence for the language arts.[15]

(In my discussion of chapter 15 earlier in this chapter, I called

14. It is awkward, in this context, to use *arts* to include what I have been calling the verbal arts. I am here using *art* or *arts* without quotation marks to indicate our common use of the word, which would include the verbal arts, although Longinus's intention is to restrict "*art*" (which I am putting in quotation marks) to the plastic arts or crafts (his *techne*), leaving what we call the verbal arts to "nature."

15. This notion of art as internalized vision—with the final externalized work itself relegated to mere craft, seen as a less lofty talent dependent upon the artisan's external know-how with materials—remains an essential part of the expressionist tradition of which Longinus is usually acknowledged to be the source. Even a neoclassicist like Sir Joshua Reynolds reflects this notion in his insistence, at the start of his "Seventh Discourse" (1776), that art is not what he terms "a *mechanical* trade": "I wished you to be persuaded that success in your art depends almost entirely on your own industry; but the industry which I principally recommended is not the industry of the *hands*, but of the *mind*." There are many twentieth-century examples, usually

attention to Longinus's distinction between rhetoric and poetry, that is, between the merely credible or vividly real and the marvelous or enthralling. I suggest that we may be able to read that distinction into the terms of his present distinction between the arts of art and of nature—or, put another way, between the arts of exactitude and of grandeur. Might we then also see in the present distinction Longinus's suggestion that rhetoric is closer to "art" [unfailing correctness] and poetry closer to "nature" [a greatness beyond accuracy]? But there are problems in the suggestion of this echo of the earlier distinction since we must remember also that rhetoric, after all, is also an art of language for Longinus, and the present distinction would appear to treat all the arts of language similarly, without regard to genre. Nevertheless, within the arts of language Longinus's earlier distinction does linger as a projection onto this one, and within its shadow poetry does seem to be privileged above rhetoric.)

I am not proposing that Longinus is literally asserting the antithesis of what is asserted by the natural-sign aesthetic about which art is or is not a natural-sign art. Indeed, he is not concerned with sign relations at all, whether natural or non-natural. He is, instead, searching for quite different criteria, unrelated to semiotics, for bestowing the term "natural" on one of the arts and denying it to the others. Thus we must observe, in this apparent reversal of the way nature relates to the verbal arts on the one hand and to the plastic arts on the other, that Longinus is talking, not about the resemblance between artistic representation and its external object, but about the relation between the work of art and how it is created— whether by the natural gift of language in the verbal arts or by the manufacturing of an artifact in the plastic arts. He does not see the art object as a representation of another object but looks for the point of origin of the art object; and that point of origin has been shifted from the external object of imitation to the internal, natural endowments of the human mind.

The art that is designated as a natural-sign art, when the arts are viewed as forms of representation, is different from the art considered closest to nature, when the arts are viewed as modes of human expression. In the latter consideration, nature itself, as it realizes itself in the expressions of human nature, dictates that what other-

---

in some ways related to the work of Croce. Among the more important, see R. G. Collingwood, esp. *The Principles of Art* (Oxford: Clarendon Press, 1938).

wise was called the natural-sign arts be consigned to the category of artifice dependent upon external materials and implements. From these claims of Longinus – and of those, such as Addison and Burke, who later take up the Longinian tradition – it will follow that drama is a far less appropriate literary kind for "natural" human expression than are those verbal arts that are the external (and "natural") expression of a single internal voice. Here clearly is an invitation to the lyric, and the late eighteenth and nineteenth centuries took it as such.

No one took up this invitation with more theoretical enthusiasm than Shelley did, late in the history of this tradition, in his *Defence of Poetry* (1821). I want here to concentrate upon one side of this complex essay even though viewed in full, it reveals more than one conception of language as a poetic medium. Only this one side is needed here to extend what Longinus, Addison, and Burke have shown us so far about the unmediated, expressive powers of poetry. In Chapter 6, I will provide the fuller and more balanced treatment that Shelley's document requires, since it is both a major – if two-sided – statement about the role of language as an aesthetic medium and a troublesome example of the theoretical difficulty encountered in the attempt to assign that role with consistency.

In his *Defence* Shelley gives us a more explicit version of the Longinian claim for poetry's uniquely natural status, privileging lyric poetry among the arts because of its "natural" relation to its author as an immediately expressive vehicle for his internality. This relation can be traced to poetry's intimate alliance with the imagination, "whose throne is curtained within the invisible nature of man."[16] Inner human nature supersedes external nature as the nature to which art – a freer art – is responsible. Shelley sees language as "a more direct [i.e., unmediated] representation . . . of our internal being . . . than colour, form, or motion" because it is "more plastic and obedient to the control" of the imagination. Indeed, "language is arbitrarily produced by the imagination," unlike "colour, form, or motion," produced as a result of the "materials, instruments, and conditions" of the other arts, the non-verbal and more tangible arts. In these other arts, their materials, instruments, and conditions

16. The passage discussed in this paragraph appears in *The Complete Works of Percy Bysshe Shelley,* ed. Roger Ingpen, vol. 7 (New York: Gordian Press, 1965), pp. 112–13. It is quoted in full and discussed at greater length in Chapter 6, below, on the poetic medium.

"limit and interpose between conception and expression," while, more ideally, language as the instrument of the imagination in poetry acts "as a mirror which immediately reflects" the first ("conception") in the second ("expression"). By contrast, the arts other than poetry, far from reflecting "the light" of the imagination, dependent on the manipulation of materials external to the human mind, are relegated to functioning only mediately, "as a cloud which enfeebles" that light.

We can well understand, then, that Shelley considers the verbal art as the very "hieroglyphic" of thought, its character a natural emanation of human internality, almost as if he were endorsing some sort of automatic writing. On the other hand, it is the more physically based arts, those that have set out to work with external instruments and materials, that must reconcile themselves to being distanced from, and related only by way of a transforming medium to, any internal source in human intuition.[17] So again the relation among the arts proposed by the natural-sign aesthetic has been inverted: with Shelley as with Longinus, the ground for assigning immediate and natural, rather than mediate and artificial, roles to the several arts rests not on representational transparency (as in the natural-sign aesthetic) but on closeness to the source of expression. Signs are to be related internally to their author (subject) rather than externally, as vehicles of representation, to their object. Once within poetry, when one is making a preference among literary kinds, the ascendancy of lyric poetry over the older notions of drama is a necessary accompaniment to this shift in both semiotics and epistemology.

We have arrived, then, at an aesthetic that emphasizes the work of art as the emanation of human internality rather than as the reflection of an external reality. It sponsors another version of the "natural" that appears opposed to the aesthetic of the natural sign, but not quite; for we cannot properly relate this one to the natural sign, since it functions in the realm of genesis rather than of semiotics. Nevertheless, here too authority is being claimed for "nature"

17. I remind the reader of my need to concede—and to address the concession—that Shelley presents another, apparently contradictory position in the same essay just two paragraphs later. There he treats the language of poems, not as automatic expression, but as he here treats the media of the other arts: as a medium in which manipulations are required among the verbal sounds to adjust the relation that they have toward "each other." Still, Shelley's primary and usual allegiance is to an immediate relation between thought or vision and the words that carry it. I will address these alternatives and the theoretical problems they create in Chapter 6, below.

over the arbitrariness of convention. Unlike the other arts, which depend upon the mediation of the making process, poetry, as the unmediated cry of the human heart, is nature itself—*our* nature—speaking. As the cry of the heart, complete and authentic in itself, it can only suffer by being imposed upon by the inhibitions produced by the arbitrary conventions of making poems.

In this extreme form, the aesthetic of subjectivity, by its simple reversal of the terms of the natural-sign aesthetic, seems to be in flight from any control by form in its promotion of an unrestrained expressiveness. This reversal of the positions of the pictorial arts and music as model for poetry is indicative of the shift in emphasis from referential precision to referential obscurity. Whether, for example, it is Burke's encouragement of a wilful vagueness to stimulate the reader's emotional suggestibility or Shelley's encouragement of an automatic writing to carry out the poet's visionary license to seek instant voice, this aesthetic threatens to become an anti-aesthetic whose rejection of too narrow a conception of form may lead to the total abandonment of form. As a less extreme corrective, the expressive emphasis of the human being as a visionary creature will be joined to the making emphasis of the human being as craftsman-poet—but not until the aesthetics of organicism comes to be formulated at the end of the eighteenth century and the start of the nineteenth and then develops toward modernism. Moving beyond the crude replacement of a static reality with the self-indulgent human subject as the source of art, more systematic organicists will seek to complete the transfer of central concern from the *objects* out there being individually represented by natural signs to the constructed *objects* produced by mind *and* labor, as these express themselves in the signs they work to put together. Chapter 6, below, dealing with theories of language as poetic medium, will pursue this attempted synthesis into the articulation of the modernist poetic and, in doing so, will address Shelley's own movement in this direction by exploring the complications of his essay that have been evaded here.

But stopping for now with the view I have been tracking in this chapter, which sees poetic language primarily as an unmediated instrument of expression, we can find in it a forceful, if exaggerated, alternative to the longstanding primary concern with the poem as a reflection of external reality, one that rejects or at least utterly transforms that concern. Further, we have seen that the tradition from Longinus to Burke to Shelley has sought to claim that only its sort of product, as a verbal product, is the "natural" one, even though we must redefine what "nature" is—from nature out there as reproducible to human nature as internal but expressible—in order to make the connection work. Shelley's extreme version of these arguments permits the tradition to progress toward its ultimate formulation in twentieth-century intuitionists like Benedetto Croce, for whom all of nature is human nature as created, or projected, in the idealistic identity of intuition and expression, which is fully projected in the sublimity of poetry.

Before leaving this tradition of theorizing, however, I should also mention here another and more recent extension that emphasizes a different aspect of it and yet seems ultimate in its own way. It leads, by way of Bergsonian intuitionism, to the so-called "consciousness criticism" of the mid-twentieth century (especially in the sixties), most influentially represented in the Geneva School by Georges Poulet. The emphasis emerges out of the doctrine of empathy (*Einfühlung*)—a feeling-into that subjectifies every object as a receptacle for an ever-transforming subjective self—the doctrine that I claimed to find earlier in this chapter behind Longinus's shift from *enargeia I* to *enargeia II*. Indeed, I placed the beginnings of the doctrine of empathy there. In contrast to the classic distance that is maintained when the object is seen out there *as* object—in clear distinction from the observing and evaluating subject—what is being called for in an empathic relation is the dissolution of the subject-object dichotomy. Indeed, nothing less than a total identification is to be achieved between author and text, between reader and text, and hence between reader and author meeting in the fusion of consciousness (between self and other, the self made other as the other is made self) that is the text as read.

This pursuit of an identity, in overcoming the distinctness between self and other, overcomes the definition of—and separation between—beings and entities. It is, as I earlier said, the opposite of the classic sense of distance between subject and object, the former in the position of observing and measuring and judging the latter as a differentiated entity on its horizon. In sympathy with Bergson and many Continental existentialists and personalists, a critic like Poulet sees objectification, like the spatializing which accompanies it, as the enemy: as that which freezes consciousness and so impedes the breakthrough and the melting as the proper reading response. Clearly, any suggestion of pictorialism is to be rejected: we are not to succumb to those discrete objects of imitation that are the source of *enargeia I* (as traced in my Chapter 3), since they are, in their bounded fixity, enemies of the flow of a released consciousness. Such a surrender to stasis must be resisted. The only distance to be entertained is an always supple "interior distance," with exterior distance internalized as it is dissolved into the realm of "human time."[18]

Yet, as in Bergson, in Poulet's concern for temporality there seems to be no way—even in the ever-changing movements of consciousness and self—to escape the danger of resorting to the spatialization of time itself. There is discoverable in every text a still point after all, the "point of departure," the Cartesian *cogito* into which the reader seeks to allow the self to flow. For one to attain an identity with the other (no longer quite other), there must be a "place" in which it can occur. Through the *cogito*, consciousness has for Poulet become a god-word. By the breakthrough, via the *cogito*, to a shared consciousness, the reading experience has attained a mystical presence, transcending difference, that, for the duration of the experience at least, dwells in a sacred place. This is, surely, the ultimate act of empathy.

Such a sacralizing act carries a cost with it, since it emerges out of the desire to dissolve the limits of the spatializing imagination and is subverting that desire in the act of being realized. As in all the privileging of temporality since Heraclitus, even in the melting of objects into the experiential flux, time must have a stop: language fights with itself—its aspirations for perpetual motion with its logocentric limitations—in the war between movement and stasis that has been with us since Zeno's paradox first blocked all ultimate thinking about the temporalizing of space. What is left is an attempt to return to the text as object, but only on new—and newly liberated—terms. And beyond what has been offered by those we have examined here from Longinus to Burke to Shelley to Poulet, this attempt is to be the subject of my later chapters.

18. I am referring to Poulet's major works, *Studies in Human Time* and *The Interior Distance*, both translated by Elliott Coleman and published by the Johns Hopkins Press in 1956 and 1959, respectively. I should note also the monumental work whose central concern most closely approaches my own in this book, *The Metamorphoses of the Circle*, trans. Carley Dawson and Elliott Coleman (Baltimore: Johns Hopkins Press, 1966). Here Poulet traces through history those motions of consciousness that dissolve the circle as a fixed figure while falling under its power. Much in his treatment of the figure anticipates the crucial role that I claim the circle plays in modernism (see Chapter 7).

5
THE VERBAL
EMBLEM I
The
Renaissance

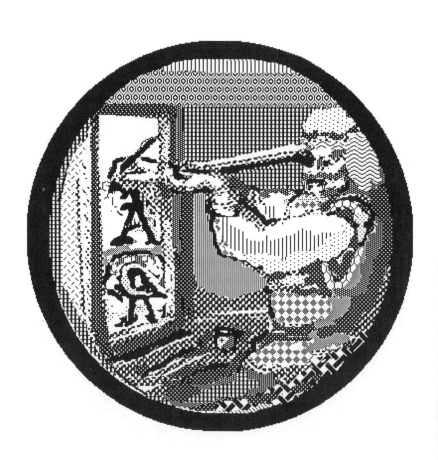

The symbol that presents to us a revelation cannot be said to have one identifiable meaning assigned to its distinctive features. All its aspects are felt to be charged with a plenitude of meanings that can never be exhaustively learned, but must be found in the very process of contemplation it is designed to engender. . . .

Thus the mysterious hieroglyph of the monster devouring itself sets the mind a puzzle which forces it to rise above the image. Not only can we not think of the sign as representing a real creature, even the event it represents transcends the possibility of our experience—what will happen when the devouring jaws reach the neck and the jaws themselves? It is this paradoxical nature of the image that has made it the archetypal symbol of mystery. We are certainly not tempted to confuse the painted enigma with its manifold meanings. . . .

It is this kind of mystery that is "condensed" into the image of the serpent biting its own tail which is a metaphor not only of time but of the inscrutable enigma of the universe that can only be expressed through contradictions. It does so precisely because the sense of sight provides an analogue to the non-discursive mode of apprehension which must travel from multiplicity to unity.

E. H. Gombrich, "Icones Symbolicae"

In the two preceding chapters I have concentrated upon debates concerning the function of the verbal arts in their relation, positive or negative, to the referential function of what were looked upon as the natural-sign arts. But while these debates were being pursued over the centuries, there was also, outside them, a long-standing interest in the word—first as spoken, then as written—as itself a magical instrument, whether of invocation or of mystic symbolism. And from this developed an alternative ekphrastic theory that sometimes ran alongside the other and sometimes intersected it in ways that enormously complicated several crucial moments in the history of aesthetics.

Although the chant of a sacred invocation could at moments convert the spoken language into a magical instrument to summon the gods, words could have bestowed upon them the total power of self-containing things only when—no longer mere sounds displaced by their successors and disappearing into the air—they occupied a space and became the fixed, graphic object of study. The movement of words toward thinghood was thus facilitated by the shift from oral literature to written texts. The word on the scroll was fixed out there, occupying a physical place, and the scroll, eventually—early in the Christian era—was cut into separate pages, which, handsomely inscribed, were lovingly put together and ornately and expensively packaged into the aesthetic objects we came to call books.

The book in the Middle Ages was an extensively decorated work of visual art, a weighty physical object to be treasured for the painstaking craft as well as the precious materials that went into it. From its ornamented covers to its "illuminated" pages, gold and, more rarely, silver and even jewels combined with the artisan's creativity to produce a treasure to hold and behold as well as to read: everything seemed to contribute to the physical there-ness of this complex object. And the equally treasured texts within were scripted with similar care and beauty. The initial letters were especially enriched in the highly colored and often gilt drawings in which they participated, under the artist's hand becoming intricate and often enigmatic emblems in their "illuminated" state. As applied to the manuscript, and especially to its initial letters, the very word "illumination," with all of its connotations of Platonic light, encouraged the letter, as well as the word and the text into which it opened, to take on a transcendent character that could allow it to make its transcendent claims. Thanks to its pictorial adornments, the letter, basic unit of an arbitrary code, carried within itself, and into the beautifully scripted words it introduced, some of the natural-sign virtues without surrendering to the sensible limitations of a merely visual sign. Its complicated mode of being thus suggested a both/ and claim to superiority that allowed it to function as the visible threshold of a sacred text and a supernal realm. It is no wonder, then, that the words that composed the manuscript could grow into a verbal emblem, in which the arbitrary sign usurped many of the most exciting elements of the visual, while retaining its contact with the sacred-intelligible order. Here was a foundation for the extraordinary function sometimes permitted language in medieval and Renaissance poetics.

The shift from oral to written texts had the additional effect of restricting their audience to those who had the resources to learn to read. As the physical container of the word, the book, with a material richness to match its spiritual richness, was the rightful possession of this limited group, those in the literate class, privileged by theological or economic restrictions to be its readers. Spiritual riches thus deserved material riches and vice versa, by Neo-Platonic analogy, as it were. The ornamented book and pages thus helped justify the wealth or station of the reader and the riches, material and spiritual (the one in effect justifying the other), carried on the body of, and within, the valuable thing the reader possessed in possessing the book.

With the advent and spread of printing and—with the progressive developments in movable type—the gradual standardizing of the printed letter, the written word, no longer an individually crafted product of the graphic art and hence less of a desirable physical entity worth treasuring for itself, was, by the late seventeenth century, gradually being emptied out. Its function was thinned to the self-effacing referential sign assigned the word by the least imaginative protagonists of the natural-sign aesthetic, who called for a merely descriptive and hence mnemonic function for non-dramatic poetry, the primary art of the word, which was now made into a less satisfying—because less sensuous—substitute for painting. In the preceding two chapters we have seen the arguments on both sides of the alternatives provided by this stripped-down semiotic.

I have been creating here a brief, melodramatic, and perhaps causally reductive narrative that claims, too melodramatically, to represent the history of the fortunes of the written and the printed word. But with it I hope to introduce a mysterious semiotic of the word that, in the Renaissance, becomes an important alternative to the two often opposing ways of tying the verbal arts to what I have been terming *enargeia*. In this chapter I want to move from them to this third and more difficult way of conceiving the function of the word as sign, as an intelligible sign that is yet invested with its own weighty substance.

In my discussion of *enargeia* in Chapters 3 and 4 there was a major lacuna: as I jumped from the ancients to seventeenth- and eighteenth-century neoclassicism, I passed over the wide range of Renaissance critics despite the fact that for most of them something like *enargeia* was very much a part of their mainly Neo-Platonic call for imitation, the definition of which, like Plato's, was accompanied by a strong visual emphasis. As Neo-Platonists whose doctrine derived from Plato's attack on sensible experience, they saw as their task the need to justify, even to celebrate, the mimesis—and the *enargeia* at its root—that Plato condemned. And they could do so only by separating mimesis from its dependence on sensible experience and relating it to the intelligible as the supersensible. It led them to an apparent paradox in which they urged that the poet use language to produce pictorial vividness—*enargeia*—like the visual artist, even while they condemned the sensible realm as unworthy of imitation. If it was a paradox, it was one that resulted in the language arts, through their inability to function as a natural sign, coming off as specially privileged in contrast to the visual arts.

In no Renaissance critic was the interest in *enargeia* stronger than it was in Jacopo Mazzoni, whose language seems pretty well to identify *enargeia* with imitation itself.[1] Indeed, in his major critical work in defense of Dante's *Commedia*, his definition of "imitation"—which he claims to be the primary end of poetry, as well as its means—is from the outset limited to the construction or representation of "the image or idol."[2] But for all his insistence on "imitation" and the "image," we will see that his is an "imitation" with a difference, a major difference.

Perhaps no critic in our history speaks more consistently of the pictorial character of the verbal artist's objective. In a single extended

1. I have a fuller and—I acknowledge—a more balanced exposition of Mazzoni's work in my *Poetic Presence and Illusion: Essays in Critical History and Theory* (Baltimore: Johns Hopkins University Press, 1979). In that volume, see "Poetic Presence and Illusion I: Renaissance Theory and the Duplicity of Metaphor," pp. 5-7, and "Jacopo Mazzoni: Repository of Diverse Critical Traditions or Source of a New One?" pp. 28-38. My treatment here is more partial, emphasizing—perhaps overemphasizing—the way in which Mazzoni lends himself to the development of the ekphrastic, and even the emblematic, tradition. As I concede in my earlier treatment, there is another side to Mazzoni in which he is in retreat from the license he sometimes appears to give to the free imagination (that which creates freestanding images). He is, after all, a Renaissance critic in the Neo-Platonic tradition, and as Sir Philip Sidney similarly turns out to be, he is at crucial moments pulled back from his more extravagant (wrongly thought of as pre-romantic) indulgences. If in earlier work I treated the contradictions, indeed the blockage, between his two sides, here I want to let loose the side that, in a more complete treatment, Mazzoni would be seen as reining in.

2. My discussion of Mazzoni is indebted, as all studies of Renaissance theory must now be, to Robert L. Montgomery's translation and critical edition of Jacopo Mazzoni, *On the Defense of the Comedy of Dante: Introduction and Summary* (Tallahassee: University Presses of Florida, 1983), from which I have quoted freely. The care and fullness of the translation allow it to supplement in important ways the pioneering anthology selections of Allan H. Gilbert in his *Literary Criticism: Plato to Dryden* (New York: American Book Company, 1940) as well as the impressive selection of translated passages interspersed in the exposition of Baxter Hathaway in his *Age of Criticism: The Late Renaissance in Italy* (Ithaca: Cornell University Press, 1962). However, since the Montgomery translation is restricted to the introduction and summary, I shall also have to make use of the other translations, especially for passages occurring later in the treatise. And books 1 and 3 have some remarkable passages. In subsequent passages quoted from Mazzoni, I will indicate the source—among the above volumes—in parentheses after the quotation.

sequence he recapitulates sympathetically and in considerable detail, with generously interspersed quotations, the history of the pictorialist tradition from Plato through late classicism and even, with Philippo Beroaldo and Cardinal Paleotti, well into the sixteenth century. Between these, the list includes—each justified as a pictorialist by quotation and paraphrase—Aristotle, Longinus, Lucian (at considerable length), Hermogenes, Pliny the Younger, Demetrius Phalerius, Philostratus, Horace (using the *ut pictura poesis erit* phrasing), Plutarch (citing the usual reference to Simonides), and Cicero. In each case Mazzoni cites the critic's appeal to the power of the narrative poem—as an alternative to the immediate representational power of the drama (according to Plato and Aristotle)—to make "particularized" images or idols or icons. These are often characterized as "visible" images, like those of the sculptor and painter, since they, in effect, depict "things so that they seem to be right in front of the gaze of the reader."[3] In his list of authorities we find the major names associated with the Hellenistic second sophistic and, through those writers in whom Mazzoni obviously read widely, the emergence of ekphrasis as a translation of *enargeia* into a specific verbal device.[4]

"On the basis of all this authority," Mazzoni concludes, "we can in my judgment confidently admit that poetry, when it is narrative, may resemble a speaking picture. Almost all good poets are forced in their narrations to report things with such clarity that we virtually see them before our very eyes." We recognize the spirit of *enargeia I* in these appeals to the poet to put the image, in all its vividness, before our eyes, as if it were a painting. And in book 3 the word itself appears: "that *enargeia* that Hermogenes called poetic imitation" is the ultimate criterion for the verbal art as a mimetic art.[5] The image presented by the poet to the eyes of the mind must be as vivid as the image presented by the visual artist is to the eyes of the body: "For with this mode one makes good resemblances and presents clearly to the eyes of the intellect that which is distant either in space or in time and allows us to see it no otherwise than if it were put right before the eyes in our face. In this way there comes into being that particularization which we have declared to be the proper instrument of poetic narrative" (Hathaway, p. 201).

---

3. Mazzoni's quotation here, with its emphasis on the language associated with *enargeia* (and, later, with ekphrasis in its broadest sense), is from Philippo Beroaldo.
4. See Chapter 1, above.
5. See my discussion of Hermogenes in Chapter 1 and n. 8 to that chapter.

Nevertheless, as I have repeatedly noted in my preceding chapters, the image placed before our eyes by the words of the poet cannot be the same as the image placed there by the visual artist, just as the intelligible cannot be the same as the sensible. Mazzoni, as Neo-Platonist, makes the most of that difference, so that despite his visual imagery, the analogy between the verbal image addressed to the eyes of the mind and the visual image addressed to the eyes of the body is heavily weighted on the side of the verbal image. Mazzoni is too controlled by the Platonic distinction between the sensible and the intelligible, as well as by Plato's condemnation of the sensible because of its limitations, not to realize the special power of the word as an intelligible entity that can imitate the activity of a sensible entity without paying the price that the sensible must pay.

It is with a shrewd awareness of the potential advantage for language as the intelligible medium that Mazzoni traces the special praise given Homer by pictorialist critics for giving the audience visual images though he himself was blind. Thus Cicero, Mazzoni reminds us, praised the blind Homer because "he made us see what he himself did not."[6] To Mazzoni it is evident that what Homer showed us, as a blind man's images, must be images for "the eyes of the intellect" rather than for "the eyes in our face." He turns his quotations from Lucian in this direction, agreeing that images in a "poetic narration" "will be much more steadfast and will last a longer time" than images of visual artists. "And that will show itself more pleasing to spectators which is not formed by hue, wax, or color, but portrayed by the ingenuity of the Muse [whom the poet] has called forth. This will without any doubt be found to be the most perfect of all images, making visible at once both the beauty of the body and the virtue of the soul" (Montgomery, pp. 50–51). The greater accomplishment, clearly, is to make visible the virtue of the soul – the intelligible realm itself – and the verbal image can attempt this as the sensible image, within a literally mimetic aesthetic of sculpture or painting, cannot. With this special privilege, the verbal artist can triumph over the mimetic even as he appears to be subject to it. But he will need to be authorized to move beyond the naive

6. Mazzoni's entire quotation from Cicero reads: "It is moreover the tradition that Homer was blind. But we see this in a painting of him, not in his poetry. What region, what coast, what part of Greece, what appearance of things, what battle, what formation, what rowing, what movement of men and of animals, is not so depicted that he has made us see what he himself did not?"

literalism of a pictorialist aesthetic of poetry, and Mazzoni's work is largely directed to justify such an authorization.

The apparent pictorialism of Mazzoni's continuing call for "images" asks less that the absent realm of sensible experience be made present—as it is with the painter—than that the poet create with his verbal "images" an analogue to the visible images of the painter, though an analogue that is empowered to refer to the invisible realm of the intelligible. We may well be reminded of the "images" called for by Longinus (see Chapter 4), who used the language reserved for *enargeia* to commend the "image in [the poet's] mind" of the Furies, created for us and put in our minds by Euripides. This metaphorical use of "image," as an analogue of the sensible in the intelligible realm, posits that which is not quite image because it is, for Mazzoni as for Longinus, more than image. In Neo-Platonic fashion it claims the advantages of the sensible image while insisting upon its access to the intelligible, which it alone can make available to the senses, if only in the figurative way of language. Thus Mazzoni can ask that the poetic image be fashioned so that it may be seen by "the eyes of the intellect" with a precision like that of the painting seen by "the eyes in the face." This is to make the intelligible accessible to human "vision," if we accept the metaphorical stretch of this word.

We see, then, that Mazzoni's repeated use of the word "image," or even "idol," does not make him the pictorialist that he seems, and it is for this reason that I reserved him—and the Renaissance tradition behind him—for this chapter instead of including him in Chapter 3. Although his "image" seems to mean a verbal picture, his use of the word dictates that it rather indicates an illusion that helps us create in our minds the sense that something is being described that ought to be visually apprehensible. It is true that even an actual picture, as a representational "image," is only an illusion of the object behind it, but the pictorialist—or natural-sign—aesthetic accepted that illusion as a visually adequate mimesis. It is an "illusion" in a sense of that word different from what we mean when we refer to the "illusion" we receive from words that encourage us to feel that there somehow is an "image" out there—in effect, an "illusion" of an illusionary image of an object, an "illusion" to the second power. This is a notion to be developed later in this chapter.

A single, though striking, example of Mazzoni's commentary on Dante should show how dependent his use of "image" is on poetic metaphor, how thoroughly grounded it is in analogy. It is figural itself and can be realized only through the use of the figural. Mazzoni chooses from the *Paradiso* (33, 115-20) the following description of the Trinity to demonstrate the particularized, singular, and even perceptible character of the poetic "image" as it seeks to represent by being an "idol," a "sensible simulacrum":

> Within the profound and clear substance
>   Of the exalted light three circles appeared to me,
>   Of three colors and one magnitude.
> And one in the other, like a rainbow in a rainbow
>   Seemed reflected, and the third seemed like
>   Fire breathed forth equally from the one and the other.[7]

This *is* a brilliant image, surely, though hardly one that is (to use Lessing's term) "picturable,"[8] or even "sensible," although the reader needs the previous experience of color and shape and other sensations to appreciate it, or indeed to understand it. Its very brilliance, in its attempt to convey the miracle of the Trinity, depends on its evasion — and transcendence — of the limitations of precise sensory definition. We could not represent it accurately on canvas, or even — in our mind's eye — quite *see* it, and yet somehow we are moved by it as if we could. Of it can be said what I have said about Homer's shield of Achilles (in my Foreword, above) or about any ekphrasis that I have defined as a fictitious mimesis: it is not quite an "image" — that is, a visual image — and yet it serves as one, indeed exceeds what a precisely visual image could be for us.[9] It satisfies our

7. This is Montgomery's translation, p. 77 (see n. 2, above).

8. For my discussion of Lessing on the unpicturable character of the images that words create for us see Chapter 2, above.

9. E. H. Gombrich, in "*Icones Symbolicae:* Philosophies of Symbolism and Their Bearing on Art," reprinted in his *Symbolic Images: Studies in the Art of the Renaissance* (London: Phaidon Press, 1972), pp. 123-95, comments in a similar way on the extended, brilliantly detailed description of the figure of Philosophy in Boethius's *Consolation of Philosophy:* "The passage not only illustrates the method of arousing curiosity through certain mysterious features which the reader has to ponder, it also explains why much of the method remained for a long time confined to verbal descriptions. The elusive character of the figure who seems to grow and shrink like Alice in Wonderland could not be represented; artists could do little more than show a matron with the ladder between the mysterious letters standing for practice and theory woven into her garment" (p. 134). Here again the verbal picture, for all its apparent appeal to the senses as something to be perceived, is "unpicturable." Lessing's term seems especially appropriate here.

craving for the "credible" in that the words create in us the satisfying illusion (though only an illusion) that in them there *is* an image. Yet Mazzoni, apparently untroubled, repeatedly refers to these lines as "sensible" in their appeal — as in their way they are, and are not — thereby revealing his confidence in the transferability (even with a surplus) of the Neo-Platonic system of analogies.

Thus, for all of Mazzoni's tributes to his pictorialist forebears, I have been observing a crucial theoretical difference between his appeal for images and the appeal for images found in many of those precursors he summons for testimony (most of them, like those I have discussed in Chapter 3, exponents of *enargeia I*). Despite Mazzoni's continual use of terms such as "imitation" and "representation" and "image" or "idol," it is not, for Mazzoni, only — or even principally — external reality (things or perceptions of things) that the imitations or images or representations are to reproduce, at least not in the kind of poetry Mazzoni most admires. By borrowing Plato's distinction between "icastic" and "phantastic" poetry, while reversing the order of preference between them,[10] Mazzoni can free the poet from a bondage to the mimetic, free him to exploit the special powers of the verbal imagination. The "image" is to represent "things that are truly derived from some work already existing" only in the case of "icastic" poetry, which is clearly not Mazzoni's favored kind. After all, his treatise is written in defense of the *Commedia*, an uninhibitedly "phantastic" poem, made up of "pictures that are made by the caprice of the artist." Indeed, we cannot forget that Mazzoni's "Defense" is addressed against Bulgarini's attack on Dante for creating an action that imitates no possibly real action in

10. This reversal is easily explained by the difference between Mazzoni's and Plato's notions (Mazzoni's Neo-Platonism departing from a mere Platonism) about the role of the mind's private phantasies. In the *Sophist*, we recall from Chapter 2, above, Plato strongly condemned the phantastic because of the delusions about reality that it imposed upon us, while he praised the icastic as giving us a true image. He saw the phantastic as Mazzoni — and we — do not: as that which reproduced exactly the phenomenal experience of the object with all the subjective distortions produced by our position in time and space. Since for Plato all imitations were literal and undeviating in their reproductive fidelity, the phantastic, as most idiosyncratic, was also the truest to our sensory experience at the expense of being untrue to the thing in itself. Mazzoni rather saw the phantastic in our more common usage as that which produced the private phantoms of our inventive imaginations. There is no "caprice" in Plato's "phantastic," while Mazzoni's is all caprice. Hence Plato can attack the phantastic for being all too mimetic, while Mazzoni praises it for its freedom from mimesis.

the world but only an action existing in the poet's mind—in effect, a "phantastic" action, controlled only by the poet's "caprice." It is, then, precisely the "phantastic" character of the *Commedia* that Mazzoni is celebrating.

Indeed, at many moments in his treatise, in his desire to defend the "phantastic" narrative that is his subject, Mazzoni seems to equate poetry with the "phantastic," pretty well relegating the "icastic" to rhetoric. For him, at least at this stage of his argument, rhetoric—and history too, which Mazzoni seems to include within rhetoric as an "icastic" art—is as much a form of verbal imitation as poetry is, though a very different form. Although Mazzoni allows poetry to be either "icastic" or "phantastic" when he introduces his distinction between the two, he gradually comes to restrict poetry to the latter: to the representation of the fabulous—of that unlikely event which we must be persuaded to accept as "credible" in spite of our wonder at it—leaving the less remarkably "credible" to the straightforwardness of rhetoric. This is a distinction that we saw anticipated in Longinus, in quite similar if far sketchier form, in Chapter 4.

Yet, as in Longinus, poetry and rhetoric, both of them modes of imitation for Mazzoni, are equally to present us with the "credible," which Mazzoni defines as particularized and hence as "verisimilar" (*like* true) images, the result of the writer's attempt to "show" rather than merely to "tell." But for him rhetoric is to deal with "the credible as credible," while, by contrast, poetry is to deal with "the credible as marvelous." The latter qualification would seem to tie poetry to the "phantastic" alone. The key passage from the introduction is worth quoting in full:

> And so the credible is the subject of poetry. But because it is also the subject of rhetoric we must necessarily see in what way it can be made to become proper to both poetry and rhetoric. . . .
>
> I say therefore that the credible insofar as it is credible is the subject of rhetoric and the credible insofar as it is marvelous is the subject of poetry, for poetry must not only utter credible things but also marvelous things. And for this reason when it can do so credibly, it falsifies human and natural history and passes beyond them to impossible things. . . . So that, if two things equally credible were offered to the poet, one of them more marvelous than the other, though false, not just impossible, the poet ought to take it and refuse the other [the less marvelous, though possible and even true]. (Montgomery, pp. 85–86)

The appeal of the verbal arts, I repeat, is in their production of the "credible," by which Mazzoni means the furnishing of particularized, sensible, and hence verisimilar (*like* true) images that remind us of what we see in our perceptual experience. But the "credible" is to be quite different in rhetoric and in poetry. In this passage—in addition to the echo from Longinus that I have mentioned—Mazzoni is obviously invoking Aristotle's distinction between poetry and history and, more precisely, Aristotle's preference for the probable-though-impossible over the improbable-though-possible. Aristotle's precedent helps furnish the grounds for Mazzoni to assign poetry the role of aiming at the "credible," while remaining indifferent to the question of whether it is true or false.[11]

By book 3 (chap. 3) Mazzoni's distinction between rhetoric and poetry seems to have hardened, as does the exclusion, by implication, of the "icastic" from poetry and the identification of the "phantastic" with it.

> A striking objection comes up . . . namely, that rhetoric cannot be distinguished from poetry, since the two have the same object (i.e., the credible). I say then by way of reply that the credible can be considered in two different ways. The first is when the credible is dealt with in so far as it is credible and persuasive; then it is the proper subject of rhetoric. The second is when it is considered as the marvelous, and thus becomes the proper subject of poetry, since poetry always seeks for a marvelous subject. . . . Pontanus has not said badly . . . that the end of the poet and of poetry is to speak in such a way as fill the hearers with wonder. This comes about when the hearers accept what they did not believe could happen. (Gilbert, p. 388)

What is too easily credible, then, is beneath the ambition of the poet, whose task it is, through the employment of the "marvelous," to force the audience to enlarge the domain of what they find credible. By appealing to their "wonder," the poet can force them to believe what was—except for this poem—beyond being believed by them. This is the reason for the poet's continual need to invoke the

11. There is, of course, a significant shift in Mazzoni's appropriation of Aristotle's "probable" for his own "credible," but the slippage from one term to the other is allowed to occur as if they were the same, though they function very differently in the two systems. Aristotle's "probable" refers to the temporal and causal relations among the several parts of the plot, while Mazzoni's "credible" refers to the verbal "images" or "idols" that we can believe in as we believe in the sensible world itself.

"phantastic." In his book 1 (chap. 67) Mazzoni has already moved beyond the alternating distinctions of the introduction to tighten the connection between poetry and the phantastic in a way that seems totally to eliminate the icastic from poetry:

> I say, then, that the phantasy is the common power of the mind for dreams and for poetic verisimilitude. . . . The verisimilitude . . . sought after by the poets is of such a nature that it is feigned by them according to their wish. Then it is necessary for it to be fabricated by the power that has the capacity for forming conceptions in harmony with the will. . . . We see clearly, then, if I am not wrong, that phantasy is the true power over poetic fables, since she alone is capable of those fictions which we of ourselves are able to feign and put together. From this it follows that poetry is made of things feigned and imagined, because it is founded on phantasy. (Gilbert, pp. 386–87)

Mazzoni's distinction between rhetoric and poetry, based on the distinction between the merely credible and the marvelous as credible, is, as I have earlier maintained, a clear echo of what I found in Longinus in Chapter 4, above. And if, as I have traced it, this distinction is projected into a distinction between the "icastic" and the "phantastic," between, that is, the mimetic dependence on an object outside the text and the text's independence of everything except the human mind that creates it, then it is a projection also of what I have claimed to be the distinction between *enargeia I* and *enargeia II*, between vivid (i.e., transparently clear) representation and vivid (i.e., intensely empathy-provoking) presentation.

But what moves Mazzoni beyond the claims for *enargeia II* that I traced in Chapter 4 is his willingness, through his extravagant claims for the "phantastic" image, to identify the poem's power over its reader with its capacity both to create and to sustain that image as one with itself as text. In this he provides a theoretical ground for the emblematic tradition that grows out of the ekphrastic impulse in its developing need to provide an alternative to the simple—and static—desire merely to transcribe verbal imitations of pictures. And the Neo-Platonic tradition, especially in the Christian modifications upon it produced in the Renaissance, furnished just the metaphysical structures for a radical semiotic whose mystical equations could allow this development to be crowned, in emblem and in theory.

I could trace a similar, if less systematically thorough, Neo-Pla-

tonic commitment in Sir Philip Sidney's *Apology for Poetry.*[12] Sidney
converts Aristotelian "imitation" into a "figuring forth" of "speaking pictures" that the poet finds within "the zodiac of his own wit."
Consequently the poet can produce a "golden world" that rides free
of the "brazen" world of our normal reality, although this world of
the poem turns out also to be contained within the transcendent
realm of Platonic moral universals.[13] (As in Mazzoni, though perhaps even more so in Sidney, the conservative ideological needs of
the moralistic inheritance from Plato drew him back from his more
adventurous moments of indulgence.)

With Sidney as with Mazzoni, such pictorial visions, as verbal,
are more appropriate to those forms of the poetic art that are non-
dramatic, conveyed to us, in epic or lyric, through the poet's own
voice. (The implicit connection that I have demonstrated between
the drama, as a literally representational art, and the natural-sign
led theorists to the non-dramatic when they sought to license a verbal art that would be independent of a mimetic obligation.) And it
is the epic—Homer's or Virgil's for most, Dante's for Mazzoni and
others—that is for the Renaissance Neo-Platonist the home of this
"golden world" of the poet's imagination, although clearly it is an
imagination that reflects, almost automatically, the transcendent
realm of the Platonic virtues.[14] This Neo-Platonic theory shifts the
burden of the poem from its dependence on external objects of imitation and places it on the verbal inventions that respond to the
visions produced by the poet's "wit." Once the reproduction of
external objects is replaced by the capricious creations of internal

12. Although Sidney's essay reflects the thinking of many earlier Italian theorists,
I do not mean here to suggest any influence from Mazzoni, since Sidney's is the earlier essay (probably written in the early 1580s, though only published posthumously
in 1595). For all its brilliance, Mazzoni's work appeared so late in the development of
Italian theory that its importance must be measured by its argument, not by its contemporary influence.

13. This passage is quoted and fully discussed later in this chapter.

14. I refer the reader to *Theory of Criticism: A Tradition and Its System* (Baltimore:
Johns Hopkins University Press, 1976), pp. 74–77, where I trace step by step how Sidney manipulates his apparent invocation of a free and independent imagination
("the zodiac of his [the poet's] own wit") into being the same as Plato's supernal
world of universal virtue. Because the poet's "wit" is drawn to the universal realm
of the "ought to be," its "zodiac" is lodged in heavenly morality. Thus what appears
like freedom is, a priori, overdetermined by a conventional ethic that is here given an
ontological sanction.

phantasy (and it is a replacement more easily attributed to narrative than to drama), the ascendancy of a self-standing verbal object, and the deprecation of mere visual surrogates, must follow.

But such a call for the narrative rather than the dramatic is consistent with Mazzoni's call, in my last quotation from him, for a poem that inspires and justifies a belief that goes beyond what for us had, before the reading of this poem, been the limits of the credible. By charging the epic to bring the marvelous within the realm of the credible—and thus to make us credit what, except in this poem, we would reject as *in*credible—Mazzoni justifies the common Renaissance practice of assigning to the epic the role of arousing wonder in its audience.

We should recognize this assignment as an extension—and transformation—of Aristotle's differentiation in chapter 24 of the *Poetics* (as noted in my Chapter 2, above) between tragedy and the epic. There Aristotle enlarges the scope of the epic, in contrast to tragedy, thanks to the freedom enjoyed by narrative from the constraints of the stage—in effect, from the constraints of natural-sign mimesis. "The element of the wonderful is admitted in tragedy. The irrational, on which the wonderful depends for its chief effects, has wider scope in epic poetry, because there the person acting is not seen." In the epic an "absurdity passes unnoticed" which would be at once evident were we to seek to mount it onstage. "Now the wonderful is pleasing: as may be inferred from the fact that, in telling a story, everyone adds something startling of his own, knowing that his hearers like it. It is Homer who has chiefly taught other poets the art of telling lies skillfully."

It is perhaps ironic that this passage occurs in the last chapters of the *Poetics*, when Aristotle is ending his treatment of tragedy by seeking, through a comparison with its chief rival for supremacy, to show its superiority to the epic. Yet here he is extending a license to the epic that he must deny to the drama because of the restrictions of the stage and the illusionary natural-sign version of representation that the stage imposes. As we can see from the final chapter of the *Poetics* (chap. 26), which serves as the conclusion to the several chapters of comparison, the restrictive—because it leads to a greater compression—is for him a criterion for the superiority of tragedy: "And superior it is, because . . . the art attains its end within narrow limits; for the concentrated effect is more pleasurable than one which is spread over a long time and so diluted." But in several places in his discussion of the epic, as we have seen, we can sense

Aristotle's half-grudging admiration of its greater field of representation, because its words present themselves to us free of the limits imposed by real people occupying real space. Most of his Renaissance readers were also captivated by the greater expansiveness and inclusiveness allowed the epic by Aristotle, though without qualifying their enthusiasm as he did, so that they support the granting of the palm to the epic in all of its fabulous wanderings. Mazzoni himself inserts Aristotle's authority in the midst of the discussion I have quoted from book 3: "As Aristotle has testified . . . Poetics is directed to the credible marvelous by means of sonorous and dignified verse, and of fables and conceptions that are new and extraordinary" (Gilbert, p. 388). Indeed, a wide array of Renaissance critics used Aristotle's brief observations about the epic to project, within a general theory of poetry, the claim that the production of wonder or admiration or astonishment—as the result of the marvelous—is the end of the epic, just as pity and fear together serve as the end of tragedy. It is a claim that finds support in Mazzoni's more systematic formulation. For these Renaissance theorists, the requirement that the epic produce wonder in the audience so frees the poem from its responsibility to historical reality or like-historical reality[15] that the poet is licensed, in flight from such realities, to indulge the monstrous. (And epic monsters fall well within the extended license that Aristotle allows the narrative poet.) Hence the well-known quotation from Sidney's *Apology for Poetry*:

> Only the poet, disdaining to be tied to any such subjection [to nature], lifted up with the vigor of his own invention, doth grow in effect into another nature, in making things either better than nature bringeth forth, or, quite anew, forms such as never were in nature, as the Heroes, Demigods, Cyclops, Chimeras, Furies, and such like: so as he goeth hand in hand with nature, not enclosed within the narrow warrant of her gifts, but freely ranging only within the zodiac of his own wit.[16]

15. In accord with Aristotle's praise of Homer for teaching poets "the art of telling lies skilfully," Mazzoni explicitly licenses the poet to transgress historical truth with his verisimilar, though phantastic, images: he speaks favorably of a kind of "impossible credible taken from history . . . when the poet transmutes and falsifies history that is true or at least recorded in some writer; this procedure is also according to my opinion fitting to the poetically credible" (bk. 3, chap. 3 [Gilbert, p. 390]).

16. *An Apology for Poetry or The Defence of Poesy*, ed. Geoffrey Shepherd (Manchester: Manchester University Press, 1973), p. 100.

The poet, not subject to nature, is free, in making fictions, to invent unnatural creatures. The use of words to describe a monster, or an action involving monsters, is a fictitious imitation, as unpicturable as the shields of Achilles and Aeneas which I treated as fictitious ekphrases in my Foreword. And it is just this transcendence of the picturable that, in the spirit of Burke, I would argue contributes to an effectiveness beyond the finitude of representational precision. We can all recall the disappointment, or embarrassed feeling of inadequacy, if not absurdity, that accompanies our response to an attempt to reduce a literary monster to the visual dimensions of pictorial representation. No, it is better to allow the words to sponsor our creating in our minds an illusion of the sensible features of the monster as if we could reproduce them in visual form, though we must avoid trying vainly to do so. This is precisely the illusionary trick of ekphrasis, we have seen: to produce the "picturesque" that cannot, and ought not, be "picturable," as Lessing would say.[17]

The interest in a mode of representation that avoids mimetic fidelity in order to exploit the more indirect semiotic power of the aesthetic sign is consistent with the claim being argued, on behalf of Renaissance theory, by E. H. Gombrich in the landmark essay to which I have already referred more than once.[18] Gombrich's exploration of the power bestowed on "symbolic images" (*icones symbolicae*) by Renaissance Neo-Platonists leads him to their celebration of religious pictures that go "the apophatic way of mysterious monstrosity" (Gombrich's brilliant phrase, p. 152) rather than the idolatrous way of divine imitation. Although acknowledging the obvious aesthetic of emulation, which celebrates the attempt to capture the divine within the sensible media available to us as humans, Gombrich pays more attention to those pious Neo-Platonists who, when dealing with the attempted representation of the sacred — even in dealing with pictorial representation — declared war on the natural sign in order to replace it with a theologically controlled code.[19] And though he is focusing upon the visual arts, Gombrich's histori-

17. I discuss this distinction in Lessing in Chapter 2, above.

18. *"Icones Symbolicae."* To establish Gombrich's early and influential role in discussions of Renaissance Neo-Platonism, I should mention that the essay first appeared, in a shorter version, in the *Journal of the Warburg and Courtauld Institutes* in 1948.

19. Gombrich persuasively argues that the crucial addition made to Neo-Platonism by the *Christian* Neo-Platonist was the insistence upon God's desire for the divine to make itself known to us. "In Plato himself there is certainly no hint that the higher world wishes to be known by us dwellers in the dark" (Gombrich, p. 148). Hence

cal analysis can be transferred helpfully to the development of the aesthetic of the verbal arts as these relate to the movement of the visual arts toward a coded rather than a simply mimetic form of representation.

We can read this division into the quotation from Sidney, above: the poet can directly seek to emulate those beings "better than nature bringeth forth," like the heroes and demigods, or he can invent beings "such as never were in nature," like cyclops, chimeras, and furies, as signifiers of his moral message. Or later: "If the poet do his part aright, he will show you in Tantalus, Atreus, and such like, nothing that is not to be shunned. In Cyrus, Aeneas, Ulysses, each thing to be followed" (p. 110). Here, clearly, are consequences of the opposition between "apophasis" and "kataphasis." Indeed, Sidney's definition of the various literary genres and their functions reflects this distinction. He treats pastoral, the elegiac, the iambic, the satiric, comedy, and even tragedy as forms that treat what is to be avoided: "Now, as in geometry the oblique must be known as well as the right, and in arithmetic the odd as well as the even, so in the actions of our life who seeth not the filthiness of evil, wanteth a great foil to perceive the beauty of virtue" (p. 117). And on the other side, he treats the lyric and epic as forms that directly represent what is to be imitated. The lyric is that which deals with virtuous acts or even "the immortal God," and the heroic that which "teacheth and moveth to the most high and excellent truth" through displaying "champions [epic heroes] who maketh magnanimity and justice shine" (pp. 118–19).

Gombrich presents these two ways that aesthetic signs, as sensible products of a worldly humanity, can try to represent heavenly reality, which can be intelligible only. As with Sidney, a sensible image of an intelligible reality can be either *like* it or *unlike* it, can seek either to resemble it or to avoid resembling it. In the latter case, however, the image can seek to refer to the supersensible indirectly, through a mediating code, whether language itself or pictures functioning as a language. It thus has resort to allegory, produced by "symbolic images." To the extent that an otherworldly Christianity fears idolatry, it would call for this second way, that which flees from any attempt to reproduce the sacred in the stuff of the world

---

the symbolic hermeneutic is given us by God as an aid in reading the Book of Nature, which He has written in order for us to read it.

that alone is available to the human being. What must be chosen for the apophatic, then, is an aesthetic medium that is visually self-ab-negating, that does not use its own features to attempt any *immedi-acy* of representation, that contents itself with pointing toward the sacred as a sign whose only power is referential, with no pretension of being in itself *like* its object. Indeed it must be as unlike its object as possible so as to avoid any charge of idolatrous ambition. Hence the painter, in avoiding the temptation to be directly mimetic in creating idols, may well resort to monsters as being at the greatest distance from the divine, though these are monsters richly endowed with allegorical meanings, with mystery. So they are "mysterious" monsters serving the "apophatic" function of representing, through mediation, what their very figures seem to deny they represent.

In the opposition between the imitation by like (apparently nat-ural-sign imitation) and the imitation by the unlike (apparently arbi-trary- and conventional-sign reference) we can find the two opposed methods of relating the divine to the earthly realms, two concep-tions of the veil between them and of the degree to which that veil can be penetrated. When the Christian painter is encouraged to press all his mimetic talents toward forcing his materials to dupli-cate the sacred on canvas—God, Christ, the angels and saints—the assumption is that the veil between heaven and earth is very thin, indeed approaches transparency, at least with the help of the sub-limely mimetic artist. In using the mental pictures and materials afforded him by his earthly existence, such an artist must choose only the richest and most beautiful in the hope that somehow these, by coming as close as humanity can to the transcendent rich-ness and beauty they would represent, *can*—by analogy, as it were—succeed in representing them to us. Thus, for example, the use of nothing less than 24-karat gold for the saintly halo may, if anything can, catch the superlative character of what we would bestow upon the more-than-human wearer. And in view of the systems of anal-ogies matching microcosm with macrocosm that we find commonly set forth in the work of some Neo-Platonic philosophers, such a vis-ual imitation of divine richness and beauty by the earthly analogy is a permitted mode of revelation in art. Its own richness and beauty, almost a breakthrough glimpse of the divine, give us a kind of ac-cess to it, bringing us to the very threshold because of its represen-tational power to imagine the sensible equivalent of the divine and because the veil between human and divine is thin enough for such

aesthetic penetration. Whatever the risk of idolatry, the pictorial—
or the attempt at a verbal imitation of the pictorial even to the point
of *enargeia I*—would, under the aegis of this theology, be encouraged as the exalted objective of the artist or poet.

But theology in this period can also foster an asceticism to counter such aestheticism by calling upon the artist to avoid seeking to
represent supernal beauty by mimesis. In the more dualistic and
hence more puritanical view, one more imbued with the original
anti-mimetic spirit of Plato, the veil is conceived as much denser, to
the point of impenetrability, thus blocking any visionary access to
the divine by the human. Here, in order to avoid the vain and dangerous service of idolatry, the Christian painter is to distance his representations from the divine by turning to the apophatic, which
uses the "symbolic images" of allegory and, where useful, the monsters that his culture and he fill with mysterious meaning, so that
they can point us, despite the self-denial they bear on their faces,
toward the invisible sacred realm from which they, and all of us, are
shut off. The mystery of such hermetic equations, their inaccessibil-
ity to the human—beyond our vision as they are beyond our understanding—is preserved, even while the humanly created painting,
with its mimetic ambition reduced, serves only as the encoded text
that points to that very mystery, though without quite enlightening
it. One does the best one humanly can by means of an allegory that
polarizes the distance between signifier and signified. Within that
distance the inventiveness of the artist is free to choose from all the
visible universe, as well as its magical transformations—so long as
it cannot be mistaken for the sacramentally invisible that is under
taboo. We can well understand the attraction felt by Renaissance
Neo-Platonists for the Egyptian hieroglyphs, which Ficino, after
Plotinus, treated as pictorial representations of intelligible ideas.
They were thus models for those looking for a precedent for picture-
writing. During the Renaissance there were many widely distrib-
uted collections of Egyptian hieroglyphs, beginning with that of
Horapollo (Ficino's "Horus," cited in Chapter 1, above).[20] It is not
irrelevant to note that the term "hieroglyph" recurs at several impor-

20. For a full discussion of the collections and attempted interpretations of Egyptian hieroglyphs in the Renaissance, as well as of their importance, see Don Cameron Allen's chapter, "The Symbolic Wisdom of the Ancient Egyptians," in his
*Mysteriously Meant: The Rediscovery of Pagan Symbolism and Allegorical Interpretation in
the Renaissance* (Baltimore: Johns Hopkins Press, 1970), pp. 107-33.

tant moments in the later history of theories pressing toward formulations of the verbal emblem.[21]

Even Mazzoni, who, as a defender of poetry as "sensible image,"
usually opposes an allegorical justification, reveals, in a passage
from book 3 (chap. 6), a moment of pious dualism that would seem
to place constraints on the poet's "caprice." He proposes that the
Song of Solomon "be called phantastic with respect to the literal
sense, but icastic with respect to the allegorical sense" (Gilbert, p.
390).[22] To put it more technically, he is asking the poem to be regarded as phenomenally phantastic (subject to a poet's invention
that is at some distance from the truth of its referent), while remaining ontologically icastic, in revealing ultimate truths about the unseen world. Gombrich's exposition of Dionysius the Areopagite, in
speaking of the role of the Scriptures, deals similarly with representation by "apophasis":

> There are two ways of approaching the Divine. Through affirmation (*kata-
> phasis*) and negation (*apophasis*). Revelation makes use of both ways. It
> represents spiritual entities by way of analogy through such dignified
> concepts as Logos or Nous or through the image of Light. But there is a
> danger in this kind of symbolic language. It may lead to the very confu-
> sions the religious mind must avoid. The reader of the Scriptures might
> take it literally and think that the heavenly beings are really god-like
> men, radiant figures of transcending beauty, clad in shining robes . . . or
> similar figures through which the Revelation has given a sensible repre-
> sentation of the heavenly spirits. It is to avoid this confusion that the holy
> authors of the revealed writings have deliberately used inappropriate
> symbols and similes so that we should not cling to the undignified literal
> meaning. The very monstrosities of which they talk, such as lions and
> horses in the heavenly regions, prevent us from accepting these images
> as real and stimulate our mind to seek a higher significance. Thus the
> apparent inappropriateness of the symbols found in the Holy Writ is in

21. See, e.g., my discussions of Diderot and Shelley.
22. In this distinction among levels of meaning, we recognize the imprint of the
four levels (the literal, the allegorical, the moral, and the anagogic) distinguished by
Dante in his well-known "Letter to Can Grande della Scala" and in more detailed
fashion in his *Convivio* (Second Tractate). I claim that a Renaissance theorist such as
Mazzoni also borrows from Dante the transcendentally mystical notion of the anagogic and adds it crucially to the first two in order to move beyond the dualisms I have
been tracing. How appropriate it is that Mazzoni should be dependent for his theory
on speculations of the poet whose masterwork he is here defending.

effect a means through which our soul is led on towards spiritual truth.
(P. 151)

Behind these two opposed views, the mimetic and the apophatic,
we find two ways of relating the birth of language to the doctrine of
the Fall; these lead, in turn, to two semiotic systems. For those who
would thin the veil between heaven and earth almost to the vanish-
ing point, mimesis is an original and natural grace, and the Fall is
marked by the introduction of language-as-code as a distancing intruder upon the natural-sign reflection of the signified in the signifier. The fall from a pictorial substitute into an arbitrary code
marks the end of a language of pure presence, of immediate representation, in which, as Ficino put it, "the pure and firm shape of the
thing itself" is replaced by signs that are "multiple and shifting."[23]
Fallen humanity must use an empty, conventional sign system for
what in the state of grace had been the fullness of the mimetic picture. But on the other side, for those who see the earthly as hopelessly cut off from the divine, those in whom the spirit of Plato
condemns any pretension by the sensible to ape the intelligible, the
indirection of a mediating code is the only way of approaching the
sacred. Consequently, it is rather the attempt at a sensible mimesis,
a pictorial rendering that would claim to be a surrogate, that characterizes the Fall, a fall into idolatry, an anthropomorphic reduction
that would seek to bring God down from the skies and transform
Him into the false priests who would represent Him on earth.

But we must remember that in describing these alternatives Gombrich is writing as a historian of art, not literature. On both sides of
his opposition between the mimetic and the apophatic he is com-
menting on the visual and not the verbal arts, even when he sees
the visual as partaking of the semiotic function of the verbal once it
rejects the mimetic function of the naive view of painting as natural
sign. Thus he is referring to pictures rather than words, even when
they are pictures that, like words, turn from the natural-sign obligation of an unproblematic visual duplication of its object to its function as a system of signs, a language, in need of being interpreted.
In demonstrating the extent to which the pictorial itself becomes a
conventionally controlled sign rather than an immediate, "natural"
equivalent, his analysis directs our attention to the claim that the

23. See Chapter 1 for discussion of the entire passage from Ficino. The reference for
it appears in n. 17 to that chapter.

doctrine of the natural sign is indeed a myth that ignores the yawn-
ing gap—a gap filled by arbitrary codes conventionally sanctioned—
between the object and its representation. Perhaps nowhere are the
consequences of this myth more tellingly revealed than in the
sacred art of the Renaissance. Indeed, Isidore of Seville anticipates
this distrust of painting's mimetic fidelity many centuries earlier (in
the early seventh century) with this warning about its deceptively
fictional character: "*Pictura* is a representation expressing the appearance of anything, which when it is beheld makes the mind
remember. *Pictura* is, moreover, pronounced almost *fictura*. For it is
a feigned representation, not the truth."[24]

Even where there *is* painting, then, for the historical commentator on symbolic images, the picture, now dedicated to the apophatic
rather than the mimetic, becomes a pictograph, often representing
a symbolic animal or invented creature. Such representations of sig-
nifying monsters function as an opaque semiosis rather than a transparency: they are full of meaning, though it is a coded referential
meaning and no longer a meaning contained and readable within
the inherent form of the represented objects themselves—literally
phantastic but allegorically icastic, as we saw Mazzoni put it. But
because of its ambition as a code that addresses the intelligible mysteries, this meaning, in its freedom from the limits of sensory perception, can display endless complications as a pictographic code
that defies human logic and the dimensions of human seeing. It is
as a supreme example of "mysterious monstrosity" in its apophatic
function that Gombrich, after Ficino, cites the *ouroboros* as the Egyptian mystical symbol for the paradoxes of time and human life.[25]
However, in this case it is *in* this circular image itself—the winged
serpent with its tail in its mouth—that its meanings begin, so that
we may see it as moving from image to emblem, with a symbolism

24. This passage is quoted in Jean H. Hagstrum, *The Sister Arts: The Tradition of Literary Pictorialism and English Poetry from Dryden to Gray* (Chicago: University of Chicago Press, 1958), p. 38.

25. See my discussion of this remarkable image in Chapter 1, above. I remind the
reader, as Ficino did, of the role played by Renaissance commentaries on Egyptian
hieroglyphs in tracing the fall from natural signs first to a pictorial code (often of symbolic animals) and then to the letters of an arbitrary alphabet. Allen's chapter in *Mysteriously Meant* (see n. 20, above) is an especially useful summary. I mention here
only the example he cites from Athanasius Kircher (in his *Obeliscus Pamphilius* of
1650), for whom the letter *alpha* is prefigured by the Egyptian picturing of a crane
bending and passing its neck and bill across its legs (as represented in the emblem
provided at the head of this chapter).

emerging from its own complexity. And here is the change that moves us beyond the dualism of the allegory in the direction of semiosis as emblematics.

The mysteries behind the attraction to an emblematics rest in a magical Neo-Platonic universe, full of reflecting microcosms within a reflecting macrocosm, with this mutuality of reflections producing an anagogic realm of identity. Here the arbitrary signs of allegory are transformed, despite what appears as their enormous difference from their sacred references (the more enormous for their being apophatic), so that strangely incongruous, dreamlike—if sometimes nightmarish—equivalences abound in the redemption produced by monstrosity: "To make of monsters and things indigest / Such cherubins as your sweet self resemble" (Shakespeare's Sonnet 114). In a form of supersensible memory that we carry with us from before and beyond this world, a form of memory that metaphysically authorizes this bizarre dream, *mnemosyne* is still to function, though now via Platonic "reminiscence" rather than sense impressions. A supersensible authority thus bestows an ontological sanction upon the hermeneutic and turns it hermetic. From this perspective, all readings end in an identity—despite the great discrepancy—between sign and referent, an identity that yields a presence of the invisible-sacred within the visible-apophatic, making the profane picture sacredly pictographic.

What is being claimed is that the encoded signs, apparently arbitrary and conventional, are, through an ontological sanction, authorized to become, in effect, *meta*-natural signs after all, full of the presence of the transcendental meaning they carry, though we cannot specify or translate them with confidence lest we reduce their mystery to sensible dimensions. This hermeneutic system has its alchemical home in the transmutation of base elements into gold and its ontological home in a pool of being in which separate entities, from the monstrous to the sublime, are dissolved into identity. The signs that such a hermeneutic is prepared to read evade the "natural" equivalence that would arise from their being matched, through perceptible similarity, to their referents and instead attain a metaphysically sanctioned identity with them, thereby achieving a meta-natural, intelligible status. This mystic hermeneutic of Christian Neo-Platonism treats God's creation as His written Word: His Book of Nature is thus wholly interpretable in accordance with principles of a persistently teleological reading that leaves no element of the sacred macrocosmic text out of the system of magical equivalences.

Within such an overwhelmingly universal theory of interpretation, what is true of apophatic images is, for similar reasons, true of words. Thus we can link the claims of Gombrich to those of Mazzoni urged in defense of Dante: the picture-magic of the *ouroboros*, offering itself as a magic text, translates into the word-magic of the verbal emblem.

We have seen from several sides the claim that what Mazzoni calls verbal "images," whether the image of the Trinity that he quotes from Dante or Homer's description of the shield of Achilles, which I have discussed, are images only in a metaphorical sense.[26] The poet is using something that strikes us as if it were an image (largely because our visual sense has been trained by actual images), but it is not an image so much as it is an analogy to what an image would be if words could literally make one. The poem, we have known since Plato's version of mimesis, stands at a distant remove from the painting of an object: if, within the natural-sign aesthetic, the visual image gives us the illusion of the absent *object* as if it were present (as Lessing put it at the opening of his *Laokoön*), the verbal "image" (Lessing to the contrary notwithstanding) gives us only the illusion of the absent visual *image* of the object as if it were present. The ostensible object in the latter case evades picturability and, for the Neo-Platonist, is the better for that evasion.

As the argument from analogy has it, the picture relates to the sensible as the word relates to the intelligible. The illusion permitted by the words (the illusion of an image) liberates the mind and gives it access to the intelligible, while the illusion permitted by the natural-sign image (the illusion of an object) locks it within the sensible.[27] This is why the apophatic visual image helps belie the notion of the natural sign and can move beyond its limitations: playing its

26. I remind the reader of Plato's precedent for this metaphorical use of "image" in his comparison of verbal and pictorial "images" in the *Cratylus,* to which I called attention in Chapter 3.

27. Mazzoni uses Plato's *Sophist* extensively (though often sifted through the second sophistic of Hellenistic rhetoricians) and derives his notion of the illusionary "image" from it. For Plato, of course, illusion is to be condemned for its deceptiveness, so that his attack on poetry in this dialogue is one with his attack on painting and sculpture. For he sees all of them hopelessly married to the sensible. By distinguishing the phantastic verbal "image" from the icastic, Mazzoni is able to free the former from its dependence on the realm of human experience in order to allow it access to the intelligible realm from which Plato excluded all the imitative arts. In defending Dante's phantasies, Mazzoni can be seen as creating a special role for poetry as a phantastic art within the Platonic aesthetic, though clearly at the expense

fictional role within a complicated code, the apophatic visual image opens out onto the semiotic possibilities of the verbal image. The fact that the poet is not literally a painter, as this argument goes, becomes the poet's strength: the linguistic sign, insofar as it is not a "natural sign" because it does not resemble its object, is therefore free to appeal to the mind's eye rather than the body's eye. And the mind's eye, through which the intelligible is "glimpsed," is of course superior to the body's, restricted as the latter is to the sensible.

But the Neo-Platonic proponent of the magic semiotic had to go beyond the Platonic dualism that ties the natural-sign image (the picture) to the sensible and, by contrast, the verbal image (the poem) to the intelligible. The magic of the Neo-Platonic aesthetic lay in its claim for art to make the intelligible susceptible to human vision—at least metaphorically—without suggesting that it could succumb to the empirical limitations of the sensible. The apophatic image, in the monstrousness of a visual or verbal form, was to be made into that magical force. Note, for example, the language in which Sidney couches his praise of David's psalms as productions of the poet as *vates* or seer:

> Lastly and principally, his handling his prophecy, which is merely poetical. For what else is the awaking his musical instruments, the often and free changing of persons, his notable *prosopopeias*, when he maketh you, as it were, see God coming in His majesty, his telling of the beasts' joyfulness, and hills leaping, but a heavenly poesy, wherein almost he showeth himself a passionate lover of that unspeakable and everlasting beauty to be seen by the eyes of the mind, only cleared by faith. (*Apology,* p. 99)

Through *prosopopeia*, we are told, David creates a presence of what can never be present to the senses. He makes us as readers "see God coming in His Majesty." But not quite: such "unspeakable and everlasting beauty" can be seen only "by the eyes of the mind," and only insofar as they are "cleared by faith," so that we are made, "*as it were*" (and only "as it were"), to "see God coming in His Majesty." Such an importation of God, however equivocal (and its equivocal character, its dependence on the joyfulness of the beasts

---

of icastic poetry (the only kind defended by Plato) as well as what the mimetic tradition has treated as the natural-sign arts.

and the leaping of the hills, is indispensable), can occur only through the workings of David's poems, which help us attain a "faith" that can "clear" the "eyes of the mind." We "see" God as we "see" the Trinity in the three circles of Dante's image or the divinely authorized Greek culture in the shield of Achilles: we "see" these with the "eyes of the mind," which can respond to the words because, in being less than a picture, they stimulate so much more "seeing" than the picture can. Through the poem we join the poet as *vates*.

Because the words produce an "as it were" picture addressed to the mind's eye, they can bring before us "that unspeakable and everlasting beauty" otherwise out of our reach. It is by means of this indirect, metaphorical sort of "speaking picture" that the poet's words can give us the "golden" world of "our erected wit" to replace the "brazen" world of sense—the fallen world of "our infected will"—in which we otherwise dwell (*Apology*, pp. 100–101). The Neo-Platonist takes this common metaphor of the golden world seriously: through the alembic of his words the poet achieves his function as alchemist.[28] In Shakespeare's Sonnet 114, from which I quoted earlier to demonstrate the illusionary metamorphosis of "monsters" into "cherubins," what the poet's eye sees has been transformed by the mind's power to superimpose its own seeing upon it, under the power of love that teaches the eye "this alchemy," thus "Creating every bad a perfect best / As fast as objects to his beams assemble." Nowhere does this alchemical process reveal itself as it does in the poetic "image," the metaphor through which words exercise a rare power of transmutation by turning themselves substantive, becoming one with the changes they perform: "Kissing with golden face the meadows green, / Gilding pale streams with heavenly alchemy" (Shakespeare's Sonnet 33). It is not just that the poem represents a metaphorical transmutation of objects; in its own action as a verbal system in play, it becomes itself the place in which the representation of the change of the language process into the process of metaphorical alchemy is embodied. The *ouroboros* and the emblem poem—the poem as image—work the same way: the poem and the accompanying emblem are mutually explicative in

28. This metaphor served powerfully for many Renaissance thinkers, perhaps chief among them, for my purposes, Ficino and Pico della Mirandola. The controlling notion of poet as alchemist and poetic image as alchemical transmutation is carefully and helpfully explored by Luminita I. Niculescu, *From Hermeticism to Hermeneutics: Alchemical Metaphors in Renaissance Literature* (Ph.D. diss., University of California at Los Angeles, 1981).

an unfolding series of interpretive possibilities whose intertwinings are full of mystery. Yet each, poem or emblem, can be seen as its own free-standing interpretive crux. And the verbal artifact itself can be read and reread, interpreted and reinterpreted, as within itself the most inexhaustively mysterious emblem of all.

It should now be clear why I wanted to reserve the Renaissance interest in poetry as image for treatment in a separate chapter, distinguishing it both from the rest of the theoretical tradition that emphasized the primacy of the visual in the writing or reading of poetry (Chapter 3) and from the theoretical tradition that opposed it (Chapter 4). Under the influence of the Neo-Platonic mind, the concept of poetry as a "speaking picture" received a radically different cast: instead of trying vainly to be like a picture in reflecting sensible reality, the verbal object, as its own emblem, accepts its independent — indeed superior — function of speaking and picturing an intelligible reality.

By contrast, the unqualifiedly pictorialist view of poetry (*ut pictura poesis erit*) that I traced in Chapter 3 and saw opposed in Chapter 4 — the view that achieves its fullest expression in the late seventeenth and eighteenth centuries — may seem to be a backward step toward naiveté after the richness of the views I have been tracing here.[29] Of course the richness was a by-product of doctrines of religious mystery that would be seen by a more scientific age as having its own naiveté. The rationalist and the empiricist sides of the neoclassical period joined to reject mystical Neo-Platonism and mystical Christianity alike in favor of doctrines that encouraged a more straightforward trimming of the poetic image to the dimensions of our normal worldly vision. The simpler versions of empiricism were especially responsible for firmly establishing the reductive theory of memory as a storehouse of pictures, a series of distinct individual snapshots of prior sensory experiences. What follows, as we have seen, is the claim that it is the function of all art, including poetry, to stimulate that memory and bring forth those renewed snapshots.

With this claim we are returned to the assumption that I claimed to be the ground for Plato's anti-aesthetic argument: that there can be a single object of imitation for all the arts, visual or verbal. From this assumption the call for *enargeia* I produced a pictorialist aes-

---

29. We may also note the thinned version of Neo-Platonism that, by the eighteenth century, produced the tamely spatial, indeed static, appeal to intelligible universals that we find, for example, in Winckelmann.

thetic for picture and poem alike. For Renaissance Neo-Platonists, on the other hand, moved by a desire to save poetry and make it an instrument for our salvation, the potential object of imitation was, in the main, to vary with the art: a sensible object for the visual arts and an intelligible object for the verbal arts. Still, the intricacies of their thinking led to some crossing over, so that we saw some authorize the visual arts, by invoking apophatic mysteries, to use their sensible objects to approach the intelligible. And from the other side, in his historical parade of pictorialist theorists of literature that we followed earlier, Mazzoni mingled theorists for whom poetic pictures were to emulate painted pictures and theorists for whom poetic pictures were "images" that yet eluded the senses. But his Neo-Platonic defense of poetry, and especially of phantastic poetry to the neglect of icastic poetry, indicates the extent to which he recognized the distinction between the intelligible and the sensible that I have been pressing.

After these Renaissance doctrines, the empiricist's reduction of all possible experience to the sensible had the consequence of once again reducing the object of poetry to that which was immediately reproducible by the visual arts, thereby once more reducing the mission of poetry to the emulation of those arts. The internal emblem was lost in the restoration of the external object as the archetype and controlling agent of the poetic image. But once the uncritical notion of brute empiricism came to be rejected, and the narrowly visual notion once more rejected with it, the exciting possibilities of the verbal emblem introduced by the Renaissance would be there to be picked up again, well after Kant, and carried farther along for being less dependent on the extravagant metaphysical demands of Christian Neo-Platonism. This reborn version of the verbal emblem will be the subject of Chapter 7.

6

LANGUAGE
AS
AESTHETIC
MATERIAL

There must be not only a partnership, but a union; an interpenetration of passion and of will, of *spontaneous* impulse and of *voluntary* purpose . . . this union can be manifested only in a frequency of forms and figures of speech (originally the offspring of passion, but now the adopted children of power). . . . The rules of imagination are themselves the very powers of growth and production. The *words*, to which they are reducible, present only the outlines and external appearance of the fruit. A deceptive counterfeit of the superficial form and colors may be elaborated; but the marble peach feels cold and heavy, and *children* only put it to their mouths.

Coleridge, *Biographia Literaria*, chap. 18

I believe we will find that at least on the surface, the principal difference between the conception of the verbal emblem in the Renaissance and in the nineteenth and twentieth centuries is that in the latter the formative role of the theological and the Neo-Platonic comes to be replaced by the formative role of linguistic manipulation by the poet. In order to prepare the way for our passage from the Renaissance version to the modernist version of the verbal emblem, I am pausing for a chapter to pursue, in the history of literary theory, several ways in which the relationship between language as a generally discursive instrument and language as a medium of a literary discourse has been characterized. Accepting, for expository purposes, the assumption of the critics I discuss that such a distinction between these uses of language exists, I can then examine the relationship between language as a medium of literary works and the media of the visual arts. For when literary theory, after the neoclassical diversion, or rather *re*version, to naive pictorialism, begins again to move toward the emblematic, creative powers are attributed to the aural as well as the symbolic functions of language in poetry in a way that ties this theory to the lately arrived (mid-eighteenth-century) discipline of general aesthetics. It is this theory that I must seek to explicate.

I am aware that beginning with its title, the interests of this chapter may seem to run counter to most, if not all, of what my theoretical colleagues have recently been writing. The suggestion that language can function as an exclusively aesthetic material implies that it can, through being appropriately manipulated, serve as a medium for the privileged mode of discourse we call poetry. On these grounds it would be more important to relate the language of poems to the media of the other arts than to relate it to language as it functions outside the poetic, and hence outside the aesthetic, realm—to language that is seen as less special. But these days our most fashionable tendencies in theory argue, to the contrary, for an undifferentiated, monolithic notion of the way language works. Whether the particular theoretical version dwells on spoken language or on writing—that is, on *parole* or on *écriture,* on speech as discourse or on textuality—all is under the control of a uniform semiotic that would allow for no privileged medium for poetry.

Nevertheless, because it affects the ekphrastic and emblematic capacities attributed to language, I want to begin here by seeing what theorists have made of the claim that under certain circumstances and with certain manipulations it acquires the peculiar capacity to function as an aesthetic medium, thereby giving poetry the special features of an art, the primary language art. This is a concept systematically developed by the dominant tradition of aesthetics in the West for more than two centuries as it moved toward its modernist apotheosis well into our own century. I have already alluded to recent moves that would subvert, if not invert, that tradition, but those will be taken up later in our story. Let me begin, then, with those considerations that led to our concern with aesthetic materials and their conversion into aesthetic media. The very notion of such materials dictates that such considerations must arise out of a logically prior concern that ties the arts to sense perception. And that leads back to the original sense of the term "aesthetic" itself.

The invention of "aesthetics" not only as a term but also as a discipline governed by the term wedded the study of the arts at once and for good to the perceptual and, more broadly, to the sensuous. Conceiving aesthetics as the science of perception (or of "sensuous cognition"), Alexander Baumgarten—from his early work in 1735 and firmly in his *Aesthetica* (1750)—set apart the study of works of art from other studies on the ground of its primal dependence on art's appeal to our sensory receptors. This literal meaning of "aesthetics," as an etymological borrowing from the Greek, remained attached to the term in the tradition that, leading through Moses Mendelssohn to Kant and beyond, used the sensuous character of aesthetic objects to distinguish their realm from the other two realms, the realm of knowledge and the realm of action. As late as Benedetto Croce's continual use of the term and his development of the discipline named for it, the aesthetic retains that restricted meaning, apparently still bound by its etymological origin, so that the bond between the aesthetic object and the sensuous basis of its entrance upon our experience remains secure. Indeed, Croce's magically omnibus term, "intuition," which he declares synonymous with the aesthetic, has sense perception as *its* originary meaning. It proceeds to spread its meaning to include our more restricted notion of intuition, though Croce finds it theoretically necessary for this high-level intuition to be continuous with his minimal and broad notion of ordinary sense perception, differing only quantitatively from it.[1] So also is it with his term "aesthetic," which for him is interchangeable with "intuition."

From the outset, such thinking about aesthetics led with consistency from these definitional assumptions about the sensuous basis of art to a concern about the "aesthetic senses," the several senses that act as receptors for the several arts. Of course, the notion of "perception" had to be broadened so that we could account for the reception of stimuli by senses other than the sense of sight. (I say this despite the fact that the earlier eighteenth century too often continued to assign the primary role to the visual—a habit of Western epistemology since Plato—as we observed in noting the dominant position of the pictorial arts in relation to their sister arts in neoclassical criticism.) The other senses had to be brought into play as theorists looked beyond painting and drawing to those "sister arts." In the eighteenth century, but more systematically by its second half, a number of thinkers—Diderot and Herder perhaps chief among them—related the different arts to the different senses in an effort to move toward a general aesthetic.

In his *Letter on the Deaf and Dumb for the Use of Those Who Hear and Who Speak* (1751), Diderot moves toward distinctions among the senses and, however unsystematically, gives early hints of the analysis that in later theorists would derive an aesthetic from such distinctions. He proposes "to decompose a man, in a manner of speaking, and to consider what he gets from each of his senses."[2] He goes

1. Between "ordinary intuition" and the intuition "which is generally called artistic, . . . the whole difference, then, is quantitative, and as such is indifferent to philosophy, *scientia qualitatum*." This discussion appears in Croce's *Aesthetic*, trans. Douglas Ainslie, rev. ed. (1922; reprint, New York: Noonday Press, 1953), p. 13.

2. My translation is taken from Denis Diderot, *Lettre sur les sourds et muets à l'usage de ceux qui entendent et qui parlent*, in *Oeuvres complètes de Diderot*, ed. J. Assézat, vol. 1 (Paris: Garnier Frères, 1875), pp. 352–53. Even earlier (1749) is his *Letter on the Blind*

on to characterize the temperament of each of the five senses and playfully suggests an experiment: assembling a society of five persons of whom each would have only one sense and would perceive and judge everything by means of it. Diderot implicitly relates each art to its proper sense by acknowledging the inadequacy of using an inappropriate sense to respond to an art that is addressed to another sense; thus he rejects the idea of representing music to those who cannot hear by seeking to find equivalent colors for the various sounds. This matching of the arts to the several senses becomes an important part of the systems of aesthetic developed in the later eighteenth century by more ambitious theorists such as Herder.[3]

Indeed, the fuller and more persistently pursued, if less easily grasped and still only seminal, development of these ideas in the work of Herder becomes a crucial influence. Like Diderot and others who preceded him, Herder sought to distinguish among the arts, one by one, according to the sense to which each appealed: painting to the eye, music to the ear, sculpture to the touch.[4] From these differences later aestheticians could work their way—as Diderot had already suggested—to each art's distinctive medium, the perceptible material that could address the appropriate sense. But Herder's idealistic tendencies, concerned more with mental receptors than with material stimuli, often came to rest upon the aesthetic sense to be struck and provoked to respond rather than upon verbal manipulations.[5]

One might expect that to the extent that the arts depended on the

---

(*Lettre sur les aveugles à l'usage de ceux qui voient*), but in this one there is little extension to the realm of the aesthetic.

3. Among those immediately influenced by this separation of the senses by Diderot, one could also mention his friend Etienne Bonnot de Condillac, whose *Treatise on the Sensations* (1754) works similarly to treat the senses one by one.

4. For example, the influence of James Harris's very early *Three Treatises* (1744) is both extensive and substantial throughout Herder's theorizing on these issues.

5. My discussion of Herder is drawn from several places and several periods in his writings. His one work devoted exclusively to this problem is *Plastik* (1778), but the more complicated discussions to which I am here referring occur throughout the *Kritische Wälder*. My generalizations about Herder's aesthetic are derived from my attempt to assemble what often seem to be piecemeal observations, though it is evident that he has global ambitions for systematic theory. Yet, because at different places he displays different and sometimes almost contradictory emphases—sometimes on the intelligible character of words, sometimes, in brilliant detail, on their aural qualities—I have had to reflect my confusion in my remarks. Whatever my difficulties with him, I find his importance to developing theories about the sensuous

senses, music and the plastic arts would be privileged, while poetry would have to be disadvantaged, since the language to which we are to respond in poetry, as we have seen extensively in previous chapters, has traditionally been thought of as primarily an intelligible rather than a sensible instrument. Where, then, within the context of a sensuous aesthetic could Herder find a place for poetry as an art? In his earlier work he reserved a special place for poetry by suggesting that it was an art beyond mere sensuous response. Although in dealing with the other arts he focused upon the sensory responses of the viewer or auditor, Herder managed to rescue and even privilege poetry precisely because it was free to transcend the limited function of assailing our senses, as the more obviously sensuous arts did. A resistant Platonism, such as we have witnessed in the Renaissance, still permitted poetry to be different—but higher for that difference—from the other arts because its effects upon us could not be reduced to its sensory properties. By defining poetry as the art that strikes—and involves—the "soul," as the other arts strike the appropriate sense, Herder argued for it as the transcendent art, supreme because it *was* more than sensuous.

But fortunately for theorists of poetic language who followed him, though Herder privileges poetry as an art that transcends its temporal nature by appealing to the soul, he does not exclude considerations of its initial sensuous impact. He thus comes to be alert to the strangely double character of language as a sensible as well as an intelligible material for art. We find in him many passages in which he tries to be faithful to his theoretical need to tie the arts— even including poetry—to sense perception by revealing a special responsiveness to the pattern of sound produced by poetry's words. In the course of remarkably seminal suggestions scattered among his writings, he often works out detailed systems of sound structure, and hence temporal structure, for poetry.

Nevertheless, Herder counters the temporality of poetry as an art of sound, like music, by rejecting Lessing's attempt to distinguish cleanly between arts of time and arts of space, with poetry treated exclusively as a temporal art. Poetry has for Herder a unique power, deriving from its appeal to the soul as well as the ear (i.e., to the soul beyond, though by means of, the ear), to turn time into space. The

dimension of the poetic medium to be indispensable to my attempt to follow that development here.

very sensuous basis of poetry as an art of sound-in-time heard by
the ear is overcome by its capacity, as an art of arbitrary signs read
by the mind, to transcend time by coming together all at once for us.
Though poetry, like all speech, "works in time," as a speech *art* it
works on the "soul" or mind through words that, though created in
time, are apprehended, as a "whole," in space. Poetry *is* a "sensuous presentation," but one that is modified and transformed by the
intelligible intrusion of the mind that receives it instantaneously as
a spatial completeness.[6]

Thus, despite Herder's concessions to the sensuous by-product
of poetry, his placement of poetry as special among the arts mainly
reflects his awareness of the tradition that treats words as arbitrary
signs that function intelligibly rather than as natural signs that function sensibly; that is, words, for all the sensuous pleasure they give,
in the end function mediately, through the intervention of the mind,
rather than immediately (literally, without mediation) through our
waiting sensory receptors. Because poetry is unlike other arts in
that its signs, as arbitrary and conventional, have meanings that are
not connected to the realm of sensory stimuli, it has the correlative
blessing of appealing to the realm of the intelligible, the Platonic
realm of the "soul," Herder's term that prefigures the "imagination" of the nineteenth century.

In its direct appeal to imagination poetry conquers temporality,
thereby (Lessing to the contrary notwithstanding) overcoming the
consecutiveness of verbal sequence. Herder's opposition to Lessing's limitations upon the arts—to Lessing's insistence on poetry's
consecutiveness—is complete: for Herder, poetry, by transcending
the sensuous, can achieve an instantaneity in the oneness of imagination's grasp. It is thus the art that frees itself from the very limits
that define the other arts, indeed from the limits that define the
realm of the aesthetic itself. In this way Herder forces poetry as the
transcendent art into the framework of aesthetics, which, because
of its basis in sense, might seem to deprive poetry of the status of art
altogether. An art beyond art, poetry is to override both sense and
time.

Of course, as my discussion of Diderot demonstrates, Herder was
hardly without precedent, though his double-edged formulation

6. For this spatial transcendence of temporal elements see Herder's criticism of
Lessing in his *Erstes Kritisches Wäldchen* (1769), which I discuss in my treatment of the
work of Patrick AE. Hutchings in Chapter 7, below.

did present a novel challenge that became a major influence upon romantic and idealist theorists. It must be noted, however, that in the early essay I have already introduced, Diderot had already proposed more single-mindedly, and with an impressive display of "close reading" of poetic texts, the grounds on which language can be converted into a medium for poetry. In Diderot's *Letter on the Deaf and Dumb,* his special concern for the role of sense perception leads him to focus—though it is remarkably early for him to do so—upon the function of the aural dimension of poetry. In a claim that foreshadows modern "deviationist" theories of poetic discourse (put forth, for example, by Russian Formalists), Diderot finds a poetic medium within the special manipulations of language that he sees as the defining feature of the poem.

> In all discourse in general we must distinguish between the thought and the expression: if the thought is rendered with clarity, purity, and precision, that is enough for ordinary conversation; join to these qualities the selection of words with rhythm and harmony, and you will have the style that is suited to the pulpit; but you will still be a long way from poetry, especially the poetry used by the ode and the epic poem in their descriptions. In poetic discourse there is a moving spirit that gives life to every syllable. . . . [Through that spirit] things are said and represented all at once: at the same time as the hearing seizes them, the mind is moved by them, the imagination sees them and the ear hears them, so that the discourse is no longer only a string of energetic terms that expose the thought with force and nobility, but it is a tissue of hieroglyphs heaped up one on the other that pictures it. I would be able to say, in this sense, that all poetry is emblematic.[7]

The succession from ordinary discourse to oratory to poetry is cumulative, each retaining the virtues of the preceding while adding special virtues of its own. Poetry, atop the rest, retains the referential

---

7. *Lettre sur les sourds et muets,* p. 374. All translations from this essay are my own. Diderot later in the essay (pp. 381–82) uses these distinctions to suggest, in accordance with a rather naive idea of progress, a theory of the historical evolution of language, consisting of stages (from primitive language to formed language to perfected language) that reflect the development from elementary speech to the conscious use of verbal harmony and "syllabic imitation." Still a proper neoclassicist, Diderot takes a position very different from the romantics', and especially from Shelley's (as we shall see later in this chapter), in precluding poetry, which is for Diderot a learned and technically sophisticated art, from appearing in the primitive (*naissant*) stage.

obligation of ordinary discourse as well as the stylistic energy of rhetoric but has something that it alone can offer: a way of selecting its words as aural entities that yield "syllabic hieroglyphs," which fulfill what Diderot sees as the "emblematic" function of poetry. The hieroglyph is a moment in (or out of?) the flow of words: its very syllabic sound seems, as if by a kind of onomatopoetic immediacy, to depict its object, thereby momentarily stopping that flow of words as a sequence of merely intelligible signs. Diderot provides a number of examples from poems (pp. 374–82) in which the sound of a syllable, as if functioning sensibly on its own within a word, has a directly mimetic power, apart from the intelligible function of the word. Again and again he searches for the hieroglyph that permits the syllable, as an aural element, to "resemble in sound" what its word is supposed to mean. As we have seen, for him it is this unique capacity that sets poetry apart from the rest of discourse.

Given the distinctions he has already suggested among the arts and the respective senses to which they are to appeal, Diderot can conclude his discussion of the operation of emblematics by extending it beyond poetry to make a general aesthetic claim: "Since each mimetic art has its own distinctive hieroglyphs, I would very much like some learned and discriminating intelligence to undertake a comparison among them . . . to assemble the common beauties of poetry, painting, and music to show the analogies among them . . . to seize upon the fugitive emblems of their expression."[8] And he proceeds to elaborate upon the emblematic differences in the aesthetic operations of poetry, painting, and music in confronting a similar object to be represented.

As for the discrete poem itself, Diderot surprisingly anticipates later theory by explicitly claiming that the syllabic hieroglyph makes every poem untranslatable into other words, since no synonym can carry over the aural element of the word it would replace.

> I used to believe, like everyone else, that one poet could be translated by another: that is an error of which I have disabused myself. One can ren-

8. Ibid., p. 385. Diderot is here suggesting to Abbé Batteux, to whom the *Letter* is addressed, how he should be changing the aim of his *Beaux-arts réduits à un même principe*, to which I refer by its English title in Chapter 3. Instead of, like Batteux, concentrating upon similarities, Diderot is here urging the discovery of the differences among the kinds of hieroglyphs in the several arts, with their different sensory appeals, even if, as a proper eighteenth-century theorist, he would grant the sameness of what they were seeking to represent (*la même image*).

der the thought; perhaps one can even have the good fortune to find the
equivalent of an expression . . . that is something, but it is not all. The
liberated emblem, the subtle hieroglyph which governs an entire description, and which derives from the distribution of longs and shorts in languages measured by quantity, and from the distribution of vowels
between the consonants in the words of every language: all that necessarily disappears even in the best translation. (P. 376)

Taking a position that anticipates the theoretical line culminating in
the New Criticism, Diderot is claiming that it is what cannot be
translated that makes the poem a poem and not another kind of discourse. Based on his statement quoted above, we must assume that
Diderot would make similar claims of indispensability for the ana-
logues to these hieroglyphs that he would allocate to the other
mimetic arts.

The rising interest in the aural dimension of poetry by Diderot,
Herder, and others called attention to the sensible potential that
accompanies poetry's intelligible character. As a result, poetry's relation to the other arts was radically changed now that it, like the
others, could be seen as being created by means of a perceptible
medium—even as it retained its intelligible character, of course. It is
true that from very early in the century poetry had been shown to
have this double character, at once distant from the other arts and
yet facing a similar representational challenge—that is, as an intelligible art strangely free of their sensory immediacies and yet somehow borrowing them. But the grounds for asserting such a relationship were totally different: in the early eighteenth century it was the
problematic character of poetry as a non-natural-sign art that provoked critics as they sought to relate poetry to the other (natural-
sign) arts. Within this framework, we have seen, poetry had to enter
into the family of arts as a disadvantaged child and on the terms of
the "sister arts" of the natural sign, but always with the acknowledgment that poetry was at a great distance from those arts.

I have already discussed more than once (briefly in Chapter 1 and
more extensively in Chapter 3) the spectrum of the arts developed
by Addison in his *Spectator* papers on "The Pleasures of the Imagination" (1712). This spectrum, used by Addison to demonstrate the
distinction between natural and arbitrary signs, was based not, as
in Diderot or Herder, on the medium of sensory reception but on
the character of the representation; not, that is, on the relation
between the work of art and its spectator or reader but on the rela-

tion—the degree of immediacy—between the work of art and its object of imitation in the world of actual experience.[9] I want here to move beyond my previous exposition of the spectrum (which runs from sculpture as the most "natural" of the arts through painting and literature on the way to music as the least) to note explicitly the impact it has on the theoretical development of the word as poetic medium.

In Addison's passage we see, well before Herder, the association of sculpture with the sense of touch, although in Addison it is sight as well as touch that sculpture can satisfy, provided that it is literally mimetic of its object—and Addison, of course, could conceive of no other kind of sculpture. Accurate representational painting can satisfy the sight but not the touch, since its three-dimensionality is illusory. So sculpture is the most natural of natural signs because in it the representation is closest to the thing itself, an unchanging substitute for it, indeed almost able to be mistaken for it. Painting may trick our sight into taking it also as a natural sign, if not as the object of representation itself, although in producing the illusion of the third dimension on the flat picture plane, technical devices enter that bring the painterly medium into prominence. In writing descriptions (and Addison limits the verbal and the musical arts to the attempt to reproduce the visual world in non-visual media), the verbal medium takes over totally if the poem is to bring into the reader's mind images that the words as signs in no way resemble. But such images *can* be made available, since words are intelligible and can thus lead the mind to use them as a medium, stimulating it to produce its own pictures from them. At the other end of the spectrum, farthest from the natural-sign end, is music, with arbitrary signs that do not carry the conventional meanings we find in language, signs that indeed do not have clearly specifiable meanings of any kind.

The character of this spectrum is such that primacy is given to the immediacy of the natural sign in a semiotic that rewards iconic similarity between the sign and its referent. In this unambiguously mimetic aesthetic, that which least impedes the pure imitation is best. And imitation is pure to the extent that it does not require intervention by a medium to allow the mind to make the comparison between the imitation and its "real" object. Addison has taken from Locke the concern that unlike pictures, language, in its distance from

9. The passage from Addison is quoted in full in Chapter 3, above.

our visual experience, does indeed mediate—and by mediating ob-
fuscates—the world it seeks to represent. Locke's characterization of
"the difficulty with language," because it functions as a medium, is
well known: "[Words] interpose themselves so much between our
understanding and the truth which it would contemplate and
apprehend, that, like the medium through which visible objects
pass, the obscurity and disorder do not seldom cast a mist before
our eyes, and impose upon our understandings."[10]

It is one of the fatal, often unacknowledged assumptions of the
mimetic aesthetic inherited from Plato that imitation is a downward
movement, so that each imitation must be inferior to its object, as a
copy is to the original. This direction is similarly assumed in Lockean epistemology. After all, as I have noted earlier, the relative values attributed to nature and to art are evident enough in Addison's
Lockean distinction between the "*primary* pleasures of the imagination" (those provided by our "sensation" of natural objects) and the
"*secondary* pleasures of the imagination" (those provided by our
"ideas," the stored memories of original sensations, especially as
they are jogged into our awareness by artistic representations of the
originally stimulating objects). The closer the imitation comes to its
object, the closer it comes to fooling us into believing that it is the
original, or at least to satisfying us that it is an adequate substitute.

Surely, then, art is less than life, and, even more surely, poetry is
less than painting. For poetry would seem hopelessly disadvantaged in its dependence on arbitrary rather than natural signs as it
seeks, nevertheless and however imperfectly, to lead the mind to
grasp the mimesis. Even painting, we saw, finds itself at some distance from its object because of its need to employ the illusionary
devices provided by its medium (a conventionally manipulated and
a conventionally perceived medium, Gombrich much later would
remind us) if we are to apprehend its mimetic equivalence. Should
we suggest, as Addison does not, that sculpture, because it is both
hard—in either metal or stone—and unmoving, is less completely a
natural sign than the live actors onstage in drama? This suggestion
would not hold for Addison, for whom the visual is paramount;
and within the visual, immediacy would seem unchallenged, even

10. This appears in chap. 9 ("Of the Imperfection of Words") of bk. 3 ("Of Words")
in Locke's *Essay Concerning Human Understanding,* ed. Alexander Campbell Fraser,
vol. 2 (Oxford: Clarendon Press), p. 119. See Chapter 3, n. 10, above, for an earlier discussion of this work.

if it is the result of the illusionary tricks worked by the medium. On these grounds the natural-sign appeal of sculpture or painting remains secure. According to the natural-sign aesthetic, once the viewer of a painting makes the adjustment that converts the two-dimensional canvas to the three-dimensional illusion, or the viewer of a sculpture is struck by the human form and overlooks the marble, the act of perception for such a viewer is as immediate as if it is confronting the thing itself.

If in Addison's extreme version of the natural-sign aesthetic, immediacy is all in the illusionary identification between the imitation and its object, then there is an inverse relation between the immediacy of representation and the function of the medium: the more unimpeded the mimesis, the less we use, or want, a medium to apprehend it. This is what "*im*mediacy" means. As distance increases between the imitation and its object—as immediate resemblance between them decreases—the more the medium must be brought into play as a middleman to help our minds make the comparison that leads the memory to recognition. It is in this sense that the medium is seen as an unfortunate necessity called forth by our falling away from natural-sign representation. We must remember, after all, that ever since the theorizing of a much earlier Neo-Platonic tradition, the movement from natural-sign to conventional-sign representation—from pictures to writing—has been conceived as a fall, analogous to and accompanying the Fall of man in theology.

It is no wonder that within this aesthetic the natural-sign arts have supremacy, and writing is seen as disadvantaged, seeking through its medium to achieve some small part of what comes naturally, and immediately, to the visual arts, which are, for all practical purposes, taken to be medium-free. But I hardly mean "for all practical purposes" as a negligible qualification, and to give it its due I must interrupt this presentation of an aesthetic that I am in danger of making too simple. In the passage just preceding the delineation of the spectrum—really an implied hierarchy—of the arts receding from sculpture to music, Addison makes a momentary but highly significant concession to the need for mediation by the perceiver's mind in any of the representational arts, including sculpture and painting. The concession is a necessary and reasonable one, though it puts in jeopardy his entire argument for the natural-sign immediacy of the visual arts. Addison is aware that the object imitated by the artist is not likely to represent the particular object previously experienced by the observer, but he invokes the empiri-

cist's unproblematic notion of how universals are induced from particulars to bridge the gap between them:

> When I say the ideas we receive from statues, descriptions, or such like
> occasions, are the same that were once actually in our view, it must not
> be understood that we had once seen the very place, action, or person
> which are carved or described. It is sufficient, that we have seen places,
> persons, or actions *in general*, which bear a resemblance, or at least some
> remote analogy with what we find represented. Since it is in the power
> of the imagination, when it is once stocked with *particular* ideas, to
> enlarge, compound, and vary them at her own pleasure. (*Spectator* 416
> [my italics])

This need for the intervention of the interpreting mind to mediate
between the object previously known by the observer and the
object being imitated should be enough to persuade Addison to
give up the quest for the natural sign in sculpture or painting,
though it isn't quite—at least to this point. He proceeds to his spectrum of the arts as if he had not undermined his assumption about
the visual immediacy of sculpture and painting by having introduced an interpretive role for the perceiver in all the arts. Having
returned to this assumption, he leaves to verbal representation the
mediating process that, presumably, pictures do not require.

Thus Addison must invoke the injunction *ut pictura poesis* with a
special urgency. Since he at this point supposes natural-sign representation to be the unquestioned objective of all the arts and still
treats the visual arts as if they functioned without a medium, he
will require that poetry, which is all medium, struggle against being
cut off from nature by its signs. If, because its signs are arbitrary
rather than natural, there must be a medium, there should, to the
extent that the poet can manage it, be no awareness of the medium
even in poetry. In this light we can better understand Addison's
attack on "false wit" (*Spectator* 58–62): "True wit consists in the
resemblance of ideas . . . false wit in the resemblance of words."[11]
His charge is that in "false wit" our consciousness of words *as*

11. *Spectator* 62. Earlier in this paper Addison has a lengthier description of the
"false wit" he would reject in favor of its opposite. "As true wit generally consists in
this resemblance and congruity of ideas, false wit chiefly consists in the resemblance
and congruity sometimes of single letters, as in anagrams, chronograms, lipograms,
and acrostics; sometimes of syllables, as in echoes and doggerel rhymes; sometimes
of words, as in puns and quibbles; and sometimes of whole sentences or poems, cast

words is forced to intrude upon what should be the unimpeded transparency of "wit" (here, happily, "true wit"), in which words are the self-effacing, naked pointers to "ideas," the latter defined as the mental residue of previous sensory experiences. "False wit," then, is that sort of writing in which the medium seems too conscious of itself. Instead, the medium, as an artificial and conventional intruder, should seek to thin itself into transparency, as it does in "true wit," in this way emulating (and fooling us into accepting it as a substitute for) natural-sign immediacy. Writing, poor thing that it is doomed to be, has its only hope in using its resources to come as close as it can to its more fortunate sister arts, though it will of course even at its best remain distant from them.

If we feel secure about the natural-sign ground to Addison's argument, on which the verbal arts stand diminished, we should indeed be startled by the theoretical inversion, beginning in the very next paragraph, to which I have called attention in Chapter 4, above. It is, as I have noted, a happy confusion that enters Addison's argument as he turns to defend the powers of the verbal art, even suggesting that for a number of reasons, poetic description may well "get the better of nature." Further, any claim that the verbal description is superior to the natural object of representation carries with it, *a fortiori*, the claim that the verbal description is superior to the faithful representation of the object in the natural signs of sculpture or painting. By this argument, a faithful ekphrasis would exceed *its* object. The very arbitrariness of arbitrary signs carries with it a freedom from absolute fidelity, together with a freedom of response to them by the reader, that may well permit the imitation to outdo its object. By inverting the hierarchy of value between original object and imitation—a hierarchy inherent to mimetic theory—the hierarchy of value between natural and arbitrary signs is similarly inverted. The verbal medium of poetry is thereby elevated, since it is given the power to raise art above nature. This position will lead with consistency to the claim that the media of all the arts (even the visual) should be given a role beyond the transparently representational, so that the very conception of unmediated natural signs would disappear. In the competition among such newly licensed media, it is the verbal that would then appear to have the advan-

---

into the figures of eggs, axes, or altars." Addison repeats this comparison, some of it almost verbatim, in the argument I am tracing in *Spectator* 416.

tage. The hierarchy of Addison's earlier passage has indeed been totally reversed.

Free of the pictorial artist's need to represent finite objects with visual precision, poets can use the very vagueness of their instrument—the fact that different readers will interpret words differently, will *see* different things, have different "ideas," on hearing the identical words—to work upon the reader's *emotions*. I have examined this claim at some length in Chapter 4, where it was urged more single-mindedly and extravagantly by Burke as part of his clear preference for the sublime over the beautiful. In Burke, as less single-mindedly in Addison, once the critic moves from the pictorial imperative—moves, that is, from the obligations of the *ut pictura poesis* tradition—which accompanies the mimetic theory of representation, language takes on certain advantages over the plastic and visual, the natural-sign, arts. This shift elevates poetry by creating a special value for its medium, whose virtue is its capacity to function just where mere picturing leaves off.

In creating this shift, Addison, and later Burke, set the grounds for an expressive aesthetic that begins to flourish when mimesis is abandoned. Mimesis, we remember, depended on the desire to de-emphasize all media, so that representation was to approximate, as best it could, a natural sign in its immediacy, without concern for mediation by the materials of art. The undoing of literary mimesis arose from a new concern for the verbal medium, which led to an interest in the functioning of other artistic media as well. Such an interest would lead one to wonder, as Gombrich later urged us to wonder, how representations are *made* so that an illusion of resemblance might occur. So my earlier statements about the "unambiguously mimetic aesthetic" of Addison were, of course, too hasty in that it is not unambiguous at all; and in its ambiguity it helped open the quest for a different aesthetic.

Let me return to my comparison of Addison with Herder. Addison's distinction between natural-sign art and arbitrary-though-conventional-sign art can be seen as an earlier version of Herder's distinction between the sensible and the intelligible arts, but only so long as we are aware of the difference between the two and the ambivalence in Herder's attitude toward his own distinction. The difference, I repeat, is that Addison is concerned with distinctions among ways in which the several arts relate to the objects they would represent, while Herder is concerned with distinctions among ways in which, in the several arts, the stimulating object relates to the sensory responses of percipients. Still, Addison, who is operating within what is later to become Herder's "aesthetic senses," similarly characterizes literature as an art trapped within the double nature of its signs, so that his placement of it eventually becomes equivocal. Indeed, we have seen Addison disrupt and subvert the simple coherence of his system in order to free the poem from the sensory limits of the finite object of representation—and to find in the poet's medium, language itself, the agent of that freedom.

Nevertheless, Herder's increased concern with art's appeal to the senses bestows a special importance upon the doubleness of linguistic sign functions, because despite the exemptions he bestows upon poetry as an intelligible medium, Herder, like Diderot before him, emphasizes the aural character of words, thereby allowing poetry to take on a uniquely ambiguous role. This ambiguity will continue to trouble the theory of poetry, in contrast to the unambiguously sensible arts, for some time. But it is a problem that will also open opportunities for that theory to make special claims for poetry.

Among those who soon follow, we find Shelley especially troubled in dealing with the problem. Within two pages of his *Defence of Poetry* Shelley gives us two apparently contradictory definitions of poetry as it relates to its sister arts: one stresses language's intelligible nature in contrast to the sensible nature of the other arts, and one stresses language's own sensible nature. In Chapter 4 I focused upon the first of these, ignoring the second because my objectives there were limited to tracking the tradition deriving from Longinus as an alternative to the natural-sign aesthetic. Here I want to provide a more balanced and hence more adequate treatment to what is a very complex document. Such a treatment calls for an exposition of the two concepts that examines both the extent to which they are mutually contradictory and the possibilities of their being reconciled.

We saw in Chapter 4 that Shelley's more romantic and idealist definition was an outgrowth of the Longinian conception of poetry as the one natural—because immediate—expression of human nature, in contrast to the distancing of poetry from nature in the natural-sign aesthetic. According to this definition, poetry ("those arrangements of language, and especially metrical language") is seen as the unmediated creation of the imagination, in contrast to the other arts, which have to do their business within the sensory limitations of their respective media. For this Shelley, the imagination speaks in language immediately and without obstacle, so that language is described as the very "hieroglyphic" of thought. Hence poetry is superior to the arts that are dependent on external media. Language, Shelley tells us (and I quote this passage in full here),

> is a more direct representation of the actions and passions of our internal being, and is susceptible of more various and delicate combinations, than color, form, or motion, and is more plastic and obedient to the control of that faculty of which it is the creation. For language is arbitrarily produced by the imagination, and has relation to thoughts alone; but all other materials, instruments, and conditions of art have relations among each other, which limit and interpose between conception and expression. The former [language] is as a mirror which reflects, the latter [media of the other arts] as a cloud which enfeebles, the light of which both are media of communication. Hence the fame of sculptors, painters, and musicians, although the intrinsic powers of the great masters of these arts may yield in no degree to that of those who have employed language as the hieroglyphic of their thoughts, has never equalled that of poets.[12]

Though poetry is seen as metrical language, it is still claimed to be "more obedient" to the imagination than other media are: in poetry "conception" speaks at once as "expression," without the interposings that limit the expression of conceptions in the other arts. The less an art suffers a limitation of this sort, the better, for Shelley is lodging the creative power in the conception that precedes the expressive act. Consequently, "sculptors, painters, and musicians," though of "intrinsic powers" equal to the poet's, cannot come up to the accomplishments of the poet, because they are fated to accept the enfeebling clouds cast by their media, each carrying the limits imposed by its internal relations, while in the poet the imagination, unconstrained by physical limits, can freely speak. Language, then, is a universalizing as well as an instantaneous medium that transcends the differentiations displayed by the media of the sensible arts.

Shelley has turned around the order of the arts because he has proceeded on a different basis for their ordering. Like others (Diderot and Herder) whom we have examined in this chapter, he is ordering the arts on the basis of the relations of each to its medium rather than on the basis of the immediacy with which each can represent an external object. Unlike those others, however, Shelley still

---

12. *A Defence of Poetry,* in *The Complete Works of Percy Bysshe Shelley,* ed. Roger Ingpen, vol. 7 (New York: Gordian Press, 1965), p. 113.

separates poetry from the other arts, but now because it alone, as language, is close to the conceptual source of artistic expression, suffering no interference by what apparently is an unresisting and uncontributing medium. The other arts, by contrast, are distanced from that source, each impeded by too independently ordered a medium that has its own resistant ways.

If, in Addison's ordering of the arts, poetry was a less "natural" and hence more mediated art in its contrast to the transparency of the unmediated arts of the natural sign, in Shelley (at least in these paragraphs) it is the plastic arts that have too much medium in contrast to the immediacy of poetry as an automatic act of imagination. But this reversal can occur only because the source of artistic obligation for Shelley has shifted to the imagination and has turned away from any external object of representation, which was the source of artistic obligation according to mimetic doctrine. So long as that source was the object of representation, as it was in the natural-sign aesthetic, any medium that did not produce a sensible resemblance was an obstacle to the immediacy of representation, and it was poetry alone, with its dependence on the arbitrary and hence unnatural instrument of language, that was shut out. But once the poet's imagination becomes the source, then it is the other arts that are seen as shut out, because of their dependence on alien media, while it is poetry alone that is blessed with immediacy, since it shares its language with an imagination that automatically speaks it. Language, as the instant evocation of the imagination, confers an unmediated naturalness upon poetry as its art.

But once Shelley has permitted "metrical language" to enter his definition of poetry, he must open himself to a difficulty that forces him, just two paragraphs later, to take back the exemption—the special freedom from interference by a medium—that he has claimed for poetry. Shelley now must turn about and follow Diderot in acknowledging that meter is a device that a poet must fashion the poem to accommodate: it is a device that will distinguish poetry from other uses of language by converting language into a perceptible medium that is no longer the automatic speech of the imagination but a hard-won series of verbal adjustments. In other words, Shelley is now also attributing to poetry the same sensible character that he had before seen as limiting its rival arts and thus differentiating them from poetry, which he had before privileged by insisting on its lack of just such a sensible medium. The resistant internal relations that order the other media, thereby limiting "sculptors, painters, and musicians," are now found challenging the poet in the language of poetry as well.

> Sounds as well as thoughts have relations both between each other and towards that which they represent, and a perception of the order of those relations has always been found connected with a perception of the order of the relations of thoughts. Hence the language of poets has ever affected a certain uniform and harmonious recurrence of sound, without which it were not poetry, and which is scarcely less indispensable to the communication of its influence, than the words themselves, without reference to that peculiar order. Hence the vanity of translation; it were as wise to cast a violet into a crucible that you might discover the formal principle of its color and odor, as seek to transfuse from one language to another the creations of a poet. The plant must spring again from its seed, or it will bear no flower—and this is the burthen of the curse of Babel. (P. 114)

In acknowledging "the vanity of translation," Shelley is apparently echoing Diderot and anticipating the critical tradition that leads to mid-twentieth-century modernism. According to this conception, all products of language, each of them a version of the infinite possible dispositions of language, must be radically differentiated from one another. If the first Shelley insisted upon the uniquely *universal* character of poetry as language, emphasizing its capacity to unify all discourse by speaking as the immediate voice of the unfettered imagination, this second Shelley insists upon the uniquely *particular* disposition of words that is the untranslatable poem, emphasizing its differentiated status in relation to all other verbal entities. Even at the cost of self-contradiction, then, Shelley wants to maintain the doubleness of language as the medium of poetry, wanting it to explore and exploit its own order even as it seeks to represent the external order of reality (though always for Shelley, we must remember, as revealed only by the internal order of thought).

The contradiction seems absolute. On the one hand, we find the Shelley (whom I am calling the first Shelley) who sees the language of poetry—created as an immediate expression responding to the desire of the imagination to express its autonomous conception—as the "hieroglyphic of [the poet's] thoughts." This conception, apparently already complete, only seeks expression as translation and hence seeks to ride roughshod over any resistance from language-making during the expressive act. It thus operates independently of the poet's will as maker and is not the product of technical labor. Conception, once conceived, automatically translates into expression, although unfortunate disparities are introduced during the making (expressive) process. Linguistic intrusion is an unhappy necessity for the pure visions of the poet.

> Poetry is not like reasoning, a power to be exerted according to the determination of the will. A man cannot say, "I will compose poetry." . . . when composition begins, inspiration is already on the decline, and the most glorious poetry that has ever been communicated to the world is probably a feeble shadow of the original conception of the poet. I appeal to the great poets of the present day, whether it be not an error to assert that the finest passages of poetry are produced by labour and study. (Pp. 135–36)

On the other hand, we find the Shelley (my second Shelley) who sees the language of poetry as a creatively resistant medium of art, which, subject to its own operational rules, is to be worked by the poet into a single, unique, and untranslatable verbal sequence. Only in that special expression can the poet's conception be found. The first Shelley, as a proper romantic, divorces poetry from a dependence on the shaped verbal object and thus can see poetry as a universal reflected in all human activity, a primitive instinct that is active "even in the infancy of society" (p. 110); the second Shelley seems closer to the neoclassical Diderot who allowed the technical accomplishments of the poet to enter only when the primitive stage of language had been sophisticated into a more formal stage, in which rhythmic and harmonic orders could be imposed upon what had been the elementary language of ordinary conversation.[13]

But a more sympathetic reading, I want to suggest, may find a way to reconcile these oppositions while preserving their antithetical relation to one another. As in the dialogues of Shelley's master, Plato (and especially in that masterful model dialogue, the *Symposium*), what we may be dealing with is not so much contradiction as a controlled dialectic in which the key terms reflect different and apparently contradictory definitions as they move from level to level. Shelley himself, perhaps borrowing Coleridge's distinction between "poetry" and "poem" (but using the term "poetry" for both), explicitly distinguishes "poetry in an universal sense" from "poetry

13. See n. 7, above.

in a more restricted sense." This is a distinction between the poetry that may occur here and there in all uses of language and the poetry of those special verbal forms that we call poems.

These two uses of "poetry" represent distinct and opposed semiotic systems as well as distinct historical moments both in collective human culture and in their reflections in the individual human psyche. And Shelley's *Defence* is organized as a treatise in a sequence that flows from the broad, universal "poetry" through ever-narrowing banks to the restrictive dimensions of the single, technically defined poem, then broadens outward again to the unlimited domain, the infinite sea of all human life and thought. There is also the alternative metaphor of the circle, which Shelley explicitly calls upon: he makes it narrower and "still narrower" until, enclosed about the individual, untranslatable poem as a circumscribed form, it "distends, and then bursts the circumference," moving outward once more to the poetic transformation of the cosmos itself as universally moral in its rhythm and harmony and hence "perpetual sympathy" (p. 115).

Within these ever-moving alternatives there is also a half-hidden myth of origin—the source, the fountain—followed by the myth of the Fall. (I anticipated these two above, in suggesting a comparison between Shelley and Diderot in how they related poetry to the primitive and the formal.) The first Shelley makes the claim for an original, universal language of identities, a language that "is vitally metaphorical," in which every word is a metaphor—a creatively poetic leap into naming a universe—is being continually invented during "the youth of the world": "In the infancy of society every author is necessarily a poet, because language itself is poetry." Consequently, "every original language near to its source is in itself the chaos of a cyclic poem" (pp. 111–12). Here indeed is a universal poetry, in which the "poet participates in the eternal, the infinite, and the one" with "conceptions" in which "time and place and number are not. The grammatical forms which express the moods of time, and the difference of persons, and the distinctions of place, are convertible" (p. 112).

It is only later, following the Fall, represented here by "the burthen of the curse of Babel," that Shelley (now the second Shelley) must come to terms with endless differentiation as it strikes both the human professions and human works. "Distinctions," like "grammatical forms" themselves, are no longer "convertible." The division into single poems and, worse, poems made untranslatable by their construction out of different language systems becomes inevitable. Rhythm and harmony are reduced from the most universal to the most individualized: reduced from immediately apprehensible cosmic powers—or at a lower, human level, from political or moral powers, or lower yet, from the powers of all language—to the limited harmony achievable within the metrical forms of the single poem.[14]

Once the Fall is invoked to splinter the original unity, then only the poem, as the microcosmic remnant of universal rhythm and harmony, can lead us back out toward a reestablishment of macrocosm. Through its own single nature each poem still can—or rather, must—recreate the essence of rhythm and harmony so that, breaking the circumference of that narrow circle of locked-in meanings, that rhythm and harmony can again establish themselves in the moral, the political, and the cosmic reaches of the human imagination, now capable of being re-unified by this act of an ever outward-opening linguistic act.

So the apparent contradiction in the two Shelleys I have sketched may be seen as two semiotic formulas or two mythic phases that, in their opposition, reflect two ways of conceiving the relation between language user and language itself, as a consequence of the changing relation between language and cosmos. Apparent opposition between the two conceptions may thus yield to complementarity, or at least to a pseudo-historical alternation between the myth of origin and the myth of loss, each reflected in its own semiotic and in conflict with the other for control of the essay. The prelapsarian claim for a language that is beyond "time and place and number" is a reversion to a Neo-Platonic mythic anthropology, reminiscent of Vico and Blake, in which all differences are dissolved, or rather have not yet come to exist. It is in this state that language can be claimed as the one "natural" medium that can express our innermost being in its act of capturing all that is outside it, here and now or everywhere and for all time. We can read the first Shelley within this semiotic of a unitary linguistic state before the Fall. In it language, as the

14. In his own discourse here Shelley himself seems alone privileged to retain original linguistic powers that confer an unlimited verbal reach: in Platonic fashion, he allows the loose metaphorical potential of his words "rhythm" and "harmony" to run, uncritically and without differentiation, through all the levels of their literal and figurative meanings from the most tightly poetic [the metrical rhythm of the line] to the most openly cosmic ["the echo of the eternal music"], presumably operating with identical applicability on each of the levels (pp. 114–15).

direct and unimpeded evocation of imagination and thought, needs
no mediation and thus stands apart from the materials of the other
arts. But after the Fall marked by the splinterings of Babel, the differentiated languages, now denied universality and resigned to particularization, require the mediating act of poem-making to speak; in
this they join the other arts, which are dependent, each of them, on
their own mediated languages, that is, on the graded orders of the
various sensible media.

Although the first, Neo-Platonic Shelley clearly seems to domi-
nate the essay, my concerns here and in what follows lead me to concentrate on that second Shelley, who, like the rest of us, must make
peace with language in its (and our) fallen state. Until well into our
own century, aesthetics has had to consider each of the aesthetic
media, now also including the words of poetry, as having what Shelley termed a "peculiar order" within whose requirements artistic
creation must undergo its refining process. Thus in tracing the making of the art object, in poetry as in the more unambiguously sensible arts, critics have had to complicate all questions about representation by moving beyond naive mimesis, which apparently depended
only upon natural signs, which, in their assumption of resemblance,
precluded the formative role of any medium. And arguments like
that of the second Shelley pointed a direction for later theorists.

Poetry had been isolated in a *disadvantaged* way from the family of
the other arts under the terms of a natural-sign aesthetic that responded to a naively mimetic interest in the objects to be represented;
and poetry came to be isolated in a *privileged* way from the family of
the other arts in the expressive aesthetic that responded to an exclusive interest in the means by which the imagination can speak directly. In both extremes poetry's separation from the family of arts
was accompanied by its essential oneness with the family of verbal
discourse at large. But once a conception like that of the second Shelley restores poetry to the family of arts, it must leave the family of
other forms of discourse—and indeed thrives on its differentiation
from them. Theory is moving toward a third aesthetic in which all artists can be seen as struggling with their medium for an expression in
which that struggle plays a shaping role.

By reminding us that poetry also has its aural aspect, the theorist
turns its words into a sensible medium also, thereby joining it to the
other arts in pursuing a common aesthetic intent: to emerge out of the
artists' engagement with the several "peculiar orders" that constitute their respective media. In contrast to the natural-sign aes-

thetic, which separated poetry from the sensible arts because its intelligibility required mediation, the aesthetic that puts the medium at the center of artistic creativity not only restores poetry to the arts but gives it a central place among them. (It may, indeed, occupy a preferred place in view of the fact that poetry cannot, whatever its special relations to its medium, completely lose its referential character as a piece of language, not altogether unlike other pieces of language. So theorists moving in this direction are not likely to give up an imperialistic desire to allow poetry—uniquely among the arts—to have it both ways.)

In order to trace this development beyond Shelley, then, I will leave the first Shelley and go forward from the second, less Neo-Platonic Shelley, the theorist for whom poets are to seize upon the plasticity of a fallen language to make it into a medium, one among the several media of the arts. This Shelley, though endangering his own theoretical consistency, anticipates that direction in twentieth-century aesthetics which has concentrated upon the role of the medium as that recalcitrant element in all the arts whose manipulation by the artist opens expressive opportunities for creating a special object.[15]

In retrospect, we can trace a rather obvious sequence among the exemplary figures I have thus far treated. In Addison's principal position, which asserts the immediacy of natural signs and the priority of natural-sign art, there is a naive philosophical realism that grounds the dependent relationship between the artistic imitation and its point of origin, the clearly discerned and authoritative object in the world of our visual experience. But Addison draws back from the consequences of such claims, which are so detrimental to the place of poetry, and smuggles in a contrary scheme that moves toward idealism: it suggests that the priority belongs, rather, to the appeal to imagination in the stimulus of signs that achieve an independence from, and thus a potential superiority to, their referents. In Burke, several decades later, we found an exaggeration of these latter claims. Herder in several places extends this idealism by means

---

15. I could trace in Coleridge a precedent for Shelley's inconsistent treatment of poetry—sometimes as an expression of private vision, sometimes as an expression of an aural medium. For Coleridge as idealist, the poem would be an expression of the primary imagination; for him as a more technical critic, the poem would be an expression of the secondary imagination, which, in order to exercise its creativity, "diffuses, dissolves, and dissipates" all that it receives from the primary. See my extended treatment of this problem in *Theory of Criticism: A Tradition and Its System* (Baltimore: Johns Hopkins University Press, 1976), pp. 95–97, 114–31.

of his theory of "aesthetic senses," which begins with sensation but ends in the soul or imagination, so that poetry may transcend sense as *the* Platonic art beyond art. (I am here passing over those moments in Herder, as in Diderot before him, of strong commitment to the aural, and hence the sensible, dimension of poetry, since this interest was, for the most part, passed over by romantic theorists in their gnostic pursuit of transcendence.)

It is this exemption of poetry from the sense-bound and hence medium-bound arts that permits Shelley, even more the idealist, to proclaim the special role of poetry, which like all language is "arbitrarily produced by the imagination" to be its very "hieroglyphic." But in the striking turnabout we have investigated, Shelley also finds in poetry, as a meter-bound language, a dependence on the "peculiar order" of a sensuously limited medium similar in function to the media he earlier—as idealist—had attributed to the other arts as their inhibiting materiality. Here is a concession to the sensory basis of the poetic art that moves back toward material reality, although it is only a subsidiary concession in Shelley, who for the most part reverts to his idealistic attachments.

But this momentary recognition by Shelley foreshadows the central concern early in our own century about the creative role played by medium in all the arts, including the poetic. What Shelley has briefly glimpsed—and, before him, what Diderot and Herder had forcefully, if sporadically, proposed—is ignored through long decades during which idealist fervor about the imagination and poetry's magical appeal to it continued largely unabated. The absolute character of this idealism is perhaps climaxed in Benedetto Croce's anti-materialistic insistence on the identity of "intuition" and "expression"; and we must remember that he kept "expression" totally distinct from the process of "externalization."[16]

It was another intuitionist philosopher, Croce's contemporary Henri Bergson, who, unlike Croce, distinguished intuition from ordinary expression and thereby accorded a special role to the arts—and especially for the language of poetry as a specially empowered medium—in giving us access to an otherwise unavailable vision. For Bergson intuition, as a contemplative activity, can occur only when we break through the veil created by the practical activities that respond to our everyday needs. The arts permit that break-

16. See Croce's *Aesthetic*, chaps. 1–4 and the different position taken in chaps. 13–15. I treat this difficulty in *Theory of Criticism*, pp. 52–53.

through. But still in the wake of Diderot, Bergson would classify the arts according to the several senses: "Even for such of us as she [nature] has made artists, it is by accident, and on one side only, that she has lifted the veil. In one direction only has she forgotten to rivet the perception to the need. And since each direction corresponds to what we call a *sense*—through one of his senses, and through that sense alone, is the artist usually wedded to art. Hence, originally, the diversity of arts."[17]

The poet has the special problem of dealing with language, which, in the service of practicality, normally consists only of the stereotyped labels that freeze the flow of our experience ("the strains of our inner life's unbroken melody" [p. 150]) in order for us to function successfully in our daily tasks. Thus, Bergson claims, "words—with the exception of proper nouns—all denote genera. The word, which only takes note of the most ordinary function and commonplace aspect of the thing, intervenes between it and ourselves, and would conceal its form from our eyes, were that form not already masked beneath the necessities that brought the word into existence" (p. 153).

To break through to intuition, then, verbal artists must struggle to make words function abnormally, in spite of their normal tendency, as it were:

> They contrive to make us see something of what they have seen: by rhythmical arrangement of words, which thus become organized and animated with a life of their own, they tell us—or rather suggest—things that speech was not calculated to express. Others delve yet deeper still. Beneath these joys and sorrows which can, at a pinch, be translated into language, they grasp something that has nothing in common with language, certain rhythms of life and breath that are closer to man than his inmost feelings, being the living law—varying with each individual—of his enthusiasm and despair, his hopes and regrets. By setting free and emphasizing this music, they force it upon our attention; they compel us, willy-nilly, to fall in with it, like passers-by who join in a dance. (P. 156)

Here is a philosophically grounded statement that re-emphasizes the special task, as well as privilege, reserved for poetry alone among the many uses of language. Having grown out of the tendency I

17. Henri Bergson, *Laughter: An Essay on the Meaning of the Comic*, authorized trans. Cloudesley Brereton and Fred Rothwell (New York: Macmillan, 1911), p. 155.

have traced from Longinus to Mazzoni, Diderot, Herder, and their heirs among the romantics, it is the basis for the theory of poetry as a fruitful deviation from normal discourse, a theory that was developed into the critical practice of high modernism. The way to this practice was cleared by a number of English theorists who, in the first three decades of this century, answered Crocean idealism with a firm commitment to the poet as manipulator of words: among many others by A. C. Bradley (in "Poetry for Poetry's Sake," 1909), by T. E. Hulme (in "Romanticism and Classicism" and "Bergson's Theory of Art," written in the teens and published posthumously in 1924), and, perhaps most strongly and systematically, by the distinguished British philosopher Samuel Alexander (in "The Creative Process in the Artist's Mind," from *Beauty and Other Forms of Value,* 1933, though many of the ideas first appear in his *Art and the Material,* 1925).

As the following composite quotation should make clear, Alexander's attack on the position, which we recognize as Croce's, that would deny the formative role of the medium in the making of the art object is explicit; explicit also is his inclusion of poetry among the arts that share this making process.[18]

> The external work being an organic part of the creative process, it ceases to be possible to hold that the external material is needed merely in order to communicate the artistic experience to others (p. 59). . . . it follows that Wordsworth was, I must believe, mistaken, when he said that there are many poets in the world, who have "the vision and the faculty divine; yet wanting the accomplishment of verse"; as if verse were a charm superadded to the real poetic gift (p. 60). . . . In general when the artist paints from his image or describes it in words, he is moulding it, in the product itself (p. 69). . . . The material of the art is a vital part of the artistic process. In poetry for instance the sound of the words, their rhythm, metre, etc., are integral to the work, and perhaps the element of prior value (p. 72). . . . The work of art being the expression or embodiment in material and contemplated for its own sake and not merely as a sign, however much it owes its form to the artist, reveals to him his own meaning, and the artistic experience is not so much invention as discovery (p. 73).

18. The quotations are taken from *Beauty and Other Forms of Value* (London: Macmillan, 1933).

It was David Wight Prall, a distinguished American aesthetician of considerable influence some decades back (however neglected he has been for some time), who completed the shift from an idealistic concentration upon mental creation to a realistic concentration upon a plastic, indeed a physical, medium. It was he who most precisely addressed himself to the role of the medium, at once sensuous and recalcitrant, an independent force requiring the artist to work toward finding a desired shape within its own resistant orders. He thus carried out the injunctions of Bradley and Alexander by exploiting and specifying the "peculiar orders" we saw delineated by Shelley. Further, by analogizing poetry to the other arts, though only while specifying its crucial difference from them, he created a theoretical space for poetics which later critics would seek to fill.

Prall's major contribution to conceiving of language as material for art was his analysis of what he termed "aesthetic surface," with the word "aesthetic" restricted to its original meaning in the realm of immediate sensation.[19] According to Prall, aesthetic surface, as it functions in art, is composed of "elements of sensuous content" (p. 59), which "in themselves fall into any known or felt natural order or arrangement." Within this order are "variations defined in and by such an intrinsic natural structure, as the variations in color and sound and shape give rise to in our minds" (p. 62). Prall finds these orders to possess "a complete and well-defined objective native character, clearly discriminable specific natures, often even very subtle and refined and exciting" (p. 63). So a sensuous surface, if it is to be adequate for artistic manipulation, must possess "relations objectively clear in given orders and a defining structure of variation" (p. 64). It is on these grounds that he excludes tastes, odors, and bodily feelings from the domain of art because—lacking this objective, discriminable, intrinsic order—they cannot present eligible aesthetic surfaces. But those "materials" that are eligible—color, sound, and shape or spatial form—"present objective structural orders intrinsic to their qualitative variation, through which we have control over them to build them into the complex formal beauties characteristic of the human arts and no longer the beauties of elements alone or of merely accidental natural combinations" (p. 68).[20]

19. This discussion occurs in his *Aesthetic Judgment* (New York: Thomas Y. Crowell, 1929).

20. Aesthetic surface thus becomes the ground for Prall's distinction between natural and humanly created beauty, between nature and art.

Further, there must be no confusion among the orders that function within each of the arts, no metaphorical cross-attributions that
lead us to speak, for example, of the "color" of a sound: "Colors have
as hues neither shape nor direction but only hue, sounds may move
in space and time, but only sounds have pitch, and pitch itself has
neither dimensions nor shape nor direction, nor is even duration of
sound its actual intrinsic quality. Thus we have marked and distinguished from one another these three orders of variation, each intrinsic to its own realm" (p. 75). We may well hear an echo here of the
distinctions among the senses made by Diderot. Herder's "aesthetic
senses," together with his characterizations of the several arts in accordance with them, also seem still to be functioning, although Prall
has transferred them to the physical realm of his "natural" orders, at
once "objective" and "discriminable."[21]

Whether created by nature or by convention, the intrinsic, discriminable order within the artists' medium is a given, is something the
artist discovers as being there without being asked for, something
within whose limits the artist must work. Prall sees the sensuous
properties of the medium as possessing a measured variation that
permits invention and manipulation, disposition and redisposition,
although its own gradation has some degree of inflexible resistance
built into it. Whether it is the spectrum of colors or the tonic scale, it
functions in accordance with its own principles of measured variation, and it is come upon by the artist—outside and independent of
the artist and the creative project at hand—so that there is no choice
but to work within what the "peculiar order" permits.

But when we observe Prall's concentration upon the orders of
color, sound, and shape, we must once more ask, what about poetry? For we may well suspect him of repeating the exclusions or exemptions with which poetry has been cursed or blessed by earlier
theorists. So long as the "orders" are defined as Prall defines them,
he will have trouble with poetry's strange medium. He may grant
that the aural aspect of words, exploited in meter, rhyme, and other
phonic devices, constitute such an order, but he argues that these elements alone do not account for poetic language. Though he attends
to the force of poetry's musical character, it is the intelligible force of

21. I will not here question, as I will most strenuously in another place, whether the
orders so confidently called "natural" by Prall are really any more than conventional.
For here it is the capacity of their sensory elements to be manipulated, rather than
their metaphysical or human origin, that concerns me.

its words, and not their sensible force, that he claims to be their primary determinant: "The content of verse is not, even as directly perceived, mainly tonal or even mainly sound" (p. 168). "Poetry has an audible aesthetic surface, but it is not appreciated as this surface alone, as the very slightly poetic effect of poetry read aloud in an unknown language is enough to convince us" (pp. 168–69). It fails "as properly musical composition" because it is instead "the printed discourse of the human mind, which, though it feels and hears, finds its proudest and most dignified satisfaction in functioning as the strictly knowing intellect" (p. 168).

Even if we isolated the rhythm of a poem, he would have us find that pure measure must give way to the cadences of normal spoken language:

> On the other hand, rhythm in the elementary sense of time-pattern in measured intervals, if it is to fit intelligible discourse at all, must be variable and subtle enough, along with establishing felt recurrence, not to interfere with such prior demands in the same sensuous realm as give meaning to verse. At least verse rhythms must be free enough of numerically measured regularity not to distort into unrecognizableness the natural linguistic, and hence symbolically significant, time-values and stresses of words and sentences in discourse. (P. 170)

This discussion appears in the midst of Prall's attempt to add rhythm as a temporal aesthetic order, an attempt that leads him beyond the aesthetic. What he discloses here about poetry leads him to question whether rhythm is an appropriate order to be handled, like the others, as exhibiting merely an aesthetic surface or whether it is an expressive order. This introduction of the expressive as a higher order than the aesthetic leads to a devaluing of the distinctions he has worked hard to establish. The aesthetic, limited to sensuous surface, indeed remains superficial next to Prall's interest in the expressive, which probes beneath it. He has undermined the artistic importance of aesthetic surface, which for him is not even an inevitable gateway to the expressive.

Like the two-in-one art of poetry, rhythm itself "is on the border between the sensuous materials of beauty and the expressive beauty of structure, and we may appropriately proceed from our account of rhythm to the meaning of beautiful form in general as distinguished from material sensuous beauty, and so to the relation which aesthetic surface bears to the nature of art" (p. 176). What he concludes is that "artistic value," deriving from the beauty of "expressive" elements, overrides "aesthetic value," which derives from sensuous "surface." It is evident that Prall's is an expressive theory in which artistic beauty, as expressive, transcends the "aesthetic," which we have seen him condescendingly limit to the sensuous, in the usual way we have been shown by Platonists. He has been forced to turn upon his own earlier sensuous principle for distinguishing among the arts, perhaps *because* he could not capture poetry within it. Thus he gives up what he earlier sought to establish, using poetry as the wedge to move beyond the sensuous to the expressive, just as language, with its sensible-intelligible duality, must do as it leads the arts in the breakthrough from the aesthetic to the artistic.

Prall has, after all, turned out less of an improvement upon Herder than I suggested above. Indeed, he has repeated Herder's move of following a hard-won, sensuously based distinction among the arts by using a transcendent poetry to undo it. The difficulty that Prall has not been able to overcome is the mechanistic relation he has established between aesthetic surface and artistic expression. For him the first does not begin to account for the second: our analysis of the first provides no purchase for an analysis of the second.[22] Because, like Herder, he is led on by his special devotion to poetry's peculiar nature, Prall is primarily dedicated to an expressive theory that leads him to an idealistic departure from the sensuous, whose measurable qualities he has analyzed so precisely. In the end, then, the arts are conceived as "more than their sensuous content," so that Prall must ultimately deny the validity of his distinctions among the arts, as arts determined by their sensuous surfaces. Instead of such material distinction-making, it is the idealistic, *je-ne-sais-quoi* sameness of expression, as applicable to all the arts, that is the quality that brings them together. At the same time we must note that they are brought together on grounds that Prall believes more suited to poetry than to the others.

Nevertheless, Prall's interest in exploring the limits and dimensions of the aesthetic medium, even if finally incomplete, will con-

22. I am indebted to Eliseo Vivas, who as my teacher first (in 1946) initiated me into the mysteries of aesthetics, for pointing out the special importance of the work of Prall in any discussion of aesthetic media. He also first warned me of the need to extend the role of the "aesthetic" beyond the limits Prall imposed upon it and to allow it to merge into the "artistic," from which Prall kept it separate. See Vivas's discussion of the matter in "The Artistic Transaction," in *The Artistic Transaction and Essays on Theory of Literature* (Columbus: Ohio State University Press, 1963), esp. p. 31.

tinue to shape discourse about aesthetics. We have seen him abandon his own effort to find a linkage between poetry and the other
arts based on sensuous surface, so that he ends by granting poetry
its usual exemption to permit it to lead the escape to the expressive;
but his failed attempt has proceeded with a care that justifies the attention that literary critics will continue to pay to language as a manipulable medium. To the extent that poetic language is treated as
an aesthetic medium, it is torn from its relations to language outside
poetry, so-called normal language, and is instead related to the
other arts. That is, poetic language is not to be treated as if its functions were those of words operating in discourse generally. Instead,
as properly poetic, it becomes a medium with a sensuous and manipulable surface that can influence its other functions, though we
can interrelate these only as we insist on treating the poem as something other than just language. But because it *is* language, after all,
theorists from Herder to Prall draw back from treating the poetic medium *only* as it functions like the media of the other arts, reserving
for it some of the exemptions obviously present in all language, *including* the poetic, as an intelligible instrument.

Still, through an insistence like Prall's on emphasizing the initial
(for him the pre-expressive) role of the sensuous surface, the temptation to treat poetic language as another aesthetic medium and not
just as another piece of language, and thus to treat poetry as one of
the arts on these grounds, will nag at the theorist. And the way is
open for others who, with a more organic theory, will get beyond
Prall's separation of the aesthetic from the artistic and allow a breakthrough into the expressive by the sensuous surface. That move will
bring the poetic closer to the other arts in its aesthetic functioning (in
the original sense of "aesthetic" defined at the outset of this chapter)
and thus bring it further from the rest of linguistic functioning.

What I have been tracing in theorists since Herder is a tendency
to move poetry from its role as a purely intelligible art to its role, at
least in part, as one of the sensuous arts. It has been a gradual shift
in emphasis from the "mind's eye" to the ear, from the indirect visual effects of poetic words to their direct aural effects. This tendency
will be intensified in those I treat after Prall. Accompanying it is a
shift in emphasis from the poetic word's referential function to its
sensuous function, from its function of directing our mind away
from the word and toward the realm of things to its function of having an immediate sensory impact and thus directing attention to itself as if it were a thing.

(This shift in emphasis occurs despite our awareness that since poetry has been established as a written art for centuries, the effects of the poem as read are rarely, if ever, really oral or *im*mediately oral. They are graphic too, indeed sometimes immediately graphic, and there may be some immediately sensuous responses to graphic relationships. Even if at other times we make imaginatively aural transfers from the graphic effects, these are hardly directly sensuous, so that aesthetics must treat them as illusionarily or metaphorically aural at best and hence as mediated — perhaps as mediated as we found the pictorial function of words to be under the natural-sign aesthetic. As the role of aural elements has receded, critics of poetry, more and more conscious of themselves as readers rather than listeners, have come to respond to the various elements of graphic play, so that the poetic medium is seen as more subtly textual. However they adjust the consideration of poetry as speech with that of poetry as writing, formal critics have concerned themselves with an aural-graphic dimension that allows poets to engage the developing text *as if* they too had a sensuous medium. I return to this thorny issue a bit later in this chapter.)

Part of the shift that I earlier noted was the changing of the model art from the visual arts (at the natural-sign end of Addison's spectrum) to music (at the non-natural-sign end). That shift was important in recognizing the aural element (even if only as a graphic illusion) as an "aesthetic surface" that helped create our awareness of the need for a manipulable medium for poetry. Now theory could move on from the fact that the indirect visual impact of the poetic "image," as realized in words, was not related to the sensuous (and hence immediately "aesthetic") character of the poetic medium, as the aural impact was. The pictorial model, which Burke had helped us see would only inhibit what the word can "naturally" perform in its affective role, was rejected because it had to subordinate the art of poetry to those plastic arts for which the pictorial role was not only appropriate but immediate. And it is the special advantages of the verbal art that theorists subsequently work to establish. The aural, or "musical," element may have been introduced as part of the poet's material, but that material has attained a dual power by retaining its other element, the word's lingering referential power, though now influenced, if not transformed, by its aural impact. In taking on this double character, this kind of language turns into a complex medium that would justify establishing poetry, once it has been granted a unique semiotic, as the newly ordained model art.

Consequently, this developing line of theory, with its debt to the lingering Platonism of Herder, sought to realize for poetry that grand merger of the sensible and the intelligible—the sensible rendering of the intelligible—which was the dream of the Renaissance Neo-Platonists we surveyed in Chapter 5. This line now could work to achieve the uniquely privileged status of words as aesthetic material in their combining of the sensible appeal of music and the intelligible appeal of non-natural sign "images." But more had to be done. The introduction of the sensible into poetry via aural stimuli still would not make it like the other sensible arts unless its sensible characteristics could somehow yield meaning, as the visual does within natural-sign theories of the visual arts. For the signs of which poetry consists, as arbitrary, are unlike the signs of the traditionally representational visual arts in that they presumably seek, through the mediation of the hearer's or reader's mental ideas, to represent the intelligible only. But if their access to the intelligible is made attainable through meanings created by the aural interrelations among words, then poetry can indeed achieve that grand merger of the sensible and the intelligible and thus the status of the master art. Theory would have cleared the way to establishing the ultimate verbal emblem. What the theorist dedicated to poetry's unique privilege must demonstrate, then, is the organicist insistence that the semantic dimension of the poetic word can be transformed by its aural dimension, so that there can be no satisfactory substitute—no synonym—for the word. In its fixity the word is itself to become the indispensable object of study, with the full meanings we seek locked within *it*, so that we need not look through it for a transparency that permits us to use it to look beyond.

Theory, now well conditioned by the tradition of aesthetics, seems ready to insist upon the place of poetry's medium among the media of the arts, and perhaps chief among them. But not quite yet. Before such systematic attempts to find that sensible-intelligible union in poetic language, there were some theorists who explored elements in the poetic workings with language that distorted it beyond its usual referential intelligibility, but they would not press their discoveries to a newly unified system of meaning and value. For example, the early Russian Formalist critics, roughly contemporary with Prall, sought to reveal the many devices that permit language to become "poeticized": the devices by means of which words are no longer what they are as we normally interpret them, by means of which they are "defamiliarized" or made "strange" so that a "literariness" may be achieved. But as in Prall, too often in this work the material elements of the medium seem isolated in analysis, since the Formalist operation—whether in the Russians or in the Prague group that follows them—is an exercise in "descriptive poetics," a would-be scientific account of how "poeticity" is created by ordinary words, of how their conversion is brought about.[23] These critics are somewhat less cautious than Prall about moving to more ambitious claims that could allow these poetic phenomena to open words outward into other dimensions. Further, through concepts such as "defamiliarization," they make clearer than he the disruption of what is termed "normal discourse"—the violations perpetrated upon it—by the "deviations" produced in the interest of "poeticity." Their influence is later joined with that of the more organicist American New Critics to produce the ultimate modernist apotheosis, which I trace in Chapter 7.

In the United States it is John Crowe Ransom who in the 1930s draws our awareness to the aural attractions of poetic language, although his usual practice is to treat the dimension of sound as being quite independent of the other dimensions of word-functioning in poems. It was this separation by him of sound and meaning that led his more organically minded cohorts among the New Critics to charge his theory with being mechanistic because it did not pursue an interaction between the "local texture" of words and the "logical structure" of meanings constituted by them. This unbridged distinction is Ransom's version of the double view of poetic language that sets forth conflicts in function between words as sounded and words as interpreted agents of meaning—in older terms, between words as sensible and words as intelligible.

Though everywhere revealing his absorption in textural matters, especially as related to meter and rhyme, Ransom for the most part refuses to allow them any role in affecting meaning; indeed, he sees such elements, however aesthetically effective they may be, as not contributing to the central argument of the poem, so that to his

23. Among many possible examples, I suggest some obvious ones: for Russian Formalism, Boris Eichenbaum, "The Theory of the 'Formal Method'" (1926), in *Russian Formalist Criticism: Four Essays*, trans. Lee T. Lemon and Marion J. Reis (Lincoln: University of Nebraska Press, 1965); for Prague School Formalism, Jan Mukarovsky, "Standard Language and Poetic Language" (1948), in *A Prague School Reader on Esthetics, Literary Structure, and Style*, trans. Paul L. Garvin (Washington, D.C.: Georgetown University Press, 1964). As a recent development of these methods see Michael Riffaterre, *Semiotics of Poetry* (Bloomington: Indiana University Press, 1978).

phrase "local texture" he prefixes the further modest qualifier "irrel-evant." It is, he means, irrelevant to the meaning being established by the "logical structure." Like the sound of a word in relation to its meaning, the sound texture of the words of a poem is "arbitrary" in relation to *its* meaning. (Ransom urges this notion without any awareness, I believe, of Saussure. But it is already firmly established in the tradition we have observed of poetry as an arbitrary-sign art.) Left to its own devices in its arbitrariness and its logical irrelevance, the aural surface seems to produce its own effects, though quite in-dependently of the poem's intended meaning:

> A formal meter impresses us as a way of regulating very drastically the material, and we do not stop to remark (that is, as readers) that it has no particular aim except some nominal sort of regimentation. It symbolizes the predatory method, like a sawmill which intends to reduce all the trees to fixed unit timbers, and as businessmen we require some sign of our business.[24]

But he does not need to be quite as modest as he is here, since it is clear that meters are to be manipulated and the regimentation made to yield to plasticity, though Ransom cannot yet get to the point of making the creative game significant:

> In this poem I think the critic ought to make good capital of the contrast between the amateurishness of the pleasant discourse as meaning and the hard determinate form of it phonetically. The meter on the whole is out of relation to the meaning of the poem, or to anything else spe-cifically; it is a musical material of low grade, but plastic and only slightly resistant material, and its presence in every poem is that of an abstrac-tionist element that belongs to the art.[25]

Yet Ransom concedes also that the attention given to aural struc-tures, by poet and reader, helps loosen up the rigidly determinate logic of the poem's structure of meaning. That meaning would be a loveless Platonic tyrant, imposing itself on the words and overdeter-mining them, except for the fact that prearranged sound patterns have a rival determinateness of their own. So the arbitrary play

24. "Poetry: A Note in Ontology" (1934), in *Critical Theory since Plato*, ed. Hazard Adams (New York: Harcourt Brace Jovanovich, 1971), p. 877.
25. "Criticism as Pure Speculation" (1941), in ibid., p. 890.

forced upon the poem's language by, say, meter and rhyme creates a space for indeterminacy and, with indeterminacy, for a break in logical efficacy and for the lingering, the pauses, that lead to a self-justifying attentiveness to the otherwise fleeting details themselves. By the end of *The New Criticism* (1941) Ransom presses this more positive role: though logically seen as a distraction, meter and rhyme may change the ground for meaning after all, by subverting it, and thus in the end by changing the meaning itself.

The importations which the imagination introduces into discourse have the value of developing the "particularity" which lurks in the "body," and under the surface, of apparently determinate situations. When Marvell [in "To His Coy Mistress"] is persuaded by the rhyme-consideration to invest the Humber with a tide, or to furnish his abstract calendar with specifications about the flood and the conversion of the Jews, he does not make these additions reluctantly. On the contrary, he knows that the brilliance of the poetry depends on the shock, accompanied at once by the realism or the naturalness, of its powerful particularity. But the mere syllabic measure, and not only the rhyme, can induce this effect. When the poet investigates the suitability of a rhyme-word for his discourse, he tries the imaginative context in which it could figure; but the process is the same when he tries many new phrases, proposed in the interest of the rhythm, for their suitability, though his imagination has to do without the sharp stimuli of the rhyme-words. And by suitability I mean the propriety which consists in their denoting the particularity which really belongs to the logical object. In this way what is irrelevant for one kind of discourse becomes the content for another kind, and presently the new kind stands up firmly if we have the courage to stand by it.

Thus all becomes "overshadowed, and we are absorbed by the power of his positive particulars, so unprepared for by his commonplace argument."[26] The two independent determinacies to which Ransom sees the poet precommitting himself, those of sound and of meaning, here interact so as to create mutual indeterminacies that alter, and expand, all that the poem can mean and do.

Fellow New Critics fail to catch those moments in which Ransom allows textural elements to be absorbed into a poetic whole. Instead, as organicists, they lament the dichotomy they consistently

26. "Wanted: An Ontological Critic," in *The New Criticism* (Norfolk, Conn.: New Directions, 1941), pp. 314–16.

find in Ransom between sensuous form (texture) and verbal meaning (structure), though they learn from him how healthy it is for criticism to confront poetry's material basis in sound patterns. In many
places in his work, the committed organicist Cleanth Brooks seeks
to convert Ransom's dichotomy into a monistic union that redefines
what poetic meaning can become as a newly achieved structure
earned in and through what Eliot termed "the right words in the
right order." As an absolute configuration read and internally heard
and felt—and all of these interpreted all at once—the poem was
finished into a fixed and irreducible absolute.

Two decades after Ransom's work of the late thirties, it was Sigurd Burckhardt who put at the center of his critical system Ransom's momentary observations about the phonetic invasion of the
realm of meaning. Burckhardt may in a number of ways appear to
be echoing what Diderot was proposing two centuries earlier with
his notion of the hieroglyph, except that where Diderot was only
suggesting an imitative relationship between sound and its object
("syllabic imitation" is one of his phrases for it), for Burckhardt
aural elements can create, or at least radically complicate—and open
new ranges of—meaning. Even more, aural elements can lead us
from our notion of the word as an intelligible referring tool to our notion of it as itself a sensible entity. Let me quote from my own description elsewhere of Burckhardt's contribution:

> As Sigurd Burckhardt . . . forcefully maintains, words as we normally
> use them and think of them are not a proper medium both because of
> what they have and because of what they haven't: they already have
> meaning before the poet picks them up, while a medium should be inert
> matter that achieves meaning only as the artist works upon it; and they
> do not have the "body" or "corporeality" a medium ought to have for the
> artist to work upon. Words come to the poet apparently stuffed with the
> meanings their histories have burdened them with, as if this is all they
> could be. Thus Burckhardt's poet, in order to remake them, must strip
> them down to raw physical matter, using their sounds to reduce them to
> *being* things rather than meanings that—though empty themselves—*refer*
> to things. Having so stripped them, forcing us to see them as if for the
> first time, he can begin to remake them into materials for his art, like any
> plastic artist. Unsatisfied by the generic and the minimal, he uses their
> physical characteristics to make them serve, as they create, their own
> unique context, forged by their arbitrary sounds and their newly emerg-
> ing possibilities of meaning. Such notions represent a development out

of Ransom's earlier claim that the poet used the phonetic character of words to turn them into physical entities, thereby reminding the reader that they *were* entities and not just counters; that they had sensory elements, capable of being manipulated, just like the elements of which the other arts were composed.[27]

The following passage is one of several I might cite from Burckhardt in which he sets forth this relationship between poetry and its medium:

I propose that the nature and primary function of the most important poetic devices—especially rhyme, meter, and metaphor—is to release words in some measure from their bondage to meaning, their purely referential role, and to give or restore to them the corporeality which a true medium needs. To attain the position of creative sovereignty over matter, the poet must first of all reduce language to something resembling a material. He can never do so completely, only proximately. But he can—and this is his first task—drive a wedge between words and their meanings, lessen as much as possible their designatory force and thereby inhibit our all too ready flight from them to the things they point to.[28]

Submissive to the poet's defamiliarizing tactics, we are trained to read poems in ways that search out elements, often phonetic elements, that can "disturb" our reading and interpretive habits outside poetry. Having been sensitized to words as sensible things, though only as we are blocked from seeing through them as intelligible signs to be interpreted, we look for ways in which language departs from its mode of operation in "normal" discourse—look especially for devices that force phonetic elements to modify, if not to transform, meaning. Within this productively deviant behavior of words, Burckhardt finds puns (or "true ambiguities") especially provocative.

[Empson] made us aware that one word can—and in great poetry commonly does—have *many meanings*. I would rather insist on the converse, that many meanings can have *one word*. For the poet, the ambiguous

27. *Theory of Criticism*, pp. 29–30.
28. "The Poet as Fool and Priest: A Discourse on Method," in *Shakespearean Meanings* (Princeton: Princeton University Press, 1968), p. 24. This essay was first published (in *ELH*) in 1956.

word is the crux of the problem of creating a medium for him to work in. If meanings are primary and words only their signs, then ambiguous words are false; each meaning should have its word, as each sound should have its letter. But if the reverse is true and words are primary—if, that is, they are corporeal entities the poet requires—then ambiguity is something quite different: it is the fracturing of a pristine unity by the analytic conceptualizations of prose. The poet must assume that where there is one word, there must, in some sense, be unity of meaning, no matter what prose usage may have done to break it. The pun is the extreme form of this assumption, positing unity of meaning even for purely accidental homophones, such as the sound shifts of a language will happen to produce.

Ambiguity, then, becomes a test case for the poet; insofar as he can vanquish it—not by splitting the word, but by fusing its meanings—he has succeeded in making language into a true medium.[29]

So what is especially provocative about the pun is that it houses opposed meanings within a single phonetic entity, thereby forcing them into a substantive identity that at once sustains and dissolves the polarity of difference: the sensible coincidence of sound denies the intelligible polarity it asserts. Indeed, in every shrewdly drawn pun, the self-contradictory doubleness of poetic language in effect emblematizes itself, and is in the emblem unified. Led by the pun as the extreme example, other phonetic similarities or near-identities—from alliteration to assonance to rhyme or near-rhyme to zeugma—create overlappings among differential elements that complicate their logical distinctness.

But we would not be doing justice to Burckhardt's incipient skepticism if we took his claims too literally, since to do so would allow us to charge him with mystifying poems and their behavior. We should keep in mind that his requirement for the poet to "reduce language to something *resembling* a material" (my italics) carries with it the concession that the reduction cannot go beyond resemblance only. Hence his acknowledgment in the very next sentence that the poet "can never do so completely, only proximately"—even in the realm of resemblance, which is to say, appearance, illusion. As readers, we cannot forgo our awareness of words as empty intelligible *signs* (like other words), whatever the poet may do to press us to a new awareness of them as full, sensible *things* (like the materi-

29. Ibid., pp. 32–33.

als of the other arts). The unsubstantial character of the first awareness (of words as intelligible signs), which seeks to point us toward
a reality elsewhere, surely is at odds with the substantial character
of the second (of words as sensible things), which seeks to keep our
attention locked within themselves. But it is the second in which we
are being subjected to an aesthetic illusion, thanks to our habit—
perhaps derived from traffic with other arts—of allowing the sense
data to which we respond to be converted into the manipulated materials of aesthetic objects.

Burckhardt may press strongly—almost exclusively, I fear—the aspect of poetic language functioning as aesthetic medium, and he
does so at the expense of the aspect of poetic language functioning
as part of the general linguistic code. Still, he steadily concedes our
inevitable awareness that words take on the aspect of "things" only
under the illusionary inducements of aesthetic dispensation: except
under the extraordinary response forced upon us by the behavior of
words in this present poem, we retain our generic knowledge of
them as coded tools of intelligibility. Still, for Burckhardt the notion
of the aesthetic has provided the justification that leaves words
fighting for privilege—the privilege of "corporeal" presence—as
they undergo the process of being turned poetic as we watch, or,
more candidly, as we license them to do so. To engage in this struggle they must be forcibly turned away from those prosaic functions
which, we may be sure, there is little danger of our losing sight of.
Are we not tempted to claim that thanks to the internally embattled
double life led by the remade language of poetry, words functioning
in poems may indeed be the most privileged of media, though only
by being the will-o'-the-wisp of media?

But as I suggested earlier, the heavy theoretical dependence on
the aural effects of language has been more pervaded by illusion
than is generally conceded by those pressing the material aspect of
words in poems. We must respond to theoretical suggestions like
Burckhardt's only while reminding ourselves not to be misled into
applying the language of surface sensation to poems in anything
like a literal way. For a long time now in our culture—a culture of
writers and distant readers—poems have been silently read rather
than heard, so that they have less regularly depended upon performance than has the drama. As recent theorists constantly remind
us, we must remember to see poems, with comparatively few excep-
tions, as forms of *écriture* rather than of *parole*. The aural elements to
which a Burckhardt has been responding usually do not literally

reach us through the ear. In effect, we read the aural effects that are to be heard, once poetry becomes a written rather than a performed art. And to *read* sounds, to apprehend aural effects without hearing them, requires of the reader the very act of mental transference from visual signs that the mediating process performs in all interpretation. For this too *is* a mode of interpretation.

The fact that so much has been made by theorists of the function of sound in the poetic medium is clear enough evidence of the primary role of illusion in aesthetic response: we react as if we are hearing what we are silently reading. Or are we rather reacting interpretively to what is written as it provides graphic (sometimes orthographic) as well as (illusionary) aural stimuli? Perhaps it is this mixture, this confounding, of visual and silently aural stimuli, habits, and memories that adds to the confusing duplicity of the sensible and intelligible orders of language and makes it so special a poetic medium in the complexity of its appeal and the multiple tensions that sustain it. But far from any literally sensuous immediacy, it rests upon these illusionary stimuli of several kinds that require a broad and strenuous interpretive response. What stimulates and justifies this response is a manipulation of the verbal medium that, once understood as illusionary, is seen to range well beyond the powers attributed by Prall to verbal surfaces.

This extension of the workings of the verbal medium suggests others: within the essential principles of this theoretical tradition, the study of aesthetic media in literature has been expanded beyond language to other elements of representation, often varying from genre to genre, and often ad hoc. Anything is seen to serve the author as a medium to the extent that it can be worked into a similar duality between meaning and illusion, between an apparent intention and an independently structured resistance that obstructs and complicates, thus leading it to serve an other-than-normal form of discourse. In the lyric, language—with its surfaces—is often the principal "material" to be worked. But even here other elements may also serve: narrative elements or confessional or autobiographical models that are forced into purposes that verbal play may create. In other genres elements not primarily linguistic may lead the way. For example, in drama it may be the stage space or dramatic structure, at once creating its own reality and reflecting ours, the two realities related to one another ambiguously in that they are at once mutually dependent and mutually exclusive. Or in prose fiction it may be narrative sequence, narrative time, or the mode of narration, at once fabrication and either "history" or "biography" (at least as a model, as a mimed or parodied form). Indeed, the development of prose fiction in the later nineteenth and twentieth centuries reflects an attempt to make the novel into a self-consciously artful literary genre by creating for it the medium of narrator manipulation that came to be termed point of view. This allows us to get inside a character's vision of his or her reality, but only while undercutting it by our guided awareness of the fictional limits (and the limiting fictions) of that vision. So the duality that I have found dogging the critical career of the verbal art as language and as representation may take several forms, but it continues to distinguish the art, so long as the poet works the medium into its Janus function, a complex doubling of the representation that outside the arts is intended to face one way only.

Within the formalist doctrine of defamiliarization, then, the poet's medium is whatever is found, in the world of meanings that precedes the poem, that can be made into a neutral space for working changes upon it, in effect whatever can be subjected to the poet's forge. I have pointed out, in critics from Addison to Burckhardt, the growing theoretical consciousness of the poet's task of giving a special shape to what otherwise is not so special, the growth, in other words, of the deviationist aesthetic that makes the poem a privileged object only because privilege has been molded into it through materials transformed for that purpose. Thus, because of the peculiarly hybrid nature of its materials, poetry comes to lead the way for the other arts instead of trailing behind them. The semiotic it teaches us may then be applied to the interpretive techniques we develop for reading the sister arts. From my earlier chapters it might easily be argued that I could find the start of my story by going back as far as Aristotle and his view of the poet's struggle to convert to art the neutral materials received from what he thought of as history (or myth, or myth-as-history). Indeed, I suppose I have done just that in making this a continuous story.

But I have been too long, if still insufficiently detailed, in tracing this development of a poetics that elevated poetry into an art with a manipulable medium. I may have lingered too long over it in view of the fact that, as I began this chapter by acknowledging, the movement at the end of this development has for some decades been pretty well deserted and superseded by other movements deeply antagonistic to it. But it is only by way of this development that I can get to the renewed championing of the ekphrastic impulse in the past two centuries. Through the 1950s the modernist culmination of this development flourished, invigorated philosophically by Bergson's attack on language that especially valued poetry as a verbal art arising out of, and in spite of, the debased operation of normal discourse, seen by him as no more than the deadening representations of those social stereotypes we require to serve our practical activities.

However, especially since the rise of structuralism and its heirs, antithetical theorists have sought to tear poetry from its hard-won home among the arts in order to return it to its home in language: they have sought to reduce poetry to the place permitted it by a general semiotics at the expense of the place earned for it by aesthetics. In the eyes of such theorists, the aesthetic tradition I have traced has allowed the "literary art" (a phrase they must question when it is used to classify an exclusive canon) to become affiliated with the wrong family, largely because it has degraded the other one. There are two families beckoning. One, the family of the arts, is elegant, privileged, beyond the reach of common life and its common language. But the other, the family of language, no longer is to be relegated to the disadvantaged role assigned it by the post-Bergsonians: though it is seen as all-inclusive, a democratic denier of privilege, for structuralists and post-structuralists it sustains alike all its levels of usage and finds a universal tropological basis that binds all verbal manifestations as close relatives. It is now being charged that at least since the systematic dispensation of Kantian philosophy, theorists have unfortunately chosen the first—and, presumably, the wrong—family with which to give poetry a snobbish and socially irresponsible attachment.

It is Kant's theory of the aesthetic and the notion of disinterestedness that post-Kantians associated with it that are now held responsible for the idolatry of the arts and their segregation from the actual business of living. From this tradition emerges the growing interest I have traced in how artists exploit the potentialities of their several aesthetic media (including, of course, language by the poets), distorting them into shapes unanticipated by their pre-aesthetic order. For the medium to be manipulated in special ways is for it to be created into a special object, one that is subject only to its own principles of "internal purposiveness," in the language of Kant. It is, of course, this claim for the specialness of the special object that has now come to be rejected as both false and dangerous. The freedom of the object from externally imposed interests is easily viewed as an irresponsible escape from the practical world, the world of interests aroused and either satisfied or frustrated.

It is the role assigned by the aesthetic tradition to working the medium that is charged with wrongly taking the object beyond the reach of the workaday world. So for antithetical contemporary theorists, literary critics in this tradition compound the error of formalist critics of the plastic arts by insisting that poetry follow the model of those arts in finding a sensuous medium and, in analogous ways, exploiting it in order to create integral objects, which are in turn used as semiotic models for those other arts. Poetry is thus led (it is charged) into the rarefied, unworldly realm of privilege, the elitist preserve of canonized works. Such, it is claimed, are the consequences of the deviationist aesthetic as a separatist aesthetic, both created and supported by theories that give priority to an aesthetic mastery produced by the poet's struggle with the medium.[30]

The alternative proposed by recent antagonists would turn poetry from the aesthetic to the less restrictedly semiotic. The Kantian moment and its theoretical consequences, carried well into their modernist apotheosis in the twentieth century, are seen as a wrong turn, and Nietzsche is made into a replacement prophet. To reject the aesthetic as a separable category leads to the rejection of any attempt by poetry to move into that sacralized realm through claiming parallels with the guiltier arts. It is the universal realm of writing (écriture) that now claims poetry for its own, though for many of these critics poetry—in spite of their theoretical hopes—still leads the way, because it creates the tropological and narrative models that the rest of writing is also shown to exhibit. For all writing is brought to share the domain of the new rhetoric, the shaping thrust of all language that denies any "normality" from which any so-called art can deviate. The separateness of discursive kinds and even the integrity of distinct verbal objects are replaced by the indivisible pool of writing that flows into and through them all, dissolving those falsely closed boundaries established by the fetishizing that would select and elevate individual texts out of an unbroken textuality (in effect, a seamless inter-textuality).

30. Of course, recent anti-deviationist theory makes similar arguments about the fetishistic insistence on elitism in earlier theories of the plastic arts. Most recent products of art clearly reflect this thinking. I discuss these similar attacks on poetry and the other arts in *Arts on the Level: The Fall of the Elite Object* (Knoxville: University of Tennessee Press, 1981). See my Supplementary Note to this chapter.

The new supremacy of linguistics over poetics means that the latter is no longer to be viewed as a branch of aesthetics. (Indeed, aesthetics itself is pretty well deprived of any legitimacy.) With no allowable distinction between normal usage and deviation, the poem is captured within the metaphorical conception of language as an unbroken system of signs controlled by a single kind of encoding and decoding operation. This metaphor precludes any notion of a verbal medium that can be worked with and struggled against to produce a special order of words wrought to be as special as they can convince us, in our compliance, that they are. But of course it is just this depriveleging of poems, this wiping out of the literary as a class, that the attack on the Kantian perspective has been intended to accomplish. Whatever texts may be produced under the pressure of our current demystifications, we may well wonder what will happen to the role in our culture of those texts long treated as most deserving of privileged interpretations once those interpretations have been stripped of their aesthetic ambition. Must even those works produced under the aegis of an aesthetic tradition, from the classical to the modernist, be re-read—and under-read—under the postmodern dispensation? This is the question that occupies the chapters that conclude this study.

As I have presented the recent decriers of the aesthetic, they have, at least implicitly, accepted an *either/or* choice between the aesthetic and the semiotic, and they have chosen. But as I earlier presented the later stages of the aesthetic tradition, it seemed possible for critics to manage both. Or at least we saw theoretical support for critics who would try to manage both, perhaps because they too recognized the mystifications attendant upon taking literally the objectivity of the object and, with it, the manipulability of the medium as if it were—even in poetry—a physical thing. As I try to demonstrate in Chapter 7, a fully self-conscious modernist aesthetic always remembered the uniquely double nature of the language of poetry, remembered that however special the configuration resulting from manipulations of the poetic medium, its elements remained part of a coded system of intelligible signs, and only through our wilful interpretation could its (*apparently*) sensible elements be read as if they were immediate, so that they were indeed to be treated as mediate only, just as all writing is. Words that are seen as if they are being heard, I have said earlier, are, like other words, signs that must be "read," or interpreted, so that they too are intelligible. With such an awareness, the contemporary critic who persists in clinging to the aesthetic tradition may still insist on the power of the medium, as manipulated by the poet-as-artist, only so long as the illusionary character of that power is acknowledged. To say it is illusionary is no more than to say it is aesthetic, no more than to say it is functioning within an experience that is different from others and serving different ends. But of course it is just this mode of experience that the anti-aesthetic theorist is impatient to deny. In denying it he willingly, even anxiously, disengages all considerations of the aesthetic medium that have emerged in the history I have traced here. I ask again whether these can be disengaged without depriving us of some of the major interpretive tools we need to take full account of the texts that history has left us to account for.

I think it is worth summarizing my narrative of the role of the poetic medium as it affects the fortunes of poetry viewed as a mode of language and/or as a mode of art. It is an uncertain narrative of the alternating families—of aesthetics and of semiotics—that adopt it and of its ambiguous and meandering path, which has led it to isolation and back. This mixed history has contributed to poetry's unique—and uniquely duplicitous—place among the arts. I can distinguish three stages, though I will end by trying to blur them.

First, beginning with Addison, we have a struggle between representation and expression. I have found here a grouping of the arts depending upon an inverse relation between unmediated representation and the need for a medium: the less you have of one, the more you require of the other. The distinction between natural and arbitrary signs is secure, with natural-sign art dominant and arbitrary-sign art (like poetry) seeking to emulate the effect of natural signs through faithful verbal description. *Ut pictura poesis erit*, as poetry creeps mimetically after painting, like a poor relation.[31] Yet the other side of this inverse relation is also pressed from time to time, with poetry, as an art in need of exploiting its medium, able to achieve levels of expression closed to arts of unmediated representation. In either case, poetry is maintained as the art with a medium, for better or worse, because of its arbitrary signs, while natural-sign arts (painting and, even more so, sculpture) simply reproduce, with no awareness of a medium at all. Direct involvement with the mate-

31. I remind the reader of Hagstrum's review of that unfortunate misrepresentation of Horace's *ut pictura poesis* as the more compelling *ut pictura poesis erit* in *The Sister Arts: The Tradition of Literary Pictorialism and English Poetry from Dryden to Gray* (Chicago: University of Chicago Press, 1958), pp. 59–60. See Chapter 3, above, for an earlier reference to this matter.

rial world that yields immediate sensation has sensory advantages, and yet these may well pale before the imaginary ideality of poetry. It is here that Herder was brought into my narrative. No less than Addison, he sees the unlikeness between poetry and the other arts, but whether it should try to be like them in their relation to the material world or cultivate its own differentness is an issue left somewhat unsettled. Shelley is seen as reflecting a similar uncertainty.

Second (and here Shelley, at least in one passage, leads the way), the increasing awareness of the sensuous character of the verbal medium leads to the attempt to return poetry to the family of the arts by exaggerating its sensuousness, so that the artist may achieve a relationship to the poetic medium parallel to the exploitation of the medium by the plastic artist. But we have shifted the ground for comparing the arts from the question of direct or indirect representation (or "imitation") of objects to the question of how the artist manipulates the peculiar sensuous order of the medium. As this second stage becomes more sophisticated, theorists become increasingly aware of the two-sided character of language in poems, so that its sensuous, material side may be taken as illusionary, without denying its continuing obligations as an intelligible instrument. Poetry, then, is brought back into the family of the arts, but always with this difference: it does have a manipulable medium after all, which creates an awareness of its plasticity, though always qualified by its need to be read — and interpreted — as a language if we are to attribute this awareness to it. Yet throughout this second stage there remains a post-Kantian insistence on the act of shaping, of forcing materials into paths that are deviant and yet, in the end, patterned — newly patterned — after all. And the pattern is one we could not have had without the remaking of the "materials" that created it.

Third, we have seen the attempt to withdraw poetry from what it shares with the arts by opposing the very notion of the arts as that elite shaping force in our culture that gives us the forms of our vision. Instead, all written texts are to be interpreted as serving that function similarly. The claim to transform language into a poetic medium is denied, seen as no more than a mystifying grandiloquence, since, with no "normal" discourse, all writers come upon language as already transformed. Consequently, language is to claim its snobbish secessionist child from its equally pretentious companion fancy-arts and bring it home to the generic verbal codes that modernist critics cajoled it into deserting.

I have more than once urged the concessions that should have been made to the common linguistic obligations of even the most carefully wrought poem by modernist criticism, however keenly it may embrace the poet's working of the medium. On the other side, in postmodern critics we now see the application to all texts, including the theoretical and critical, of tropological and narratological categories formerly reserved for the interpretation of poems. Might not these two cross-tendencies promise a negotiation of the issue? Is not the obliteration of the aesthetic itself obliterated by the elevation of all texts to the tropologies of fiction? I would suggest that in modernism and postmodernism alike we find a commitment to self-conscious illusion (whether as the aesthetic or as that which undoes the aesthetic) that may well reconcile some of the oppositions that have been tearing critical theory apart in recent years. How anti-aesthetic can any theory be that finds all writers, including even the theorist, working the medium, weaving illusions through the play of words? I conclude my argument here by allowing it to shield the hope that it may reveal these theoretical oppositions as themselves only an illusion, an illusion at times disguised by the artistic—if not poetic—pretensions of some contemporary theorists.

Still, I must concede that the attacks on the aesthetic, and thus on the claims for a specially plastic medium, are serious and persistent beyond this fond hope, although it is important to face them only after having given the aesthetic its due, especially since the fate of the ekphrastic is clearly at stake as well. We are now ready, in the final two chapters, to extend the arguments of defenders and attackers to their most extreme forms by examining both modernist and postmodern claims and illusions.

A SUPPLEMENTARY NOTE

Shortly after working out my argument in an earlier—and quite different—version of this chapter, I was made aware of the extraordinary exhibition mounted by Jean-François Lyotard at the Centre Pompidou (the Beaubourg) in Paris in the spring of 1985. Although it was not explicitly directed to the issues I discuss here, from its title onward I see its mission as bearing profoundly on the primary philosophical assumptions underlying the narrative I have traced in this chapter, although—I must add—only by way of negation. I thus cannot resist bringing it into this discussion, if only in this subsidiary way. As indicated by its title, "Immaterials" ("*Les Immatériaux*"), as well as by the documents written to justify the exhibit,

what Lyotard put together was radical in its commitment to undermine the "material" notion of the aesthetic that my chapter has
been dedicated to describing.[32]

What was there to engage us was not the anticipated exhibition of
things, of whatever kind, constructed by a human being's manipulation of materials. Instead we were invited to a participatory experience that at every step violated our museum-formed expectation that
we would confront a display of made "objects"—or, indeed, that
what we would confront would be "objects" at all. We entered wear-
ing sound-equipped helmets that surrounded us with many varieties of music, or with words in innumerable languages—some quotations, some apparently random—or with miscellaneous noises, all
the sounds coordinated, and thus changing, with the many zones of
the exhibit. We thus wandered from zone to zone, encountering a
bewildering succession of electronic effects, functioning computers,
films of comedy and terror, quotidian items, sensory stimuli (visual,
auditory, even olfactory). Here and there traditional museum objects and artifacts were scattered, though inevitably amid incompat-
ible companions, so that, within so deconstructive a context, they
functioned only as parody. In this exhibition all was intended as disruption, unsettling our traditional (i.e., pre-postmodern) expecta-
tions derived from a Cartesian museum model that has each of us
behave as a subject among a display of the passive constructs displayed before us as objects.

The "immateriality" of the exhibition demonstrated Lyotard's
idea of the postmodern. This idea is at war with what he sees—and
what I in this chapter have treated—as the dominant aesthetic tradition from the Enlightenment through modernism: the tradition
that privileges the artist as the creator who uses aesthetic media to
transform raw matter into made "objects." But according to Lyotard,
we have such "objects" only because—and so long as—we constitute them as such by means of the *human* perspective, in accordance
with its Kantian (and, earlier, Aristotelian) obligation to be such a
constitutor through both the mind and the will operating upon and
shaping external, unformed materials. The purpose of his exhibition, then, was to get us beyond, or at least outside, that perspective
by dissolving those objects into dispersive fields of energies, a postmodern realm that disdains materials as the substantive basis of

32. Besides the brochures published for the exhibition, see "A Conversation with
Jean-François Lyotard," in *Flash Art*, no. 121 (March 1985): 32–35.

made objects, which it disdains equally. (I observe once more in this case that just as in the aesthetic tradition now being bypassed the language arts sought to take on sensuous attributes that would ally them to the plastic arts, today language is given the role of leading the other, apparently material arts, by analogy, onto the undifferentiated, "immaterial" semiotic field that can be seen, at least initially, as its own. And the technology for disseminating information is seen as our new "immaterial" medium for whatever may go by the name of art.) It was for me especially appropriate that this exhibit was held in the Pompidou, which, as a people's center, played a principal role in the discussion of these very issues in my *Arts on the Level: The Fall of the Elite Object*.[33]

Clearly, Lyotard and I might well agree about the formative role of the material medium in the artistic creation of the "objects" authorized by the "aesthetic" tradition since, let us say, Baumgarten, which as it was formed still remained within the precincts of the subject-object epistemology created by Descartes. And we might agree too about the recent revolutions in culture and in theory that would undo both the "aesthetic" and the tradition. We might well disagree, of course, about the enjoyment we take in these developments of our recent history or the sadness—might he condemn it as the mere nostalgia?—we feel. We might disagree, in other words, not only about how we should respond to these newly exhibited, value-free "stimuli"—what else should we call them in the absence of "objects"?—but, even more, about how we should continue to respond, with enquiring admiration or political resentment, to those older, demanding aesthetic objects that have been our treasured relics produced under the earlier dispensation. For we might further disagree about the extent to which we should cooperate with the fate imposed upon us, and accept as utterly deterministic, beyond the activity of human will, those crushing historical forces that, in the name of "democratic despotism" (Lyotard's phrase), would impose that fate.

33. See n. 30, above. I refer especially to pp. 57–58, as well as to Joan Krieger's emblem (*"Les Baux > Beaubourg"*) on p. 50.

7
THE
VERBAL EMBLEM II
From
Romanticism
to
Modernism

Words move, music moves
Only in time; but that which is only living
Can only die. Words, after speech, reach
Into the silence. Only by the form, the pattern,
Can words or music reach
The stillness, as a Chinese jar still
Moves perpetually in its stillness.

T. S. Eliot, "Burnt Norton"*

I n Chapter 4 I traced the arguments of those who created a tradition out of their countermovement to pictorialism. They
sought to use the freedom of the word from the limits of the
natural sign in order to claim a special power for it—in its way also
authorized by "nature"—and they sought to use the sequential character of the verbal text in order to open the spatial enclosure of the
visual arts to the free flow of temporality. But in the later stages of
the tradition that I traced back to Longinus, in notions I there associated with Burke or Shelley or Poulet, I claimed to see a wilful
neglect of form and the precision of outline (in Burke's terms, the
forsaking of the "beautiful" in favor of the "sublime") in order to allow words to be absorbed by the undemarcated reaches of our inner
life. Because such theorists as these desire the verbal arts to oppose
the restraints of visual representation instead of emulating them,
their interests lead their theory to move in an anti-formal, if not an
anti-aesthetic, direction.

The force of this opposition leads to a polarity that less anti-
formal theorists in their wake seek to mediate. For the latter, language, as we saw in Chapter 6, need not be regarded as an anti-
formal element just because it is not to be reduced to its visual appeal, nor does it have to be associated with imprecision. They
would argue that the aesthetic game need not be given away to the
visual arts, nor need it be condemned. The growing interest in
words as a potential aesthetic medium, unlike the media of the
other arts yet functioning in analogous ways, can for them yield an
aesthetic synthesis that builds on the manipulative possibilities in

*It seemed appropriate to use for my epigraph here a quotation that was central
to my earlier essay (see the Appendix), since this chapter seeks to systematize the
world of that essay of many years ago.

197

language to create an object free of natural-sign limitations that can yet stand forth as a construct that is always in motion and yet continually contained.

So there is in the late eighteenth and early nineteenth centuries a growing attention both to the "making" power of words in the hands of an able poet and to the object those words "make," the space they create for themselves out of their temporal character as elements in motion. Having, in the name of temporality, won their battle against the closed eighteenth-century spatial imagination and now enjoying the freedom from enclosure that accompanies their victory, theorists, perhaps looking for a formal principle that can replace visual form, soon begin to work their way back to space. And this is to work their way back to *form*, since form, at least for the romantic-modernist thinker, is achieved by the poet's imposition of spatial elements on a temporal flow, with that temporal flow somehow preserved even as it is captured. What emerges, in the aesthetic from Kant through the New Critics, is the possibility of a rebirth of the notion of the verbal emblem. But because there is, at least since Herder (as we observed in detail in Chapter 6), a newer and more self-conscious awareness of the potential role of language as aesthetic medium, there must be significant differences between the Renaissance verbal emblem (my "verbal emblem I") and what I will here treat as "verbal emblem II." My purpose in this chapter is to explore the development of this emblem and with it the ultimate modernist return to a newly dynamic spatiality.

The return to a newer conception of form under the control of the verbal imagination is related, in the last two centuries, to the dominant role of the metaphor of organicism in descriptions of poetic production. The introduction of the doctrine of organic form allows the theorist to deny that the final determination of what the poem is to be is derived from any object or code external to the developing verbal creation, while still insisting that there are formal controls exercised upon that creation, even if those controls must be internally developed in the course of the creative process. Not coincidentally, it was in the course of many idolatrous studies of Shakespeare as both master poet and model poet, creator of works whose perfection had continually to be reaffirmed and justified, that many of the romantic discussions of organic form were pursued.

Most notably in the appreciations of Shakespeare by August Wilhelm Schlegel and the derivative (if not directly borrowed) essays of Coleridge, organic form, in contrast to the superficial form disparag-

ingly termed "mechanical regularity," is introduced as the only
principle that can account for Shakespeare's accomplishment. In a
lecture appropriately named "Shakespeare's Judgment Equal to His
Genius," Coleridge argues against neoclassical censure of Shakespeare's art because it violated certain sacred dramatic principles. It
is not, he argues, that one must choose between genius and judgment, and praise Shakespeare as a genius though acknowledging
that he is without judgment, but rather that genius must include
judgment, though Shakespeare's judgment is too intricate for legalistic minds to judge. It is not that Shakespeare's work is lawless because it does not obey their universal laws but that it is responding
to more subtly imposed laws that it is itself generating. I am, obviously, using Coleridge to provide the alternative that would mediate between the extremities (*enargeia I* and *enargeia II*) that I was left
with at the close of Chapter 4. I cannot resist quoting Coleridge's own
picturesque defense against the charge that a poet must either satisfy a narrow and externally imposed formal demand or be charged
with formlessness:

> No work of true genius dares want its appropriate form, neither indeed is
> there any danger of this. As it must not, so genius cannot, be lawless; for
> it is even this that constitutes it genius—the power of acting creatively
> under laws of its own origination. How then comes it that . . . whole na-
> tions have combined in unhesitating condemnation of our great drama-
> tist, as a sort of African nature, rich in beautiful monsters—as a wild heath
> where islands of fertility look the greener from the surrounding waste,
> where the loveliest plants now shine out among unsightly weeds, and
> now are choked by their parasitic growth, so intertwined that we cannot
> disentangle the weed without snapping the flower? . . . The true ground
> of the mistake lies in the confounding mechanical regularity with organic
> form. The form is mechanic, when on any given material we impress a pre-
> determined form, not necessarily arising out of the properties of the
> material;—as when to a mass of wet clay we give whatever shape we wish
> it to retain when hardened. The organic form, on the other hand, is in-
> nate; it shapes, as it develops, itself from within, and the fullness of its de-
> velopment is one and the same with the perfection of its outward form.
> Such as the life is, such is the form. Nature, the prime genial artist, inex-
> haustible in diverse powers, is equally inexhaustible in forms.[1]

1. The quotation is taken from "Shakespeare's Judgment Equal to His Genius," in
Coleridge's Essays and Lectures on Shakespeare and Some Other Old Poets and Dramatists

At the close of Chapter 4 I anticipated this theoretical move that would join the expressive human capacity inherited from Longinus, emphasized in that chapter, to the making emphasis inherited from the Aristotelian conception of *poesis*. Its aim was to evade the alternatives of a dictated mimetic precision at one extreme and a freely subjective obscurity at the other, as it sought to justify the poem as a constructed *object*, a whole that exceeded the sum of the individual representations within it. And yet, because the metaphor was pressed to the extreme, it was to be conceived as a "natural" object, product of an organic process of growth.[2]

In this literalized version of the organic metaphor, the poem as a "natural" object was to go beyond the automatic flow of human speech by developing, under human guidance, into a formal completeness, as if as part of the natural process, or at least in emulation of it. As the above quotation has shown us, nature, working through the human creator, is the form-maker, that "prime genial artist . . . inexhaustible in forms." Hence the number of poems, each with its own form, is endless. Coleridge has learned from Burke, as well as from the German philosophers who led him to his position, that the direction of all representation (or should we in the present instance change "re-presentation" to "presentation"?) must be from inside the human mind outward to the world rather than, as with the natural-sign tradition, from the outside world inward to its re-presentation in the human mind.

As organicism is most consistently defined, the work of art, now shaped as it emerges from the human creator instead of imitating a pre-ordained shape in nature, yet achieves its own special relation to nature. Captivated—and captured—by the organic metaphor, theorists attribute to the work the natural form, the integral system of internal relations, of a biological entity. Signs that in their derivation

---

(London: J. M. Dent, 1906), pp. 42–47. (I cannot resist calling attention to the similarity of Coleridge's vegetation metaphor to Johnson's in his description of Shakespeare's lawless tendencies in the "Preface" to his *Shakespeare*.) I join Coleridge in arguing for a greater complexity in organicism than is usually granted it in chap. 2 ("The Typological Imagination and Its Other: From Coleridge to the New Critics and Beyond") of my *A Reopening of Closure: Organicism Against Itself* (New York: Columbia University Press, 1989), pp. 31–56. I perhaps echo Coleridge's lament in arguing that those who too quickly condemn organicism for requiring closed poetic systems fail to respond to the subtleties that, in its best proponents, open it up.

  2. In Chapter 8 I trace the critique, at once semiotic and political, of this notion of the "natural."

may have been arbitrary and conventional are so arranged and transformed by the poet that as they emerge from the creative process, they take on a sense of inevitability and necessity aroused in us by the organic forms of living nature. Here, then, is the third version of "nature" we have entertained, different from either the doctrine of the natural sign (Chapter 3, above) or the vision of nature speaking through the poet (Chapter 4). It sees poem-making as an imitation of nature's creative force, proliferating into an infinity of biological forms. The organic metaphor, pressed literally into becoming the model for poetic form, turns the poem into its own sort of natural sign.

This is essentially the role given the poet by Aristotle, who is the first to adapt the biological model to literature, more specifically in him to the description of the forms of dramatic plots. He finds the power of these forms within their capacity to reshape their external objects, the casual realities of historical events as they occur, into the causal probabilities of the poem as it ought to be constructed—into the poem, that is, as a made object, a complete system of mutually dependent internal relations operating in accordance with our logic rather than with the chronology of happenstance.[3] If we remember Aristotle's desire to elevate the "probable" over the merely "possible" (*Poetics*, chap. 24), we can understand that the controlling principle behind the sequence of incidents in drama requires that the coherence of human logic triumph over chronological accident; it is to persuade us as aroused witnesses that the humanly created order *is* the natural order, at least insofar as nature operates in accordance with the teleological principles at the heart of the Aristotelian metaphysic.

Aristotle shifts easily from the drama as an objective structure to audience response without concerning himself about the differences required by this shift. He seems to expect us to accept the shift from what is logically "probable" in the action to what the audience can be induced to find "credible," believing the order to be "natural" because it is logical, as logical as the principle of coherence, without aporia, that he claims to find in nature.[4] Thus the audience

3. Among the many places I could point to in the *Poetics*, I need mention here only Aristotle's argument for logical, rather than chronological, definitions of "beginning," "middle," and "end" in chapter 7, as reinforced by his defense of "unity of plot" over "unity of the hero" in chapter 8 and by his calling in chapter 23 for an epic structure that presents "a single action" and not, as history does, "a single period."

4. This shift from the "probable" to the "credible," anticipated by Aristotle as he

response, far from arbitrary, is to be controlled by the teleological pressures exerted by the poem through its objectively formal properties. The Aristotelian action, then, should be taken as the idealized version of the natural order and, as a logical transformation of it, an improved order that we should accept instead of the nature we see, that we should accept as nature's ultimate form.

The proper drama is, in effect, more than a natural sign as nature's transparent representation; it is, as substitute for visible nature, the primal creation that speaks for nature itself. As an object *for* imitation, it is as fixed and absolute as nature itself *seems* to be for the Platonists—no, more so, since it has behind it the philosophical authority of Aristotle's teleology, his final cause, to lend it substance. Consequently, as I pointed out in Chapter 3, the apparent appeal to temporality in Aristotle's view of the plot as a sequence of incidents is deceptive, since that sequence is frozen into the pattern fixed by the logical structure of probabilities. And the logical superimposes itself upon the chronological and changes it, subdues it to order by removing all chance from it, so that—as Aristotle makes clear in *Poetics* 7—the sequence is ruled by "causal necessity," by procedures governing antecedents and consequences. Aristotle may seem to focus upon chronology in his central concern for the role played in dramatic form by the terms "beginning," "middle," and "end," but these terms here have only a logical force: the "middle" of a tragedy follows the "beginning" because it logically follows *from* it, not just because it comes after it; and the "end" is the logical conclusion to the drama, the end of its consequences, not just the temporal moment that arbitrarily comes after the others.

The poet thus fosters within the viewer or reader the illusion that human logic has produced a self-sealing organism, what nature—or a natural history—true to its teleological principle, ought to be, even if in the experiential realm we inhabit, accidents intervene to thwart the realization of potentiality inherent in nature's substance. We need the arts, it can then be argued, in order to teach us what nature (or nature's version of history) might be if it were unimpeded by accident. If the dramatic system of causal relations is all it should be, then, it creates the impression of biological nature's growth and

moves uncertainly back and forth between the two in chapter 6, becomes a commonplace in sixteenth-century Italian criticism, which often calls itself Aristotelian. As a shift in focus from dramatic structure to audience response, it helps foster those Platonic intrusions that distort the shape of Renaissance Aristotelianism.

fulfillment. As Aristotle claims in his *Physics,* chapter 2, the artist partly imitates nature and partly surpasses it.[5] The objects borrowed for imitation from the outside world must be made to appear as if they develop *naturally* into what becomes their fixed pattern, as if they develop *naturally* into "the finality of [their] form," if I may borrow Kant's words for my purposes.

It is this suggestion that Kant functions for Coleridge and later post-Kantians as a second coming of Aristotle that shows the form-making doctrine of the *Poetics* to be relevant to romantic organicism. The imposition worked by the Aristotelian poet upon his materials from a position outside them is forced by poetic form to seem to us like a flowering from inside. (My vegetation metaphor is intended as an echo of the common language of organicism.) It is this infusion of organic vitality into otherwise inert materials that for the later organicist Coleridge turns the poet's act into an imitation of God's. The poet's own I AM gives life to its objects, transforming them into the mutually sustaining elements of the self-sufficient world it has created, in effect giving birth to what Renaissance critics would have called a "second nature," in its way an improvement over the first.

So here is a return to nature by signs that, as arbitrary and conventional, had begun their career in alienation from it. The vision of the poem as a perfect emblem of organic nature requires a totalized concept of the aesthetic object resting on a teleology (what Kant termed "internal purposiveness") that converts every wayward element into an inevitable and indispensable part of the created pattern. Before turning beyond the romantics, however, I must note again that this need to claim a holistic structure, a system of inevitable interrelations, undermines and renders deceptive the introduction by Aristotle (and Coleridge after him) of an apparently temporal model to counteract the stasis behind all of Plato's discussions of the arts, including the verbal arts. By insisting that the poet imitates an action, a sequence of incidents, rather than individual personages,

5. Richard McKeon's commentary in his "Literary Criticism and the Concept of Imitation in Antiquity" (in *Critics and Criticism, Ancient and Modern,* ed. R. S. Crane [Chicago: University of Chicago Press, 1952], p. 161) is instructive here: "Art imitates nature, Aristotle was fond of repeating, and, at least in the case of the useful arts, the deficiencies of nature are supplemented in the process of that imitation by art following the same methods as nature would have employed. 'Generally, art partly completes what nature cannot bring to a finish, and partly imitates her.'" He is quoting from *Physics,* chap. 2.

Aristotle seemed to be substituting a temporal notion of form for Plato's spatial and thus static notion. He thus positioned critics to move beyond the obvious pictorialism behind Plato's concepts in order to exploit the special powers of literature as a temporal art. But the firm commitment to teleological structure turned the action—as a sequence fixed in its system of mutual inevitabilities, in which the beginning was as dependent on the end as the end was on the beginning—into a spatial form after all. Hence we can understand the attractiveness of Aristotelian organicism for romantic theorists, who would recapture for space the temporality let loose by the revolution against neoclassicism, though in doing so they could yet resist the analogy to the visual arts in order to work for poetry's superiority as a time art. They could, they thought, have the dynamics of temporality without having to give up the fixity of structure.

As criticism in our own century systematically projected this formalism that would impose its spatial fixity upon literature's temporality, the mystifications of organicism expanded into the worship of form by literary modernism. In the formalist tradition from Aristotle on, the conflict in literature between the temporality of sequence and the spatiality of the form that freezes this sequence is resolved on the side of space. As the New Criticism turned the claims of the Coleridgean formulations into an ultimate critical method, the spatialization of temporal sequence in literature became the object of aesthetic worship. The attachment to myth as human narrative (at the expense of history as an indifferent, inhuman out-there) in a T. S. Eliot or a Cleanth Brooks or—more explicitly for my purposes—in the valorization of "spatial form" by Joseph Frank may be seen as the crowning idolatry of fixed poetic structure in the modernist movement in both poetry and criticism.

As we have seen, the idolatry of the spatial in the theory sponsored by the modernist tradition springs from sources far different from the neoclassical desire, also spatial, for a natural-sign art in the seventeenth and eighteenth centuries. After all, the discrediting of the natural-sign aesthetic—indeed the very notion of the natural sign—was accomplished during that late eighteenth-century moment, and the modernist certainly would do nothing to restore its credit. As I have sought to show, ever since the work of Edmund Burke and even before, the rejection of the hierarchy among the arts that was based on the hegemony of natural signs led theorists to turn from the limiting precision of visual representation, to turn to the verbal arts as superior to the plastic, and, as this theoretical direction developed through the nineteenth century, to turn to music—the art farthest removed from natural-sign representation for Addison—as the condition toward which all the arts should aspire.

But literary theorists, however anxious to exploit the auditory character of the poetic medium, were not about to give up its semantic function. Further, we have seen that aesthetic theory does not stop with Burke's denial of the natural sign and the celebration of an unrepetitive temporality: having freed literature from a dependence on visual precision so that it can explore the wider and less controlled range of reader associations, having allowed literature to escape spatial fixity in order to indulge temporal expansiveness, the history of theory, now under the modernist dispensation, reverses itself under the pressure of the organicist commitment to closure and encourages literature, still retaining its devotion to time, to become spatial after all. But this return to spatiality is now to be made on the terms of the verbal arts rather than on those of the visual arts, in that the spatiality achieved in words is to be a hard-won victory over the inherent transience of verbal sequence.

The rise of semiotics in our century brought modernist poetics to their concentration upon language as the seat of poetry's special powers. This linguistically based version of organic theory transformed the workings of the criticism it sponsors. I have just traced the use of the organic metaphor in criticism from Aristotle. However, perhaps because of his exclusive interest in the dramatic imitation of an action as a substitute natural sign (see my Chapter 2, above), Aristotle's organicism, it must be conceded, was restricted to interrelations among the parts of the plot, defined by him as the arrangement of the incidents. Because for Aristotle language, as material cause, was relegated to a subsidiary role serving the various moments of the plot, its only requirement was that it be appropriate to a prior something else (to a speaking character who, in turn, was determined by what the action required). Consequently, the language of the poem was not given a formative role within the growing organic entity: it determined nothing else and was determined by almost everything else. Since it did not participate as a generative force in the growing organic entity, it had, as it were, a one-way, mechanistic relationship to those elements that were generative. And organicism was reserved as a way to describe the relations among the broadly structural elements of the action alone, as if these could proceed—in synopsis form—without the language that, in the work, actually carried them along.

As the nineteenth and twentieth centuries take up the organic metaphor for the poem, they increasingly transform it in order to introduce an active, indeed a primarily active, function for language.[6] For the modernist, language is to have it both ways, sharing the temporality of experience and yet giving it the unity of human comprehension by imposing spatial form upon it. If the natural-sign aesthetic was doomed in part because by the nineteenth century a temporal epistemology, sensitive to history, replaced the spatial ontology of rationalism, modernism returned spatiality to aesthetics only while continuing to recognize experience as irreducibly temporal, thereby holding out to poetry the special task of running along like experience and yet rebounding like a human shape. The conception of time as abandoned to Bergsonian fluidity only heightens the aesthetic achievement that seizes it and then displays what it has seized. And poetry becomes the one place in which that victory over time *in* time can again and again be represented.

Poetry sits atop the hierarchy of the arts by virtue of this double power, allowing its creator the most formidable of displays precisely because of that which leaves language as the least natural (i.e., most arbitrary and most conventional) of media. The special and two-sided role assigned the language medium in poetry allows it to supervise the paradoxical coexistence of time and space, of the sensible and the intelligible, of mimesis and free-ranging expression. In the now obsolete spectrum of the arts we saw poetry caught between the extremes of the visual arts and music, and facing both ways. The old hierarchy among the arts emerging from such a framework first led to the *ut pictura poesis* injunction, then started an opposed movement all the way to music in pursuit of the non-mimetic. With modernism the verbal arts ascend to the status of model—in the center and facing both ways, toward the plastic arts and toward music, and absorbing both ends into themselves. Now it is the visual arts that are to ape the semiotic duplicity of the verbal arts (*ut poesis pictura*),[7] though they can do so only at the cost of distancing

6. The need to emphasize the generative role of language in the creation of poetic form is very likely heightened by the fact that in this period critics are dealing mainly with lyric poems, with the emerging form in each of them seen to be primarily dependent on verbal manipulation. Once the methods of linguistic analysis of the New Criticism were firmly entrenched, efforts were made to extend them to certain kinds of prose fiction as well.

7. This is a far different version of *ut poesis pictura* from the one I suggested toward the end of Chapter 3, above. That one represented the neoclassicist's attempt to force

themselves the more self-consciously from any attempt to function as natural signs, that is, by accepting their role as sign systems within an aesthetic constructed, according to poetry's requirements, on a semiotic basis. And abandoning naive mimesis, theorists have increasingly argued for all the arts, including the visual, functioning as linguistic signs requiring interpretation.

For many decades now in the plastic arts, *all* aesthetic signs have come to be taken as both arbitrary and conventional, as anything but natural, since the natural sign has been abandoned as a possibility for even the few kinds of art for which it might appear to be at least superficially appropriate. Indeed, so-called realistic paintings and sculptures, like so-called realistic dramas, are not exempt from this toppling of any remnant of the authority of mimesis, of the natural-sign dream, even as we might have applied it to the few remaining cases in the arts that might still seem to be obvious candidates. Theorists could point to the formidable work of Gombrich in the history of the visual arts as authorizing their increasing awareness of the need to subordinate any mimetic function of the arts (even in what seemed to be the least problematic of the visual arts) to the conventions governing the way art was both made and perceived. Emphasizing "the beholder's share" and the role of the visual habits, both optical and cultural, in shaping what that beholder sees, in *Art and Illusion* (1959) Gombrich encourages the reader to attend to the devices, derived from convention, that create what we, as human perceivers within our historically bound cultural habits, see as pattern. Aware of these devices, we will not be deceived by what presents itself to our naive response as if it were a natural sign. Gombrich playfully confronts the Socrates of the *Cratylus*, attacking his support for the mimetic pretensions of the would-be natural sign: one should account for form, Gombrich argues, by relating it to function rather than to the external referent.[8] Hence the Gombrichian motto, Making before Matching.

Even paintings produced within consciously realistic movements, such as the seventeenth-century Dutch, indeed, the very still-life

---

seventeenth- and eighteenth-century narrative painting, by means of the *punctum temporis,* into the static doctrine that had already captured poetry. Here I am suggesting the reverse as a consequence of the modernist aesthetic: that the semiotic notion of art as a language system, most obviously seen operating in poetry, be applied—on the poetic model—to the sister arts as well.

8. *Art and Illusion* (London: Phaidon Press, 1959), pp. 305–6.

genre itself,[9] can be seen as forcing us to sense the fact that they *are* paintings, representations that create the illusion of their apparent objects through the manipulation of alien, quite unrelated materials, artificial materials. Unless we are taken in and subject ourselves to a delusion promulgated by the myth of the natural sign, the paintings are to be perceived as self-referential demonstrations of the illusionary powers arising from the workings of the painterly medium, rather than to be accepted as transparent imitations of—or, worse, substitutes for—an apparently identical, or at least matching, "reality." This "reality," with which the natural-sign painting is supposed to have a one-to-one relation, cannot be asserted to have been there to check the painting's "accuracy," since the reality we see has been created for the viewer *by* the painting, that compound of canvas and pigment whose clues have worked with the viewer's eye and the viewer's previous experience to create what is now serving as the viewer's illusionary "reality."

As I tried to show in Chapter 3, the *trompe l'oeil* is the case *a fortiori* for the would-be natural sign: a representation so transparent that we are presumably to mistake it for a piece of reality; but the Gombrichian perspective can be seen as reversing the function of even so manifest an instance of realism. Instead of actually being fooled, as birds were said to be by Zeuxis, we are to see that we could *almost* be fooled by so artful a manipulation of painterly devices that demonstrate their illusionary power, though not by altogether fooling our never totally "innocent eye." Because we are not birds but rather are attuned to the conventional nature of the medium, we do not take it as an unqualifiedly natural sign—as a representation so transparent that we mistake it for reality, as not art at all—but instead respond to the *trompe l'oeil* as a demonstration of total artifice, as an ultimate display of the un-real character of illusion, an illusion that threatens to become a delusion but always remains only on the verge.

As Chapter 2, above, should have amply revealed, the application of this turnabout to the theater is obvious, since from this perspective we can view "realistic" drama—or even more what today might be called a "happening"—as a continual and moving *trompe l'oeil* only for the hypothetically innocent spectators (human "birds"),

9. I would prefer here the more strongly self-contradictory French *nature morte*, though both the English phrase and the French emphasize the oxymoron they contain.

who, unaware of dramatic convention, might be free to mistake art for life, to mistake the constructed play for a series of living incidents they have happened upon. But as in the case of the would-be natural-sign response to apparently literal representation in the visual arts, the perspective that theorists like Gombrich awakened in us has alerted us to the self-conscious theatricality that, in conventionalizing the illusionary natural sign, should disrupt and complicate the natural-sign response to even the most "realistic" of dramas. As we see in the *trompe l'oeil* tendency of each "realistic" painting or drama, no agent of disruption is more effective than the self-reference that hides within even the most apparently lifelike representation.

Once the breakthrough occurs that transforms our response so that it addresses self-conscious art rather than natural-sign innocence, then, too, in our experience of even the most apparently static of paintings, time intrudes upon space, Lessing to the contrary notwithstanding. Gombrich once again takes the lead in justifying this invasion in his "Moment and Movement in Art" (1964), in which he shows how the *punctum temporis* (see Chapter 3, above) is violated by the observer's narrative propensity to impose movement on it.[10] We are moving toward a semiotic—and hence a verbal—model, in which time invades space in the arts Lessing treated as spatial no less than space invades time in the arts Lessing treated as temporal.

Rosalie Colie extends this notion in "Still Life: Paradoxes of Being," a central chapter in her *Paradoxia Epidemica* (1966), which is deeply indebted to Gombrich's seminal essay, "Tradition and Expression in Western Still Life."[11] Her chapter builds on the space-time, stasis-motion paradox inherent in the phrase "still life," which she relates to my oxymoron "still movement," from my original essay on ekphrasis (see the Appendix). The chapter begins by describ-

---

10. Gombrich, "Moment and Movement in Art," *Journal of the Warburg and Courtauld Institutes* 27 (1964): 293–306, reprinted in *The Image and the Eye: Further Studies in the Psychology of Pictorial Representation* (Ithaca: Cornell University Press, 1982), pp. 40–62.

11. *Paradoxia Epidemica: The Renaissance Tradition of Paradox* (Princeton: Princeton University Press, 1966), pp. 273–99. "Tradition and Expression in Western Still Life" appears in Gombrich's *Meditations on a Hobby Horse and Other Essays on the Theory of Art* (London: Phaidon Press, 1963), pp. 95–105. See also the pioneering work on the subject, which influenced both Gombrich and Colie, Charles Sterling, *Still Life Painting from Antiquity to the Present Time*, trans. James Emmons (New York: Universe Books, 1959), chap. 5, esp. pp. 50–56.

ing in imaginative detail a still-life painting in which the objects statically disposed to be imitated are represented as being so delicately
transient (thin, transparent, even "partly consumed") that they are
seen as only momentarily present: "They seem only barely there,
only barely real" (p. 273). The artist wants us to see them as evanescent, as illusions only. In Protestant northern Europe, with its asceticism, the "representation of the transient" is a *memento mori*, a
reminder of the illusory, flimsy, and ultimately unreal character of
the things of this fading world in the face of death's eternity (p. 275).
No wonder the painting that represented such things was called a
vanitas, deceiving the senses as reminders of the deception produced by the vain objects themselves, especially when juxtaposed
to the death's head. The static representation, so fixedly out there,
is belied by the transitory nature of the material objects of this van-
ishing realm. Time gives the lie to this vain attempt to stop it, this
vain attempt to give it permanence by fixing it in the painting. As an
object concerned exclusively with the realm of appearance, then,
the painting, a material thing composed only of empty representations—optical illusions—becomes an allegory of the deceptions of
the material world represented by the material things it is imitating.

Colie is thus suggesting a daring—even reckless—universalizing
and thematizing of this claim. All artists, having become skeptical
epistemologists persuaded by their art of the illusionary character
of reality, foster the illusionary tendencies of their paintings as self-
contradicting objects. "The illusionism that all still-life painters
strive to achieve brings to a focus the illusion of all painting and all
art" (p. 273) and, by implication, of all material reality too—just the
universal theme of seventeenth-century Platonism. A way of reading paintings, and literary works as well, becomes the authority for
sanctioning a single metaphysical and moral judgment aimed at the
illusionary character of the material—and the materialistic—world:
"All pictures are, somehow, *vanitates*; all pictures demonstrate, not
just the weakness and deceits of our senses, but also the relative
meaninglessness of things" (p. 298). "Things point to the meaninglessness *sub specie aeternitatis*; being alive is a *memento mori*" (p.
291). Here, in this modernist move to substantialize an interpretive
method dedicated to the ubiquity of aesthetic illusionism, there is a
puritanical discomfort that reveals the striking persistence of Platonic moralism.

Colie's generalization also expands her claims beyond the illusionary plastic arts to the illusionary verbal arts by turning from exam-

ples from painting to examples from drama. She thus reminds us of Cleopatra's subtle and strangely prophetic acknowledgment in Shakespeare's *Antony and Cleopatra* that her role centuries later is to be acted—as before our eyes it is indeed being acted, and the very lines being spoken—by a boy: "And I shall see / Some squeaking Cleopatra boy my greatness / In the posture of a whore" (V.ii.219–21). "The playwright's grasp upon his craft was tight enough to permit the risk of breaking the illusion," of breaking into "self-reference," just as "the illusionism involved in the still life risks the painter's art by drawing attention to the artifice" (pp. 273, 362). Once again, as in the history of natural-sign theory and the history of the rejection of natural-sign theory, the would-be realistic visual arts and the drama are linked, this time by the self-referential devices that, in turning them inward, cut their ties to their references.

In this chapter and in a later chapter, "Problems of Self-Reference," Colie pursues the self-referential habit of the aesthetic object that has art "drawing attention to the artifice." As one might expect, she is especially interested in the role of the mirror in paintings and comes to concentrate on involute works such as Jan van Eyck's wedding portrait of Arnolfini and his wife (with its specially reflective mirror in which the artist appears in front of the couple) and, inevitably, that other painting with a famous, problematic mirror, Velasquez's *Las Meniñas*, a painting that appears to represent its own act of being painted.[12] Such paintings, she tells us, leave us balancing between what are simultaneously "two points of view" (pp. 358–59). It is what Gombrich, referring to Escher as well, calls "visual deadlock," the painterly analogue to the self-contradictory verbal pun.[13] When she transfers her insights to the verbal arts, Colie focuses upon the use of mirrors or mirrorlike elements first in drama, then also in other literary genres, particularly the lyric. In all these she

12. Colie discusses the van Eyck painting in *Paradoxia Epidemica*, pp. 282, 362, and the Velasquez on pp. 358–59. The latter discussion in 1966 was among the earliest of many studies during the past two decades, studies that have set off a number of debates. I will mention only a few of them: Michel Foucault, *The Order of Things* (in French *Les mots and les choses*) (New York: Vintage Books, 1973), pp. 3–16; John R. Searle, "*Las Meniñas* and the Paradoxes of Pictorial Representation," *Critical Inquiry* 6 (Spring 1980): 477–88; Joel Snyder and Ted Cohen, "Reflexions on *Las Meniñas*: Paradox Lost," *Critical Inquiry* 7 (Winter 1980): 429–47.

13. Gombrich himself uses the phrase "visual pun" as synonymous with "visual deadlock" and "visual paradox." All of them are attempts to describe perceptual "stalemate," "the hidden complexity of all picture reading" (see his 'Illusion and Visual Deadlock," in *Meditations on a Hobby Horse*, pp. 153–56).

finds a similar and insistent reflexivity, which is to remind us of the make-believe illusion that is both art and art's reflection of an equally illusionary material world.

Her interpretive method traces the circularity—indeed, celebrates the vortical principle—of works that continually turn back on themselves, confessing themselves only art and not the actual things. But the method has from the outset been thematized in the metaphysical and moral implications of her appeal to illusion, which ends by suggesting a justification for art. It suggests that all worldly existence is to be seen as *de*lusion, leading us astray, *except* for the conscious self-referentiality of the work of art: the work's confession that its *il*lusion (in the sense I attributed to Johnson in Chapter 2) reveals itself to us as a self-conscious version of delusion that can serve as our metaphysical beacon through these shadows and snares. In reminding us of its own status as illusion, as soothsayer of our universe, the work of art may be the only thing we can trust, even as it self-consciously retreats before itself. The credibility of Colie's interpretive method, unfortunately, may have to rest on the ontological justness of her claims, and yet, as an aesthetic, it reaches out to proclaim the evidence that argues for them. As we will see, those who follow the modernists worry about so primary a role being assigned the aesthetic, about its arrogating to itself nothing less than universal cognition—about, in short, its aestheticization of the world of knowledge and action.

The ultimate paradox of the modernist commitment to the poem as a "work of art" arises from its confidence that however self-contradictory its ontological status, in its very airiness it is the one sure thing, indeed a solid, reified "body"—there's that word again—in a world that otherwise falls, or ought to fall, away. It is also the one sure thing that the commentator can talk about with precision, so that the critic as analyst-interpreter becomes a major guide for us all. Hence our sense of the object as a spatial out-there, as having its place, was a necessary assumption, despite the fact that we were dealing with a sequence of words, which—as we learned after the fading of our neoclassical overconfidence in their visual power—have neither an immediate physical reality nor even a claim to carrying us with transparency to a mediate physical reality. This renewed commitment to the spatial in modernist theory, I have more than once observed, refers to a very different version of the spatial from that which is related in any way either to natural signs or to picture-making. Instead, in a manner that resembles Renaissance emblema-

tics rather than neoclassical pictorialism, for the modernist aesthetic it is the "body of the poem" itself that claims spatial character.
The metaphor of "body," for all its incarnational implications, is
taken almost literally and, for this reason, is revealed as another
modernist method that thematizes itself. It is worth examining in
detail how it does so, since this transforming of a poetics into a subliminal metaphysics is what postmoderns find to be the danger of attributing an independent power to the aesthetic.

As I anticipated in Chapter 6, the spatial is now to be achieved by
a transformative use of language as a poetic medium that takes arbitrary signs and *literally* changes their nature in spite of their pre-
poetic tendencies, freezing them into a spatial fix, making them into
their own emblem, though hardly a picturable one. So the spatial is
no longer defined by way of the visual so much as by way of the material, as taking up its own place: the art object, as spatial, is now to
lead, not elsewhere to a something seen, but to its own naturelike
organic thinghood, rooted in its own integrity. In my examination of
Burckhardt's claims for the verbal medium in Chapter 6, I traced the
process by which words in poems were to take on a substantive "nature," turning from the arbitrary and conventional to the inevitable
and indispensable. Such a change in their function calls for a description that introduces metaphors that treat words as if they were
bodies, that treat them as living things, occupying spaces that grow
into a pattern, instead of as passing, empty sounds in an endless
string coming before and going after. If the sound of words, as
poetry's sensible element, has no meaning when the poet picks
them up, he is to work it into giving us a special access to meaning
before he is finished with them. The trick, as we saw Burckhardt advise, is to take those arbitrary sounds and, through aural or graphic
devices, to tie them down, to give them a material character, to force
them, despite their accidental character, to take on substantive consequences.

For this theoretical tradition, the aesthetic illusion of the poem's
materiality is not, as in theology, a matter of faith but has been constructed by what the poet succeeds in making the medium perform
for us. The aesthetic thus becomes the way that modernist theory allows for the secular, textually "earned" equivalent of a semiotic
formed out of the Christian mystery: the equivalent of the incarnation, of the "corporealizing" of language, the substantiating of
words—allowing them to take on flesh—before a readership whose
semiotic habits have been formed by the workings of that mysteri-

ous divine-human paradox in its culture. It is indeed a final carrying out of Matthew Arnold's call for a literature that is a substitute for a defunct religion, a literature that can give us the psychological lift without requiring the price of a faith that cannot withstand the assaults of modern scientifically induced skepticism. Yet, however unmetaphysical a theorist such as Burckhardt may mean his poetics of corporeality to be, the desire to have poets endow the word with "body" (by my earlier use of the word "flesh," I have already revealed the metaphor for what it is) does reflect the persistence of Christian semiotic in the tradition after Coleridge, for whom, we must remember, the term "symbol"—a major source of modernism's "symbol"—derives from his need to find an interpretive method for the Bible. Nor, as I feel the sequel will amply demonstrate, can this tradition altogether cut itself off from its theological source in its attempt to find an independent secular method.

The coupling of the dynamics of a flowing sequence and the capturing of it within a form, though an always responsive and yielding form, is consistent with the advocacy of the emblematic in poetry, with the call for the poetic "symbol."[14] It is an appeal to poetically empowered words to turn substantive and to hold within themselves the moving world of words and references that are recreated into their text. This paradoxical fusion of historical time and metaphysical space within the word springs from the dependence of organicist poetics upon the form, if not the substance, of the primary Christian metaphor.[15] Its central divine-human paradox in the figure of Christ represents both the impossible union of our chronological time with heaven's eternal *now* and, when projected into the realm of language, the transfiguration of many running words into the Word. Modernism attempts to secularize this paradox into the poetic metaphor that, from romantic theory on, becomes both symbol and emblem, the device that creates a magical mode of lan-

14. See Coleridge's original definition of "symbol," in contrast to "allegory," in *The Statesman's Manual, The Collected Works of Coleridge, Lay Sermons*, ed. R. J. White (London: Routledge and Kegan Paul, 1972), p. 30; and my discussion of this distinction in Coleridge and those who follow in my "'A Waking Dream': The Symbolic Alternative to Allegory," in *Allegory, Myth, and Symbol*, ed. Morton W. Bloomfield, Harvard English Studies 9 (Cambridge: Harvard University Press, 1981), pp. 1–22.

15. See chaps. 1 and 2 of my *A Reopening of Closure*. In the first chapter I examine the semiotic of the Renaissance love lyric as a secularization of the Christian semiotic, and in the second I deal with Coleridgean and later organicism as a development of this metaphorical habit that has grown out of what I term the "typological imagination."

guage behavior, containing the moving world (and world of words) within a specially created verbal form. For all its inventiveness, the poetic imagination is thus a secular projection of what, after Renaissance practice, I have called the typological imagination.

Adapting the Bergsonian paradox about temporality, the theorist seeks to maintain both the sequence of words (linguistic analogue to the moving sequence of existential moments) and the formal capturing of this sequence in its consummate verbal form (linguistic analogue to life's epiphanic moment, what I term elsewhere an "eschatological punctuation" upon historical sequence).[16] Mutually exclusive as these two may seem, they must paradoxically coexist: the moment must be grasped and sustained as its own space, but without forgoing the sequence of moments, so that, instead, it provides an all-enclosing home for that sequence even as the latter still wanders into the darkness of an ever-unwinding future. The dependence of this paradox in organicist aesthetics upon the two-in-one paradox of the primal Christian metaphor is persistent and, alas, too often uncritical. It accounts, in criticism that follows this line, for the frequency of terms associated with body, corporeality, incarnation—the word made flesh (as Word). Armed with this borrowed metaphor, this criticism moves, with its mystifying appeal to the verbal miracle, beyond the alternatives of monism and dualism—and even beyond a continuing tension between the two—to an insistence on sustaining them, despite their mutual exclusivity, as a both/and.

As just one example, quite late in this theoretical tradition, while it is quite secure in its claim to authority, we find one of the more explicit references to this metaphor, which ties secular criticism to at least the *form* of theological metaphor, in the culminating resolution that W. K. Wimsatt and Cleanth Brooks pronounce to their ambitious history of criticism. Their rejection of the two disjunctive alternatives, as well as of a sustained tension between them, follows the model I have just described.

The writers of the present history have not been concerned to implicate literary theory with any kind of religious doctrine. It appears to us, however, relevant, as we near our conclusion, at least to confess an opinion

16. In "*Murder in the Cathedral:* The Limits of Drama and the Freedom of Vision," *The Classic Vision: The Retreat from Extremity in Modern Literature* (Baltimore: Johns Hopkins Press, 1971), pp. 337–62, esp. pp. 344–48.

that the kind of literary theory which seems to us to emerge the most plausibly from the long history of the debates is far more difficult to orient within any of the Platonic or Gnostic ideal world views, or within the Manichaean full dualism and strife of principles, than precisely within the vision of suffering, the optimism, the mystery which are embraced in the religious dogma of the Incarnation.[17]

The Renaissance way of moving toward the verbal emblem in theory (see Chapter 5, above), like its contemporary borrowing of theological metaphors to accommodate the miracles of courtly love, had long before established a useful precedent for organic theory.[18] And Coleridge, picking it up in order to define his poet as a godlike wielder of the I AM, clearly derived his most influential claims for the mastery of experience and language by poetic form from the hermeneutic demands of the Book of books, the Bible.[19] As he turns to poetry he retains his concern for infusing language with substance, modeling the semiotic of poetry after that of the sacred Word: he seeks mental faculties and linguistic means that will allow the poet-creator to make words "esemplastic" or "coadunative" (to cite only two of his unfortunate neologisms desperately invented as descriptions of that mysterious process by which the poet must use words to make many into one, to achieve "unity in multeity"). In retaining the *form* of the Christian metaphor as its model, the Coleridgean aesthetic sets its modernist followers on a path that ties their aesthetic to a metaphorical formula that must threaten to carry its own doctrinal thematization (as the formula for a *Christian* semiotic) within it.

The modernist aesthetic has many ways of asserting the unifying character of poetic form as it acts upon both existential temporality and the flow of words. But these too can be seen as thematizing their aesthetic claims through a semiotic that may be seen as borrowing its form from the Christian metaphor. As an ultimate modernist, Patrick AE. Hutchings reconstructs a poetics that is an emblematics, collapsing time within a verbal form, by appealing to Coleridge's precedent. From chapter 15 of the *Biographia Literaria* he quotes as an

17. *Literary Criticism: A Short History* (New York: Alfred A. Knopf, 1957), p. 746.
18. Once again I call attention to *A Reopening of Closure*; see esp. chap. 1, "The Figure in the Renaissance Poem as Bound and Unbounded."
19. I am referring to Coleridge's influential definitions of "symbol" and "allegory," with the former clearly reserved by Coleridge for the highest poetry (see n. 14, above). This distinction, from *The Statesman's Manual*, occurs during Coleridge's discussion of biblical interpretation.

epigraph to one of his essays, "Images become proofs of original genius . . . when they have the effect of reducing multitude to unity, or succession to an instant."[20] The title of this essay, "Imagination: 'as the Sun paints in the camera obscura,'" refers to a passage in which Coleridge uses the activity of the camera obscura, its contraction of light into a visual image, as a metaphor to describe the instantaneity of the poetic imagination. In the body of the essay Hutchings quotes the sentence in which Coleridge calls for poetry to display the sort of verbal "painting" that is not an attempted reproduction of the visual object by the fancy but an imaginative creation, "with such co-presence of the whole picture flashed at once upon the eye, as the sun paints in a camera obscura."[21]

Hutchings consistently seeks, in opposition to Lessing and as an echo of the voices of Diderot and Herder, to claim for the poem the power to "escape the serial nature of its medium"[22] by forcing the reader to apprehend it at an instant—*tout à coup*. He cites the precedent of Herder, who, in his argument with Lessing, argues that the poem "works in space, so that it makes its whole speech sensuous." It is also true that since it is speech, "it works in time" and thus shares the temporal succession of words and ideas with other kinds of speech; but it is distinguished as poetry because we perceive it spatially as a "whole, which is expressed little by little by its parts" ("the whole that it constructs through time").[23] This whole, for Hutchings as for Herder, is the meaning that we grasp from the ver-

20. Quoted as the epigraph to "Imagination: 'as the Sun paints in the camera obscura,'" *Journal of Aesthetic and Art Criticism* 29 (1970): 63–76. It is quoted also in his "'Words After Speech': Phenomenology and Symbol in T. S. Eliot's Quartets," *Philosophical Studies* (National University of Ireland, Dublin) 22 (1973): 17–37; the quotation appears on p. 19.

21. "Imagination," p. 67. The quotation from Coleridge appears in *Biographia Literaria*, ed. J. Shawcross, 2 vols. (London: Oxford University Press, 1907), 2:102–3.

22. Hutchings, "Meaning and Simultaneity in Poetry," *Australasian Universities Language and Literature Association, Proceedings and Papers of the Tenth Congress* (Christchurch, New Zealand, 1966), p. 295. Also on this page: "There is a categorical difference between the signs, serial and temporal, and the *meaning* of these signs, which is in some sense a-temporal." And later (p. 299): "What we read are words in a serial order: but what we understand is something which, though it may dawn on us progressively as we read, is not itself essentially a thing of parts which follow parts. Neither the meaning, nor the meaning of the meaning are 'objects which succeed, or the parts of which succeed to each other.'" For a much earlier version of such statements see the quotation from Diderot below.

23. Quoted by Hutchings in "Imagination," p. 64. This is one of the passages in Herder that I discuss in Chapter 6, above. See *Herders Werke*, ed. Theodor Matthias,

bal sequence, which we grasp in a flash. Hence Hutchings's principle: "It takes time to say but not to mean" (p. 65). The sequence of
instants that is the text—*if* it is a proper imaginative whole as Coleridge would have it—collapses into our grasping it all at once.

Hutchings could as usefully have quoted Diderot's earlier argument on behalf of the instantaneity of our mental response that transcends and unites the sequence of words:

> The state of mind, in an indivisible instant, was represented by a mass of
> terms that the precision of language required, and that distributed a total
> impression among several parts; and because these terms were pro-
> nounced successively and were only understood in the order in which
> they were pronounced, one was led to believe that the feelings of the
> mind that they represented had the same succession. But that is not at all
> the case. The state of our mind is one thing, the account we render of it,
> whether to ourselves or to others, is another; the complete and instan-
> taneous feeling of this state is one thing, the successive attention . . .
> that we are forced to give to it to make ourselves understood is another.
> Our mind is a moving tableau . . . : we spend much time rendering it
> with fidelity, but it exists in its entirety, all at one time: the imagination
> does not proceed step by step as verbal expression does.[24]

Here indeed is precedent for Hutchings's motto, It takes time to say
but not to mean.

This concept may remind us also of the interest of eighteenth-
century critics of painting or sculpture in the *punctum temporis*,
which I discussed toward the close of Chapter 3.[25] But their "point
of time" was to be a single isolable instant that any spatial art had to

---

vol. 1 (Leipzig: Bibliographisches Institut, n.d.), p. 258. I have altered Hutchings's
translations to make them more literal.

24. Diderot, *Lettre sur les sourds et muets à l'usage de ceux qui entendent et qui parlent*,
in *Oeuvres complètes de Diderot*, ed. J. Assézat, vol. 1 (Paris: Garnier Frères, 1875), p.
369; the translation is mine. Diderot's argument for instantaneity in the midst of temporal succession is related to the function he assigns to the "hieroglyph" (see my discussion in Chapter 6) in fulfilling the mission of the poem to interrupt what, in
discourse other than poetic, is for him the mere flow of words as intelligible signs.

25. I remind the reader of Gombrich's key discussion of the *punctum temporis* in his
"Moment and Movement in Art." As I pointed out earlier in the present chapter,
Gombrich, speaking of painting, disputes the *punctum temporis* by insisting that it
cannot prevent the intrusion upon it of the temporal by the observer's narrative imagination. Hutchings, speaking of poetry, is making the opposite point: that the tem-

extrapolate out of a sequence of such instants in a narrative in order to represent it. Given a series of still frames, each changing just a bit, so that together they make up a picture in motion, the eighteenth-century artist devoted to the *punctum temporis* must choose the one frame that, at the apex of the line of probabilities, can freeze the action most significantly. That artist, acting as a good empiricist who sees experience as a sequence of perceptible snapshots, is claiming to find that one crucial frame in the series, pick it out, and project it. On the other hand, the instant designated by Hutchings, as non-empiricist, is not one pulled from the flow of instants but the one by means of which the perceiving mind, without stopping the flow, collapses all into one. It is the one instant in which a totality of meaning is grasped as "some indefinite specious present" (p. 65). In his subsequent discussion here and in his companion essay, Hutchings makes it clear that this is an instant which is, as a *tout à coup* instant, out of time.[26]

It is this concept of the moment that is outside the temporal sequence yet somehow contains it all that leads Hutchings to call upon the Christian figuralism that projects a miraculous simultaneity between the moment in a historical sequence and the eternal moment out of time. He thus turns to Eliot's *Four Quartets*, which for him is the poem that makes his claim by in itself being the embodiment of that claim: the poem says it by enacting it. From the epigraph to his essay onward, Hutchings relates his comments on the *Quartets* to my own earlier discussion of "the still movement of poetry," a discussion largely dependent on my study of the *Quartets* (as well as Keats's "Grecian Urn") that develops the paradoxical relationship between stillness and movement in the way poems—at least ekphrastic poems—function.[27] The *Quartets* permits Hutchings to move, as Eliot does, from the capture of movement by stillness in the language of poems to the existential and metaphysical—that is, the thematic—extensions of this temporal paradox.

The *Four Quartets* serves Hutchings, as it served me in the essay

---

poral sequence of words cannot prevent the reader's unifying imagination from collapsing it into a single moment of meaning ("It takes time to say but not to mean").

26. See my own discussion, in Bergsonian terms, of the words "instant," "instance," and "instantaneous" in *The Classic Vision*, p. 9.

27. I am referring (after Hutchings) to my essay *"Ekphrasis* and the Still Movement of Poetry; or *Laokoön* Revisited" (see the Appendix). The Hutchings essay I am referring to is " 'Words After Speech.' " The quotation from the *Four Quartets* that serves as my epigraph to the present chapter is a central passage for Hutchings's discussion.

that helped to prompt his, as more than an example: the poem is an extended, moving argument for the intersection of time and the timeless, of the historical and the eschatological, in the miraculous transformation of the human story under the Christian dispensation, which is analogous to the similarly miraculous transformation of the verbal sequence by the inspired poet. The endless movement of words within a timeless pattern that still preserves their movement is a semiotic reflection of the sequence of our existential moments within the eternal presence of the Christian meta-narrative. "Except for the point, the still point, / There would be no dance, and there is only the dance" ("Burnt Norton"). For Eliot the "dance" is at once a dance of the language of the poem and the dance of life, both all still form and yet all movement. As if explicating the symbol of the *ouroboros*, the reflexive meta-narrative conceives of time both as running out, each uncapturable moment succeeded by the next, and as redeemed, the redemption turning time back on itself, changing the graphic figure for time from line to circle. Whether we are speaking of time's moments or their semiotic echoes in the poem's words, the circle is the ideal emblem of that doubleness, since in its completeness it represents an ultimate closure and in its rotating it represents an endless motion to escape stasis.[28] There are no points on a circle, so that any point we try arbitrarily to impose upon it is never at rest but, dissolving into its companions, seems always to be running from itself, though only as part of the process of making the circle complete — as Donne puts it, of making one's circle "just." In this conception, time's moments are in ceaseless flight, as, inescapably, they retrace the circle by coming around (dust to dust). Hence the opening and closing words of Eliot's "East Coker": "In the beginning is my end. . . . In my end is my beginning." Hence also the closing verse paragraph of the *Quartets* in "Little Gidding":

> We shall not cease from exploration
> And the end of all our exploring
> Will be to arrive where we started
> And know the place for the first time.

28. I again refer the reader to Georges Poulet's remarkable work, *The Metamorphoses of the Circle*, trans. Carley Dawson and Elliott Coleman (Baltimore: Johns Hopkins Press, 1966), esp. pp. xi–xxvii, 1–14, and 342–47.

Eliot captures the divine-human paradox of time as both still and moving, indeed as still moving, in his figure of the wheel, from the circular movement of its hub to the repetitive cycles of its rim. It is the ever-turning wheel of human history, which is tied to the "still point" of the wheel's hub by God's saints, who, like Christ, share the human and divine worlds and the concept of time appropriate to each. The world on the rim, for all the illusion of its forward motion, moves round and round like the repetition of the seasons traced in the *Four Quartets*, finding the meaning of their paradoxical motion in their relationship to the center that holds them, but only by means of those saints, like Thomas Becket, who tie them to the center, that still, turning (still turning) point. The two worlds, then, with their respective concepts of time, are so linked that every moment is doubled—even self-contradictorily doubled—in its meaning.[29] Thus the Christian Easter is both one day in the disappearing year and an always recurring event in the transcendent present: "That the pattern may subsist, for the pattern is the action / And the suffering, that the wheel may turn and still / Be forever still" (*Murder in the Cathedral*, pt. 1). What is true of the lived moment of the saint's life can also be true of the written word of a text, or for that matter, of the text itself in its relation to the divine Master Text. Thus, through the figure of Becket, the many lines of transferred text—especially those that carry further the figure of the wheel of time that authorizes Becket's dual role as man and saint—link *Murder in the Cathedral* to *Four Quartets*, which becomes its meta-text, reflecting back on the play and giving new meanings to the gleanings from the play that it contains.

In such modernist commentary as Hutchings's, the formal is being treated as just the other side of, if not actually one with, the thematic. How, apart from a Christian semiotic, does a running verbal sequence get "redeemed"? We consistently find, in the modernist-formalist, a redemption for the word in a text's echoes, juxtapositions, foreshadowings, and returns, which together constitute what Joseph Frank will term "spatial form," ostensibly unrelated to the-

29. One may be reminded of a parallel doubleness, much earlier in Eliot's career as critic, in the theory of history that he introduces in "Tradition and the Individual Talent," where he develops a relationship between the unrolling sequence of literary works and the sudden emergence of the masterpiece that transforms the past as well as the future: "What happens when a new work of art is created is something that happens simultaneously to all the works of art which preceded it" (*Selected Essays* [New York: Harcourt, Brace, 1950], p. 5).

ological doctrine. But the role of Eliot's work in the development of modernist criticism suggests otherwise. Can these metaphors that seek to account for a moving text returning upon itself, circularizing its linear movement, become persuasive without a notion that permits a claim for the redemption of time, a notion that, because it cannot escape its theological source, firmly ties down the formal to a universal thematic?

This poetic, then, seems to require sustenance by the model provided by Christian orthodoxy, so that its claims for the behavior of words in the texts it reads may require support from a Master Text whose mysteries can be earned only by faith, a faith not easily transferred from the religious to the poetic except by the faithful. Clearly, in Hutchings as in Eliot, the paradoxical coincidence of time and the timeless—of time spent and time redeemed—in verbal representation is a pattern that is dependent on the theological formula. The aesthetic thus may not be much more self-sustaining in this version of modernism than we saw it in the Renaissance, although many critics after Eliot, closer in humanistic spirit to the Arnoldian impulse to secularize the religious, try to drop the theological substance even as they maintain the model. Nevertheless, as we shall see in Chapter 8, their antagonists have reason for their concern that there is at least a quasi-theological mystification—and implicitly a reactionary political agenda—at the base of the verbal miracles proclaimed for poetry by high modernism. I have dwelled on Hutchings here because in him, especially when he uses Eliot as his metatext, the easily traced relationship between the poetic and the theological, as regards both existential time and textual time, instructs me when I turn to critics who are less explicit about such a relationship, probably because they are less aware of a connection they would prefer to avoid.

Central to the modernist's emblematic quest is the desire to transform history into myth, a myth whose verbal symbols, like Christianity's, are filled with presence. And as we saw in the appeal to the Christian metaphor in the passage I quoted from Wimsatt and Brooks earlier in this chapter, the New Criticism, as the ultimate rationalization of modernist poetic practice, required the transformation of history into mythic (i.e., for them, poetic) form to build the "well wrought urn" as their critical emblem.[30] Again there is the

30. I am speaking, of course, of Donne's "well wrought urn" (in "The Canonization"), which Brooks made his own.

need to complement the linear with the circle of eternal return. Other mythic structures sometimes served as well as the Christian: one only need think of the mythification of history in a meta-poem such as Yeats's *A Vision* or at many points in the work of Stevens. The poetic transformation and redemption of the merely sequential in event or in text is a constant objective, and the pressure toward secular transubstantiation retains suggestions of Christian parallels.

As a young, sympathetic companion to this effort, Joseph Frank, strongly influenced by Eliot, sought to produce a justification as well as a philosophical genealogy for a poetics of "spatial form." His definition of modernism—as art that favors spatial juxtaposition over temporal succession, the formalistic over the historical—is drawn largely from Wilhelm Worringer's grouping of periods by their emphasizing flatness or depth in art, from Mircea Eliade's conception of "sacred time" as made spatial through the ritual recurrence of moments that redeems them and sets them apart, and from Ezra Pound's definition of the image (to which Hutchings's formulation may be indebted) as "that which presents an intellectual and emotional complex in an instant of time."[31] I find few examples that demonstrate as clearly as Frank does the critic's, and especially the modernist critic's, habit of adapting metaphorically (and uncritically) for the verbal arts terms that are used literally in formalist criticism of the visual arts.[32] Frank's discussion of what he claims to be the spatial character of literary form in modernist literature—"word groups [that] must be juxtaposed with one another and perceived simultaneously," or a poem that "dissolves sequence" and "the inherent consecutiveness of language"—moves easily, too easily, into

31. The quotation from Pound appears in Joseph Frank, *The Widening Gyre: Crisis and Mastery in Modern Literature* (Bloomington: Indiana University Press, 1963), p. 9. These influential essays on "Spatial Form in Modern Literature" originally appeared in 1945. Although Frank has written later both to defend and modify his views on the subject, it is these early essays that, in the reckless extremity of their claims, help us appreciate the modernist critic's spatial bias in trying to collapse verbal sequence into formal structure. The rest of my comments on Frank are drawn from this group of essays.

32. In "Spatial Form in Literature: Toward a General Theory," *Critical Inquiry* 6 (1980): 539–67, W. J. T. Mitchell explores the complications of the notion of spatial form and the unfortunate reduction implied in the simple opposition of time and space in the rhetoric of criticism. He rejects any exclusive claim to temporality that is unaware of the intrusion of spatial elements, as well as the reverse claim. He raises a series of important questions to pursue those complications. I hope my efforts in this volume go some way toward answering those questions.

the thematic spatializing of history in such works: works like *The Waste Land, Ulysses,* and the *Cantos,* which "maintain a continual juxtaposition between aspects of the past and present" (pp. 15, 10, 12).

Frank's key notions, the juxtaposition of represented elements and the simultaneity of perception, are borrowed from Lessing, who, using them literally, reserved them for the spatial arts and thus denied them to the verbal arts. In rejecting Lessing's distinction while borrowing his notions—and even, in the case of "juxtaposition" and "simultaneity," his terms—Frank hopes that they can be made to exert enough figurative force for him to apply them to the temporal art of literature. His call for the "juxtaposition of word groups" in modernist writing may begin only as a metaphor for the spatial (because, as Lessing has told us, a text is in fact not a canvas and can only be read word by word, page by page), but it comes to be literalized, in transforming not only the temporality of our reading experience but the very representation of time itself: verbal juxtapositions slip into temporal juxtapositions that undo actual chronology.[33] Following Eliade, Frank moves from the formal to the explicitly metaphysical, from the dissolution of verbal sequence to the mythic dissolution of history:

> By this juxtaposition of past and present . . . history becomes ahistorical. Time is no longer felt as an objective, causal progression with clearly marked-out differences between periods; now it has become a continuum in which distinctions between past and present are wiped out. . . . Past and present are apprehended spatially, locked in a timeless unity that, while it may accentuate surface differences, eliminates any feeling of sequence by the very act of juxtaposition. . . . What has occurred, at least so far as literature is concerned, may be described as the transformation of the historical imagination into myth—an imagination for which historical time does not exist, and which sees the actions and events of a particular time only as the bodying forth of eternal prototypes. (Pp. 59–60)

This language, in moving into the thematic, still reverberates with the absorption of time into the timeless that has been embedded in the Western structure of figuration at least since the late Christian

---

33. Even the criticism of Wordsworth, hardly an ideal poet for the modernist, was affected by the spatializing of the temporal, so that there was for a time considerable emphasis on the "spots of time," as well as the "genius loci," used by Wordsworth to collapse temporal distances (see esp. Geoffrey H. Hartman, *Wordsworth's Poetry, 1787–1814* [New Haven: Yale University Press, 1964]).

Middle Ages. And as elsewhere, its habit of metaphysical projection has been hard to resist. Indeed, in the timelessness proposed by Frank we find little of the paradoxical dynamics of circularity, with its still movement, that I have observed in Eliot.

Cleanth Brooks, in his study of one of our great ekphrastic poems, the "Ode on a Grecian Urn," makes a similar claim about the transcendence of history (as mere facticity) by the mythopoeic. The title of his essay, "Keats's Sylvan Historian: History Without Footnotes," anticipates the modernist argument.[34] It enables him to explain the urn's lack of interest in answering the factual questions being asked about the figures represented on it and their actions: "Mere accumulations of facts . . . are meaningless. The sylvan historian [the urn] does better than that: it takes a few details and so orders them that we have not only beauty but insight into essential truth. Its 'history,' in short, is a history without footnotes. It has the validity of myth—not myth as a pretty but irrelevant make-belief, an idle fancy, but myth as a valid perception into reality" (p. 151).

Now such an ontological claim is a good deal for critics like Frank and Brooks to make. They may begin, apparently as freestanding modernist critics with a formalist bias, by turning poems into spatial entities whose form triumphs over sequence, changing befores and afters into the simultaneity of juxtaposition. They can perform such analysis only by means of a controlled parade of modulations, repetitions, and echoes, all of which, through a loose metaphor, are pressed to serve them as temporal equivalents of juxtaposition, as if juxtaposition could have a temporal equivalent. But as they betray the metaphysical grounding of such claims that would freeze the temporal into the spatial, they bring even their strictly formalist practices under the suspicion that they rest on a prior thematic commitment. In retrospect we can see that they present an obvious target for the theoretical demystifiers who follow. In the modernist moment, then, there returns to the poetic word the renewed attempt to earn for it the status of verbal emblem, of the letter as substantive. Unlike the formulation of the verbal emblem in the Renaissance, however, the modernist formulation relies on an appeal not (at least not ostensibly) to the mysteries of Christian Neo-Platonism but to the craft of the poet, who struggles with a medium—at once aural, graphic, and both referential and self-referential—to allow it

34. *The Well Wrought Urn: Studies in the Structure of Poetry* (New York: Reynal and Hitchcock, 1947), pp. 139–52.

to achieve dimensions that will persuade us to set the poem and its complex workings apart from other discourse. In Chapter 6 we saw these strange labors and their marvelous products most tellingly set forth for us by Burckhardt, as we will see them condescendingly denied by the postmodern skepticism we will meet in my final chapter.

It is hard to see how even those of us who would like to see such claims made believe they can be made metaphysics-free. Yet for all the smuggled metaphysics that thematizes the modernist critical method, let us concede that it can often allow a winning, impressive, and persuasive account of what it wants to find going on in many poems—those splendid works, most of them of high estate in a limited elitist canon—that the modernist method has with least strain accommodated to its extraordinary analytical instruments. We should not lightly dismiss such profitable and pleasurable accomplishments as we wrestle with the cost of having them, or the cost of abandoning them.

Critics must have the substantive notion of the poem as body to make good their attempt to turn the poem into emblem, Renaissance or modern. The emblem is the ultimate ekphrasis, as natural-sign mimesis—even of works of the visual arts—was not. In the ekphrastic emblem what is to be imitated is not just an object external to the poem, as the individual work of sculpture or the painting *was* the object of imitation for the ekphrasis in the most literal use of that term, with which I began. What is rather to be imitated is the status of the sculpture or painting as a physical art object. That status is achieved for the poem by its making a claim to an integrity like that of an object created by the plastic arts, an integrity marked by the wholeness of that spatial character which results from the exploitation of a sensuous (or an illusionarily sensuous) medium. The poem, then, would, if it could, imitate the spatial object by being one too.

Thus, so long as the merely figurative sense of this concept is acknowledged, this theoretical tradition can redefine the proper ekphrasis—conceived as verbal emblem, whether Renaissance or modernist—as the poem that imitates the completeness of form of its visual object of imitation by seeking its own form, indeed by shaping itself as a similar form. Tracing it back to the *ouroboros*, I have already indicated how, with its potential for paradox, the circle is made to serve this tradition as the most likely shape both for the object of imitation and for the form of the poem that uses it for its theme and its own shape. Since probably no shape so clearly as a circle represents the closure of form that the modernist seeks, it becomes a major formal principle for modernist criticism. On the thematic side I have already emphasized—in Eliot's beginnings and endings, in Frank's adaptation of Eliade to texts and history, in Brooks's commentary on the round surface of the urn—the idea of the circle of eternal return that controls their conversion of chronological time into mythic time. (With Yeats we could retain a circular shape so long as we changed the circle into a spiral, thereby once again combining progressive movement with eternal recurrence.) And we have seen, especially in Colie, that self-reference, in its reflexive turnings, leads to a circularity of form that has illusion multiply itself into a disappearing vortex.

The special relation between ekphrasis and the circular figure (literal in the form of spatial objects, metaphorical in the form of verbal objects) is emphasized in Leo Spitzer's seminal essay, which I have leaned upon from the very beginning of my efforts in this book. Speaking of Keats's "Urn," Spitzer observes that the structure of the poem imitates the urn's shape: "The poet describes an urn . . . bearing in typically Greek fashion a circular 'leaf-fring'd' frieze (and it is, I submit, mainly for that reason that the poem is circular or 'perfectly symmetrical' . . . thereby reproducing symbolically the form of the *objet d'art* which is its model)." The balance of the paragraph follows the stanzas of the poem to demonstrate that circularity. It concludes: "The circular form of the frieze makes it necessary for the main elements of the first scene to reappear in stanza v." Like the modernist-formalist that he is, Spitzer, in a footnote to this passage, extends his perception to cover the ekphrastic impulse itself: "Since already in antiquity the poetic *ekphrasis* was often devoted to circular objects (shields, cups, etc.), it was tempting for poets to imitate verbally this constructive principle in their *ekphraseis*. Mörike's poem on an ancient lamp shows the same formal circularity motivated by the form of the model as does Keats's ode on the urn."[35] One could add, as I have elsewhere, that Keats's shows a thematic circularity revealed by the urn as symbol: the circularity of the human life represented by the urn as both womb and tomb, holder of life and receptacle of death.[36] It is a paradoxical circularity reminis-

35. All the quotations from Spitzer in this paragraph are from "The 'Ode on a Grecian Urn,' or Content vs. Metagrammar," in his *Essays on English and American Literature*, ed. Anna Hatcher (Princeton: Princeton University Press, 1962), p. 73 and n. 5. See the epigraph to the Foreword, above.

36. Once again I refer to my original essay on ekphrasis, which serves as the Appendix to this volume.

cent of what I have several times observed in the tail-eating serpent that, from my frontispiece, has recurred throughout this book. The modernist, Spitzer or Brooks, views the enactment of this theme of paradoxical circularity in the form of Keats's ode as being a paradigmatic realization of the verbal emblem. In this continual reference to the circular, both in modernist formalism and modernist thematics, the mythopoeic assumption is that chronological time must be bent into circular time. Mythic temporality, converted to space, is shaped like a poem, which in its self-enclosure becomes the verbal emblem of temporality as mystery.

It should not be surprising that I feel a similar temptation concerning the shape of my own book on ekphrasis *as* a book, a temptation that has led me to complete *my* circle by coming back in the end to the circular shield, and to Spitzer's circular claims, with which I began. But I must resist: here, in modernism, where we are trapped in a static formalism, is not the place for me to end my book, since my insistence that the ekphrastic object is in endless motion counteracts any one-sided commitment to its stillness. Not that I mean to make modernism into a single, fixed theoretical category. Within modernist theory and practice there are varying degrees of satisfaction with the collapsing of time into spatial pattern and thus with the circle as the figure of formal closure. I would distinguish three varieties within this range of attitudes, moving from (1) the overemphasis on timeless form suggested by Spitzer or Frank to (2) the paradoxical insistence on both temporal and spatial claims in Eliot or Brooks to (3) the shifting of dominance to the temporal almost to the rejection of spatial form by those who verge on the threshold of the postmodern. I should quickly add that each of these in his own way alludes to the precedent of Keats.

Within the third group I would point especially to Wallace Stevens, even as early as his anti-ekphrastic ekphrasis, "Anecdote of the Jar" (1919).[37] The "gray and bare" jar is a considerable comedown from Keats's urn, with its "leaf-fringed legend," its "brede / Of marble men and maidens overwrought." And as a jar it demands none of the special semiotic deference we pay to the urn as symbol. Further, Stevens is writing a mere "Anecdote" and not a far-reaching "Ode": as an anecdote his is only one of the small stories (*petites*

37. The poem appears in its entirety in the Appendix (see p. 286). My present purpose requires me to give it a far more extensive reading here.

histoires) that Lyotard calls for in his postmodern assault on any master narrative.

Yet even this minimal jar insists on the unifying act of enclosure performed by its circularity as an artifact, though only at the same time as the poem attests to its existential insufficiency. The jar's roundness is the emblem of the formal control it forces upon whatever would resist form, so that however "slovenly" the "wilderness" may be on its own, it is made to "surround"–to group itself as a circle–around the hill, itself shaped round by the jar's presence. Closing the first quatrain by repeating the word "hill," now controlled by "surround," emphasizes the shaping power of the jar.

The brief poem seems to be directed by the playful persistence of the "round" both in that very word (lines 2 and 7) and in the companion words governed by "round": "Surround" (line 4), "around" (line 6), and even "ground" (line 7). Indeed, its final appearances in line 7 ("The jar was round upon the ground") are most telling: the word "round" reminds us of its presence in "ground," although it turns that word into a self-contradiction, at once the earthy wilderness and yet with the formal reshaping literally within itself. The "round upon the *ground*" permits us to witness the verbal transformation of the wilderness.

The final quatrain has no variety of "round" in it, and needs none, since the jar has by this point taken "dominion everywhere." Now the repetition has for the first time shifted to rhyme ("air," "everywhere," "bare"). The hard-won dominion everywhere has left everywhere bare, thanks to the gray bareness of a form that, unlike Keats's, has no representation of life on it, only the emptiness of that form itself. Late in his "Ode" Keats may have addressed his object with the harsh words "Cold Pastoral," but they would resound as being far more desperately earned in the Stevens poem. The rhyme of "everywhere" and "bare" in the shadow of the jar's dominion is a deadening echo. The final two lines might have been free of the jar's circle with the mention of Tennessee's life in bird and bush or anything else, except that they are utterly negated in their very statement ("did not give," "Like nothing else"). Even as the universal dominion of the gray and bare form is established, the jar is revealed to be isolated from the natural reality it would reshape, in its deadness to be the very opposite of what it would emblematize.

If the final two lines appear to break the circle by introducing bird and bush, the persistent negations keep the wilderness ("no longer

wild") still under the jar's dominion. The circularity of the poem itself is restored and made "just" by the final word, "Tennessee,"
which is the very word, and world, that concluded the poem's opening line. It should be needless by now to add that in this negative
and circular context, "Tennessee" here at the end is only a word in
the poem, referring to the word in the poem's first line rather than
to that real living place existing beyond the jar and the poem. In
bringing the poem around, Stevens has satisfied Spitzer's claim
about the metapoetic circularity of the ekphrastic poem that seeks
to emblematize its circular object.

But we must remember, too, that Stevens has written a poem far
more devastating in its concern about the existential emptiness of
aesthetic form and the ekphrastic itself. If I earlier delineated a spectrum running from those modernists who are less uncomfortable
with, or are even seeking, the stillness of the still point to those who
are restive in their awareness of temporality and, even further, to
those who reject the stillness of form, while still in the end coming
to terms with it, the Stevens of this poem is in the latter group, trying to beckon what is beyond the circle without being free of that circle himself. The poem, in short, recuperates what it would destroy.
Stevens, as a poet with an acute interest in the plastic arts, suc-
cumbed to—while he struggled to reject—his own ekphrastic inclinations. Is this, then, a poem by a modernist who beckons the
postmodern to destroy the circle of form or by a postmodern who
still must surrender to its formal persistence? Whichever way we an-
swer this question, we are in effect projecting a postmodernism that
is continuous with modernism, in contrast to the more severe postmodernism that surrounds us, which would disrupt history by totally deconstructing the totalizations of its predecessor and would
permit no remnant of spatial form to stand.

I would justify my decision, on this one occasion, to dwell at an
incommensurate length on this single brief poem by citing it as an
appropriate response to the verbal economy practiced by modernism at its most intense. For me too there is always the inner resistance of words, which insists upon the incapacity of the circle to
hold. Not only does Stevens's jar attest to its own insufficiency to
hold what it claims to contain but it reminds us that even in its circularity, Keats's urn, whose beauty may be all there is to know, displays still-moving figures who, in their uncapturable historicity,
leave forever open their unanswerable questions. But this is to move

beyond modernism in all of its several varieties and to my next chapter. As it is my final chapter, my discussion there must deal with those for whom any figuratively circular shape—together with the circular process of ekphrasis—is broken open in the very process of being formed,[38] its contents dispersed, floating off, like this book, on the unpredictable wings of the postmodern.

38. My *A Reopening of Closure: Organicism Against Itself* deals principally with the extent to which the closure imposed by organicism carries within itself the counter-movement that would explode it.

8

A POSTMODERN RETROSPECT

Semiotic Desire,
Repression
in the Name of Nature,
and a
Space for the Ekphrastic

>   . . . and now long needy Fame
>   Doth even grow Rich, naming my Stella's name.

>   Sir Philip Sidney, *Astrophil and Stella*, 35

>   Oh absent presence, Stella is not here;
>   False flattering Hope, that with so fair a face
>   Bare me in hand, that in this orphan place,
>   Stella, I say my Stella, should appear.

>   *Astrophil and Stella*, 106

The ekphrastic impulse in literary theory, as I have been trying to demonstrate, is companion to the semiotic desire for the natural sign. This latter is the desire to use the word to control the presence of either the god or the lover, perhaps more explicitly so in the Renaissance, when metaphor works to make the lover into the verbal equivalent of the deity. In Chapter 7 we looked into the various ways by which modernist critics used their organicist theories of closure to sacralize the work (the work as *word*) itself, thus turning it into the ultimate container of verbal presence. It is at this moment, when a culture is seen as totally containable within its shaped word, that the postmodern (in the arts or in theory) strikes to explode that stuffed package.

Theoretical developments since the New Criticism, developments usually grouped together as "postmodern," have attacked its formalistic overconfidence in the poet's spatializing power to impose closure despite the usual way words work, despite, that is, the unending openness of what that criticism took to be "normal" discourse. I have tried to anticipate those attacks in Chapter 7. But more single-mindedly than I do there, postmodern theorists have unpacked Joseph Frank's spatial metaphors—especially, perhaps, his anti-temporal seizing upon "juxtaposition" as a literary effect—and lamented the self-mystifying consequence of taking them literally. These theorists have recognized the extent to which modernism represented a completion of the project undertaken by romanticism. What they are resisting is the aesthetic desire for the poem as a totalized verbal system, a notion that is the very heart of aesthetic organicism from the first. Their resistance reflects the postmodern desire to deny to the poem the opportunity to be accorded the status of a privileged object that is a unique product of a unique working of language, an idealized—indeed a *naturalized*—object, emblem of teleological fulfillment. Instead, poems, like verbal compositions of any sort, are to accept the general fate of language as arbitrary, temporal signs and not to seek to inflate metonymic modesty into metaphoric grandiloquence, justified only by metaphysical bad faith.

There has been perhaps no more forceful attack against the claims for the power of the poet and the poet's shaped word to contain its object within it than in the essays of Paul de Man, both before and after his encounter with the work of Jacques Derrida. Much of de Man's most trenchant writing constituted a polemic against the pretensions of a poetics of verbal presence, speaking instead in a minor key for aporia and an open temporality, for the necessary gap between word and hope in a textual universe at the mercy of a self-abnegating law that rules only in the name of the arbitrary. We have observed the thematic move by which Frank uses his spatial form (the juxtaposition of temporally separated textual elements) to achieve a "juxtaposition of past and present" that rescues us from history by converting it into the "timeless unity" of myth. It is a move not inconsistent with the "natural supernaturalism" of romanticism traced for us by M. H. Abrams. In a countermove designed to awaken us from the aesthetic dream, de Man insists that these delusions of a so-called aesthetic realm that celebrates the transformational power of the created symbol must be dissipated. He reminds us that the myth of an achievable identity between word and world is indeed a myth, as he drags us back to the human condition as the verbal condition of unbridgeable difference, finally an impotent condition trapped in the sequence of unrepeatable, unredeemable befores and afters that constitute both every human text and human existence itself. (We can observe too in de Man a thematic extension of the textual, much as we did in Chapter 7 in the position under attack, though here, of course, it takes a thoroughly negative direction.)

Those in the deconstructionist line whom I have represented here by de Man have been offering an alternative way of grappling with the workings of texts: they reject the claims of any who would inflate those workings and their consequences out of a metaphysical ambition for the extraordinary manipulation of a language that would grant it special entry into the domain of aesthetics. But there are other recent critics who are more interested in reading through texts to their sociopolitical subtexts, and they would deconstruct those claims (even if they might prefer not to use that word) in another way: from a point of view that focuses on the unrelenting shaping power of institutionally controlled discourse to impose itself on all texts. These critics, whether deriving from Marx or Foucault or both, would expose the fetishizing of "nature"—and, consequently, of natural authority—in the rhetorical subservience of language to the sway of forces vying for power, forces that seek to validate that power by an ideology for which they claim a natural sanction.[1] In their different ways, then, postmodern critics remind us to be wary of the metaphysical dream behind the timeless myth of "nature" and wary also of the post-romantic voluntarism, the humanistic aggrandizement, the hidden quest for private power, behind the modernist's will to totalization, to genesis revisited.

Any of these ways of stirring us out of the romantic-to-modernist dream based on the verbal conquest of temporality and difference, any of these several textual or sociopolitical versions of deconstruction, would will an end to ekphrasis, with its implications about form, as they have sought to will an end to the aesthetic itself. Wary of the dependence of the aesthetic on a nineteenth-century organicism that called for a totalizing discourse, these joined from their several directions in a war on the aesthetic, which was now outlawed as a false construct created for the evasive and dangerously complacent comforts of discursive and ideological unity. Yet, as I have already indicated, there remains a significant difference between the deconstruction of texts based on a new way of reading them and the deconstruction of texts based on a way of reading through them to a subtext controlled by the dispositions of social power.

Although in Chapter 7 my ambivalence was intended to be quite evident, and my rejection of modernism anything but complete, I did intend to acknowledge and confront those weaknesses that aroused the concerns that we have been hearing voiced far more negatively in the de Man version of deconstruction, in its charges against the so-called formalistic aesthetic, charges that would reveal the inevitable thematic, and thus the metaphysical, accompaniment to this aesthetic. In the current chapter, then, I am concerned primarily with that other direction from which anti-aesthetic objections, even more forcefully, come. If I am to look back on my subject from our most recent perspectives and see what of it is left standing, I still

1. W. J. T. Mitchell emphasizes and persuasively develops this aspect of my subject in *Iconology: Image, Text, Ideology* (Chicago: University of Chicago Press, 1986).

must take into account the sociopolitical rejection of the tradition of the aesthetic that culminates in modernism. This is the commonest of the voices we are currently hearing. Indeed, it is one that complains also about the textual version of deconstruction I have here associated with de Man, charging that it too is, in the end, no less formalist than its organicist precursor-enemies and thus is equally, if unwittingly, a servant of repressive political forces. I do not mean to argue the issue here so much as to recognize my need to address this recent widespread assault upon the very assumptions that permit my subject to be treated as I have treated it.

So let me here rehearse the several stages of the history I have traced in these chapters—the history of the natural-sign aesthetic in its several alternative versions—from a perspective that provides an awareness of sociopolitical undercurrents. Are these to be regarded as causes, or accompaniments, or consequences? And what effect should they have on our judgment of the theories being set forth, whether independently of these undercurrents or in subservience, conscious or unconscious, to them? My problem is how to give fair due to the sociopolitical without accepting a complete reduction to it, so that some space may be saved for the aesthetic and, as a corollary, for the ekphrastic. I am making this move, I must hope, not merely to save my subject for this book's sake but to discover it as a subject that, for society's sake, should be seen as saving itself.

I will begin by suggesting a broad—but I hope not too easy—analogy between literary doctrine and political force and then will try to limit its analogical reach. Such an analogy, I believe, can be proposed between the more or the less repressive tendencies in the prescriptions of literary theories and the more or the less repressive tendencies in the sociopolitical attitudes and institutions that may be seen as sponsoring, or at least as finding comfort in, these theories. This analogy can be seen in the ways that a culture imposes its semiotic, transferring its dependence on the natural sign from the realm of the arts to the political realm. It is a transfer from apparently innocent play to surreptitious manipulation. To enforce this transfer, aesthetic theory must use whatever repression is necessary to preserve the transparency of natural-sign reference in art, carrying it over to its political analogue, thereby justifying a general repression in the name of nature.

This subliminal political interest may help account for the restrictiveness of dramatic theory as I trace it in Chapter 2. What controls this analogy is the myth of the natural sign, with its appeal to our semiotic desire for the natural sign, which I here suggest has been functioning in the realm of the arts in order to help promulgate the legitimation of natural signs in the sociopolitical realm. This myth and this desire, once embodied for us in art, are—though indirectly, of course—to persuade us of the "natural" ground of claims in the sociopolitical realm as these are institutionalized in those other, power-imposing discourses that, nevertheless, may take their semiotic habits from texts whose objectives, as predominantly aesthetic and hence apparently more innocent, cultivate a receptivity in us for that semiotic appeal. Hence we have become generally vulnerable when cultural claims call us to obedience to nature's order.

Throughout this study I have acknowledged that our semiotic desire for the natural sign is a reflection of our ontological yearning: our anxiety to find an order or structure objectively, "naturally," "out there"—beyond society as well as ourselves—that would authorize the signs and forms that our subjectivity projects and that we then want—nay, require—others to respond to and acknowledge as being there. It is an anxiety exploited by all holders of power and bearers of doctrines that they seek to impose through a claim to a natural authority. This attempted imposition so often succeeds because it meets and satisfies our semiotic desire for the natural sign, as it confers the special privilege of nature upon the conventional—and arbitrary—signs dictated by various motives, most of them politically suspect. These are the signs that, however deceptively, function for a culture as its "nature," signs that are extrapolated in order to be insisted upon as everybody's "nature" and to be thus acknowledged universally.

The arts, in their illusionary character, may well lead the semiotic parade in the culture's cultivation of its signs as "natural." It was this illusionary objective for the arts (mimesis in its most extreme, and innocent, sense) that made the arts of sculpture and painting—intended, presumably, as transparent representations of, or even as substitutes for, "real" objects—the model arts for the other arts to emulate. We have seen the primacy of the visual in Plato lead, in his more literal followers, to a "visual epistemology" that would have the arts, in their naive mission to function as natural signs, aspire to the *trompe l'oeil*.[2] In other words, the arts, as would-be natural signs,

2. Again I am invoking the phrase "visual epistemology" from Forrest G. Robinson, *The Shape of Things Known: Sidney's Apology in Its Philosophical Tradition* (Cambridge, Mass.: Harvard University Press, 1972), esp. pp. 1–59.

were to seek an ever closer resemblance to their referents (their "originals in nature," the eighteenth-century theorist would say), a semiotic accord that would approach equivalence. And through much of the earlier history of aesthetics we have seen that even the verbal arts were encouraged—as best they could, despite their conventional and arbitrary materials—to join in this illusionary mission.

It would seem to be a strange and severe requirement to insist upon for the verbal arts, though from their earliest days critics found one kind among these arts—the dramatic—that could emulate or even exceed the more "natural" non-verbal arts, the visual arts, in an apparent dedication to the natural sign. Indeed, the very mimetic arguments that called for such emulation, arguments fashioned in accord with the unproblematic resemblances to their objects that this criticism claimed to find in sculpture and painting, would raise the drama beyond even those arts in its capacity to produce an illusion of "reality." The drama, with its flesh-and-blood creatures, is constituted by signs that far more closely resemble the moving, live world beyond—that consequently could far more easily fool the naive among us—than does sculpture or painting, as unmoving replicas in a lifeless material medium. We can say with Lessing that drama is more faithful than the spatial arts to our ineluctably temporal experience, since it presents "moving pictures" instead of still pictures. Indeed, in the captivating spirit of illusion as *trompe l'oeil*, we could go further and say that drama presents not pictures at all but the persons and things themselves.

My point about the extension of the natural-sign aesthetic to poetry has been this: the need to link the verbal arts to the obvious arts of visual illusion narrowed the range of what could be represented in the drama as the one explicitly visual verbal art. We have seen this as the point of seventeenth-century French dramatic theory. The restriction of represented objects to the visible was thereby also intended as a restriction of them to natural signs. If, then, all the arts, and the dramatic art preeminently, were to be only illusionary—"airy" embodiments of nature—then those arts were to fool us, to trick the eye, thereby showing the way to non-aesthetic forms of discourse, which were to parade their claims as if they were naturally authorized—and they alone, to the exclusion of all other claimants. In this way the arts could serve the ambitions of ideology in its quest for domination, so that the verbal arts, at least in their dramatic form, could become emblematic of the illusionary function of would-be natural signs in a culture that could use such signs to authorize its exclusionary force.

The conclusions of Chapter 2 would, I believe, support the claim that those using Plato's natural-sign argument against drama (though for the opposite purpose of approving it) were making it our most restrictive literary genre as an aesthetic correlative of the tightest of those ruling discursive institutions of which it is to function as an indirect representation. The drama is seen as the most restrictive in that it is the verbal genre most rigorously tied to the "natural sign," the genre whose fictions most nakedly seek the status of natural sign, so that it overcomes the arbitrary stuff of its composition. Throughout the history of literary theory we have seen critics distinguishing drama by this special representational character that they see in it, in contrast to narrative and lyric genres. In this establishment of the conventional notion of drama as a natural-sign art and thus as the most restrictive of genres, I must again call attention to the critical concern about the difference between drama and narrative, between actions we are allowed to witness and actions that are reported to us by a narrating character. The actors stand as natural signs in their semiotic relation to their characters (who stand as natural signs, thanks to the actors, in their semiotic relation to "real" persons); by contrast, a narrative voice, spoken or written, only supplies the words that our interpreting minds must convert to the actions we seek inwardly to "see."

Dramatic representation, in other words, is the only true verbal imitation if by "imitation" we mean—as Plato only sometimes, and most narrowly, does—the literal mimicking of persons in real life. I have shown in detail that this attribution of generic specialness sets in motion, from Aristotle onward, a poetics of drama set apart from poetics at large; and it is a poetics that remains privileged so long as painting and sculpture, as natural-sign arts, remain the model for poetry to seek to emulate, so long, in other words, as the mimetic aesthetic remains in force and the notion of the mimetic is taken narrowly and literally.

To summarize, the literal restriction of "imitation" leads to a highly exclusive regulation of the drama: only what is visually representable may be represented. The natural sign is to be a transparent sign, transparent and thus immediate to the senses. The stage can represent only the limited things that can be shown, in contrast to the almost unlimited things that, by way of narrative, can be told.

Since, however, for Aristotle compactness, efficiency, and exclusion are prized aesthetic virtues, it is not surprising that not only are those unrepresentable marvels admissible in the epic outside what is permitted the drama but their inclusion in the epic, for all the wonder they inspire, helps Aristotle judge the epic to be a genre inferior to the pristinely exclusive drama. In the ambivalence of chapter 24 of the *Poetics* we saw Aristotle adopt Plato's equation of "imitation" with impersonating another's speech and attribute unqualified imitation to drama alone among the verbal arts, thereby cutting drama off from the other verbal arts – from the representation of anything that is not, in more than one sense of the word, "sensible."

The narrative poet, whose represented persons are not seen, may indulge fantasies that could not be brought onstage; even if they could, they would appear ludicrous. Though Aristotle thus bequeaths to Renaissance theory the notion that the marvelous or wonderful is the proper end of epic, he means no elevation of that genre by it. The drama dare not be monstrous (i.e., dare not, in imitation of the epic, include the representation of monsters as the unreal) in so restrictive a doctrine. Instead the drama was to exclude all that was not representable onstage without straining a sensible audience's credibility.

Thanks largely to their Neo-Platonism, Renaissance theorists treated the wonderful and marvelous more favorably (see Chapter 5). With their elevation of the intelligible over the fallen domain of the sensible, they looked to poetry to represent those things that exceeded the domain of sense and of sensible representation and thus, because of epic's power to do so, treated it as superior to drama. On these arguments, which raised the epic to becoming their model literary art, they could even encourage Renaissance dramatic practice to loosen restrictions in hopes of emulating the epic by expanding into the realm of the monstrous the limits of what might be represented onstage. The pursuit of the wonderful, as part of the Platonic rejection of the sensible for the intelligible, brought with it the abandonment of the limited natural sign and license to explore the freer realm of the arbitrary. For the Renaissance preference for narrative marks the transcendence of the finite picture by the infinite potentialities of the word.

We have seen an exemplary version of this theoretical transformation in Jacopo Mazzoni's defense of Dante's *Commedia*. The attack against which he formulates his defense, Bulgarini's, charged that Dante's visionary poem eludes the world of palpable action, the realm of human history, in order to indulge the private phantasms of his mind. In order to counter this argument, Mazzoni reformulates and, in the process, distorts Plato's distinction between the "icastic" (now seen as limited to the external world of the senses) and the "phantastic" (now seen as the mental images limited only by "the caprice of the artist"), though he does so for what he considers to be Platonic purposes. Despite his Platonic desire to elevate narrative over drama, the reasons he offers for this non-Aristotelian conclusion reveal, instead, an Aristotelian influence, even if in an inverted way: he prefers narrative to drama on the grounds that narrative, with its unseen actions, is the more appropriate instrument of the phantastic, while drama, controlled by the sensible limits of the stage, is the more appropriate instrument of the icastic. Much like Aristotle in *Poetics* 24, Mazzoni, in restricting the drama to the sensibly representable, reserves for narrative the freedom to explore the domain of the wonderful without worrying about credibility, since, composed of non-natural, intelligible signs, it does not concern itself with the visible. But in the Platonic hierarchy, if not the Aristotelian, this is a transcendent virtue. Hence the phantastic can be inscribed in narrative without concern for the necessary exclusions that dramatic representation inevitably carries within itself.

Mazzoni is therefore theoretically comfortable about defending the *Commedia*, since for him the defense of narrative is one with his defense of the phantastic, a free-ranging domain well beyond the mundane (icastic and thus mimetic) restrictions indigenous to the drama, even the stretched versions of drama permitted in the Renaissance.[3] In that comfortable relationship between his theory and the poem used to demonstrate it, Mazzoni is in a more fortunate position than Lessing was to be in his *Laokoön*. Especially as we compare Lessing's statements there with what we found him saying elsewhere, we find a certain theoretical embarrassment accompanying the *Laokoön*. For given his subject in that treatise, Lessing has to construct his argument by constant reference to the epic, even though his major claim—that poems must use their arbitrary signs to create an illusion of natural signs—must rest upon his appeal to the drama, which he elsewhere does acknowledge to be the one

3. See the series of distinctions in which Mazzoni couples all the variables involving the two opposing pairs, drama versus narrative and phantastic versus icastic. These appear in the "Introduction" to *On the Defense of the Comedy of Dante* (1587), trans. Allan H. Gilbert, in *Literary Criticism: Plato to Dryden*, ed. Gilbert (New York: American Book Company, 1940), esp. pp. 360–62.

poetic form that deserves to be taken for a natural sign.[4] Despite the similarity we find in the use by these two theorists of the Aristotelian (based on the earlier Platonic) basis for their distinction between drama and narrative, we see that Lessing must return to the primacy of drama in his desire to return to the sensible realm of the natural sign.

But Lessing's distinctions are recognizable as essentially the same as Mazzoni's, except that the preferences are reversed. By now I have traced a series of these distinctions that slide into and support one another. They can be summarized as follows: in the two critics it is the conjunction of the *sensible* with the *natural* sign, at once *icastic* and *representable*, that both enables and tightly limits the functioning of the *drama;* on the other side, the *intelligible* is conjoined with the *arbitrary* sign, the *phantastic* as that which is sensibly *unrepresentable,* to permit the freer realm of *narrative.* The preference clearly depends on the value to be bestowed upon or withheld from the sensible world.

In the Renaissance the one crossover between these opposing pairs occurs when, because of the primacy granted the epic as the model literary art, the drama is by some less restrictive critics encouraged to expand its own tight bounds in the direction of what narrower dramatic theory would have considered unrepresentable, in the direction, that is, of narrative inclusiveness, indeed of the monstrous. This violation of narrow criteria for dramatic propriety is hardly surprising when we consider the contempt for the enclosing finitude of the sensible that the Renaissance inherited from Plato. So long as the sensible defined the limits of drama as would-be natural sign and the intelligible rather than the sensible was the proper object of poetry, Neo-Platonic critics would elevate the narrative over drama and the verbal over the visual.[5]

As our exemplary Renaissance Neo-Platonist, Mazzoni reveals his favoring of narrative over drama to be an appeal to a freedom of vision over the icastic-dramatic imitation-as-limitation. But can we not see it also, if only subliminally, as a political appeal for the poet's visionary freedom? And the liberalizing of literature, by the move

4. See my discussion of Lessing's letter to Nicolai in Chapter 2 and in n. 12 to that chapter.

5. There are, of course, several other, more frequently cited reasons for the elevation of epic over tragedy in the Renaissance by far more conservative, more Horatian critics. Their appeals to the didactic and to "Virgil-worship" are well documented in the standard histories of Renaissance criticism.

from the sensible to the intelligible through the attempt to represent the unrepresentable, permitted narrative benefits that could even, by extension, be bestowed upon a loosened version of drama that might now indulge its own monsters. I have been trying to suggest, by this appeal to the political, an image of drama as an overregulated body politic in need of liberalizing, if not of revolution: in need of being freed from its bondage to the limited world of one-to-one sensible representation. This is the political extension of the natural-sign repressiveness—in the drama as in a culture's ontological claims—that I claimed to find behind the analogy with which I introduced this discussion.

One can find implied political metaphors strengthening the pleas for greater imaginative freedom elsewhere in Renaissance writings. I think especially of the language used by Sidney (in a passage examined in Chapter 2) to defend the poet's "freely ranging only within the zodiac of his own wit."[6] Fighting for equality with nature, which is the governor of all other human discourse, "only the poet, disdaining to be *tied to any such subjection*, lifted up with the vigor of his own invention . . . goeth *hand in hand* with Nature (p. 100, my italics).[7] More than a hundred years later, we find even in as conservative a critic as Alexander Pope (a major example of conservatism for me later in this chapter) an impressive metaphorical defense against a legalistic criticism that would condemn Shakespeare's own monstrosities: "To judge therefore of Shakespeare by Aristotle's rules, is like trying a man by the laws of one country, who acted under those of another."[8]

It was this broadening of the criterion of what was includable in the drama that prompted—as a reaction against it—the ultimate restrictiveness of seventeenth-century French dramatic theory that I examined in Chapter 2. In its quest for the ultimate theater of illusion (really for a theater of *de*lusion capable of imposing its literal

6. *An Apology for Poetry or The Defence of Poesy,* ed. Geoffrey Shepherd (Manchester: Manchester University Press, 1973), p. 100.

7. The subjection of the other human sciences is clearly indicated by the language that precedes this quotation: "There is no art delivered to mankind that hath not the works of Nature for his principal object, without which they could not consist, and on which they so depend, as they become actors and players, as it were, of what Nature will have set forth" (pp. 99–100).

8. The sentence appears in Pope's "Preface" to his *Shakespeare,* in several ways a foreshadowing of Johnson's (see "Preface" to *The Works of Shakespeare,* ed. Alexander Pope, 6 vols. [London: Jacob Tonson, 1725], 1:vi).

reality upon the naiveté of its audience), that restrictiveness rejected as a monstrosity even the slightest extension of a minimalist notion of what was representable. Not only does that purest of theoretical moments return to the restrictions of the sensible world but it reveals the most extreme and most literalistic version of drama as a would-be natural sign, caught within the narrowest limits upon what is permitted to be visible onstage. It thus puts forward the most extreme identification of the natural sign with the sensible sign, by implication leaving for Platonists the opposing identification of the arbitrary sign, as supersensible, with the intelligible sign of narrative.

In Chapter 2 I dwelled on the unfortunate insistence on seeking, in the name of a naive notion of credibility, a verisimilitude that would push drama toward being so complete a natural-sign representation that it was, in effect, a continuing *trompe l'oeil*. Paradoxically, we saw that such a drama was commonly charged with producing the very opposite: an utterly conventional display of artifice that defied audience credibility. In my recounting of the narrative adventures of seventeenth-century French dramatic theory, we saw an even more important peripety in its fortunes: an intended purity of generic form, through that very purity, turned into the impurities of *genera mixta*. We found an inverse proportion between the dramatic and the narrative: the less the drama can show, the more frequent and fulsome the intrusions of what must be told. Thus, in this French dramatic theory, exclusions imposed by the dramatic form must result in necessary inclusions allowed to narrative: what was kept offstage showed up, and was welcome, in the stories that had to be reported by those who *were* onstage, so that the audience could be informed of what had to be known of the action that was not permitted visual representation. In their very restrictiveness, the principles of exclusion could not prevent—indeed indirectly required—the admission of their antagonist, the non-representable, the merely verbal, the narrative, even to the most inadmissible monster that a narrative fable could invent.

If I may continue to press the political analogue, the most legalistic conception of drama as a closed, repressive genre forced it, however indirectly, to open itself to an invasion of what was completely beyond its control. It is a self-defeating paradox: the narrative is a subversive force that intrudes itself just where the impurities it brings are most forbidden. The extreme requirements of exclusiveness permit—nay, require—the very uninhibited, monstrous inclusions it would repress. In this way even the drama, as the tightest of genres, becomes subject to the Bakhtinian carnival, the *heteroglossia* that Bakhtin himself reserved for the mixed genre (or anti-genre) of the novel. Through exclusion, pressed to its limits, the drama must let in, if only through the back door of narrative, everything that would disfigure it. As we saw, even the marvelous, and thus the visually unrepresentable, which was carried to extremes in the Renaissance anti-genre of the romance, cannot be in principle excluded from being reported, as the drama is forced to concede that the unrepresentable may be able to find a mode of representation for itself after all, even if beyond the realm of the natural sign.

The metaphor I cited from Pope is applicable: the drama, as minirepublic, must give up its hard-won sovereignty; it must yield through its own devices to the threatening, disruptive force that, far from being excluded by the form, breaks it open. From this theoretical perspective, drama, required to be exclusive if it is to satisfy the interests of order and generic neatness, invites in what it would repress. Surely the political trope beckons: by making its claims in the name of the "natural," as a model of the natural sign, drama may also be seen as reactionary—or at least as being put in the service of a reactionary aesthetic that can itself be placed in the service of a reactionary social structure in search of being legitimized as "natural" and thus as unassailable. For its own political health, drama thus stands in need of being at least in part liberated by that which destroys its purity of genre: by the narrative intrusion that, as intelligible rather than sensible, functions as a Platonically sanctioned freedom from the distorting limits of the *merely* sensible and representable, in pursuit of the visions of the capriciously unpredictable mind. The phantastic, unrestrained by dramatic propriety, breaks out of the repressive limits of the natural sign—withdrawing from the "nature" to which Plato's condemned "mimetic tribe" would bind the sign—to let loose the arbitrary sign that indulges the intelligible realm, the realm of dream, whether of nightmare or, as in romance, of nightmare overcome.

Nevertheless, as many seventeenth-century (and early eighteenth-century) theorists demonstrate—even when moving beyond dramatic theory—strong conservative forces persist, fearful of the threat from an untamed caprice in the poet's mind and blind to the self-contradictory futility of their own dedication to a universally governing "nature." They continue to work for the natural-sign aesthetic and, with it, for a mimesis that is unaware of the naiveté of its unquestioning pursuit of semiotic fidelity. As I have suggested, this conservatism reveals itself not only in their literary and aesthetic affiliations but also in their attachment to a dogmatic philosophic realism and, behind this, in their sociopolitical commitment to an inflexible notion of order.

The theoretical pressure to establish the authority of "nature" and the natural is never innocent (merely aesthetic)—not metaphysically innocent and, more insidiously, not politically innocent. Behind the effort to convert humanly created signs into an immediate surrogate for the objective natural truth, we find the ontological dependence on an unchanging, transhistorical external reality, a universal structure into which all particulars fall without remainder. That dependence arises from a confidence in that firm, spatial structure out there, whose solid objects, as objects of imitation, authorize their imitations, but only while assuring those imitations of their lesser, secondary status as mere appearances, to which, since Plato, we have habitually condescended. Still, a natural-sign art is to validate nature for us as an ontologically grounded authority to which all our activities and languages are referred for sanction. Nature, then, is both archetype and objective, the origin and measure of its illusionary representation.

We have a prideful confession of this position in its extremity in Pope's well-known injunction to critics (in his *Essay on Criticism*, 1711), with implications that are obvious for poets as well:

> First, follow Nature, and your judgement frame
> By her just standard, which is still the same:
> Unerring Nature, still divinely bright,
> One clear, unchanged, and universal light,
> Life, force, and beauty, must to all impart,
> At once the source, and end, and test of Art.
>
> (1.68–73)

The word "still" confers permanence, a rootedness to regulate whatever humanly contrived flowers we may seek to manufacture. Under such dispensation the prescribed principles for poem-making are *found* in the order of things as necessary, and not arbitrarily invented by human caprice: "Those rules of old discovered, not devised, / Are Nature still, but Nature methodized" (1.88–89). The rules are summoned in imitation of the natural order; they are discovered *in* the natural order and convert that order into literary method. Thus these discoveries permit us to transcribe nature's method into our discourse. Indeed, most of those treated in my survey of natural-sign theory, in reducing the order of signs to "nature methodized," have sought, by conversion, to make theirs into a method naturalized.

Consequently, Pope tell us, when the poet (e.g., Virgil) seeks to copy nature, he finds himself doing again what other poets (e.g., Homer) have done before: "Nature and Homer were, he found, the same." What follows? "Learn hence for ancient rules a just esteem; / To copy Nature is to copy them" (1.135, 139–40). Since nature has been, is, and remains "still the same," "still divinely bright," a natural sign is a natural sign is a natural sign, referable immediately to nature. With nature so constant a referent, the signs that would represent nature must resemble one another. One can only rediscover that which has been discovered: there can be nothing new under the sun any more than the sun can itself be new.

The critic, then, may well creep behind the scientist, subjecting the discourse in his charge to the order displayed by scientific discovery. It is no wonder that Aristotle, primal scientist ("natural philosopher"), was accepted as the critic to tame the poets: they "received his laws" because they were "convinced 'twas fit, / Who conquered Nature, should preside o'er Wit" (3.651–52). And nature as a total, and totally explicable, order could be revealed in its completeness and without aporia by the scientist-metaphysician. To the nonscientist, the foolishly prideful layman, these laws, as organizational principles for all that is, may not be properly understood, but—in Epistle 1 of his *Essay on Man* (1733)—Pope takes on the role of the all-revealing scientist-metaphysician who makes the order clear.

This epistle represents the ultimate act of methodizing nature and naturalizing method. Following the instructions given in the *Essay on Criticism,* Pope has in the *Essay on Man* become the master-critic of the master–Work of Art of the Primal Artist.[9] Viewed this way, the three concluding couplets of Epistle 1 are perfectly reasonable, indeed inevitable. The first of these makes my point:

9. I have argued elsewhere that there is a common metaphysical grounding for the *Essay on Criticism* and the *Essay on Man* despite the considerable distance of time (more than two decades) that separates them. See my *Theory of Criticism: A Tradition and Its System* (Baltimore: Johns Hopkins University Press, 1976), p. 104 and the discussion that follows.

> All Nature is but Art, unknown to thee;
> All Chance, Direction, which thou canst not see. . . .

In such a perfect spatial structure, characterized by the totalizing metaphors of the Newtonian world machine and the great chain of being, the impulse toward change is the major antagonist, instigated at once by human pride and metaphysical error. There can be no errant particulars wandering free of their home in the all-inclusive universals of the "universal frame." This frame, of course, must be conceived as utterly immune to historical contingency. Indeed, how could any metaphysical structure be conceived in which history was more completely ignored, or more irrelevant, in which time was more unqualifiedly the enemy of the unfettered spatial imagination?

One need not press this spatial language, or its metaphysical construct, very hard before sensing its sociopolitical implications. And in the sociopolitical may we not perhaps find a subliminal motive for the aesthetic and the metaphysic (really the aesthetic *as* the metaphysic, or the metaphysic *as* the aesthetic) rather than the consequence deriving from them? The rule of absolute stasis is an indispensable ideological ground for a society whose hierarchical character was to be fixed. Hence one proclaims a structure—apparently metaphysical, though founded on aesthetic norms and hiding political compulsion—whose perfection had a place for all things but, more importantly, sought to keep everything in its place.

> Vast chain of Being! which from God began,
> Natures ethereal, human, angel, man,
> Beast, bird, fish, insect, what no eye can see,
> No glass can reach; from Infinite to thee,
> From thee to Nothing. On superior powers
> Were we to press, inferior might on ours:
> Or in the full creation leave a void,
> Where, one step broken, the great scale's destroyed:
> From Nature's chain whatever link you strike,
> Tenth or ten thousandth, breaks the chain alike.
>
> (1.237–46)

At moments the political significance of the language becomes explicit and the metaphors literalized ("On superior powers / Were we to press, inferior might on ours"). The price of any aggrandizement of power is a blurring of spatial distinction that threatens to explode the entire structure:

> And, if each system in gradation roll
> Alike essential to th' amazing Whole,
> The least confusion but in one, not all
> That system only, but the Whole must fall.
> Let Earth unbalanced from her orbit fly,
> Planets and Suns run lawless through the sky;
> Let ruling Angels from their spheres be hurled,
> Being on Being wrecked, and world on world;
> Heaven's whole foundations to their centre nod,
> And Nature tremble to the throne of God.
>
> (1.247–56)

It is the ambition to achieve power ("superior" power) beyond one's station that so darkly threatens the metaphysical-aesthetic order, now revealed to be a political order: "All this dread Order break— for whom? for thee / Vile worm!—Oh Madness! Pride! Impiety!" (1.257–58). As always in this vast, machinelike structure, the proposed similarity among the operational principles that govern its many parts and subsystems permits the rule of analogical argument to go unchallenged:

> What if the foot, ordained the dust to tread,
> Or hand, to toil, aspired to be the head?
> What if the head, the eye, or ear repined
> To serve mere engines to the ruling Mind? . . .
> Just as absurd, to mourn the tasks or pains,
> The great directing Mind of All ordains.
>
> (1.259–66)

It is obvious that Pope has, on nature's transcendent and unquestionable authority, raised the status quo—the notion of place as a permanent station—to an absolute and universal principle that holds equally, through analogy, in all areas of human activity. As in the neoclassical idea of drama, the spatial structure is so complete, so perfect, in its fixity that no change can be permitted in the disposition of its parts without leaving an unfillable gap that would undermine its working altogether. There can be no unauthorized movement, no slightest alteration, that is other than utterly subversive, producing the explosion of total revolution.

This closed, totalized doctrine clearly is a politically convenient one for the protection of a static, hierarchical social order, though its appeal to the sanction of nature as god ("The great directing Mind of All") invariably rests on a secure metaphysic whose only justification seems to be a spatially complete aesthetic construct controlled by a system of analogies. Once human thought projects nature as a perfect work of art, made by the One Supreme Artist and to be interpreted by the scientist-critic, a system of signs has been constructed that denies the contingently historical conditions of its creation by declaring the system "natural" and necessary rather than conventional and arbitrary. The ideal spatial structure need suffer no modifications from the human realm of temporality. Indeed, if nature is conceived as a perfect work of art from which the possibility of all chance or change has been removed, then how dare any humanly created sign presume *not* to imitate nature and seek to attain the status of a natural sign, a sign authorized by nature to create human institutions, and not the other way around—even if our subjectivity may, in error, suggest otherwise?

It was, we saw in Chapter 2, Johnson himself who, in opposition to such dogma, pointed out the extent to which human artifacts, and the rules that govern them, are subject, not to nature, but to the conventional—and even the merely nominal—character of human invention. For example, we saw him defend the mixing of genres in Shakespeare by characterizing the pure genres of tragedy and comedy, not as justified in the nature of things, but as created "according to the laws which *custom* had prescribed," out of which "rose the two modes of imitation, known by the *names* of *tragedy* and *comedy*" (my italics).[10] These dramatic conventions, as human institutions, are anything but natural, as—according to Johnson—Shakespeare's unconventional plays reveal.

In distinguishing human institutions from nature, Johnson implicitly makes the extension from the aesthetic to the political. Thus, in his impatient and at moments even angry review of the Soame Jenyns treatise, he warns against the dangers of succumbing naively to the semiotic desire for the natural sign: he attacks the out-

10. Johnson's "Preface" to *The Plays of William Shakespeare*, in *Samuel Johnson*, ed. Donald Greene (New York: Oxford University Press, 1984), p. 423.

rageously callous claim that the several economic levels of a largely suffering humanity are justified by the permanent laws of nature that uphold the great chain of being, whose immutable demarcations between its links are beyond challenge.[11]

As Johnson's critique indicates, the naive rationalist's appeal to the universal hegemony of nature, as the all-controlling out-there, occurs within an invented narrative that repeats the myth of the natural sign. There is no provision in this "nature," transcendent protagonist of this narrative, for the constructive (*and* oppressive) role of human institutions and the transforming role of the history they create. At a later historical moment these institutions and the sense of history's role in creating them were to undo the dogma of a free-standing nature in an attempt to have it seen as no more than a projection of their own activities. From this perspective, the universal nature, "which [for Pope] is still the same," is never again the same: it not only was changed but was itself made to disappear by reductive concepts that new historical circumstances brought into play.

What we call "nature" thus comes more and more to be deconstructed into a mirror of our own historically conditioned selves, of our desires, and of our desire to validate those desires by grounding them in what we claim to be an objective nature out there. But in the words that Shakespeare, that sublime deconstructor, applies to everything except transcendent love, our several conceptions of nature, far from spatially secure, turn out to be "subject to Time's love or to Time's hate, / Weeds among weeds, or flowers with flowers gathered" (Sonnet 124). They are thrall to "policy, that heretic / Which works on leases of short-numb'red hours." Nature, untransformed by love, is thus reduced to being politically "subject" to time's caprice, *its* politics. Such political insecurity, awaiting destruction and replacement, is seen in "Time's fickle glass, his sickle hour" (Sonnet 126): a concept of fragile, temporary nature that self-destructs under the pressure of its own temporal character. This pre-Popean view of history's deconstructive and reconstructive power comes to be revived and institutionalized in the historicizing of our concepts of nature during the past two centuries.

Once nature is thus relativized, so that it loses its ontological grounding, it can of course serve no longer as the fixed referent for a natural sign. And the natural sign, no longer authorized, will be

---

11. Review (1757) of Soame Jenyns, *A Free Inquiry into the Nature and Origin of Evil*, in *Samuel Johnson*, pp. 522–43.

consigned to the realm of myth and will give way to the acknowledgment of the conventional character of all signs. There is a lengthy
history of the different semiotic and, consequently, the different aesthetic that a less dogmatic view of nature permits. Even more than
language, art as a human construct can emphasize its character as
a *made* object, product of men and women, themselves products of
history and its institutions. As such, it cannot claim to reach beyond
its system of conventional signs to find again its home in nature.

We have seen how, as the ultimate extension of the natural-sign
aesthetic, the tightest neoclassical formula for drama cannot avoid
undermining itself, proclaiming its own artificiality in the midst of
its pretension to naturalness, and breaking its form, mixing its representational modes, in the midst of its quest for an austere purity.
With narrative as the antagonistic intruder that it has invited in, the
very restraints that the drama has imposed on itself lead it to expose
its artifice, its awareness of its own failed deceptiveness, its consciousness of the doubleness—and unreality—of its illusionary pretensions. If this is the case even when the fervor of the quest for the
natural sign is so great, how much less likely the case must be in
milder versions of that quest.

For those who we saw sell themselves on the myth of the natural
sign, the drama, in light of its peculiar representational character and
its peculiar theoretical history, served as the example par excellence—
indeed as the allegory—of how the natural-sign aesthetic could turn
its deceived worshipers into willing victims of the temptation to convert aesthetic illusions into delusions of the actual, the natural. The
drama could thus serve also as a leading agent in creating an accom-
modation between the doctrines that a culture would forcefully prop-
agate and those who are persuaded to accept them as part of a naturally sanctioned system. One may see the drama—and, through it,
the natural-sign aesthetic itself—as being put to shrewd use by the
dominant culture: the illusionary naturalization of the literary sign is
to lead the way to the naturalization of other, less persuasively illusionary signs that the culture would impose upon its members.

In suggesting this political extension, I am repeating, though in
different language, the warnings of Bertolt Brecht, who in our time
related drama to the sociopolitical realm and sought to free us from
the illusionary hold on us by them both. For him, as the traditional
drama, capitalizing on the credibility produced by its verisimilitude, seizes us and takes us in, it is also taking us in on behalf of the
dominant political culture: by using its natural signs to take us in

aesthetically, it is imposing upon us a more general naturalization of the sign in order to take us in politically. As a staging of a socio-political program, it seeks to manipulate its viewers, and does manipulate them unless it is resisted by those it would persuade. Hence Brecht would replace the theater of illusion with a theater of alienation, a theater that, instead of seeking credibility, forces us to emancipate ourselves from domination by the natural sign in drama and, consequently, from domination by the natural sign in sociopolitical institutions. An alternative to illusionistic drama becomes, for him and his agenda, a political necessity.[12]

But I have been arguing that even if in spite of itself, the drama has always provided its own alternative within itself. Even in the most illusionistic version of dramatic theory as would-be natural sign, the drama it sanctions is driven to undo itself. So while it apparently is seeking to exercise what I have described as its coercive function, the drama, through its inevitable self-contradictions and self-exposure, also, as a mode of the aesthetic, produces its own model corrective, which should help us resist being taken in by the myth of the natural sign — in society as in art, though thanks to art. The fact that drama, despite its avoidance of non-natural-sign representational forms such as narrative, comes to depend on just such forms forces it to disclose its own arbitrary-conventional, its other-than-natural, character. Consequently, the drama's betrayal of itself as merely a conventionally controlled representation, emptily mimetic, and not the thing itself, reveals the illusionary character of the aesthetic sign's *apparent* (as if) pretensions to be a natural sign and stands as an emblematic warning against all claims to natural authority.

Not long after Johnson delivered the ultimate and devastating critique of the natural-sign aesthetic in the form it was given by dramatic theory in its strictly neoclassical version, that aesthetic was abandoned in its naiveté. It is an unhappy consequence (for I think it is no mere coincidence) that once the natural-sign aesthetic is displaced, the drama itself appears to suffer its own decline among com-

---

12. Using the practical language of the theater to propose his "alienation effect," Brecht makes this point again and again in his writings. In *Brecht on Theatre: The Development of an Aesthetic*, ed. and trans. John Willett (New York: Hill and Wang, 1964), something of this sort is said throughout. See esp. "Alienation Effects in Chinese Acting" (pp. 91–99) and no. 43 of "A Short Organum for the Theatre" (p. 192), which contains the following as its final sentence: "The new alienations are only designed to free socially-conditioned phenomena from that stamp of familiarity which protects them against our grasp today."

peting literary genres. In these pages we have watched a newer theory authorize a semiotic that privileges other kinds of verbal representation, mainly the novel and the lyric. But we have also seen that this theory eventually comes to justify these genres as alternatives to the apparently natural signs of the drama through a formalism that would objectify the individual text, thereby finding only another way of achieving an illusionary naturalization of *its* conventional signs. So though it turns away from the natural-sign aesthetic, the organicist-formalist aesthetic seeks in its own way to naturalize the literary sign so that, still addressed to our semiotic desire, literature can continue to work as a persuasive agent doing the coercive work of its culture. However different in its appeal, this theory may also be traced back to political sources or forward to political consequences. But we will see that as with natural-sign theory, it will have to face an unsettling rebound produced by the stubborn resilience of literary signs.

I have, in these chapters, traced three very different versions of the claim to an authorization of poetry by "nature," one picking up from the demise of the preceding version, as if poetics could not survive without such a claim. After narrating the rise and fall of the natural-sign aesthetic, I turned to the line of theory that is founded on a special power in the poet that is claimed as the direct expression of the power of nature. In Chapter 4 I found in followers of the Longinian tradition the shift from an interest in natural-sign representation to an interest in the natural expression in language of the human creature as creator of the sublime. And in Chapter 7 I described as the third version the organicist insistence on the poet as a quasi-divine maker of an object whose teleological completeness makes it an idealized realization of a natural object. Organic nature, working through the poet, expresses itself in the shaping, in and through a medium, of an object—a perfect substitute for, and improvement upon, nature's objects, and sanctioned by that natural principle of the organic that it so fully satisfies. To elaborate this claim here I could recall from Chapter 7 Coleridge's remarkable quotation on the intrinsic character of organic form as nature's. I repeat only the conclusion: "Such as the life is, such is the form. Nature, the prime genial artist, inexhaustible in diverse powers, is equally inexhaustible in forms."[13] Following upon the tradition from Longi-

---

13. Coleridge, "Shakespeare's Judgment Equal to His Genius," in *Coleridge's Essays and Lectures on Shakespeare and Some Other Old Poets and Dramatists* (London: J. M. Dent, 1906).

nus to Burke to Shelley that found nature in the language of unmediated expression, organicism—developed from Coleridge to the New
Critics—returns to the poetic object by way of a theory of forms that
also leans on a natural sanction, though it is internally rather than
externally derived. However revisionary, it even claims its special
object to be a kind of natural sign, though the concept of "nature"
being appealed to has little in common with the nature of the natural-sign aesthetic.

Thus behind modernism's myth we still find the appeal to nature,
as Schiller long ago reminded us: it is an appeal to nature as model,
if no longer as object, though it is an appeal in its way even more pre-
sumptuous than what we observed in the natural-sign aesthetic.[14]
What modernism unwittingly shares with the natural-sign aesthetic
is a flight from the arbitrary and conventional as insecure and the
desire to claim an authority beyond the fleeting vagaries of time.
Hence modernism returns to spatiality, though it does so in a metaphysical context that has acknowledged the epistemological dominance of the temporal. In following this theoretical development
and expressing my concerns about it, I have continually conceded
that the organic aesthetic carries with it a mystification with almost
as much power to deceive as those simpler claims for nature made
on behalf of the mimetic aesthetic of natural signs that we examined—and discarded—earlier.

The making of a "second nature" by the poet's I AM asserts human mastery over accident, a godlike act of genesis that subdues
the unshaped in the name of power, the creative power. Seen thus,
this relentless power, a projection of the liberated human ego,
which absorbs whatever it touches into the shapes formed in accordance with humanly imposed ends, can be viewed as an aesthetic
reflection—an idealized version—of the dream of private enterprise,
as the purest extension of a humanistic dominance produced by an
ultimate engineering. Indeed, in the nineteenth century the rising
idolatry of the national state as an organic construct, with a growth
that has been guided into the created perfection of a work of art,
may be viewed—and these days is invariably viewed—as another
reflection of a language that permits the aesthetic to be extended
into the sociopolitical realm, so that it is seen as a reflection of that

14. I have borrowed this notion, which runs through Schiller's *Letters on the Aesthetic Education of Man* (1795), and adapted it to the development of literary theory as
it moves into the nineteenth and twentieth centuries.

realm, or even, perhaps, as a product of the rhetorical motives generated by that realm.

Accordingly, we have properly come to view this theory with suspicion, and to question its claim to "disinterestedness," while fearing for the hidden political consequences of its aesthetic realm and the organicism sponsored by that realm in the nineteenth and twentieth centuries. Granted, with organicist theorists we are far removed from the world of Pope and the reactionary motives that earlier I suggested his rhetoric may have preferred to conceal, but the dubious relationship between the rhetoric of the organicist aesthetic and either its sociopolitical consequences or its sociopolitical motives can be shown to be similar. Once again the arbitrary play of institutional power seems, however subliminally, to be guiding the aesthetic much as it does the other elements of culture, all as part of an ongoing arena of conflict for control. Consequently, as the postmodern disposition examines the claims for the "disinterested" power — at once moral and normative — of the literary work, presumably backed by an objective natural authority, that disposition invokes its own rhetoric of suspicion to reduced those claims to their historically contingent, institutionally instructed biases.

In Chapter 7 we watched as critics inflated the visionary ambition of poems as modernist aesthetic objects, as verbal emblems. They used poems to project visions of temporality, collapsed within their spatial confines, into the realm of myth seen as metaphysically authorized transformations of human history. These were to become authentic visions for us all, their poetic status legitimizing them as ultimate forms of nature. The poem, then, was in the end revelatory, and what it revealed was somehow out there for us all, through careful enough reading, to apprehend. It was, finally, a simulacrum, and somewhere it had its object. For all that modernist theory would deny to earlier claims for mimesis, in making these claims it too, in its own way, could be seen as reaching for a metaphysical imitation of nature and hence as setting itself up as a natural-sign aesthetic after all.

The myth of the natural sign dies hard, and its persistence is very likely related to the unspoken sociopolitical interest in catering to it. At a number of points in this study we have seen the extent to which Gombrich's work on illusion helped to expose the potential deceptions in the illusion of the natural sign, to reveal the bankruptcy of an aesthetic that took it as truth. There may, then, be no better example for me of the persistence of the natural-sign myth than Gombrich. Even for Gombrich himself, who has been credited with burying it for good—and has been so credited by me—it never quite died. Indeed, in his later work it has been reemerging explicitly—and embarrassingly for those of us who thought of ourselves as following him. Many of Gombrich's readers saw his earlier arguments as leading to the claim that all art arises out of, and functions by way of, conventional signs. But Gombrich was himself to reject this reading of his work as part of his general rejection of what he terms "conventionalism."[15]

The temptation to hang onto the belief that the "nature" of one's own culture is *nature* for all leads its victim to believe that he or she knows what nature objectively is, what it demands, and what it looks like for all who would imitate it. It leads both to cultural provincialism and to cultural imperialism. In the face of all he contributed to the treatment of art as a series of interpretable codes, Gombrich nevertheless remains such a victim of the temptation held out by the natural-sign aesthetic, despite the fact that his distinctive authority comes from his apparent resistance to that temptation. In retreat from the denials (attributed to him) of nature's singleness, knowability, and authority, Gombrich now denies instead that his theory "lent support to an aesthetics in which the notions of reality and nature had no place." Thus he denies too that he "had subverted the old idea of mimesis and that all that remained were different systems of conventional signs which were made to stand for an unknowable reality."[16] Assured of the universal dominion of the reality established by and for the English scientific tradition extending from the original Royal Society to his colleague, the perceptual psychologist James J. Gibson, Gombrich must reject such readings of his work with the familiar charge that they represent "an out-and-out relativism," presumably the enemy to British scientific hegemony, which is here made synonymous with the pursuit of truth.

My language here makes evident my own acknowledgment of the cultural—and, beneath that, probably political—consequences of any commitment to a monolithic concept of nature. This commit-

15. This rejection was evident earlier, in his response to the work of Nelson Goodman and, more recently, in his vituperative response to my essay on him. See the following sequence of essays: my essay, "The Ambiguities of Representation and Illusion: An E. H. Gombrich Retrospective," *Critical Inquiry* 11 (1984): 181–94; Gombrich, "Representation and Misrepresentation," ibid., 11 (1984): 195–201; and my "Optics and Aesthetic Perception: A Rebuttal," ibid., 12 (1985): 502–8.

16. Gombrich, "Representation and Misrepresentation," p. 195.

ment would project the arbitrary and yet conventional product of cultural institutions into "nature," "out there," to be used by those institutions to make their claim to be universally controlling forms. Even if unconsciously ethnocentric, the commitment cannot help but try to be hegemonic, even in so innocuous a disguise as that of an aesthetic theory. As Brecht warned, in its yearning for the "natural," it can use the aesthetic for a subliminal political persuasiveness. Our desire to read the sign as natural can thus have effects that are dangerous as well as illuminating: it may reveal the idols of our culture to us but may also enslave us to them.

In my survey here I have tried to show how, under the pressures of a philosophical tradition and the hierarchy that follows from it, convention intrudes upon the arbitrary, catering to our desire to see it too as natural, and in a way that connects semiotic explorations in aesthetics to our attitudes toward sign-functioning in sociopolitical areas of human concern. Seen from this perspective, the history of sign-functioning as attributed to the arts by aesthetic theory, with its narrative of conflicts and delusions in the alternating fortunes of natural and arbitrary-conventional signs, can be viewed as an allegory—with the special illusionary purity of an aesthetic allegory, if you will—of the story of signs, with their dangerous and error-filled pretenses to authority, in society's long chase after the power of enforcement that claims to derive from "nature." But I have tried to show also that the aesthetic can have its revenge upon ideology by revealing a power to complicate that is also a power to undermine.

I have argued that these complications, and hence these underminings, are introduced into our flight from the natural sign by means of the duality of the word's power both to be and not to be an image—in an older jargon, to be intelligible without yielding up an attachment to the sensible. Whether in drama or a less visually mimetic genre, the verbal arts, more than any less ambiguous sign system, remind us of the illusion at the base of our semiotic desire for the natural sign: that it is less a desire for pure presence than for an illusionary presence, the idea of a presence that can extend, or, even more, elevate, the pleasures and prospects—while postponing the death—of the sensible. But since it occurs only in words, the attempted deception is always only half meant. So long as those shaped words, even or especially shaped into an ekphrastic form, are there to remind us that we are *not* intended to be deceived—not even when they are most like images—we should be in less danger of being taken in by the monstrous attempts, at every level of our culture from the aesthetic to the political, to claim a natural sanction for human inventions, those wayward institutions that would rule us.

Indeed, I do not mean to dissipate the aesthetic, with its dependence on the recurring illusion of the natural sign, by reducing it altogether to the interests and powers of sociopolitical reality. The history of the tenacity of the natural-sign aesthetic is more than the history of error (and, when that sign is projected into other areas, of dangerous error), though it is that. What lies behind it is the history of the semiotic desire for the natural sign, the history of the unavoidable longing, in the individual and in culture, to find and to nourish a language authorized by its mirroring of the external reality we call "nature," though, alas, always in accordance with our imperialistic tendency to see contingencies in all conceptions of what is "natural" *except* our own. It is a longing I have been noting ever since the desperate, and desperately complex, ironies of Plato's *Cratylus,* and it is one of the more potent stimuli for culture's persistent indulgence of the arts. It accounts for the pleasure that Aristotle reminds us we take in imitation and for the fact that some trace of the mimetic appeal of art pops up again each time we think it obliterated.

So we ignore this longing at our peril. The postmodern perspective reminds us that many works these days routinely play self-consciously with their status as art to the point of destroying it. Such outrageous self-consciousness, the more so for having become routine and even conventional, obliterates the subtleties of self-reference that in older works sustained the illusionary aesthetic for which I have been arguing. And yet, as our continuing fealty to older works in our tradition reveals, the longing persists, and will very likely withstand the most radical toying with it that we find today—even in the technological innovations of the film. If the longing will not go away, no matter how we deconstruct it, we will do well to try to understand it and how to live with it, to allow it its role in our anthropological fullness, though without succumbing to it. In recognizing this longing and coming to terms with it without totally yielding to it, the literary work of art thus takes on the social function of serving as a model for less aesthetic discourse. It is exhilarating and, except for its self-corrective tendencies, would be dangerously deceptive in its illusionary character. (I suppose I still think of drama as leading the way, although in this study I have tried to argue that the ekphrastic element in any literary work should allow it to be accorded similar power for those of us who will see it there.)

The literary work of art is exhilarating in its appeal to our semiotic desire for the natural sign, but it can be admittedly deceptive in the illusory nature of that appeal, as—in our best cases—it appears to confess whenever, in self-reference, it reveals its merely conventional, its artificial, basis. Following Brecht, I am claiming that we need art's self-undoing to stimulate the alienation that warns us away from a culture's delusions that would legitimize its authority by an appeal to nature. Its ideology derives from a totalizing that would delude us by denying its status as conventional only, and hence as illusionary. By contrast, it is art that is the de-totalizer by means of its self-awareness, its self-display of illusion *as* illusion. Just as an art with pretensions to being a natural sign may set an example by which a culture's other, non-aesthetic signs—reflective of power—can legitimize themselves through the claim to natural authority, so an art of self-conscious illusion may set an example for the stripping away of such claims. Thus, contrary to the charge of recent theorists, to aestheticize the political is to dis-arm it, provided we have a full enough sense of what the aesthetic can do. It would thus provide a counter-ideological, rather than an ideological, service. In this way we can make use of the semiotic desire for the natural sign instead of being abused by it. And it is the role of art to play the unmasking role—the role of revealing the mask *as* mask. Within discourse it is the literary art that is our lighthouse, serving as both beacon and warning, as it demonstrates what discourse—discourse that is less self-enveloping and self-disclosing and hence more suspect—can lead us in unwary moments to accept as "natural." By means of the literary art and the shrewd self-awareness it encourages, we can create for ourselves a second innocence, but this time one that is armed against what would take advantage of it.

This, then, is one of the major functions of art in culture: within the received language of a culture, the arbitrary-conventional comes to take on the appearance of the "natural," and its arts flourish to the extent that they create their illusionary "realities," which, under the spell of aesthetic experience, carry the conviction of their naturalness, whether on canvas, in stone, on stage or page. In sophisticated cultures they also undercut that conviction by their self-consciousness, their confession of the art they are and the reality they are *not*. It is a self-consciousness to be encouraged, for in this reflexive action they serve their culture well, as emblems of the semiotic ambivalence each healthy culture ought to have, cherishing the illusions it has created, provided it never stops distrusting them and their claims to be a "natural" reality. While it examines those illusions and those claims, a culture discovers itself through questioning its reasons for attaching itself to them. And self-discovery, with its attendant skepticism, would constitute a worthy end for the cultivation of all the arts.

But this may sound too positive as a conclusion for a chapter promising postmodern skepticism. Let me here too introduce the doubts I proposed earlier, doubts created by the fear of parochialism, as I worry about putting forth, as if it were universal, this unique cultural mission for literature: the mission of catering both to our need for semiotic illusion and to our need to see it, for all its glory, as illusionary. What if our commitment to this mission is too readily in accord with the political reasons that justify and extend our comforts? Even more damning, what if, as Chapters 5 and 7 surely suggest, we can see our language and our arts being made by poets to work in these ways for us only because they appeal to the Christian semiotic habit of metaphor built into our cultural history and thus into our private psychological and linguistic histories that follow from it? How far need we retreat, once we concede this much to our history? On behalf of at least some of those oppressed by that history—as well, perhaps, as liberated by it—how can I resist asking why we should reject such a luminous gift of illusionary verbal presence (dare I say a present of presence?), even if it is we who fill it with that presence—first our poets and then ourselves in a happy complicity?

APPENDIX

Ekphrasis
and the
Still Movement of Poetry;
or
Laokoön Revisited (1967)

L et me interpret the proposed subject for these papers, "The Poet as Critic,"[1] as referring to the poet as critic in his poem, the poet as critic in the act of being poet; which is, in effect, to rephrase the title to read, the poetic in the poem. It would seem extravagant to suggest that the poem, in the very act of becoming successfully poetic—that is, in constituting itself poetry—implicitly constitutes its own poetic. But I would like here to entertain such an extravagant proposal.

Central to a poem's becoming successfully poetic, as I have tautologically put it, is the poem's achieving a formal and linguistic self-sufficiency. I could go on to claim, as I have elsewhere, that this formal and linguistic self-sufficiency involves the poem's coming to terms with itself, its creating the sense of roundedness. That is, through all sorts of repetitions, echoes, complexes of internal relations, it converts its chronological progression into simultaneity, its temporally unrepeatable flow into eternal recurrence; through a metaphorical bending under the pressure of aesthetic tension, it converts its linear movement into circle. But in making these claims, I am being pressed to metaphors of space to account for miracles performed in time, even if—thanks to the powers of poetic dis-

1. The subject of the first conference of the Iowa Center for Modern Letters, held at the University of Iowa, October 28–30, 1965. This essay was the opening paper of that conference. It was first published in the collection of conference essays, *The Poet as Critic*, ed. Frederick P. W. McDowell (Evanston: Northwestern University Press, 1967), pp. 3–26.

course—in a specially frozen sort of aesthetic time. The spatial meta-phor inevitably becomes the critic's language for form. Many a self-conscious literary critic has been aware of the debt he owes to the language of the plastic arts—perhaps sculpture most of all—in his need to find a language to account for poetry's formal movements, its plasticity, if I may use the very word that most gives the temporal game away to space.

Very likely it was just this self-conscious necessity that created the tradition of *ut pictura poesis* from Simonides to Winckelmann, the tradition that drove Lessing to the classical good sense of his *Lao-koön* and its insistence on keeping distinct among the arts what be-longed to Peter and what to Paul, what to space and what to time. It is surely too easy to try to make poetry and sculpture meet and even fuse (as John Dewey, for example, tried to do anew in *Art as Ex-perience*) by seeing the poem's transcending of mere movement through circular form as being one with the statue's transcending of mere stasis through its unending movement. But still the language of space persists as our inevitable metaphor to account for the poem's special temporality, its circularizing of its linear movement.[2]

I would take as my model statement Eliot's words in "Burnt Nor-ton" about words and their relation to "the still point of the turning world":

> Words move, music moves
> Only in time; but that which is only living
> Can only die. Words, after speech, reach
> Into the silence. Only by the form, the pattern,
> Can words or music reach
> The stillness, as a Chinese jar still
> Moves perpetually in its stillness.[3]

2. The beginnings of the sort of study I am undertaking here were made by Joseph Frank in his essays on "Spatial Form in Modern Literature" in *Sewanee Review* 58 (Spring, Summer, Autumn, 1945), which appear in revised form as the first chapter of his book *The Widening Gyre: Crisis and Mastery in Modern Literature* (New Bruns-wick, N.J.: Rutgers University Press, 1963), pp. 3–62. But Frank is interested more in the use of these spatial metaphors by recent authors than in the generic spatiality of literary form and—even more to *my* point—in the inevitability of spatial language by the critic or by the poem as its own aesthetician. French literary critics of time-consciousness and space-consciousness, like Gaston Bachelard and Georges Poulet, also touch matters relevant to my interests here—though with a crucial difference of emphasis, as should become clear toward the end of this essay.

3. This quotation and the one which follows are from T. S. Eliot, *The Complete Poems*

These words, in turn, are an echo of the words of the Fourth Tempter in *Murder in the Cathedral*, themselves echoes of Thomas' earlier words about the Women of Canterbury:

> You know and do not know, what it is to act or suffer.
> You know and do not know, that acting is suffering,
> And suffering action. Neither does the actor suffer
> Nor the patient act. But both are fixed
> In an eternal action, an eternal patience
> To which all must consent that it may be willed
> And which all must suffer that they may will it,
> That the pattern may subsist, that the wheel may turn and still
> Be forever still.

I mean to take from Eliot's words about the still movement—like the Chinese jar—of verbal form the suggestion that the poet himself, in seeking to find an eloquence to account for the forms his words seek to turn themselves into, has done well to turn to metaphors from the spatial arts. Thus the poem that in the very act of becoming successfully poetic implicitly constitutes its own poetic may do so, as Eliot suggests, by turning itself into the Chinese jar. It violates Lessing's injunction most strenuously by claiming for itself another order than its own, by substituting the Platonic claim to oneness for the Aristotelian theory of well-policed classes of Peter's and Paul's, with mutual appropriation prohibited.

I use, then, as the most obvious sort of poetic within the poem this anti-Lessing claim: the claim to form, to circular repetitiveness within the discretely linear, and this by the use of an object of spatial and plastic art to symbolize the spatiality and plasticity of literature's temporality. Actually, of course, a classic genre was formulated that, in effect, institutionalized this tactic: the *ekphrasis,* or the imitation in literature of a work of plastic art. The object of imitation, as spatial work, becomes the metaphor for the temporal work which seeks to capture it in that temporality. The spatial work freezes the temporal work even as the latter seeks to free it from space. *Ekphrasis* concerns me here, then, to the extent that I see it introduced in order to use a plastic object as a symbol of the frozen,

---

and Plays, 1909–1950 (New York: Harcourt, Brace, and World, 1952), pp. 121 and 193, respectively.

stilled world of plastic relationships which must be superimposed upon literature's turning world to "still" it.

There are, of course, many less explicit ways for the poem to proclaim as its poetic what I might term its ekphrastic principle, if I may broaden the ekphrastic dimension beyond its narrowest and most literal employment—as I must confess I intend eventually to do. For I would like finally to claim that the ekphrastic dimension of literature reveals itself wherever the poem takes on the "still" elements of plastic form which we normally attribute to the spatial arts. In so doing, the poem proclaims as its own poetic its formal necessity, thus making more than just loosely metaphorical the use of spatial language to describe—and thus to arrest—its movements.

A critic like Sigurd Burckhardt goes so far, in attributing plasticity to poetry, as to insist—and persuasively—that the poem must convert the transparency of its verbal medium into the physical solidity of the medium of the spatial arts:

> . . . whether [a painter] paints trees or triangles, they are corporeally there for us to respond to. . . . The painter's tree *is* an image; but if the poet writes "tree," he does not create an image. He *uses* one; the poetic "image" is one only in a metaphorical sense. Actually it is something that evokes an image, a sign pointing to a certain pre-established configuration in our visual memory. . . . The so-called poetic image achieves its effect only by denying its essence; it *is* a word, but it functions by making us aware of something other than it is. If many key terms of literary analysis—"color," "texture" and "image," for example—are in fact metaphors borrowed from the other arts, this is the reason: poetry has no material cause. Words already have what the artist first wants to give them—body.
>
> I propose that the nature and primary function of the most important poetic devices—especially rhyme, meter and metaphor—is to release words in some measure from their bondage to meaning, their purely referential role, and to give or restore to them the corporeality which a true medium needs.[4]

Thus, by calling attention to the poetic function of words as substantive entities, one might extend the ekphrastic impulse to every poet in search of the sculptor's fully plastic medium.

But, as I have said, it is most useful to begin with the literally and

4. "The Poet as Fool and Priest," *ELH* 23 (December 1956): 280.

narrowly ekphrastic, the poems, which, in imitating a plastic object in language and time, make that object in its spatial simultaneity a true emblem of itself—and of poetry's ekphrastic principle. Jean H. Hagstrum, in his pioneering work *The Sister Arts*, finds his prime example of this mastery of space in time in Homer's description, in Book XVIII of the *Iliad*, of the shield of Achilles wrought by Hephaestus. Hagstrum acknowledges Homer to be a painter, but only as a poet could be:

> The passage remains faithful to the demands of verbal art and is by no means only an enumerative description. The shield becomes an emblem of the life of man: of nature and society, of the seasons of the year, and of cities at war and in peace; of agricultural scenes and the diversions of the rural day. There is obviously much that is non-pictorial: sound, motion, and sociological detail all "appear" on the surface of Hephaestus' masterpiece.[5]

In this total mastery of moving life, the capturing of it in a "still" pattern, do we not seem to have the whole of Homer's world? In this emblem all is at an instant, though it is only in time and language that its simultaneity is created. The emblem is the constitutive symbol, the part that seems to contain the dynamic whole.

From the start, as in my title, following the example of Eliot in the quotations I have cited, I have been openly dependent upon the pun on the word *still* and the fusion in it of the opposed meanings, never and always, as applied to motion.[6] Having, like Eliot, bor-

5. *The Sister Arts: The Tradition of Literary Pictorialism and English Poetry from Dryden to Gray* (Chicago: University of Chicago Press, 1958), p. 20. Hagstrum, trying to be etymologically faithful to the word *ekphrasis*, uses this word more narrowly than I do as I follow its other users. To be true to the sense of "speaking out," he restricts it "to that special quality of giving voice and language to the otherwise mute art object." The other descriptions of spatial works of art, those that are not made to "speak out," he merely calls "iconic," even as he admits this is a narrower use of *ekphrasis* than that of his predecessors (*The Sister Arts*, p. 18n). Since I confess from the start that I intend to broaden poetry's ekphrastic propensities, it would be expected that I also am using *ekphrasis* here to include what Hagstrum calls "iconic" as well as what he calls "ekphrastic."

6. There is a very different and common use of *still* in the aesthetic realm to which I must call attention since it is so single-minded in its rejection of Keats' secondary and more subtle meaning. The "still" of the genre called still-life painting unhappily means only "stilled," inanimate, even in a sense dead—as we are told in the equivalent French phrase, *nature morte*. This sense of the timeless, of the motionless, may recall, for example, Pope's use of *still* to deny change in *An Essay on Criticism:*

rowed it from Keats, I have freely used it as adjective, adverb, and verb; as still movement, still moving, and more forcefully, the stilling of movement: so "still" movement as quiet, unmoving movement; "still" moving as a forever-now movement, always in process, unending; and the union of these meanings at once twin and opposed in the "stilling" of movement, an action that is at once the quieting of movement and the perpetuation of it, the making of it, like Eliot's wheel and Chinese jar, a movement that is still and that is still with us, that is—in his words—"forever still." Thus my rendering and free borrowing of the "still" of Keats' "still unravish'd bride of quietness" in the poem which Leo Spitzer taught us profitably to view as a most splendid example of *ekphrasis.*[7] Further, Spitzer taught us to view the ekphrastic and imitative element in the poem not merely as its object but also as its formal cause. In keeping with the circular, "leaf-fring'd" frieze of the urn it describes, Spitzer tells us, ". . . the poem is circular or 'perfectly symmetrical' . . . thereby reproducing symbolically the form of the *objet d'art* which is its model."[8] In a footnote to this passage Spitzer generalizes on this practice:

> Since already in antiquity the poetic *ekphrasis* was often devoted to circular objects (shields, cups, etc.), it was tempting for poets to imitate verbally this constructive principle in their *ekphraseis.* Mörike's poem on an ancient lamp shows the same formal circularity motivated by the form of the model as does Keats's ode on the urn. . . .

So the spatial metaphor about the "shape" of the poem is not quite metaphorical, is in a sense literal. Only a little less immediately

---

> First follow Nature, and your judgment frame
> By her just standard, which is *still* the same:
> Unerring Nature, *still* divinely bright,
> One clear, unchanged, and universal light. . . .
>   (I, 68–71 [my italics])

How much less aware is this "still" than the pun which restores vitality, and an eternal vitality, to a word that means primarily to deny motion and sound. For a more profound vision of *nature morte,* one that is more just to the dynamics of the still-life genre in painting, see Rosalie L. Colie, "Still Life: Paradoxes of Being," *Paradoxia Epidemica: The Renaissance Tradition of Paradox* (Princeton: Princeton University Press, 1966), pp. 273–99.

7. "The 'Ode on a Grecian Urn,' or Content vs. Metagrammar," in Leo Spitzer, *Essays on English and American Literature,* ed. Anna Hatcher (Princeton: Princeton University Press, 1962), pp. 72–73.

8. Ibid., p. 73.

iconic than George Herbert's poems of imitative graphic form, the poem seeks to attain the "shape" of the urn. In this iconic attempt to shape itself in the form of its content, the poem seeks to perform in a way similar to the way the urns themselves, as sepulchral receptacles, sometimes sought to perform, if we can sense them as Sir Thomas Browne momentarily does in his *Urne-Buriall*. For the urn, container of ashes of the dead, seems to take on the form taken by its contents in life, thus becoming a still remaining form of a form that is no more. Browne's description is magnificently far-reaching:

> While many have handles, ears, and long necks, but most imitate a circular figure, in a spherical and round composure; whether from any mystery, best duration or capacity, were but a conjecture. But the common form with necks was a proper figure, making our last bed like our first; nor much unlike the Urnes of our Nativity, while we lay in the nether part of the earth, and inward vault of our Microcosme.[9]

In "the Urnes of our Nativity" we see a further circularity, a further reaching toward stillness (in both major senses): we see at once the end and the beginning, the receptacle of death simultaneously as the receptacle and womb of life, even while, as tomb, it takes on a spatial permanence in its circular imitation of the living form. This added circularity introduces new possibilities for temporal complexity in the use of the urn as the object of *ekphrasis*, a raising of it beyond the linear chronology of life's transience. These are possibilities that Cleanth Brooks seems to have foreseen in *The Well Wrought Urn*,[10] in which he assembles several complex uses of *urn* in poems, some of which I shall be referring to; although, interested primarily in single interpretations, he does not press their ekphrastic implications.

There is a climactic couplet in Alexander Pope's "Eloisa to Abelard" that serves at once to summarize and to symbolize this poem's studied futility. Eloisa, now denied sexual satisfaction with her lover not only by edict and by physical separation but even more irrevocably by the fact of his emasculation, becomes increasingly

---

9. *Hydriotaphia, Urne-Buriall, or A Brief Discourse of the Sepulchrall Urnes Lately Found in Norfolk*, in *The Works of Sir Thomas Browne*, ed. Geoffrey Keynes, vol. 4 (London: Faber and Gwyer, 1928), p. 23.

10. *The Well Wrought Urn: Studies in the Structure of Poetry* (New York: Reynal and Hitchcock, 1947). He discusses "urn" in "The Canonization," "The Phoenix and the Turtle," "Elegy Written in a Country Churchyard," and "Ode on a Grecian Urn." See pp. 16–20, 101, 112–13, 139–52.

and more bitterly conscious of the tragic irony in the underlying sexual meaning of her repeated imperative to him: "Come!" She reaches the bitterness of the lines

> Come, Abelard! for what hast thou to dread?
> The Torch of Venus burns not for the dead.
>
> (lines 257–58)

He is the walking dead, deprived of all flame. If he defies Church and even the laws of space, his coldness yet prevents all or anything. And as his beloved, Eloisa is doubly cursed since *her* heat has not been subdued: ". . . yet Eloisa loves." And then the masterful couplet to which I want to call attention:

> Ah hopeless, lasting flames! like those that burn
> To light the dead, and warm th' unfruitful urn.
>
> (lines 261–62)

Here "urn," in its simultaneous relations to flame and death and fruit, becomes in an instant the constitutive symbol for the multiple agonies of the speaker of this monologue. As both tomb and womb, the urn is the receptacle at once of death and of love, of the remnants of the flame and of its height, of the congealing of life and the flowing of life. And a few lines later, in as daring an image, Pope adds the needed liquid element, derived of course from her tears:

> In seas of flame my plunging soul is drown'd,
> While altars blaze, and angels tremble round.
>
> (lines 275–76)

What is left but for her to direct her flames toward God, as Abelard's rival, in the questionable frenzy of religious ecstasy?

My point is that it is the urn of line 262 that, if I may pun myself, *receives* these meanings, at once preserves and gives life to them, as it gives life to the poem. Receiver of death as it is not permitted to be the vessel of life, it is warmed by the "hopeless, lasting flames" of a desire that dare not—indeed cannot—feed it. And the flames are at once of heat and of cold: at once agent of sexuality, of the life that is its consequence, and agent of the ashes, cold residue of life's flames and death's. The enforced, permanent chastity, this death in the midst of life, is of course reminiscent of the double-edged "stillness," the always-in-motion but never-to-be-completed action that, as with Keats' urn, accompanies the introduction, in accordance with the ekphrastic principle, of spatial forms within literature's temporality.

How different at all is Shakespeare's introduction of the urn, at the close of "The Phoenix and the Turtle," to be at once the repository of the separate ashes of the ideal lovers and the guarantor of their resurrection in the "mutual flame" of their new-born union, in accordance with the Phoenix riddle? Or Donne's introduction of the "well wrought urn" in "The Canonization" as the equivalent of his poem, an ever self-renewed memorial to his true lovers? Both these uses have been properly exploited by Cleanth Brooks in his appropriately titled book.[11] Or we may move forward in time, across the centuries to William Faulkner's *Light in August*, to see the urn crucially, and similarly, functioning. It has been pointed out[12] that each of the three major strands of the novel derives its symbolic characterization in metaphorical and ekphrastic descriptions that by now should sound familiar to us. Let me cite the three passages.

The indomitable Lena Grove, in her endless and endlessly routine—even automatic—movements is, properly enough, given an ekphrastic symbol:

> . . . backrolling now behind her a long monotonous succession of peaceful and undeviating changes from day to dark and dark to day again, through which she advanced in identical and anonymous and deliberate wagons as though through a succession of creakwheeled and limpeared avatars, like something moving forever and without progress across an urn.[13]

Continual, deliberate advance, a "succession," yet a forever movement, "without progress." The rolling wheels of all the interchangeable wagons are not finally very different from the wheel spoken of by Becket and the Fourth Tempter in Eliot's *Murder in the Cathedral;* for, like that wheel, these are fixed in an eternal motion, at once ac-

11. Ibid., pp. 17–20.

12. C. Hugh Holman, "The Unity of Faulkner's *Light in August*," PMLA 73 (March 1958): 155–66, esp. pp. 159, 161, 164. There is reference here also to Norman H. Pearson's treatment of Lena in terms of Keats' "Grecian Urn" in his "Lena Grove," *Shenandoah* 3 (Spring 1952): 3–7. Faulkner's awareness of Keats' urn as a source for allusion is more explicitly shown us in *The Bear.*

13. *Light in August*, Modern Library ed. (New York: Random House, 1950), p. 6. Other references are to this edition.

tion and patience, action and the suffering of action (with the appropriate puns on *patience* and *suffering*). The eternal circularity of Lena's urn and the wagon wheels that bear her round it is further enhanced by the transcendent notion of the "avatars": the god in an ever reappearing, ever indestructible, ever freshly embodied movement, continually in touch with the world and yet remaining intact.

There are similarly definitive passages for Joe Christmas and the Reverend Hightower. First, the young Joe Christmas' vision after his discovery of the uglier facts about female physiology:

> In the notseeing and the hardknowing as though in a cave he seemed to see a diminishing row of suavely shaped urns in moonlight, blanched. And not one was perfect. Each one was cracked and from each crack there issued something liquid, deathcolored, and foul. He touched a tree, leaning his propped arms against it, seeing the ranked and moonlit urns. He vomited. (page 165)

Then Hightower's vision of the "seminary," that etymologically shrewd word, as the protected retreat from living, as the tomb of the seed killed within him:

> When he believed that he had heard the call it seemed to him that he could see his future, his life, intact and on all sides complete and inviolable, like a classic and serene vase, where the spirit could be born anew sheltered from the harsh gale of living and die so, peacefully, with only the far sound of the circumvented wind, with scarce even a handful of rotting dust to be disposed of. That was what the word seminary meant: quiet and safe walls within which the hampered and garmentworried spirit could learn anew serenity to contemplate without horror or alarm its own nakedness. (page 419)

We should note, first, that while Joe Christmas' urn and Hightower's classic vase exist as metaphorical definitions of their visions, Lena is an actual figure on an urn of our narrator's envisioning. Christmas' vision, distorted by the ugliness of human perversity, sees the foulness of death flowing from what should be the vessel of life and love. Hightower's vision, rendered bloodless by his withdrawal from the living, sees the vacancy of purity in the aesthetic containment and non-commitment of the "classic and serene vase." (And how appropriate that what Hightower sees is a vase—devoid of contents—rather than an urn, a vase as the aesthetic equivalent of the urn while resisting that latter's involvement with either life or death.) But Lena, the creature of the endlessly repetitive, generative fertility principle, is seen as an actual figure partaking of the still movement of the life on the urn. And how different an urn from those of Christmas' vision, one that holds death as part of the ongoing life process, one that—as Sir Thomas Browne saw it—holds the body of death as the womb holds the body of life, and in the symbol that recalls the womb. So there is Christmas' death-dealing vision; there is Hightower's vision that, in desperate retreat from that of Christmas, denies life as well; and there is Lena's, the vision of wholeness under the aegis of a primal sanctity. Lena's naiveté of course does not permit *her* to have this vision, as Christmas and Hightower have theirs. Instead, all-existing rather than envisioning, she must live it unselfconsciously, herself crawl round the urn's surface, and be made part of the narrator's vision—and ours.

I have already suggested that the shift from urn to vase, as we get to Hightower's life metaphor, is a significant one, confirming in this sterile symbol the shift from the pulsing, dark and deathly existential concern of Joe Christmas and the Apollonian living grace of Lena's procreative innocence to the pulseless aesthetic distance of Hightower's non-living purity. If we view the vase symbol generally as the aesthetic equivalent of the urn, the resistance to the urn's involvement with death and life—whether death-as-life (Lena) or life-as-death (Christmas)—then we can move easily to Eliot's Chinese jar and think of the latter as an echo of the "frail China jar" of Pope's "The Rape of the Lock," itself an echo of the china vases Pope speaks of elsewhere in this poem.

In "The Rape of the Lock" there would surely seem to be no place for the urns, if we take seriously their ritual involvement with the actualities of flesh-and-blood existence. Better, in this supercilious celebration of the airiness of the world of play that resists flesh and blood, to replace them with vases and jars, *objets d'art* in the toyshop unreality of Belinda's art-world. We have just seen Hightower's more serious and less successful attempt to withdraw from the consequential world-winds lead to a similar conversion from the urn to its life-free aesthetic equivalent, the vase, whose cognate term, vessel, perhaps better reminds us that it is but an extension of the urn. For, as I have elsewhere argued at length,[14] Pope's poem is created

14. In "The 'Frail China Jar' and the Rude Hand of Chaos," *The Play and Place of Criticism* (Baltimore: Johns Hopkins Press, 1967), pp. 53–68.

out of a wistful idolatry of the disengaged and—in terms of flesh-and-blood reality—the inconsequential, pure if fragile world of social play. Finally, I claim, the mock-heroic world of the lock, where empty symbols rather than bodies are the objects of rape and battle, becomes a metaphor for the poem itself, even as the "frail China jar," *objet d'art*, becomes the toyshop substitute for our blood-filled vessels of breathing life. The recurrent use of china as symbol of honor's empty equivalent for chastity was commented upon earlier by Cleanth Brooks.[15] This use is indicative enough of the transformation of the world of bodies to the wrought world of empty objects:

> Whether the Nymph shall break Diana's Law,
> Or some frail China Jar receive a Flaw . . .
> > (Canto II, lines 105–6)

> Or when rich China vessels, fall'n from high,
> In glitt'ring dust and painted fragments lie!
> > (III, 159–60)

> 'Twas this, the morning omens seem'd to tell,
> Thrice from my trembling hand the Patch-box fell;
> The tott'ring China shook without a Wind . . .
> > (IV, 161–63)

We may note that this very use of china as a generic term for ceramic objects is a metonym made in the spirit of Pope. Pope himself extends the significance of this metonymy in yet another passage in the poem, one whose brilliance sustains the others. It occurs in his description of the pouring of coffee: "From silver spouts the grateful liquors glide, / While China's earth receives the smoking tide . . ." (III, 109–10). Here in this wrought ceramic world we have the transformation of earth into art; indeed, in these earthen objects is the only earth that is admitted in this poem. China is, after all, the aesthetic form of China's earth, the aesthetic reduction of China for this social company. Again we are reminded of Sir Thomas Browne, this time his relating the purgative crematory fire to man's "earth":

But all flies and sinks before fire almost in all bodies. . . . Where fire taketh leave, corruption slowly enters; In bones well burnt, fire makes a wall

---

15. *The Well Wrought Urn*, p. 87.

against it self. . . . What the Sun compoundeth, fire analyseth, not trans-
muteth. That devouring agent leaves almost alwayes a morsel for the
Earth, whereof all things are but a colony; and which, if time permits,
the mother Element will have in their primitive mass again. (*Urne-
Buriall*, pages 30–31)

The jars and vases and cups of Pope's airy world, vessels subject
only to the smoking tides of coffee poured from silver spouts, are
the real China of that world, from which all other earth has – by the
transmuting ceramic fire – been purged. Browne helps remind us of
that more destructive purgation of earth in the fire of cremation.
And the remnants of cremation, we remember, have as their container that which also is fired out of earth. But the urn, as a created
form, is one created – as Browne has already told us – in imitation of
the living form as an echo of the womb which forms life. As a fired,
earthen icon of what its contents had been – the earthly form consumed by fire – as holder of life and death, the urn transcends both.
For it has attained the pure and permanent circularity of form and,
in its frieze, has the forms of life eternally captured as, like Keats'
figures or Lena Grove, they trace a still movement around it.

The sepulchral urn's aesthetic equivalent of breathing life, an
equivalent that at once captures life's movement and perpetuates it,
accounts for the suspended purity we have seen in the figures of
Pope and Keats and Faulkner. To appropriate the term from Eloisa,
we might say the "unfruitful urn" in one sense leads to a fruitful
urn – the fruitful poem – in another. There is an enforced chastity
binding Eloisa and Abelard, not altogether unlike the aesthetically
enforced chastity binding Keats' figures on the urn. We can see this
enforced chastity in Eloisa's description of Abelard, which precedes
her hopeless and bitter invocation to him ("Come, Abelard!")
which we witnessed earlier:

> For thee the Fates, severely kind, ordain
> A cool suspense from pleasure and from pain;
> Thy life a long dead calm of fix'd repose;
> No pulse that riots, and no blood that glows.
>
> (lines 249–52)

It is just this being "fix'd" in a "cool suspense" from the rioting
pulse and glowing blood that lends the creatures of Pope's world of
artifice in the "Rape" and the creatures trapped on Keats' urn their

precious transcendence—and their unworldly incompleteness, their dance that denies the very notion of consequence. Belinda's "purer blush," Keats' "maidens loth," the mock love-battle at the end of the "Rape," the unanswered factual questions in Keats' "Ode"— these testify to the inconsequential, unbound, free nature of the chaste aesthetic transmutation of breathing existence.

There are, then, three kinds of earth and three ways of its being fired—all finally expressive of the circular tradition that moves from earth to earth. There is, first, man's living earth—his flesh—that, fired by sexual desire, fills the earthly vessel with the flowing fruit of life, of more earth; there is, secondly, as timely consequence of the first, man's dying earth that, fired by the funeral rite, is reduced to the ashes that, in urn burial, fill the third kind: the earthen vessel, an artifact that, transmuted by the ceramic fire of human craft, becomes a permanent form. The latter is at once unfruitful and still-moving, the transcendence of earth in the earthen, the transcendence of flesh in the artifice of eternity; and—where it is urn, too—it is also the receptacle of the remnants of that other earth, the flesh, that is conceived in fire and consumed by fire. Further, the urn may, as Browne describes, imitate the shape of the human conceiving urn; still further, it may have the figures of life as a frieze forever running around it, either in pursuit of desire (the first kind of firing of man's earth which I have spoken of) or in celebration of death (the second kind of the firing of earth)—the two very actions captured on Keats' urn. And, as in the case of Keats' urn, these are captured on the object that, as the third sort of the firing of earth, is in its shape the icon of the others and their container, holding them at once within it and on its circular surface. Thus it celebrates both time past (the ashes within) and time forever now (the circular pattern of scenes that is the frieze), even as, in its shape, the container of death mimics the container of life, tomb as womb. No wonder an amazing multiple pattern is projected by the purified metonymy of sexual meanings ceramically purged and yet insisted upon in "The Rape of the Lock," where "China's earth receives the smoking tide" pouring from the "silver spouts," well heated since "the fiery spirits blaze." Here is a ceramic masque, an earthen playing out of that most earthly action. Can we resist expanding these meanings to include those which range about the china vases and jars of this poem as they relate to frail sexual purity? Or, if we can consider also the "unfruitful urn" in the abortive firing of Eloisa's desires, can we resist seeing vase as the vessel that is related, without sexual consequences, to the urn, with the jar as the semantic generalizing of the ceramic impulse? And we must marvel at the resuscitation of the urn, so unpromising an object of death, into a symbol of life in death: of art. We must marvel at the choice of the urn as the ekphrastic object *par excellence* to unite the stilled and the still-now movement by concentrating within and upon itself the several sorts of earth and the several manners and consequences of their being fired.

But all, even the most aesthetically transcendent, still remain literally movements from earth to earth, from living-dying time to time both affirmed and arrested. This is reason enough to deny that one other kind of the firing of earth as a possible fourth kind: the religious firing that is to transform man's earth to pure spirit. Eloisa, her earth now fired so unfruitfully by Abelard, claims this different kind of firing by God: "But let Heav'n seize it [the soul], all at once 'tis fir'd: / Not touch'd, but rapt; not waken'd, but inspir'd!" (lines 201–2). Nevertheless, this is a figurative firing only: it can move her toward the "flames refin'd" that "in breasts seraphic glow" (line 320) only by denying her literal earth, her earthly status as creature. Which is why Eloisa remains so ambivalent, why in seeing God as Abelard's rival and successor (". . . for he / Alone can rival, can succeed to thee" [line 206]), she must involve her sexuality in her religious impulse. She must confound the firing of her earth with the smothering of earthly fires which constitutes the religious metaphorical firing that she seeks. This denial of all kinds of earth and of earthly fires, sexual and aesthetic, replaces the movement from earth to earth with the Platonic movement from earth to heaven as the last movement, the permanent stilling of movement. It is destructive of the aesthetic, of the earthen, of the ekphrastic principle; is a fraudulent alternative and, for her, a false resolution. Time is merely stilled in the simple sense, the sense of "still life"; it is killed in the sense of the French translation of still life, *nature morte*. And the brilliant multiplicity of time's possibilities for running free and yet running around, repeating circularly, the brilliant revelations of the *ekphrasis*, of the urn at once fruitful and unfruitful—these are forever sacrificed. To alter Horace and defy Lessing, as with the urn, so with poetry.

Keats' urn, a pure *ekphrasis*, is an object especially created to celebrate the teasing doctrine of circularity. If this doctrine is aesthetically complete in creating, through enforced chastity, a fruitful urn of the aesthetic sort out of the unfruitful urn of the empirically human sort, in its chaste circularity it touches the empirically human only fitfully. In its freedom from what Yeats called "the fury and the mire of human veins," in its purging—at once Yeatsian and Aristotelian—of "complexities of fury," it asserts the transformation of the empirical into the archetypal ("the artifice of eternity"), in this way obeying the Hegelian injunction to move from the concrete to the concrete-universal. In the drama of poetry we recognize the creatures as creatures like us, like us most of all in their intense individuality, their here-and-now unique concreteness. But the motions they make—rituals of love and death—through aesthetic pattern and thus through the principle of echo, of repetition, become forever-now motions. This principle frees these motions from the singleness of chronology's linearity and of the empirical sort of finitude. Thus though concrete, the characters in this sense attain universality. They are converted from the merely individual to the casuistic; their motions achieve formal finality even if they never merely finish. Theirs is the finality-without-end, if I may so adapt Kant's definition of aesthetic experience. As creatures fixed on Eliot's wheel or Keats' urn, they show us the movements we all are and have been eternally fixed upon making, though we each make them but once, in singleness, and without awareness of our fixed turning.

To the usual notion of poetry's archetypal nature that moves too quickly from the particular to the universal, indeed that merely universalizes the particular, I would prefer this sense of the archetypal dimension of each poem as it struggles to capture the empirical in all its movement.[16] It must be at once as movement and as movement overcome, as movement joined and mastered, that the individual poem can make its movement eternal and still significant to us in our empirical singleness.

Yeats' Byzantium poems, as I have shown in my quoting from them, at once enunciate this aesthetic and create the ekphrastic symbol, the golden bird, that embodies it. The bird has been placed—indeed "hammered"—into these poems to continue with them their manufactured, artificial perfection forever. Purged, as the "images of day" with their "complexities of mire and blood" are "unpurged," the well-wrought object is both bird and golden handiwork even as, through miracle, it can be both at once, so that it is indeed "More miracle than bird or handiwork." Like the earthen urn or Pope's china, it is the product of the transmuting and purify-

16. I clearly mean here to propose an alternative view of poetry as archetype to that of Northrop Frye.

ing fires, alchemical medium of eternal creation, so different from
the destructive fire that reduces the aged man's earth to ash. As
"God's holy fire," it partakes—like "the gold mosaic of a wall"—of
"the artifice of eternity" and so can transubstantiate the "aged
man," the "dying animal," into the golden creature—both in and
out of nature—of wise and eternal song.

Without this express insertion of the ekphrastic object, there are
other birds that turn legendary under the pressure of their poetic
contexts: indeed there is a chain of them leading to Yeats' golden
bird that may be seen as their appropriate embodiment. And always it is this Platonic opposition between empirical singleness and
archetypal inclusiveness that stirs the movement toward the golden
incarnation.

In Wordsworth's treatment of his cuckoo, the poet must make a
judgment about this very duality in the bird: it is a "wandering
voice" even as it remains "bird," it is "far off" even as it is "near,"
it brings the poet "a tale / Of visionary hours" even as his sense of
reality recognizes that it is only "babbling." This duality has the experiential basis we find in many of Wordsworth's poems: the moment celebrated is a conjunction of two occasions, one far past with
one present. The recurrence of experience, of identical stimulus,
modified by the severe changes time has wrought in the experiencing subject, permits the simultaneous perception of motion and stasis that has been my concern. As his most acute commentators have
pointed out,[17] Wordsworth has himself provided just the metaphor
to express this trapping of temporal change: those moments, laden
with "a renovating virtue," he terms "spots of time" ("The Prelude"
XII, 208)—precisely the union of spatiality and temporality I have
been trying to demonstrate. The very word "spot," related as it is
here to time's movement, yet brings us to stasis, the arresting of
time, by seeming to refer to a place, a permanently defined spatial
entity. This notion accounts, in "To the Cuckoo," for the poet's capacity to transcend the limitations of literal reality in order, through
a double exposure, to blur time's movements to an identical spot.
Conscious, then, of his animistic delusion, he chooses to see the
cuckoo as "No bird, but an invisible thing, / A voice, a mystery. . . ."

17. None more incisively than Geoffrey H. Hartman. See his *Wordsworth's Poetry,
1784–1814* (New Haven: Yale University Press, 1964), esp. pp. 153, 211–19, and his
"Wordsworth, Inscriptions, and Romantic Nature Poetry," in *From Sensibility to Romanticism: Essays Presented to Frederick A. Pottle,* ed. Frederick W. Hilles and Harold
Bloom (New York: Oxford University Press, 1965), pp. 389–413.

As in other bird poems by Romantic poets, the poet moves from the fact that he hears but cannot see the bird to the self-deceptive synecdoche that the voice *is* the bird, so that the bird becomes a disembodied voice, free of the mortality that attends a single finite bodily existence. Once he has thus transcended the bird as earthly animal, Wordsworth is able to return to his childhood with the claim that this is the very bird he then heard and could not find: "The same whom in my schoolboy days / I listened to . . . / And I can listen to thee yet. . . ." Now, listening still, he must—by the conscious choice of self-deception—willfully create ("beget") that "golden time" which, in his boyhood, he shared instinctively. In this conscious decision to ignore the reality of the babbling bird for the visionary voice, he has created for the now "blessed Bird" the "unsubstantial, faery place" that is its "fit home." Dare we think the place to be his Byzantium and the recreated bird of the mature poet's imagination his golden bird? We could, if it were not that his awareness of the self-induced state of delusion leads him to remember its "unsubstantial" nature. The delusion is not firm enough to construct an object that would perpetuate itself, *realize* itself.

The poet in Keats' "Ode to a Nightingale" also undergoes the fanciful transformation of reality induced by the song of the bird. He is, even more than Wordsworth's poet, the captive of his trance, so that his fairyland demands the firm denial of the bird's material reality: "Thou wast not born for death, immortal bird!" He so uncritically accepts the magic of the synecdoche as to allow the identity of the sound of the voice to lead to the undoubted identity of occasion: "The voice I hear this passing night was heard / In ancient days by emperor and clown: / Perhaps the self-same song that found a path / Through the sad heart of Ruth . . . / The same that oft-times hath / Charm'd magic casements. . . ." Yet even here the reality principle naggingly remains. It reminds the poet that the suspension of chronological time is, for humanity, not an attribute of an aesthetic never-never land, a Byzantium, but an attribute of death's nothingness: "Now more than ever seems it rich to die . . . / Still wouldst thou sing, and I have ears in vain— / To thy high requiem become a sod." Further, the immortality conferred, by contrast, upon the bird is in effect withdrawn when the poet, awakening from the spell, admits his return to empirical singleness, tolled as he is back to his "sole self." He acknowledges the final failure of the delusion sponsored by the song of the bird, now wistfully referred to as "deceiving elf," the failure of his own fancy ("the fancy cannot cheat so well"). And the song is now permitted to depart with the departure of the physical bird:

> Adieu! adieu! thy plaintive anthem fades
> Past the near meadows, over the still stream,
> Up the hill-side; and now 'tis buried deep
> In the next valley-glades. . . .

Beyond the "still stream," for the poet it is nothing less than "buried." Keats' poet, aware of man's need for time's movement as well as his need to capture it, has—more than Wordsworth's poet—overdone the extravagance of his earlier Platonic delusions. But he has not managed to find a material object that can contain the still perfection in an earthly form (or an earthen form, if we dare fancy Keats to be searching for an ekphrastic equivalent to his urn). Since he cannot travel to Byzantium and convert his bird to hammered gold, both he and the bird return to time-bound reality to proceed with the complexities of aging. Only the moment, but that moment memorialized, preserved, stilled—and distilled—in the poem, remains. In this well-wrought residue, the ekphrastic principle asserts itself even in the turning aside from an ekphrastic object.

How different are these experiments in synecdoche, with their attempts to hold the turning world as it turns, from the simple postulation by Shelley of the other-than-material nature of his skylark. He begins at once with the flat disembodiment of the "blithe spirit": "Bird thou never wert." But the liveliness of motion is denied together with its status as bird. Its existence in human time is by fiat transcended, so that the collision of movement with movement captured is evaded. All is stilled, and there is no living movement. One thinks, by contrast, of the urging of movement in the pleas to the mistress in "Corinna's Going A-Maying"; the conflict between moving and staying is the very principle of form in the poem. The poet warns against the dangers of staying movement, culminating in the penultimate line, "while time serves, and we are but decaying." Here movement can *seem* to arrest decay and *seem* to make us the master of time, rather than—in decaying stasis—its slave, as the "while" of "while time serves" assures we shall be. This is the foretaste of that masterpoem about time, "To His Coy Mistress" ("Had we but world enough, and time"), and Marvell's invocation to action as the subduer of time, leading to the ekphrastic introduction of the physical, spatial object which is the emblem of his mastery over time even as time works its destructive power:

> Rather at once our time devour,
> Than languish in his slow-chapped power.
> Let us roll all our strength, and all
> Our sweetness, up into one ball . . .
> Thus, though we cannot make our sun
> Stand still, yet we will make him run.
>
> (lines 39–42, 45–46)

   Discussion of earthly birds turned legendary, of poems concerning birds that are at once temporal and supernal, must lead to the albatross of Coleridge's "Ancient Mariner." In few other places in literature is the opposition between stillness and motion more central to the structure, and their relation is controlled by the bird as it turns sacramental. The poem swings between the movement sponsored by the breeze and the calm, the curse resulting from its being withdrawn. We are likely to agree with the first judgment of the mariner's shipmates: that he "had killed the bird / That made the breeze to blow." Everywhere descriptions of movement in its varied paces, and of calm as the dread alternative, direct the poem's own pace. The poem moves with and among its movements and calms. The gratuitous murder of the albatross marks the fall that is to stop all movement. And the mariner becalmed finds his appropriate emblem: the albatross instead of the cross is hung about his neck. It is this static, uncreative, decaying state that characterizes the poet of Coleridge's "Dejection: An Ode." The poet, in effect the cursed, becalmed mariner, asks for the airy impulse that "might startle this dull pain, and make it move and live!" (line 20). "Dejection" is a poem that laments the becalming of spirit, that claims failure, the failure of movement, as its subject. Herrick's "Corinna" showed us forcefully the implication of decay in stillness. Far more graphically in the "Ancient Mariner," total stillness is accompanied by decay, the decay that motionlessness permits to set in: "The very deep did rot" (line 123), "the rotting sea," "the rotting deck" (lines 240, 242). The mariner's becalmed life-in-death is a surrealistic paralysis, seven days and seven nights of the unblinking curse in the eyes of his struck-dead shipmates. In his suspended state he yearns for the effortless motion of "the moving moon" (line 263), a still movement not unlike the movement we have marked in a Lena Grove. The gloss to the poem at this point furnishes a moving statement of such a natural, routine motion as the mariner requires:

> In his loneliness and fixedness he yearneth towards the journeying Moon, and the stars that still sojourn, yet still move onward; and every where the blue sky belongs to them, and is their appointed rest, and their native country and their own natural homes, which they enter un-announced, as lords that are certainly expected and yet there is a silent joy at their arrival.

Later, after the partial penance by the mariner and the partial for-giveness bestowed upon him, the return of the beloved breeze and his eventual return are not of this sublime order; he is returned to his native country and to man, but as a wandering stranger among them. And, still doing penance, he must move in ever-recurrent cir-cles among them, ever retelling his tale.

His tale, the poem proper, has movement even in the face of calm; further, as "Dejection" does not, it succeeds at last in conquering—in moving beyond—the state of being becalmed; nevertheless, it re-mains a "still," even-now movement. For it is framed by a repeti-tious, unendingly repetitious, ritual action, as the mariner must tell his tale again and again, wandering continually in search of a listener—still, even now as I talk. Thus the archetypal nature of the singular, integral poetic action in its transcendence of the empiri-cal—and thus our assurance of its casuistry, an assurance that per-mits our aesthetic pleasure in response to what in life would be unendurably painful. The "Ancient Mariner," in its emphasis on the necessity of the endless retelling of the tale, is a paradigm of this aspect in our greatest works. In its rounded completeness, in its coming to terms with itself—in short, through pattern, that which is bent on destroying its simple, linear temporality—the work guar-antees its special, its other-than-empirical realm of being. Our de-spair at tragedy, for example, while preserved as despair, is yet transfigured to comfort in our knowledge and assurance of its still and inevitable movement, of how it has been and will always be—how it must be. Oedipus must pursue his stubborn ignorance iden-tically to the identical catastrophe; Hamlet must make his always identical way to the absurd indiscriminacy of the final sword play; Lear must prance *his* always identical way to the wretched loveli-ness of the reconciliation scene that ironically lulls him and Cordelia to their deaths. And still they make their inevitable movements, even now as we talk—if I may stick at this point.

This is the final meaning of aesthetic inevitability or circularity—even as the urn demonstrates it; this is the final meaning of Aristotle's probability and necessity that bring poetry and its casuistry beyond history and the empirical world's possibility. The poem as total object has, despite its entrancing *movement*, become the fixed—or rather transfixed—object, its own urn, Yeats' golden bird that has been placed inside the poem to prove that the latter must breathe in its manufactured, artificial perfection forever. But, as the casuistic principle insists, it is always in its unique, contextual singleness that the poem so functions, not as a sign to the universal; in its finitude, its discrete discontinuity from all other poems, from poetry or from language as ideal forms, not as an opening to these.[18] *Ekphrasis*, no longer a narrow kind of poem defined by its object of imitation, broadens to become a general principle of poetics, asserted by every poem in the assertion of its integrity. Is it too much to say that essentially the same principle lies behind the employment of the poetic refrain, indeed behind the employment of meter itself? Such is largely the ground for Wordsworth's and Coleridge's justification of meter: the reduction to the sameness of repetition of that which is disparate, varied, progressive, in motion; the identity of recurrence together with the unceasing change of movement. It is the lack of such minute but systematic guarantees of recurrence that creates some of the handicaps prose fiction has in proclaiming itself a rounded object and that accounts for many of the ad hoc devices it invents to make itself into an aesthetic, a still moving, entity.

Every poem's problem as its own aesthetician, and every critic's problem after it, is essentially the problem of Keats with his Grecian urn: how to make it hold still when the poem must move. And the critic's final desperation is an echo of the outburst, at once absolute and equivocal, of the last two lines of the poem. There are unanswered factual questions asked through the course of the "Ode" ("What men or gods are these? What maidens loth? . . . Who are these coming to the sacrifice? To what green altar . . . ? What little town . . . ?"). These have guaranteed the poet's exasperation at the inadequacy of empirical data before beauty's archetypal perfection, the inadequacy of fact before artifact. The final two lines confer uni-

18. Again it is the alternative to Frye's archetypal universality that I am insisting upon.

versal absolution in that they absolve in absolute terms (to press the redundancy) the poet's need to ask such merely informational questions. We are reminded of Sir Thomas Browne's dismissal of a similar series of questions concerning the historical data surrounding his urns, "the proprietaries of these bones, or what bodies these ashes made up," questions further beyond man's resolution than those that ask "what Song the Syrens sang, or what name Achilles assumed when he hid himself among women."[19] The aesthetic of Keats' final lines, then, is the only culmination of still motion's transcendence of unarrested progression.

And so it is with the critic's desperate struggle to wrestle his slippery object to earth. It is the problem of defying the Lessing tradition, with its neat separateness of the mutually delimiting arts, and seeing the time-space breakthrough in the plasticity of the language of poetry. This language, in taking on Burckhardt's "corporeality," tries to become an object with as much substance as the medium of the plastic arts, the words thus establishing a plastic aesthetic for themselves, sometimes—but not necessarily—using the ekphrastic object as their emblem.

But in one sense the tradition from Edmund Burke and Lessing which sees a uniqueness in the literary medium *is* affirmed. For literature retains its essential nature as a time-art even as its words, by reaching the stillness by way of pattern, seek to appropriate sculpture's plasticity as well. There is after all, then, a sense in which literature, as a time-art, does have special time-space powers. Through pattern, through context, it has the unique power to celebrate time's movement as well as to arrest it, to arrest it in the very act of celebrating it. Its involvement with progression, with empirical movement, always accompanies its archetypal principle of repetition, of eternal return. The poem can uniquely order spatial stasis within its temporal dynamics because through its echoes and its texture it can produce—together with the illusion of progressive movement—the illusion of an organized simultaneity.

My earlier unfavorable claims about Eloisa's religious firing, like my few words on Shelley's "Skylark," were meant to serve as warning against the Platonic denial of the empirical, the mere stilling of movement. In the resistance to the ekphrastic impulse, it cannot too often be urged that the aesthetic desire for pure and eternal form must not be allowed merely to freeze the entity-denying chronolog-

19. *Urne-Buriall*, p. 44.

ical flow of experience in its unrepeatable variety. The remarkable nature of Eliot's "Four Quartets," we must remember, is that the shaping of their musical form into the Chinese jar never deprives existence of its confused multiplicity. For, if we may shift to his other key metaphor, life at the periphery of the wheel never stops moving, even as it radiates from the extraordinary dance at the still center of that turning world. Yet "The Rape of the Lock" reminds us that there is a clear danger from the aesthetic purification of life. We see this danger anew if we return to the urn-jar motif and refer to yet another aesthetic jar, this time in Wallace Stevens' "Anecdote of the Jar":

> I placed a jar in Tennessee,
> And round it was, upon a hill.
> It made the slovenly wilderness
> Surround that hill.
>
> The wilderness rose up to it,
> And sprawled around, no longer wild.
> The jar was round upon the ground
> And tall and of a port in air.
>
> It took dominion everywhere.
> The jar was gray and bare.
> It did not give of bird or bush,
> Like nothing else in Tennessee.[20]

The jar's roundness and—in its aesthetic "dominion everywhere"—its grayness and bareness do no justice to the sprawling "slovenly wilderness" that surrounds its hilltop heights. (Indeed, it is only the jar's round presence that forces the formal impulse to attribute the function of "surrounding" to the aimless wilderness.) Only transcendent, the jar has nothing of life—"of bird or bush"—in it.[21] Here is the warning against the deadening of life, the freezing of movement, caused by too simple and Platonic a sense of aesthetic purity, of the jar or urn motif which, in my ekphrastic mood, I have

20. *Collected Poems of Wallace Stevens* (New York: Alfred A. Knopf, 1954), p. 76.
21. For a very persuasive reading, together with a summary of conflicting readings of the poem and of corroborative passages in Stevens' work (especially those relating the jar to the urn), see Patricia Merivale, "Wallace Stevens' 'Jar': The Absurd Detritus of Romantic Myth," *College English* 26 (April 1965): 527–32.

described admiringly only. Time, in its unique empirical particularity, must always be celebrated in its flow even as we arrest it to make
its movement a forever-now movement. Or else poetry is hardened
into static, Platonic discourse that has lost touch with—indeed that
disdains to touch—our existential motions. But as poetry, even Stevens' poem, in its persistence, itself becomes the jar, though more in-
sistently involved with flowing existence than was the hilltop jar it
decries. Like Eliot's, it has absorbed a liveliness whose moving slov-
enliness it must cherish.

Writers on time in the vitalistic tradition of Bergson have commonly claimed that, in its inevitable universalizing, language tends
to give death to the dynamism of experience by spatializing it and
thus freezing its undemarcated ceaseless flow of unrepeatable and
indefinable, un-entitled units. Thus phenomenological literary critics in the spirit of this tradition have tended to anti-formalism, to
the neglect of the object and the accentuation of the subjective flow
in the transcription of their authors' consciousness of time. However just their charges against the spatializing, and thus the killing,
power of language generally, I must maintain—in the tradition of
Keats in his "Urn" and Yeats in his Byzantium poems—that aesthetic jars usually avoid the inadequacy recorded by Stevens, that
the specially endowed language of poetry frees as well as freezes
temporality, frees it into an ever-repeated motion that has all the
motion together with its repeatability, through the rounded sculp-
ture-like inevitability that guarantees its endless repetition. For this
aesthetically formalized language takes on plasticity as well as spatiality. Through its ekphrastic principle, literature as poetic context
proclaims at once its use of the empirically progressive and its transcendent conversion of the empirical into the archetypal even as it remains empirical, into the circular even as it remains progressive.

In this sense poetry must be at once immediate *and* objective:
neither the mediated objectivity of the normal discourse that
through freezing kills, nor the unmediated subjectivity that our idol-
aters of time-philosophy would want to keep as the unstoppable,
unrepeatable, un-entitled all; neither life only frozen as archetypal
nor life only flowing as endlessly empirical, but at once frozen and
flowing (like the urn), at once objective and immediate, archetypal
and empirical. I would share the interest of the Georges Poulets and
the Maurice Blanchots; but I would give the special liberating license to our best poetry, insisting on its ekphrastic completeness
that allows us to transfer the human conquest of time from the

murky subjective caverns of phenomenology to the well-wrought, well-lighted place of aesthetics. For the poetic context can defy the apparently mutually exclusive categories of time and space to become fixed in the still movement of the Chinese jar that poets have summoned to their poetry as the emblem of its aesthetic, which that poetry's very existence, its way of being and meaning, has implicitly proclaimed. The patterned and yet passing words can, as Eliot has suggested, "reach into the silence," "reach the stillness."

INDEX

Abrams, M. H., 234
Addison, Joseph, 45–46, 51, 103, 104,
    105, 108, 162, 168, 177, 187, 191–92, 205;
    Spectator Nos. 58–62, 98, 157–60; *Spec-
    tator* No. 62, 24n.21, 157n.11; *Spectator*
    No. 416, 23–25, 83–87, 98–100, 153–60
Alexander, Samuel, 171–72
Allen, Don Cameron, 133n.20, 136n.25
Aristotle, 47, 50, 58–60, 76–78, 81, 89, 96,
    102–3, 119, 125, 187, 239, 243, 247, 259,
    284; *Physics*, 203; *Poetics*, 41–44, 52–53,
    60, 77–78, 128–29, 201–5, 240–41
Arnold, Matthew, 214

Bachelard, Gaston, 264n.2
Bakhtin, M. M., 245
Batteux, Abbé, 80, 152n.8
Baumgarten, Alexander, 146, 195
Bergson, Henri, 32, 96n.2, 105, 111–12,
    169–70, 188, 287
Beroaldo, Philippo, 119
Blake, William, 166
Blanchot, Maurice, 287
Boethius, *Consolation of Philosophy*,
    122n.9
Boileu, Nicholas, 98n.6
Boivin, Jean, xiiin.1
Bradley, A. C., 171–72
Brecht, Bertolt, 62, 252–53, 258, 260
Brooks, Cleanth, 182, 204, 215–16, 222;
    The Well Wrought Urn, 225, 227–28, 269,
    271, 274
Browne, Sir Thomas, 273; *Urne-Buriall*,
    269, 274–75, 285
Bulgarini, Belisario, 123
Burckhardt, Sigurd, 50, 182–85, 187,
    213–14, 226, 266, 285

Burke, Edmund, 5, 24–26, 94, 108, 110,
    112, 130, 159, 168, 177, 197, 200, 204–5,
    255, 285; *Philosophical Enquiry*, 99–105

Cicero, 119, 120
Cohen, Ted, 211n.12
Coleridge, Samuel Taylor, 11, 26, 96n.2,
    164, 168n.15, 198–200, 203, 214, 216–18,
    284; *Biographia Literaria*, 145, 216; "De-
    jection: An Ode," 282–83; "The Rime
    of the Ancient Mariner," 282–83;
    "Shakespeare's Judgment Equal to
    His Genius," 199, 254–55; *The
    Statesman's Manual*, 214n.14, 216n.19
Colie, Rosalie, 227; *Paradoxia Epidemica*,
    209–12, 268n.6
Collingwood, R. G., 107n.15
Condillac, Etienne Bonnot de, 148n.3
Corneille, Pierre, 54
Croce, Benedetto, 107n.15, 111, 146–47,
    169, 171

Dante Alighieri, 127, 138, 140; *Convivio*,
    134n.22; *Divina Commedia*, 118, 123–24,
    240–41; "Letter to Can Grande della
    Scala," 134n.22; *Paradiso*, 122
Davis, Paul, 7n.7
de Man, Paul, 27, 234, 236
Demetrius Phalerius, 119
Derrida, Jacques, 11, 234
Descartes, René, 195
Dewey, John, *Art as Experience*, 264
Diderot, Denis, 48n.11, 80, 96n.2,
    134n.21, 150, 160–65, 169–71, 173, 182,
    217; *Les bijoux indiscrets*, 63n.25; *Lettre
    sur les sourds et muets*, 147–48, 150–53,
    218; *Paradoxe sur le comédien*, 61–62,

289

Designed by Christopher Harris/Summer Hill Books

Composed by A. W. Bennett, Inc.,
in Palacio text and display.

Printed on 50-lb. Glatfelter Supple Offset, B-05,
and bound in Holliston Roxite A
by Princeton University Press.